SECOND EDITION

HANDBOOK OF CLINICAL ISSUES IN COUPLE THERAPY

SECOND EDITION

HANDBOOK OF CLINICAL ISSUES IN COUPLE THERAPY

EDITED BY
JOSEPH L. WETCHLER

Routledge
Taylor & Francis Group
New York   London

Routledge
Taylor & Francis Group
711 Third Avenue
New York, NY 10017

Routledge
Taylor & Francis Group
27 Church Road
Hove, East Sussex BN3 2FA

© 2011 by Taylor and Francis Group, LLC
Routledge is an imprint of Taylor & Francis Group, an Informa business

International Standard Book Number: 978-0-415-80475-2 (Hardback) 978-0-415-80476-9 (Paperback)

For permission to photocopy or use material electronically from this work, please access www.copyright.com (http://www.copyright.com/) or contact the Copyright Clearance Center, Inc. (CCC), 222 Rosewood Drive, Danvers, MA 01923, 978-750-8400. CCC is a not-for-profit organization that provides licenses and registration for a variety of users. For organizations that have been granted a photocopy license by the CCC, a separate system of payment has been arranged.

Trademark Notice: Product or corporate names may be trademarks or registered trademarks, and are used only for identification and explanation without intent to infringe.

Library of Congress Cataloging-in-Publication Data

Handbook of clinical issues in couple therapy / Joseph L. Wetchler, editor. -- 2nd ed.

    p. ; cm.
Includes bibliographical references and index.
ISBN 978-0-415-80475-2 (hardback : alk. paper) -- ISBN 978-0-415-80476-9 (pbk. : alk. paper)
    1. Marital psychotherapy. 2. Couples--Psychology. I. Wetchler, Joseph L. II. Title.
    [DNLM: 1. Couples Therapy--methods. 2. Marital Therapy--methods. WM 430.5.M3]

RC488.5.H32623 2011
616.89'1562--dc22   2010035025

Visit the Taylor & Francis Web site at
http://www.taylorandfrancis.com

and the Routledge Web site at
http://www.routledgementalhealth.com

Contents

Acknowledgments		vii
Editor		ix
Contributors		xi
Introduction		xv

1 The State of Couple Therapy   1
RICHARD J. BISCHOFF

Part I   Biological and Physiological Issues

2 Brain Biology and Couple Therapy   23
THOMAS W. ROBERTS

3 Couple Therapy in the Presence of Mental Disorders   41
WAYNE H. DENTON and ANNA R. BRANDON

4 What's Love Got to Do With It?
Couples, Illness, and MFT   57
SHOBHA PAIS and MARY E. DANKOSKI

5 Couples Therapy and Addictions   75
THORANA S. NELSON and NEAL J. SULLIVAN

6 Current State of Sexuality Theory and Therapy   95
JOAN D. ATWOOD and EMILY KLUCINEC

Part II   Traumatic Issues

7 Conjoint Couples Treatment and Intimate Partner Violence:
Best Practices   115
ERIC E. McCOLLUM and SANDRA M. STITH

8 Trauma and Recovery in Couple Therapy   129
LORNA HECKER

9 The Field of Infidelity: Past, Present, and Future   145
KATHERINE M. HERTLEIN and GERALD R. WEEKS

vi • Contents

Part III Divorce and Remarital Issues

10 Divorce Therapy 165
JEROME F. ADAMS

11 Remarital Issues in Couple Therapy 189
MARCIA L. MICHAELS

Part IV Sociological Issues

12 Awareness of Culture: Clinical Implications
for Couple Therapy 207
SHRUTI S. POULSEN and VOLKER THOMAS

13 Fostering Strength and Resiliency in Same-Sex Couples 225
JANIE K. LONG and BARBARA V. ANDREWS

14 Couple Therapy and the Integration of Spirituality
and Religion 247
KAREN B. HELMEKE and GARY H. BISCHOF

15 Feminist Couple Therapy 271
ANNE M. PROUTY and KEVIN P. LYNESS

Part V Primary Prevention Issues

16 One Size Does Not Fit All: Customizing Couple
Relationship Education for Unique Couple Needs 293
JEFFRY LARSON and W. KIM HALFORD

17 Premarital Counseling: Promises and Challenges 311
LEE WILLIAMS

Part VI Training Issues

18 What Is Unique About Supervising Couple Therapists?
One Supervisor's Beginning Answer 329
CHERYL L. STORM

Index 345

Acknowledgments

As a couple and family therapist I am aware that none of us exist in isolation. We are all part of a larger system that helps us develop and survive. This book, as well, was nurtured and supported by an interconnected web of individuals who all played an important role. If any of them had not been a part of the process in some way, I am sure that the outcome would not be as good as it is. I first want to thank all of the chapter authors for their exceptional contributions. When I invited each of the first edition authors to "re-up" for the second edition, they unanimously and immediately "signed on." Moreover, all additional authors who were invited also immediately consented. It was so gratifying to know that all of them shared my enthusiasm for this project, and their excitement shows in every chapter.

I also want to thank Bill Cohen and the staff at Haworth Press who published the first edition of this book. Their nurturance of the initial project ensured that I would have the energy and fortitude for a second "go round." I am also grateful to the staff at Routledge Press, the new home of this book, for facilitating its transition to their imprint, and exhibiting a great amount of patience during the somewhat chaotic and lengthy process of bringing it to light.

I think it is also important to mention my colleagues, Lorna Hecker, Jerry Bercik, and Kathy Schultz. We worked phenomenally hard through several rocky years to see that our academic program stayed on track and continued to thrive. It was in this environment of determination and perseverance that this book evolved. Without this hardworking team, this book would not have been completed.

Further, I have a special thanks to my family, Bernie, Jorie, Diane, Sherry, Daniel, Jessica Lily, Jessica Marie, and Ryan. Their love and support has been a godsend. They cheer me on through all of my projects and remind me of what is truly important in life.

Finally, I dedicate this book to my spouse, best friend, lover, and partner for life, Carole Schwartz. She provided the initial spark for the first edition as well as numerous other projects. Our relationship has allowed us both to grow personally, professionally, relationally, and spiritually. I look forward to each new day knowing we share the adventure together. I love you, honey!

Editor

Joseph L. Wetchler, PhD, is a professor and director of the Marriage and Family Therapy Program at Purdue University Calumet, Hammond, Indiana. He is a clinical member and approved supervisor of the American Association for Marriage and Family Therapy. Dr. Wetchler was the recipient of the 2007 American Association for Marriage and Family Therapy Award for Training, the 2004 Purdue University Calumet Outstanding Faculty Scholar Award, and the 1997 Indiana Association for Marriage and Family Therapy Award for Outstanding Contribution to Research in Family Life. He served as editor of the *Journal of Couple and Relationship Therapy* from 1999 through 2008 and has served on the editorial boards of the *American Journal of Family Therapy*, the *Journal of Family Psychotherapy*, the *Journal of Feminist Family Therapy*, the *Journal of GLBT Family Studies*, the *Journal of Marital and Family Therapy*, and the *Journal of Clinical Activities, Assignments & Handouts in Psychotherapy Practice*. Dr. Wetchler is the editor of the *Handbook of Clinical Issues in Couple Therapy*, 1st edition, the coeditor (with Fred Piercy and Katherine M. Hertlein) of the *Handbook of the Clinical Treatment of Infidelity*, the coeditor (with Jerry Bigner) of *Relationship Therapy with Same-Sex Couples*, the coeditor (with Volker Thomas and Terri Karis) of *Clinical Issues with Interracial Couples*, the coeditor (with Lorna Hecker) of *An Introduction to Marriage and Family Therapy*, and the coauthor (with Fred Piercy and Douglas Sprenkle) of the *Family Therapy Sourcebook*, 2nd edition. He also is the author of numerous journal articles on family therapy supervision, family therapy for child and adolescent problems, couple therapy for substance abuse, and the self of the therapist. Dr. Wetchler has been a coinvestigator on a large project funded by the National Institute on Drug Abuse to study couple therapy approaches for substance-abusing women. He regularly consults to social service agencies and therapists in private practice, and maintains an active couple and family therapy practice in Northwest Indiana. Dr. Wetchler is a licensed marriage and family therapist in Indiana.

Contributors

Jerome F. Adams
Department of Human Development
and Family Studies
University of Rhode Island
Kingston, Rhode Island

Barbara V. Andrews
Department of Counselor Education
Adams State College
Alamosa, Colorado

Joan D. Atwood
Marriage and Family Therapy of
New York
Rockville Centre, New York

Gary H. Bischof
Department of Counselor Education
and Counseling Psychology
Western Michigan University
Kalamazoo, Michigan

Richard J. Bischoff
Marriage and Family Theraphy
Program
University of Nebraska-Lincoln
Lincoln, Nebraska

Anna R. Brandon
Department of Psychiatry

and

Department of Clinical Sciences
University of Texas Southwestern
Medical Center
Dallas, Texas

Mary E. Dankoski
Department of Family Medicine
Indiana University
Indianapolis, Indiana

Wayne H. Denton
Department of Psychiatry
University of Texas Southwestern
Medical Center
Dallas, Texas

W. Kim Halford
School of Psychology
University of Queensland
Brisbane, Australia

Lorna Hecker
Marriage and Family Therapy
Program
Purdue University Calumet
Hammond, Indiana

Karen B. Helmeke
Department of Counselor Education
and Counseling Psychology
Western Michigan University
Kalamazoo, Michigan

Katherine M. Hertlein
Department of Marriage and Family
Therapy
University of Nevada, Las Vegas
Las Vegas, Nevada

Emily Klucinec
Marriage and Family Therapy of
New York
Rockville Centre, New York

xii • Contributors

Jeffry Larson
School of Family Life
Brigham Young University
Provo, Utah

Janie K. Long
Center for Lesbian, Gay, Bisexual,
    and Transgender Life
Duke University
Durham, North Carolina

Kevin P. Lyness
Department of Applied
    Psychology
Antioch University New England
Keene, New Hampshire

Eric E. McCollum
Northern Virginia Center
Virginia Polytechnic Institute and
    State University
Blacksburg, Virginia

Marcia L. Michaels
Marriage and Family Therapy
    Program
Alliant International University
San Diego, California

Thorana S. Nelson
Department of Family, Consumer,
    and Human Development
Utah State University
Logan, Utah

Shobha Pais
Department of Family Medicine
Indiana University
Indianapolis, Indiana

Shruti S. Poulsen
Counseling Psychology and
    Counselor Education Program
University of Colorado
Denver, Colorado

Anne M. Prouty
Department of Applied and
    Professional Studies
Texas Tech University
Lubbock, Texas

Thomas W. Roberts
Department of Child and Family
    Development
San Diego State University
San Diego, California

Sandra M. Stith
Marriage and Family Therapy
    Program
Kansas State University
Manhattan, Kansas

Cheryl L. Storm
Marriage and Family Therapy
    Program
Pacific Lutheran University
S. Tacoma, Washington

Neal J. Sullivan
Department of Family, Consumer,
    and Human Development
Utah State University
Logan, Utah

Volker Thomas
Department of Child Development
    and Family Studies
Purdue University
West Lafayette, Indiana

Gerald R. Weeks
Department of Marriage and Family
  Therapy
University of Nevada, Las Vegas
Las Vegas, Nevada

Lee Williams
Marital and Family Therapy
  Program
University of San Diego
San Diego, California

Introduction

The second edition of the *Handbook of Clinical Issues in Couple Therapy* marks a slight shift in the field, from focusing on the various theoretical schools to focusing on those issues that impact couples and their treatment. The first edition was a tentative statement in that direction. That the book is now in its second edition means the field found this shift worthy of continued dialogue. To place this book in context, it is helpful to briefly examine the history of couple therapy.

The development of couple therapy is perhaps unique in the mental health field. Its founders came from outside the establishment. They were clergy, lawyers, home economists, and others who worked with, and were concerned with the stability of, married couples. In my opinion, this has affected how couple therapy has been viewed. There has always remained a second-tier status, especially when compared to the more dynamic family therapy movement (Broderick & Schrader, 1991; Wetchler, 2002). The common view still remains that couple therapy is about "saving marriages" rather than a profound way of conducting therapy with the power to impact numerous personal issues, as well as an important adjunct treatment for an array of disorders and life problems. To be sure, "saving marriages" is highly important business and deserves much more research and professional interest (Doherty, 2002). Still, a look at the broader issues that impact couple therapy, and perhaps its cutting edge, is also in order.

The purpose of this book is to focus on couple therapy as an important mental health treatment, and to provide clarity to several of the key issues dealt with by those who practice its theories and techniques. In that way, it differs from other surveys in the field. During the past decades, some highly promising treatment models have been developed with strong research programs that support their efficacy at helping distressed couples (Baucom & Epstein, 1990; Greenberg & Johnson, 1988; Jacobson & Christensen, 1996). These and other approaches are presented in several excellent overviews of the field (Gurman, 2008; Harway, 2005). However, as our field has progressed, there has been a move toward examining the common factors across theoretical models that are most helpful to couples and families (Blow, Sprenkle, & Davis, 2007; Davis & Piercy, 2007a; Davis & Piercy, 2007b). A similar trend has also emerged to examine the core competencies that make couple and family therapists more effective, and use these as outcomes within our training programs (Nelson et al., 2007). These developments lead us away from a focus on theoretical schools and more toward an examination of the issues faced

xv

by couples. In short, a focus on the clinical issues within couple therapy has the potential to inform the common factors and core competencies research in a way that a theory-based focus may not.

In their excellent decade review, Johnson and Lebow (2000) discussed the emerging issues for couple therapy at the end of the twentieth century. As several years have since passed, many of those emerging trends have become even more firmly established. It is only fitting that this work focuses on their ideas, and others, and updates them for couple therapists and researchers today.

This book begins with an overview of the field and the emerging issues by Richard J. Bischoff. It then divides into six parts: Biological and Physiological Issues (Part I), Traumatic Issues (Part II), Divorce and Remarital Issues (Part III), Sociological Issues (Part IV), Primary Prevention Issues (Part V), and Training Issues (Part VI). Thomas W. Roberts begins Part I with a review of the implications of the new research in brain biology and its significance to couple therapy. Wayne H. Denton and Anna R. Brandon follow with a discussion on couple therapy with major mental illness, and Mary E. Dankoski and Shobha Pais review the interplay of couple therapy and medicine. Finally, Thorana S. Nelson and Neal J. Sullivan, and Joan D. Atwood and Emily Klucinec, respectively, provide overviews of couple therapy and the addictions, and sex therapy.

Part II deals with areas that often prove to be particularly difficult for those in the helping professions. Eric E. McCollum and Sandra M. Stith evaluate the literature on couple therapy and domestic violence and Lorna Hecker orients readers to the issues of trauma and couple therapy. Katherine M. Hertlein and Gerald R. Weeks round out the section with a discussion of infidelity and couple therapy.

Relationship issues involve more than those tied to marital health and stability. Couple therapists are often required to provide treatment for those that are no longer in committed relationships. To that end, Jerome F. Adams discusses issues related to divorce therapy and Marcia L. Michaels surveys remarital treatment in Part III.

Also, couple therapy does not exist in a vacuum, but rather in a broader societal context. Nor is couple therapy restricted to white heterosexual couples. Shruti S. Poulsen and Volker Thomas begin Part IV with an overview of the issues related to culture and couple therapy. This is followed by more focused discussions by Janie K. Long and Barbara V. Andrews on same-sex couples, by Karen B. Helmeke and Gary H. Bischof on spirituality and couples, and Anne M. Prouty and Kevin P. Lyness on feminist issues and couple therapy.

Further, it is important that couple therapists help couples in non-distressed relationships to prevent the development of future problems. In Part V, Jeffry Larson and W. Kim Halford provide a chapter on couple education and Lee Williams presents a chapter on premarital counseling.

Finally, no review of the field of couple therapy would be complete without a discussion of issues involved in the training of couple therapists. While much has been written on the training of family therapists (Liddle, Bruenlin, & Schwartz, 1988; Todd & Storm, 1997), little exists on the supervision of couple therapists. In Part VI, Cheryl L. Storm expands her discussion, started in the first edition, to further the dialogue in the field.

My primary hope is that readers of this volume will come to appreciate the extent of the work currently being done in the field of couple therapy and that these reviews will be useful resources to practicing couple therapists and students. A second hope is that the reviews contained in this project provide the impetus for theory development and research that continues to move the field of couple therapy forward.

References

Baucom, D. H., & Epstein, N. (1990). *Cognitive-behavioral marital therapy*. New York: Brunner/Mazel.

Blow, A. J., Sprenkle, D. H., & Davis, S. D. (2007). Is who delivers the treatment more important than the treatment itself? The role of the therapist in common factors. *Journal of Marital & Family Therapy, 33*, 298–317.

Broderick, C. B., & Schrader, S. S. (1991). The history of professional marriage and family therapy. In A. S. Gurman & D. P. Kniskern (Eds.), *Handbook of family therapy* (vol. II, pp. 3–40). New York: Brunner/Mazel.

Davis, S. D., & Piercy, F. P. (2007a). What clients of couple therapy model developers and their former students say about change, Part I: Model-dependent common factors across three models. *Journal of Marital & Family Therapy, 33*, 318–343.

Davis, S. D., & Piercy, F. P. (2007b). What clients of couple therapy model developers and their former students say about change, Part II: Model-independent common factors and an integrative framework. *Journal of Marital & Family Therapy, 33*, 344–363.

Doherty, W. J. (2002). How therapists harm marriages and what we can do it. *Journal of Couple & Relationship Therapy, 1*(2), 1–17.

Greenberg, L. S., & Johnson, S. M. (1988). *Emotionally focused therapy for couples*. New York: Guilford.

Gurman, A. S. (Ed.) (2008). *Clinical handbook of couple therapy* (3rd ed.). New York: Guilford.

Harway, M. (Ed.) (2005). *Handbook of couples therapy*. Hoboken, NJ: Wiley.

Jacobson, N. S., & Christensen, A. (1996). *Integrative couple therapy: Promoting acceptance and change*. New York: Norton.

Johnson, S., & Lebow, J. (2000). The "coming of age" of couple therapy: A decade review. *Journal of Marital and Family Therapy, 26*, 23–38.

Liddle, H. A., Breunlin, D. C., & Schwartz, R. C. (Eds.) (1988). *Handbook of family therapy training & supervision*. New York: Guiford.

Nelson, T. S., Chenail, R. J., Alexander, J. F., Crane, D. R., Johnson, S. M., & Schwallie, L. (2007). The development of core competencies for the practice of marriage and family therapy. *Journal of Marital & Family Therapy, 33*, 417–438.

Todd, T. C., & Storm, C. L. (Eds.) (1997). *The complete systemic supervisor: Context, philosophy, and pragmatics*. Boston: Allyn & Bacon.

Wetchler, J. L. (2002). Couple therapy and the 21st century. *Journal of Couple & Relationship Therapy, 1*(1), 1–3.

1
The State of Couple Therapy

RICHARD J. BISCHOFF

Contents

Introduction	1
History of Couple Therapy	1
News Flash: The Eclipse of Couple Therapy	4
Glimpses Into the Shadow: Practice Patterns and the Consumer Reports Study	7
Out of the Shadow	8
Research on Couple Functioning	8
The Development of Theories/Models Unique to Couple Therapy	10
Research on the Effectiveness of Couple Therapy	15
The Future of Couple Therapy	16
References	18

Introduction

Couple therapy, in its state-of-the-art form, is currently one of the most robust treatment modalities in the field of psychotherapy. But, for many, both in and out of the field, couple therapy is a sleeping giant. Many trained as therapists, including many trained as marriage and family therapists, are not fully aware of the strong empirical and theoretical base that underlies the practice of couple therapy. The purpose of this chapter is to briefly review the history of couple therapy, placing this history in the context of the broader field of mental health care, and to identify the trends and evidences that suggest that couple therapy is currently worthy of premiere status.

History of Couple Therapy

As long as there has been coupling and marriage, there most assuredly have been people who have been willing to become involved in others' relationship problems. For many, it is difficult, and sometimes even emotionally painful, to see the unhappiness experienced by those in a bad relationship, and most people do not like to see a marriage end. So, for many, a desire to help is a natural response (if for no other reason than to just alleviate their own distress as observers). Those who select a career in the helping professions (e.g., clergy, physicians, mental health professionals, social workers, educators, lawyers) are probably most susceptible to becoming involved in others' lives and relationship problems. So, it is not difficult to understand how the origins of couple therapy are shared among the many helping professions and not just within the mental health fields.

Modern couple therapy has its origins primarily in the marriage counseling movement of the early 1900s (Broderick & Schrader, 1981; Wetchler, 2003). This movement occurred largely outside the mental health field. It was initiated by clergy, lawyers, physicians, social workers, educators, and really anyone who became involved in couple relationship problems through their primary work. Marriage counseling, in these early days of the movement, was a part-time endeavor (Broderick & Schrader): an avocation for most. At this time, a compassionate lawyer, physician, or minister, for example, would provide advice or counsel to distressed individuals or couples with whom they were working in their capacity as professionals. In many ways, this is still happening today.

It wasn't until the early 1930s that the first marriage counseling centers were established with professionals devoting full time attention to providing marriage counseling (Broderick & Schrader, 1981; Wetchler, 2003). Paul Popenoe founded the first of such centers, the American Institute of Family Relations in Los Angeles, California, in 1930 (Popenoe, 1992), thus ushering in the era of professional marriage counseling (Broderick & Schrader). On the other side of the United States, Emily Mudd's Marriage Council of Philadelphia in Pennsylvania opened its doors soon after in 1932. Other centers soon followed, with each being unaffiliated with others and with the impact of each being largely local.

With the establishment of the marriage counseling centers, interest grew in marriage counseling as a full-time profession. But, because the practice of marriage counseling emerged from outside the mental health field, being a marriage counselor was generally a second profession for non-mental health trained professionals. For example, Paul Popenoe (see Popenoe, 1992) was trained as a biologist and spent his early career studying date palms. During World War I, he developed an interest in heredity and became a eugenicist and was the editor of the *Journal of Heredity* before developing an interest in marriage counseling. Emily Mudd (see Thomas, 1998) was trained as a landscape architect. Her interest in marriage counseling probably developed during the 1920s when, with her husband—a microbiologist—she established Pennsylvania's first birth control clinic.

Recognizing the need to link professionals and advance the practice of marriage counseling, Emily Mudd and other like-minded professionals established the American Association of Marriage Counselors (AAMC) in 1942 (Broderick & Schrader, 1981; Wetchler, 2003). But, this did little to address the great diversity in marriage counseling practice, and with an increasing number of marriage counseling centers and marriage counselors, it was becoming harder to ignore both the diversity in practice and differences in the quality of services being provided. With no standards of counseling, there could be no consistency across treatments. Marriage counseling centers were generally being staffed by individuals whose training was in another field and whose qualifications for providing marriage counseling consisted of an interest in helping couples overcome marital distress. So, a joint committee of the AAMC and the National Council on Family Relations was appointed in 1948 to develop standards for marriage counselors (Broderick & Schrader). This was soon followed by standards for marriage counseling centers (Broderick & Schrader), which have become the precursor to the standards for training that exist today through the Commission on Accreditation for Marriage and Family Therapy Education (COAMFTE).

But, despite these attempts to provide standards for practice, the field continued to be dominated by a diverse group of practitioners during the 1950s and 1960s. Marriage counseling was still a second profession for most of those who saw their primary professional role as that of marriage counselor. Because marriage counselors came from a broad range of professional backgrounds, it was difficult to establish a profession and to mainstream marriage counseling within the mental health care field. Probably as a result of the second profession nature of marriage counseling, the practice also lacked a professional literature, which is necessary for legitimizing, advancing, and standardizing any treatment modality. Even as late as 1973, Alan Gurman lamented that the scholarship about marriage counseling lagged far behind the other mental health treatment modalities of the time. Consequently, the practice continued to reside on the fringes of the mental health care field. Even within the AAMC, most members during the 1960s identified marriage counseling as something that they did in addition to their primary professional role (Alexander, 1968). More than a primary professional organization, the AAMC was a place where anyone who was interested in providing marriage counseling, regardless of their primary professional role, could come together to associate with and learn from one another. But, without a membership base with their primary professional identity as marriage counselors, the AAMC struggled with its identity and consequently struggled to maintain a clear purpose and direction. So, the stage was set for marriage counseling to be overrun by something else that could be more easily mainstreamed in the mental health care field. That something else was family therapy.

During the 1960s, the AAMC saw an increase in its membership among those who had been trained in the mental health field (primarily psychiatry) and who were interested in family relationships. So, in 1970, to accommodate this increasing interest among its members for working with families, the AAMC changed its name to the American Association of Marriage and Family Counselors (AAMFC) (Broderick & Schrader, 1981; W. C. Nichols, 1992). Then, in an attempt to both elevate the practice of working with couples

4 • Handbook of Clinical Issues in Couple Therapy

and families to the status of a treatment and to further advance the emerging profession, the name was changed again in 1978 to the American Association of Marriage and Family Therapists (AAMFT) (Broderick & Schrader; W. C. Nichols).

But, it wasn't really until the publication of standards for training marriage and family counselors (and later, marriage and family therapists) in 1975 (W. C. Nichols, 1992) that an identity as a marriage and family therapist began to emerge. Without training standards, MFT would always be seen as a specialization practiced by professionals trained in other mental health fields. But, with training standards and the accreditation of graduate level training programs, graduate students were being trained as marriage and family therapists as their first profession and their primary training was in the practice of couple and family therapy. First profession status finally arrived and with it the professionalization of the field.

News Flash: The Eclipse of Couple Therapy

Professionalization was important to the field of marriage and family therapy, but it did not come without negative consequences for couple therapy. One of the most important negative consequences was that couple therapy became hidden; obscured in the shadow of its younger, more dynamic, and outgoing sibling: family therapy.

Although younger, the history of family therapy is similar to that of couple therapy. Both began as part-time endeavors by practicing clinicians and as second professions for many of its pioneers. However, it is in the differences in the histories of couple therapy and family therapy that we are able to understand how marriage counseling, as the older sibling, could be eclipsed by family therapy.

First, unlike couple therapy, family therapy has its origins more firmly in the mental health field. This may be due to the fact that it came on the scene later than marriage counseling, and after the mental health field was more developed. It may also be due to the fact it emerged in response to a recognition that family pathology was associated with psychological maladjustment and that most, but not all, of the family therapy pioneers were trained first as psychiatrists, social workers and psychologists. This positioned family therapy much differently from marriage counseling whose practitioners where trained first in the clergy, the law, education, and medicine and whose clients were primarily individuals seeking advice or guidance about the how-to's of married life (Gurman & Fraenkel, 2002). So, while marriage counseling was seen as appropriate for addressing problems in living, family therapy was seen as appropriate for addressing psychological maladjustment. Consequently, many in the field did not even recognize it as a mental health treatment modality (Gurman & Fraenkel).

Second, unlike couple therapy, family therapy has its roots in research. As "the auxiliary activity of a professional whose primary commitment was elsewhere" (Broderick & Schrader, 1981, p. 4), marriage counseling developed out of the desires of well-meaning professionals to help individuals and couples understand married life and improve their marriages. Family therapy, however, developed in response to research that pointed to the role and influence of family relationships in the development and perpetuation of individual pathology. These research findings provided both the rationale and the foundation for family intervention.

Third, unlike couple therapy, theories and models were the basis for family intervention almost from the beginning of family therapy. Techniques and strategies for intervention were derived from and pertained to these theories and models, thus not only giving clinicians a conceptual framework to aid in interpreting family functioning, but also giving them a framework for how to intervene to bring about change. These models directed how and when techniques would be used and gave clinicians a common language for talking with one another about their clinical work.

Nothing like this existed for marital counseling. Manus (1966, in Gurman & Jacobson, 1986) lamented that although there were an increasing number of therapists working with couples, that the approach was "a hodgepodge of unsystematically employed techniques grounded tenuously, if at all, in partial theories at best" (p. 1). Gurman and Fraenkel (2002) explained that because marriage counseling was without a theory to guide it, clinicians turned for direction to those theories that were dominating the mental health field at the time. For those trained to work with individuals, these were the psychoanalytic theories, with object relations being the most logical choice among them (Gurman & Fraenkel; Gurman & Jacobson). But, with an emphasis on the interaction of individuals' intrapsychic processes, the focus was still on the individual and the model gave couple therapists little practical direction about what to do in conjoint work with couples. In the late 1960s and early 1970s behavioral marital therapy came on the scene, but like object relations, it was primarily a one-dimensional adaptation of a theory originally developed to describe individual functioning and guide the behavioral modification of individuals. For those trained as marriage and family therapists, the family therapy theories were the most logical choice. After all, it was assumed that couple relationships were nothing more than just a subsystem of the family and so the family models would apply. But, this assumption turned out to be just as faulty as the one that suggested that models to guide work with individuals could be applied to relational systems because couples and families are made up of individuals. But, in the absence of alternatives, these fallacies were overlooked and couple therapy became subsumed within family therapy.

During the 1970s and early 1980s there was a proliferation of family therapy models (Gurman & Kniskern, 1981; W. C. Nichols, 1992; M. P. Nichols & Schwartz, 2007). One might think that with so many competing models, confusion and chaos would reign and the field would be diluted, but just the

6 • Handbook of Clinical Issues in Couple Therapy

opposite happened to family therapy. All this interest in model development quickly propelled family therapy to star status. The fervor over model development actually advanced the field because it increased interest in it. There was always something new and there was something for everyone. In contrast, couple therapy during the 1970s—when family therapy was quickly ascending in status and recognition as an exciting new treatment modality—was still largely just a collection of techniques in search of a model or theory. To fill this gap, the models of family therapy were quickly adopted to explain couple functioning (just as models of individual psychotherapy had earlier been adapted to explain couple functioning and to guide treatment). So, marital therapy, which was already marginalized and discounted as a legitimate treatment modality, was subsumed within family therapy.

Fourth, unlike couple therapy, family therapy had charismatic and outgoing proponents of the various family therapy models. Critics descriptively compared what was happening in the field of marriage and family therapy to a religious fervor, complete with competition among various sects for followers (see Sprenkle, 2003; Werry, 1989). The influence of these charismatic proponents was so great that it often overshadowed evidence (or lack of evidence) supporting the effectiveness of these models. As a result, inflated, and at times false, claims of model superiority were common. Many of these included claims, albeit unsubstantiated, that the family therapy models were sufficient for directing couple therapy. Because marital therapy was without a coherent theory, most in the field accepted these claims as reasonable applications of the family therapy models.

The consequence was that couple therapy became hidden behind family therapy. For many, it was so obscured that it wasn't even acknowledged as a separate treatment modality. The obscuring of couple therapy, even now, is reflected in the language that is used to talk about both couple therapy and family therapy. As will be seen from the examples below, even within the field of marriage and family therapy, marriage therapy might regularly receive top billing, but family therapy is the acknowledged star. For example:

- For many, couple therapy and family therapy are not seen as separate modalities and are referred to with the single, all encompassing phrase *couple-and-family-therapy*, which is often shortened to *family therapy*.
- Family therapy appears to be the preferred term for many when referring to any mental health treatment that is designed to intervene at any level higher than the individual.
- Many mental health professionals use family therapy as an abbreviation for the profession of marriage and family therapy.
- The most popular text used as an introduction to the theory and practice of both *couple therapy* and *family therapy* is simply titled *Family Therapy: Concepts and Methods* (M. P. Nichols & Schwartz, 2007).

- Division 43 of the American Psychological Association is named *Family Psychology* even though its members are interested in both couple and family relationships and in both couple therapy and family therapy.
- The journal and newsletter produced by APA Division 43 are named the *Journal of Family Psychology* and *The Family Psychologist* respectively.

Glimpses Into the Shadow: Practice Patterns and the Consumer Reports Study

While the professionalization of the field caused couple therapy to be under-appreciated, little-acknowledged and hidden, it did not disappear. Studies of practice patterns among marriage and family therapists and self-identified "family therapists" have reliably found that the work of these clinicians is mostly with couples (Doherty & Simmons, 1996; Simmons & Doherty, 1995; Whisman, Dixon, & Johnson, 1997) and that the most frequently occurring complaints for which clients seek help from these clinicians are marital difficulties (Gurman & Fraenkel, 2002; Simmons & Doherty).

Reflecting the state of couple therapy in the late 1980s through the mid-1990s was the much-publicized Consumer Reports' (CR) study of psychotherapy (Consumer Reports, 1995; Seligman, 1995). In this survey, consumers of mental health treatments gave couple therapy the poorest customer satisfaction ratings of any other mental health treatment modality. The study also found that for those receiving couple therapy for 6 months or less, only 22% reported major improvement in their presenting problems. The rate of self-reported improvement increased to only 34% for those receiving up to 12 months of couple therapy. While one might cheer the increased rate of improvement with more time in couple therapy, the meaningfulness of this higher rate of improvement diminishes when one acknowledges that couples attend couple therapy an average of just 11 sessions (Simmons & Doherty, 1995). Assuming a weekly session, this means that most couples would have finished, or otherwise discontinued treatment sometime between 3 and 4 months—long before the 6 month mark. When one also considers that if couples are going to notice improvement, they will most likely do so within the first 6 months of treatment (self-reported improvement increased only 12 percentage points from the 6 month mark of 22%). These findings are downright discouraging.

The CR study created quite a stir among mental health professionals and came as a shock to marriage and family therapists because it called into question the effectiveness of the couple therapy modality. But, it reflected, perhaps accurately, the status of a treatment that had been in the shadow of another for over two decades. As John Gottman (1999) described, in marital therapy we do not need "just a minor fix; rather, we need a major change" (p. 5).

8 • Handbook of Clinical Issues in Couple Therapy

Out of the Shadow

So, how did couple therapy come out of the shadow of family therapy to become the indisputable champion in the mental health field? At the same time that the CR study was being conducted both researchers and clinicians were giving increased attention to couple relationships, and for the first time, models of therapy unique to work with couples were being developed. Beginning in the 1990s, three independent noteworthy trends emerged that over time coalesced to create a robust couple therapy treatment modality. These trends continue to exert influence today. Perhaps unexpectedly, the most influential of these has come from outside the field of psychotherapy: from research about what makes marriages work. The two others, coming from within the field, are the promotion of treatment models unique to couple therapy and research designed to document the effectiveness of couple therapy.

Research on Couple Functioning

Through the proverbial backdoor, the work of relationship researchers, not that of couple therapists or psychotherapy researchers, has been the primary influence on the state of the art of couple therapy. This may seem surprising because both researchers and clinicians have long lamented the gap that exists between research and practice (e.g., Gurman, 1973; Liddle, 1991; Sprenkle, 2003) and there have been many attempts, principally by clinicians, to bridge the gap with strategies for making research findings more relevant to clinicians (Pinsof & Wynne, 2000), how clinicians can use research findings to inform their clinical work (e.g., Williams, Patterson, & Miller, 2006), and how training can be changed to bridge the gap (e.g., Crane, Wampler, Sprenkle, Sandberg, & Hovestadt, 2002; Liddle; Stith, Rosen, Barasch, & Wilson, 1991). But, with marriage and couple relationships seen primarily as a subsystem of the larger family system, as it was prior to the 1990s, there was no need to develop a model of therapy to guide couple therapy. Unbeknownst to those in the mental health field, what was needed was a scholarship of couple relationships that was informed by research about the uniqueness of couple relationships and about what makes marriages work (Gottman, 1999). The relationship science that began to mature in the 1990s provided this kind of foundation (Berscheid, 1999) that would support the development of models of therapy unique to work with couples. Currently, the connection between relationship science and couple therapy is probably better developed than in any other realm of psychotherapy.

The study of marital relationships in the past was dominated by one-dimensional attempts to study marital dissatisfaction (Bradbury, Fincham, & Beach, 2000). This early research grew, quite naturally, out of a growing awareness of marital distress and out of concerns about the rising divorce rates. An important early advancement in this research was the development of the Locke-Wallace Marital Adjustment Test (MAT) (Locke & Wallace,

1959) which allowed researchers to reliably get at marital dissatisfaction quickly and easily. The MAT is still used today. Second and third generation instruments have also been developed such as the Dyadic Adjustment Scale (Spanier, 1976) and the Revised Dyadic Adjustment Scale (Busby, Christensen, Crane, & Larson, 1995).

With instruments to measure dissatisfaction in couple relationships, researchers turned their attention to determining the factors associated with marital dissatisfaction and its relationship to divorce. The research by Mavis Heatherington in the 1970s on the effects of divorce (Heatherington, Cox, & Cox, 1978) stimulated a great deal of interest in divorce and its consequences among researchers and clinicians. More than any other research effort of the time, Heatherington's work ushered in a rapid growth in the research literature about divorce and couple relationships.

But, this burgeoning literature did little to advance the practice of couple therapy because it did little to help marriage therapists understand what made good relationships good. The most practical applications of this knowledge was to dissuade couples from divorcing by pointing out the negative consequences of divorce or to help individuals in truly horrible marriages see that divorce wouldn't be as bad as their marriage. It was not enough to know what made marriages bad; therapists and couples needed to know what made marriages good and they needed a model for how to make struggling marriages better.

The first signs that research would make a difference to couple therapists occurred when researchers moved beyond self-reports of problems and dissatisfaction to systematic observations of both happily and unhappily married spouses as they interacted with one another in both controlled and uncontrolled situations. Consistent with the emphasis at the time on couples in distress, researchers began by observing couples in conflict (Fincham, 2003). In controlled situations, researchers would ask couples to identify an issue or issues that they normally argue about or that had not yet been resolved and then ask them to discuss this issue while they would be videotaped and observed. This, for the first time, allowed researchers to begin to tease out the intricacies of couple relationship dynamics. The focus was no longer on the individual (as it was with the study of marital dissatisfaction and divorce), but on the couple as a unit. What the research revealed about marital conflict surprised both researchers and clinicians. Contrary to expectations, this research found that it wasn't the presence or absence of conflict (or things to argue about) that distinguished between bad and good marriages. Rather, the distinguishing feature was in how couples handled conflict (see Gottman, 1999). Armed with findings that suggested that even good marriages had conflict, researchers were able to turn attention toward what made a good marriage good.

As a result of this change in focus toward understanding relationship processes in both happy and unhappy couples, the 1990s experienced a dramatic increase in the number of scholarly papers on marriage and

10 • Handbook of Clinical Issues in Couple Therapy

couple interactions—a research boom if you will (Bradbury et al., 2000). With increased attention on the couple relationship, sophisticated research methods were developed that allowed researchers to get at complex relationship dynamics and that brought to light couple interactions in a way that better matches what couple therapists need to know in the therapy room. The relationship science of today is multidimensional and multidisciplinary (Fincham, Stanley, & Beach, 2007) with researchers simultaneously considering the influence and interaction of perception, physiology, and behavior—what John Gottman (1999) refers to as the "core triad of balance" (p. 37). The idea is that an understanding of each part of this triad must be balanced with an understanding of the others and with how all three interact together in order to understand couple relationships. It is the interaction of these three aspects of functioning that makes couple relationships unique. This balanced, multidimensional research perspective has led to the development of integrative models of couple therapy that emphasize the complex interaction between individual psychology (e.g., emotion, perception) and physiology (e.g., heart rate, health), and interactions that capture the uniqueness of couple functioning and couple therapy.

The Development of Theories/Models Unique to Couple Therapy

Concurrent with the movement toward advancements in relationship science in the 1980s and 1990s, there was a separate, but overlapping movement toward building theory of couple therapy. Although both were occurring at the same time, it wasn't until the latter part of the 1990s that evidence began to appear in the literature of their convergence. This movement toward theory building was spurred on by three noteworthy trends: the trend toward integrative practice, the trend toward briefer interventions, and the trend toward using research to inform model development.

The Trend Toward Integrative Practice The 1990s saw a movement among clinician-scholars away from the promotion of traditional one-dimensional models of psychotherapy toward models of psychotherapy that integrated principles across multiple theories (Gurman & Fraenkel, 2002). While it could be argued that integration (or rather eclecticism) has been a common practice for decades, the promotion of formal integrative models of intervention through professional scholarship has occurred only recently. The trend toward model integration appears to have emerged in response to a recognition that (a) factors common across therapies account for the greatest proportion of outcome variance (see Hubble, Duncan, & Miller, 1999), and (b) model superiority would not be determined by pitting one approach to therapy against another (Gurman & Fraenkel). Integrative models help clinicians to see and address the multidimensional nature of couple interactions, making intervention more effective and efficient. It is common for the integrative models of today to concurrently emphasize individual psychology, emotional expression, interpersonal dynamics, psychophysiology, and meaning and belief systems. Given the complex interpersonal and personal dynamics involved in intimate adult relationships, it is not surprising that integrative models were needed in order for move couple therapy out of the shadow of family therapy.

The Trend Toward Briefer Interventions   Beginning in the 1980s, there was a push in the mental health field for the development of shorter term treatments. This was driven largely by an effort to contain health care costs, but was also driven by a realization that lengthier treatments were not associated with better treatment outcomes than shorter term treatments. While couple therapy has been generally considered a shorter-term treatment, this trend in the mental health field influenced couple therapy for the better by encouraging model developers to make couple therapy more efficient through more targeted interventions. This was done by placing more attention on the couple interaction and the existing strengths of the relationship rather than on individual intrapsychic processes and dysfunctions. As a result of the trend toward briefer interventions, coupled with the trend toward integrative practice, state-of-the-art couple therapy treatments now capitalize on the strengths of the couple relationship in developing treatment plans designed to bring about change.

The Trend Toward Using Research to Inform Model Development   With the increased sophistication of research since the start of 1990s there has been a corresponding increase in the ability to apply research findings to clinical practice. Nowhere has this been more noteworthy than in work with couples. Research on couple relationships (see preceding text) and on the effectiveness of couple therapy (see following text) has exerted great influence on the development of models of couple therapy. This research has served to both inform the development of models of couple therapy and to demonstrate the effectiveness of this treatment modality. Research on relationships has been used to make couple therapy models more relevant by increasing our understanding of couple relationship processes. Research on change processes has been used to make couple therapy more effective and efficient through a refinement of therapeutic strategies and techniques. Research on treatment outcomes has been used to demonstrate that couple therapy works.

While there are many noteworthy models of couple therapy, we will mention only two because they exemplify how the major trends have worked to lead to the development of unique models of couple therapy.

Emotionally Focused Couple Therapy   With origins in the 1980s, emotionally focused couple therapy (EFT) is a relative new-comer on the couple therapy scene, but has risen quickly to a position of being one of only a handful of state-of-the-art couple therapy treatments. The effectiveness of EFT has been well documented (e.g., Johnson, 2007; Johnson & Lebow, 2000). EFT gained initial prominence among professionals trained as marriage and family therapists, and so filled a void among these clinicians for a model of couple therapy based on systemic principles. EFT is less well known among couple therapists trained as psychologists and clinical social workers (Gurman & Fraenkel, 2002), but this is changing as couple therapists in each of the mental health professions increasingly look for established, well-validated models to guide their work with couples.

But, EFT's rise to prominence is the result of more than just being in the right place at the right time. This rapid ascendancy to state-of-the-art status is a product of the tenacity of its model developers to understand therapeutic change processes unique to work with couples and to document the effectiveness of the model. Couple therapists Leslie Greenberg and Susan Johnson (with others) systematically observed change incidents in couple therapy to determine commonalities and processes (Greenberg & Johnson, 1988). They found that observable changes in the way that spouses interacted with each other followed periods of softening—times when spouses appeared to let down their defenses enough to take the perspective of the other person and to empathize with their emotional experience (Greenberg & Johnson). This observation led to the development of a three-phase, nine-step model of couple therapy designed to create situations where softening could occur and where the resulting change could be reinforced and integrated into the couples' everyday life.

EFT is an integration of gestalt/experiential and family systems (primarily structural and strategic) and principles. Consequently, it emphasizes both the individual emotional experience and the interactional processes of an intimate couple relationship. According to EFT, emotion is the driving force in organizing how people interact with one another. Emotion occurs in the context of relationships (it is a relationship experience) and serves the purpose of connecting people to one another and to the environment (Johnson & Denton, 2002). It is emotion that motivates people to action and is the driving force behind what people do and what they think (Greenberg & Johnson, 1988). Interactional processes are emotional processes as much, if not, more than they are behavioral processes. So, emotion must be addressed directly in order for lasting change to occur.

A central premise of EFT is that adults have an inherent need for sustained, meaningful, and intimate contact with another person (Johnson, 2007). Because it is emotion that drives the achievement of this attachment with someone else, couple therapy must emphasize attachment processes and the emotions that drive these processes. Problems develop for couples when attachment injuries occur: when attempts to get needs for intimacy, shared meaning, and self-worth are disregarded, ignored, or, worse, abused. Left unresolved, these injuries can fester and result in problematic cycles of interaction. Couples who have experienced attachment injuries will often feel that they must protect themselves from further injury by hiding their primary emotions and protecting their vulnerability. Yet, it is precisely the expression of these vulnerabilities and primary emotions that are so important to getting intimacy needs met. So, a problematic interactional cycle develops that is potentially toxic to both the relationship and to each partner.

Each person's past is alive in the present. In fact, it is really only the current experience of the past that is important to the couple. While past attachment injuries are important, it is the on-going, pervasive attempts to protect oneself from re-injury that is the focus of treatment. So, EFT emphasizes the importance of current emotional experiencing and EFT therapists work to help clients experience emotions in the present so they can be identified, acknowledged, and worked with as they are experiencing them.

The conjoint couple therapy begins with an assessment of the current interactional functioning of the couple. This is done through the use of enactments and otherwise observing the couple's interactions while talking about the couple's distress. The stage is set for softening to occur as the therapist works to deescalate problematic cycles of interaction through active redirection and intervention. This de-escalation occurs as the therapist helps spouses acknowledge primary emotions. Specific change events are created as therapists help partners identify, acknowledge, and express their primary emotions in a safe environment where vulnerabilities can be acknowledged and accepted. According to the theory, this type of emotional expression leads to action or change. So, the last phase of couple therapy is to reinforce and consolidate these changes.

Integrative Behavioral Couple Therapy As a behavioral therapy, integrative behavioral couple therapy (IBCT) "views behavior and any changes in that behavior as a function of the context in which the behavior occurs" (Dimidjian, Martell, & Christensen, 2002, p. 253). IBCT has its origin in the behavioral marital therapy (BMT) that originated in the late 1960s. Prior to the development of BMT, marriage counseling was generally done with just one spouse (Gurman & Fraenkel, 2002), and there did not exist a model of therapy to suggest that conjoint work was needed or desirable. The focus was on individual adjustment to marriage and not so much on the interactional processes of the relationship. The emphasis of BMT on seeing and changing behavior in the context of the relationship made BMT the first conjoint couple therapy.

BMT had a great deal of promise. In fact, no other couple therapy has as many outcome studies documenting its success as BMT (Dimidjian et al., 2002). However, despite this success, in the 1980s the primary developers of BMT became unsettled with the model's inability to produce what they considered to be meaningful change. Neil Jacobson and Andrew Christensen found that the positive marital outcomes associated with BMT were not

14 • Handbook of Clinical Issues in Couple Therapy

able to be sustained even 3–6 months post therapy completion, and that the improvements that were seen were probably attributable to deterioration in control groups more than improvements in those receiving treatments. So, thus began a deconstruction of the model through a systematic observation of therapy sessions and couple interactions and therapy outcome studies to determine the processes of change in couple relationships. Through research and clinical work, Jacobson and Christensen (1996) realized that traditional BMT placed too much emphasis on the behavior of each spouse when the key to a successful couple relationship was really on the perception and acceptance of the behavior by the recipient of it (the other spouse). So, they reasoned, if they were to improve the effectiveness of couple therapy, they must place less emphasis on behavioral change and more emphasis on acceptance of differences and perpetual problems.

Unlike traditional BMT, IBCT does not attempt to search for and eliminate incompatibilities and problems in relationships. IBCT holds that all couples have problems and will, in time, encounter areas of difficulty, but that these do not necessarily cause distress or lead to relationship unhappiness. Rather, distress is the result of how couples handle these problems, disagreements, and difficulties (Dimidjian et al., 2002).

Successful couples tolerate and accept differences by giving more weight to one another's contributions. They continue to see and value the redeeming characteristics of their partners even in the face of difficulty. These couples may acknowledge differences and problems—and they may even argue about them—but they are more willing to compromise, with each person trying to see the perspective of the other and with each demonstrating a willingness to accommodate the other in the areas of difference. A characteristic of successful couples is that they do not try to change each other and the paradox is that in an environment where change is not required or expected, change is more likely to occur. So, while differences continue to exist, for successful couples they become less pronounced in both perception and behavior over time.

While most intimate relationships begin with a tolerance, and even an appreciation of differences, as the relationship progresses some couples find it increasingly difficult to accept, tolerate, and compromise in areas of difference. Principally in an effort to get the partner to change (and out of frustration in not being able to get them to), these couples develop intractable, negatively escalating cycles of negative and coercive behavior. With each trying to change the other, each becomes more resolved in not changing and a polarization develops in the relationship. This often results in perceptions of the partner having character flaws.

Thus, to move couples from distressed to non-distressed status, IBCT focuses on the recipient of behavior. Focus is on partners' perceptions of one another and on acceptance of differences and perpetual problems. Rather than attempting to establish rules for governing behavior, the IBCT therapist

The State of Couple Therapy • **15**

focuses on shaping behavior through contingencies (the natural consequences of adopting the behavior).

While IBCT does not yet have the empirical support that BMT enjoyed, there is evidence to suggest that improvements of couple functioning as a result of IBCT intervention are both clinically significant and enduring—outcomes that were not associated with BMT. For example, a recent study (Christensen, Atkins, Yi, Baucom, & George, 2006) followed couples receiving IBCT and traditional BMT over a period of 2 years. While couples in both treatments experienced a decrease in marital satisfaction after treatment was completed, IBCT couples regained satisfaction sooner and were generally more stable and did better overall than BMT couples.

Research on the Effectiveness of Couple Therapy

In order to understand the impact of psychotherapy research on couple therapy, one must distinguish between the day-to-day practice of couple therapy (that which is provided by the clinician in the field) and the state of the art of couple therapy (that which is well articulated, widely accepted, and replicable across multiple clinicians with verifiable effectiveness). While it is true that the state of the art is practiced by many work-a-day clinicians, reason would suggest that it would be equally true that many, even most, clinicians providing couple therapy would not practice the state of the art. One look at the history of couple therapy would suggest that this would be true. After all, couple therapy, in all of its historical variations, has been practiced for a century, but it has only been within the past two decades that coherent theories of couple therapy have emerged and that the couple therapy treatment modality has been accepted as part of the mainstream of mental health care. So, it would stand to reason that the practice strategies of the past would persist in the day-to-day practice of couple therapy. However, reason would also suggest that advancements in the state-of-the-art therapy would, over time, be adopted by clinicians in search of a theory to guide practice and would be expected by a clientele in search of an effective treatment for couple distress and other problems for which couple therapy has been found effective.

In Pinsof & Wynne (2000), noted clinicians and researchers William Pinsof and Lyman C. Wynne, in their introduction to a special issue of the *Journal of Marital and Family Therapy* on treatment effectiveness explained that "couple and family therapy research has had little, if any, impact on the practice of most couple and family therapists" (p. 1). While I would agree with this statement, I assert that effectiveness research has been critically important, even essential, in the development of the state of the art of couple therapy and in mainstreaming this treatment modality.

Research on the effectiveness of couple therapy that has helped to bring it out of obscurity has been that which has documented (a) that certain couple

16 • Handbook of Clinical Issues in Couple Therapy

therapy approaches are effective and useful, and (b) that couple therapy is an effective treatment modality for specific conditions. This research has found that couple therapy in its state-of-the-art forms works and that it is a legitimate treatment modality for a wide variety of problems, extending beyond just marital distress (Bray & Jouriles, 1995; Shadish, Ragsdale, Glaser, & Montgomery, 1995; Sprenkle, 2002; Stith, Rosen, & McCollum, 2003).

The Future of Couple Therapy

Summarizing the current state of the field, Susan Johnson (2007), one of the developers of Emotionally Focused Couple Therapy (EFT) declared,

> For the first time in the field of close relationships, there is a rich convergence of theory, research, and practice. All the arrows have at last begun to point in the same direction. For the first time the couple therapist is walking in a territory that is predictable, explainable, and changeable (p. 7).

The future of couple therapy is bright. But, it has still not come of age, despite attempts by prominent scholars to declare that it has (e.g., Gurman & Fraenkel, 2002; Gurman & Jacobson, 1995; Johnson & Lebow, 2000). Do we have robust, state-of-the-art couple therapy treatments? Yes. Finally, we do. They are validated by a growing body of research suggesting that they are effective. They are well articulated and training in their use is widely available so that both the treatments and the outcomes can be duplicated outside of the research setting. But, to have a robust state-of-the-art treatment with demonstrated effectiveness is not, by itself, evidence that any treatment modality has come of age.

Johnson and Lebow (2000) explained that the maturity of any treatment was determined by four criteria. These criteria are as follows: (a) there is a clear description of the problems that the treatment addresses; (b) there is a clear description of what distress and adjustment looks like; (c) there is a unifying theoretical framework for the phenomena addressed; and (d) there exist interventions documented to be effective. Johnson and Lebow present convincing evidence that these criteria have been met. The maturity of the state-of-the-art treatments is not in question. But, to declare that couple therapy has come of age is premature. For, in order to declare a treatment to have come of age, it must also be the treatment of choice among clinicians. In order to have come of age, it is especially important that the majority, or maybe even a sizeable minority, of clinicians (in this case couple therapists) recognizes and practice the state of the art—something that I believe has not yet happened among those practicing couple therapy. So, I would add these four additional criteria: (a) there must be widespread acceptance of the treatment as unique and legitimate by both the field and the customers; (b) it must be the treatment of choice for certain problems and there must be clinicians who identify themselves as administering the treatment; (c) there must be acceptance of the treatment by other helping professionals, who may not be the ones administering the treatment but who might be making referrals and/or collaborating with the clinicians administering the treatment; and (d) the consumers of mental health treatments must see it as acceptable and seek out the treatment. Unfortunately, I have found no evidence to suggest that the state-of-the-art couple therapies enjoy widespread use. In fact, I suspect that many who are practicing couple therapy are not even aware that the state-of-the-art treatments exist.

But, the future of couple therapy is bright.

As a foundation on which the future of couple therapy will be built are the following:

- A sophisticated relationship science exists that is bringing to light the complex dynamics of couple relationships. Research questions are being asked that are relevant to the work of couple therapists and that are producing results that are informing both the theory and practice of couple therapy.
- Robust models of couple therapy exist that take into account the complex, multidimensional nature of couple interactions. These models are integrative, theoretically sound, well articulated, and specially designed to guide work with couples. They are easily replicable and accepted as legitimate mental health treatments.
- A science and scholarship of couple therapy exists in which the effectiveness of the treatment modality in its state-of-the-art form is documented.

With these advancements as a foundation, we offer the following four suggestions for future work which will continue to advance the practice of couple therapy:

- Continued work on what makes marriages work.
- Work on the application of state of the art of couple therapy models to different cultural groups. The established models of couple therapy have been developed and evaluated primarily with the dominant cultural group in North America (e.g., Caucasian, heterosexual, middle class). Investigating the unique application of couple therapy to minority culture groups and internationally will lead to advancements in the treatment modality. It will help to identify strengths and limitations in its application and will help to clarify the theory that serves as its foundation.
- Work on improving access to training and in getting the word out that state-of-the-art treatments exist. As we increase the numbers of therapists practicing state-of-the-art treatments, both clients and the field will benefit.

18 • Handbook of Clinical Issues in Couple Therapy

- Continued work on couple therapy for specific disorders. With the link between couple functioning and mental and physical health and quality of life clearly determined, the couple therapy treatment modality has great promise as a preferred treatment option. Applying state-of-the-art couple therapy treatments to a wide variety of disorders and problems and then determining the effectiveness of the interventions will go a long way toward helping couple therapy come of age.

References

Alexander, F. (1968). *An empirical study on the differential influence of self-concept on the professional behavior of marriage counselors*. Unpublished doctoral dissertation, University of Southern California.

Berscheid, E. (1999). The greening of relationship science. *American Psychologist, 54,* 260–266.

Bradbury, T. N., Fincham, F. D., & Beach, S. R. H. (2000). Research on the nature and determinants of marital satisfaction: A decade in review. *Journal of Marriage and the Family, 62,* 964–980.

Bray, J. H., & Jouriles, E. N. (1995). Treatment of marital conflict and prevention of divorce. *Journal of Marital and Family Therapy, 21,* 461–473.

Broderick, C. B., & Schrader, S. S. (1981). The history of professional marriage and family therapy. In A. S. Gurman & D. P. Kniskern (Eds.), *Handbook of family therapy*. New York: Brunner/Mazel.

Busby, D. M., Christensen, C., Crane, D. R., & Larson, J. H. (1995). A revision of the dyadic adjustment scale for use with distressed and nondistressed couples: Construct hierarchy and multidimensional scales. *Journal of Marital and Family Therapy, 21,* 289–308.

Christensen, A., Atkins, D. C., Yi, J., Baucom, D. H., & George, W. H. (2006). Couple and individual adjustment for 2 years following a randomized clinical trial comparing traditional versus integrative behavioral couple therapy. *Journal of Consulting and Clinical Psychology, 74,* 1180–1191.

Consumer Reports (1995). Consumer reports study on psychotherapy. *Consumer Reports,* November 1995, 734–739.

Crane, D. R., Wampler, K. S., Sprenkle, D. H., Sandberg, J. G., & Hovestadt. A. J. (2002). The scientist-practitioner model in marriage and family therapy doctoral programs. *Journal of Marital and Family Therapy, 28,* 75–83.

Dimidjian, S., Martell, C. R., & Christensen, A. (2002). Integrative behavioral couple therapy. In A. S. Gurman & N. S. Jacobson (Eds.), *Clinical handbook of couple therapy* (pp. 251–277). New York: Guilford.

Doherty, W. J., & Simmons, D. S. (1996). Clinical practice patterns of marriage and family therapists and their clients. *Journal of Marital and Family Therapy, 22,* 9–25.

Fincham, F. D. (2003). Marital conflict: Correlates, structure and context. *Current Directions in Psychological Science, 12,* 23–27.

Fincham, F. D., Stanley, S. M., & Beach, S. R. H. (2007). Transformative processes in marriage: An analysis of emerging trends. *Journal of Marriage and the Family, 69,* 275–292.

Gottman, J. M. (1999). *The marriage clinic: A scientifically-based marital therapy*. New York: W. W. Norton.

The State of Couple Therapy • **19**

Greenberg, L. S., & Johnson, S. M. (1988). *Emotionally focused therapy for couples*. New York: Guilford.

Gurman, A. S. (1973). Marital therapy: Emerging trends in research and practice. *Family Process, 12*, 45–54.

Gurman, A. S., & Fraenkel, P. (2002). The history of couple therapy: A millennial review. *Family Process, 41*, 199–260.

Gurman, A. S., & Jacobson, N. S. (1986). Marital therapy: From technique to theory, and back again, and beyond. In N. S. Jacobson & A. S. Gurman (Eds.), *Clinical handbook of marital therapy* (pp. 1–9). New York: Guilford.

Gurman, A. S., & Jacobson, N. S. (1995). Therapy with couples: A coming of age. In N. S. Jacobson & A. S. Gurman (Eds.), *Clinical handbook of couple therapy* (pp. 1–6). New York: Guilford.

Gurman, A. S., & Kniskern, D. P. (Eds.). (1981). *Handbook of family therapy*. New York: Brunner/Mazel.

Heatherington, E. M., Cox, M., & Cox, R. (1978). The aftermath of divorce. In J. H. Stevens Jr., & H. Matthews (Eds.), *Mother-child, father-child relations* (pp. 149–176). Washington, DC: NAEYC.

Hubble, M. A., Duncan, B. L., & Miller, S. D. (1999). *The heart and soul of change: What works in therapy*. Washington, DC: American Psychological Association.

Jacobson, N. S., & Christensen, A. (1996). *Integrative couple therapy: Promoting acceptance and change*. New York: Norton.

Johnson, S. M. (2007). A new era for couple therapy: Theory, research, and practice in concert. *Journal of Systemic Therapies, 26*, 5–16.

Johnson, S. M., & Denton, W. (2002). Emotionally focused couple therapy: Creating secure connections. In A. S. Gurman & N. S. Jacobson (Eds.), *Clinical handbook of couple therapy*. (pp. 221–250). New York: Guilford.

Johnson, S. M., & Lebow, J. (2000). The "coming of age" of couple therapy: A decade review. *Journal of Marital and Family Therapy, 26*, 23–38.

Liddle, H. A. (1991). Empirical values and the culture of family therapy. *Journal of Marital and Family Therapy, 17*, 327–348.

Locke, H. J., & Wallace, K. M. (1959). Short marital-adjustment and prediction tests: Their reliability and validity. *Marriage and Family Living, 21*, 251–255.

Manus, G. I. (1966). Marriage counseling: A technique in search of a theory. *Journal of Marriage and the Family, 28*, 449–453.

Nichols, M. P. & Schwartz, R. C. (2007). *Family therapy: Concepts and methods*. Boston, MA: Allyn & Bacon.

Nichols, W. C. (1992). *The AAMFT: Fifty years of marital and family therapy*. Alexandria, VA: American Association for Marriage and Family Therapy.

Pinsof, W. M., & Wynne, L. C. (1995). The efficacy of marital and family therapy: An empirical overview, conclusions, and recommendations. *Journal of Marital and Family Therapy, 21*, 585–613.

Pinsof, W. M., & Wynne, L. C. (2000). Toward progress research: Closing the gap between family therapy practice and research. *Journal of Marital and Family Therapy, 26*, 1–8.

Popenoe, D. (1992). *Remembering my father, Paul Popenoe: An intellectual portrait of "the man who saved marriages."* Retrieved July 8, 2008 from http://www.popenoe. com/PaulPopenoe.htm

Seligman, M. E. P. (1995). The effectiveness of psychotherapy: The Consumer Reports study. *American Psychologist, 50*, 965–974. Retrieved October 11, 2010 from http://horan.asu.edu/cpy702readings/seligman/seligman.html

20 • Handbook of Clinical Issues in Couple Therapy

Shadish, W. R., Ragsdale, K., Glaser, R. R., & Montgomery, L. M. (1995). The efficacy and effectiveness of marital and family therapy: A perspective from meta-analysis. *Journal of Marital and Family Therapy, 21,* 345–360.

Simmons, D. S., & Doherty, W. J. (1995). Defining who we are and what we do: Clinical practice patterns of marriage and family therapists in Minnesota. *Journal of Marital and Family Therapy, 21,* 3–16.

Spanier, G. B. (1976). Measuring dyadic adjustment: New scales for assessing the quality of marriage and similar dyads. *Journal of Marriage and the Family, 38,* 15–28.

Sprenkle, D. H. (Ed.). (2002). *Effectiveness research in marriage and family therapy.* Alexandria, VA: American Association for Marriage and Family Therapy.

Sprenkle, D. H. (2003). Effectiveness research in marriage and family therapy: Introduction. *Journal of Marital and Family Therapy, 29,* 85–96.

Stith, S. M., Rosen, K. H., Barasch, S. G., & Wilson, S. M. (1991). Clinical research as a training opportunity: Bridging the gap between theory and practice. *Journal of Marital and Family Therapy, 17,* 349–353.

Stith, S. M., Rosen, K. H., & McCollum, E. E. (2003). Effectiveness of couples treatment for spouse abuse. *Journal of Marital and Family Therapy, 29,* 407–426.

Thomas, R. M. (1998, May 6). Emily Mudd, 99, dies; early family expert. *The New York Times.* Retrieved July 8, 2008 from http://query.nytimes.com/gst/fullpage.html?res=950DEEDB1731F935A35756C0A96E958260

Werry, J. S. (1989). Family therapy: Professional endeavor or successful religion? *Journal of Family Therapy, 11,* 377–382.

Wetchler, J. L. (2003). The history of marriage and family therapy. In L. L. Hecker & J. L. Wetchler (Eds.), *An introduction to marriage and family therapy.* Binghamton, NY: Haworth.

Whisman, M. A., Dixon, A. E., & Johnson, B. (1997). Therapists' perspectives of couple problems and treatment issues in couple therapy. *Journal of Family Psychology, 11,* 361–366.

Williams, L. M., Patterson, J. E., & Miller, R. B. (2006). Panning for gold: A clinician's guide to using research. *Journal of Marital and Family Therapy, 32,* 17–32.

I
Biological and Physiological Issues

2
Brain Biology and Couple Therapy

THOMAS W. ROBERTS

Contents

Affective and Emotional States	24
Learning and Memory	28
Application of Brain Biology to Couple Therapy	32
References	38

Since the mid-1990s, brain researchers have rewritten much of what is known about brain functioning. New methods of research, such as brain imaging, have expanded the field of brain research and made it possible to observe the blood flows through the brain and to map brain activity as it occurs (Liotti & Panksepp, 2004). New insights have broken down the conventional wisdom of the mind/brain relationship. Understanding the mind requires understanding how the brain functions (Panksepp, 2004). It has also become very clear that effectiveness of any type of psychotherapy relies on changing the client's brain (Baxter, Schwartz, & Phelps, 1989; Brody, Saxena, & Stoessel, 2001; Kandel, 1998).

Researchers have found that serotonin uptake in the brain is related to the learning that takes place in therapy. Using SPECT imaging, Viinamaki, Kuikka, and Tiihonen (1998) found that after 1 year of psychotherapy, serotonin uptake was greater for those receiving therapy than it was for those in the control or the no-therapy groups. Cognitive-behavioral researchers found that therapy has an effect similar to an antidepressant medication and acts by reducing the thyroid axis. Subjects who did not receive therapy had an increase in thyroxin (Joffe, Segal, & Singer, 1996).

Other researchers, such as Schwartz, Stoessel, Baxter, Martin, and Phelps (1996), have also found that therapy produces brain change in the level of serotonin, resulting in chemical changes in the brain. Additionally, animal studies have found that rats exposed to spatial stimuli showed greater dendrite growth than rats not exposed. Enriched environments increase brain weight, cortical thickness, and size of neuronal cells (Kolb & Whishaw, 1998).

From these and other studies, the assumption is that psychotherapy changes brain structure and function (Kandel, 1999). While the above research findings are intriguing, how the brain is transformed in psychotherapy is yet to be determined. It is assumed that psychotherapy alters the neurochemistry and physiology of the brain, although how this occurs is shrouded in mystery. While neuroscience has opened new avenues of thought for therapists, it has not provided a guidebook for how to conduct therapy to maximize changes in the structure and function of the client's brain. In fact, the purpose of neuroscience does not completely overlap with the purpose of psychotherapy. The purpose driving neuroscience is to uncover objective quantitative research to develop models of how the mind functions as a process of brain activity (Cozolino, 2002). On the other hand, psychotherapy is driven by an understanding of subjective experiences and effects of social relationships on a person's emotional life. The purpose of this chapter is to bridge the gap between neuroscience and psychotherapy so that there is greater understanding of how the objective biological processes of the brain affect interpersonal relationships and how relationship therapy can affect that biology.

This chapter focuses on those brain processes that are more relevant to the study of psychotherapy, specifically couple therapy, and attempts to define how change occurs by applying neuroscience to psychotherapeutic processes. The author assumes that therapeutic change results from the modification of the brain via new experiences that stimulate plasticity of the brain. Therapeutic outcomes are viewed as the product of interactions of the emotional system, memory, and learning. While these processes overlap and are not mutually exclusive, the discussion of each as entities will allow for an examination of relevant research. The final section of the chapter will make applications to couple therapy.

Affective and Emotional States

A starting point in discussing neuroscience and psychotherapy is affect, or emotions. Generally, researchers accept the notion that affect is innate with cross-cultural universal components of emotional expressions (Amini et al., 1996). Emotions are central to understanding internal dynamics and interactions with others. Much of therapeutic practice and interventions are directed toward influencing and changing emotions. Positive outcomes in therapy are related to how one feels with corresponding changes in thoughts and behaviors.

One of the key issues emerging from neuroscience and psychotherapy is a new understanding of the relationship between rationality and emotionality, or thinking and feeling functions of the brain. These two concepts have been the foundation on which most theories rest. The conventional wisdom has been that rationality is the goal for behavior and the job of the neocortex is to control or subdue the emotional brain. Murray Bowen (1978), one of the first biosocial systems researchers and clinicians, believed that rationality held a superior or hierarchical position with reference to affect or emotions. The emotional brain, or limbic system, was viewed as archaic and the part of the brain humans share with other animals. According to Paul MacLean

(1990) the brain is composed of three parts, referred to as the triune brain, consisting of the R-complex or reptilian brain, the paleolimbic or mammalian brain, and the neolimbic/neocortex. The R-complex, comprising the sympathetic and parasympathetic nervous systems, is related to many autonomic and immunologic functions including sexual, respiratory, cardiovascular, and gastrointestinal. More importantly, the R-complex has been linked to the wide range of mood disorders, such as anxiety and depression. This link suggests that there is a difficulty of addressing these mood and anxiety disorders in therapy because it relies heavily on language and cognitive processes.

The paleolimbic, or limbic, brain system, including the hippocampus, amygdala, and hypothalamus, plays an essential role in the function of emotions (MacLean, 1990). The limbic system receives input from other brain centers and processes them relative to cognitive and behavior functions. For example, sensory input can by-pass the neocortex and go directly to the amygdala, which can stimulate a physiologic response without cognitive input (LeDoux, 1996). Panksepp (1998) postulates that humans share a basic emotional system with other animals, which includes centers for motivation, rage, fear, panic, lust, maternal care, and play.

The neocortex is viewed as the product of evolution, and is related to such tasks as language, strategic planning, cognitive, and symbolic representatives. Researchers take the position that in time, with further evolution, the noecortex will have greater control of the emotions. Research strongly suggests that the left prefrontal cortex is related to positive affective states and has a regulatory function on emotional expression through the amygdala. However, until further evolution of the brain occurs, humans will continue to be largely at the mercy of their overactive emotions (LeDoux, 1996).

In understanding these three parts of the brain as the backdrop for psychotherapy, it is not surprising that the traditional therapeutic process promotes verbal and interpretative techniques. Generally speaking, the goal of psychotherapy is emotional regulation through use of the neocortex. Therapy relies on the use of language and making connections between one's intentions and one's actual behavior. Traditional wisdom promotes the premise that gaining insight regarding how past experiences have restricted one's response repertoire will produce recognizable result in therapy. In short, the traditional outcome of therapy is a restructuring of emotions though rational means and more conscious control over forces that underlie behavior.

Based on neuroscience, this chapter takes a different view. Although no one can argue that our thoughts can influence our feelings, it is becoming clear that the boundary between rationality and emotionality represents a heuristic device for understanding human behavior rather than a real dichotomy between these two brain functions. In our limited past understanding of how the brain worked, it seemed plausible to postulate that rationality and emotionality stemmed from two independent systems. What has become clear from recent research is that the neocortex and the limbic system are well integrated in the human brain, although there do appear to be some areas of the brain that are more involved in emotional responses and other areas that are more involved in cognitive functions. Generally, the idea of the limbic system as the center of emotionality and the prefrontal cortex as the center of cognitive processes are accepted by most brain researchers (Panksepp, 2004). Recent research has revealed, however, that the two systems work together to process information. For example, researchers have discovered that the neocortex does not function adequately without input from the emotional areas of the brain (Damasio, 1994). Without emotional input, a person would be unable to make rational decisions, even as minor as what to eat for breakfast. In a sense, every choice a person makes is an emotional one because rational decisions are made on the basis of potential emotional impact on the person. Therefore, the starting point for application to therapy is to understand how the emotional system informs the rational system about current experiences. This process is called emotional or affective restructuring in contrast to a more traditional process of cognitive restructuring.

Contrary to earlier views postulating that emotions were a type of description of cognitive appraisals, neuroscientists have found convincing evidence that emotional processes in the brain can directly affect behavioral responses through the secretion of hormones, sending signals throughout the nervous system that bypass the neocortex (Kastin, Pan, Maness, & Banks, 1999; LeDoux, 1996). This bypassing of the neocortex, largely due to the structure of the brain in that there are more pathways from the emotional centers of the brain to the neocortex than vice versa, may be the underlying dynamic causing many arguments and emotional dissatisfactions experienced by persons in intimate relationships.

One of the more intriguing discoveries about emotions comes from the work of Richard Davidson (2001), who has concluded that the differences in our brain hemispheres account for much of the affect experienced by individuals. Using PET and fMRI research, Davidson demonstrated that a person tends to have a dominant side when processing emotional information, which remains constant over the person's life time. Left prefrontal dominance tends toward a more optimistic emotional expression, while right prefrontal domination correlates with negative preoccupation. According to this view, emotions as expressed in relationship dynamics are largely intrapsychic and reflect a particular recurring pattern within the brain of each partner.

Emotional disorders, especially as they are expressed in couple relationships, reflect communicative problems associated with autonomic responses. The major factor in a successful relationship may be the compatibility of the partners' autonomic systems; the incompatibility of autonomic responses may account for problems experienced by individuals in a relationship (Gottman, Murray, Swanson, Tyson, & Swanson, 2002).

Attachment bonds emanate from these ancient brain communication patterns and are implicated in relationship problems (Bowlby, 1969, 1984). According to Bowlby, the purpose of attachment was to create a sense of belonging and security in the infant. Attachment styles develop by the age of two and continue throughout life and appear to be nonconscious and pre-cognitive. The initial bonding in relationships is important for the development of psychopathology. The relationship between parent and child is reciprocal and the child's behavior equally affects how the parent responds. Researchers have found that there are early critical periods in which the environment must contain certain experiences. Bowlby (1984) maintained that attachment was much like an instinctual or motivational system that involves memory processes. The infant's inborn attachment signals are linked to the nurturing behaviors of the caregiver. According to Bowlby, the infant responds to separation by protest and despair. Protest occurs through searching, crying clinging, and, if not restored, will result in despair, which conserves energy by withdrawing from danger. The attachment bond becomes a prototype of how an infant views the world. Problem-solving behavior and reaction to stress can be predicted by the attachment bond as the child moves from childhood into adulthood.

Animal research has demonstrated long-term effects for individuals separated from attachment figures, such as social ineptness, lack of appropriate response to others in social interactions, poor mating behavior, and lack of maternal instincts (Amini et al., 1996). In addition, other animal studies have found that long-term inattentive rearing practices of monkeys produce offspring that have poor social and self-caring behavior. The data from these studies reveal that monkeys have permanent changes in their serotonin and norepinephrine levels, resulting in neurological dysfunctions (Andrews & Rosenblum, 1994).

Animal studies on attachment have led some to believe that attachment is basic to mammals in maintaining neurophysiologic homeostasis (Kraemer, 1992). This view contends that input from others, primarily attachment figures, is necessary for homeostatic balance. The ability to maintain one's own homeostatic balance is viewed as lacking at birth and severely inadequate in later life if significant attachment bonds are deficient. If attachment is the primary organizing factor of mammals, it tends to explain why adults may have relationship and personal behavior dysfunction throughout their life spans.

As inferred earlier, the neural systems undergirding affection bonds form the brain's emotional center. Researchers have found that social isolation is related to structural and functional changes in the neurochemistry systems of primates that may lead to dysfunction of these systems (Amini et al., 1996). The conclusion to these studies is that emotional experiences through attachment relationships have long-term effects on the structural component of brain systems. For mammals, the input from attachment figures is necessary for maintaining balance. In the brain, the neurotransmitters most affected by attachment include oxytocin, monoamine, and opiate systems. Humans have an inborn mechanism for communication to establish attachment, and must receive appropriate responses from others in order to develop normally. This interplay of response from caregiver to child is referred to as attunement (Amini et al., 1996). Affective attunement to others is formed early without conscious awareness. Since attachment forms outside conscious thought and conscious attempts to change it have little effect, couples relate to each other through the lens of their attachment styles without understanding the process.

Learning and Memory

Another important inquiry into the workings of the brain is how it processes, stores, and retrieves information. Memory is the core of one's self-identity. Without memory, one's continuing sense of self, including both positive and negative emotions, would be lost. According to brain researchers, learning and memory start with an understanding of synapse (Damasio, 1994). The traditional view of synapse posits that an electrical signal travels along a nerve fiber and triggers a neuron to release a chemical transmitter which bridges across a divide and links with a receptor on a neighboring neuron. Any input to the brain triggers this process of synaptic response involving millions of neurons. Much focus has been placed on understanding the chemical transmitters and their role in human behavior. The causes and treatment of mental illness, particularly from the point of view of psychiatry in the use of psychotropic medications, has been related to increasing or decreasing the activity of certain neurotransmitters. For example, imbalances in two neurotransmitters, serotonin and norepinephrine have been studied for decades for their role in the development and maintenance of depression (Mayberg, 2004).

Learning is the process of forming and strengthening synaptic connections in the brain, which may receive help from support brain cells called glia. Haydon (2001) found that glia cells are imperative for learning and memory because they play an active role in how neurons communicate with each other. Neurons grow and change as a result of the frequency of their use. Experiences and repetition of information can affect learning and memory formation. New experiences and information must be integrated into preexisting knowledge (Ramachandran & Blakeslee, 1998). The brain works to maintain a worldview of previously integrated information. New information is deleted, distorted, and changed in other ways to fit into the preexisting beliefs (Ratey, 2001).

Researchers have found that lateralization of the brain affects how it integrates new information (Ramachandran & Blakeslee, 1998). For example, the left hemisphere is more involved in maintaining the status quo, while the right hemisphere challenges the status quo and causes revisions in the belief system. An effective and largely neglected way to learn may be through overwhelming one's belief system with inconsistencies so that the right hemisphere can initiate the change process.

Learning takes place through short- and long-term memory formation. Short-term memory is usually what one is conscious of in the moment, but may not be remembered later. Long-term memory is the ability to recall something into consciousness at a later time. Researchers have found that tiny spines on synapses form and strengthen memories through repeated activation of that synapse (Shimura et al., 2001). From photographing memory formation, researchers have found that memory involves the duplication of synapses involved in the original memory. When the original memory synapses stimulate others nearby because of their repeated use, the structures of those neighboring synapses change to replicate the pattern of that memory. The implication is that "exercising" the brain can improve learning and memory because activated synapses are able to stimulate other nearby synapses.

According to LeDoux (1996) consciousness is what the mind is aware of at any given time. Since the mind can only experience one thing at a time, conscious awareness is restricted to one input at a time. However, most learning takes place outside of conscious awareness. Much learning takes place at an unconscious level. Freud (1953) postulated that the unconscious was composed of three types. The dynamic unconscious was the most common term and referred to repressed material. Another part of the unconscious related to perceptual and motor skills that is not repressed is called procedural unconscious. The preconscious referred to almost all memory because there is a lack of awareness of almost all mental processes.

Researchers have found that repetition may strengthen a synaptic connection, but may also cause the brain to tire and actually shut down. After a while, the brain recognizes familiar input and ignores it (Ratey, 2001). For the brain to remain engaged and active, information needs to be presented in different formats, such as imagery or movement (Languis, Sanders, & Tipps, 1980). Visualization improves not only learning, but also skill at performing a task. For example, researchers have found that a skill, such as playing the piano can be enhanced by visualizing imagined music or auditory imagery (Zatorre & Halpern, 2005). A person imagining the sound of music can improve his/her skill of playing the piano almost as much as the actual physical practice of playing the piano. Visual, motor, and auditory imagery activate the same areas in the brain as if a person were actually engaged in the activity.

Study of memory over the years has revised the view of basic mechanisms of memory formation and retrieval. Memory can be strengthened, weakened, changed, and distorted. In fact, researchers have discovered that there are different types of memory involving different brain circuits (Bachevalier, Brickson, & Hagger, 1993; Schacter, 2001). Declarative, or explicit memory, involves the medial temporal lobe, medial diencephalon, and ventral portion of the prefrontal cortex. Procedural, or implicit memory, engages the cerebellum and neostriatum. Since implicit memory cannot be recalled from conscious awareness, its presence must be demonstrated from experience.

30 • Handbook of Clinical Issues in Couple Therapy

Researchers found that when there was damage to the temporal lobe, resulting in inability to consciously learn new information, that new information was acquired, but the subject had no conscious awareness of having learned it (Cave & Squire, 1992). Likewise, researchers have found that damage to the basal ganglia impairs implicit memory, but not explicit memory. These findings lead to the conclusion that these two memory systems act independently from each other. Since there are different reactions to neural transmitters, it can also be concluded that they have different neuropharmacology.

The distinction between implicit and explicit memory is important because it allows for greater understanding of how memory develops in and supports intimate relationships. For example, explicit memory is derived from a conscious experience and the intention of remembering an event (Schacter, 2001). Explicit memory is what persons usually regard as memory. Implicit memory occurs from nonconscious learning and, since it occurs outside of awareness, affects behavior, but prevents one from cognitively connecting his/her actions with causes. Implicit learning would not allow persons to have insight into the underlying reasons for their behavior.

Researchers have found that implicit memory develops soon after birth, while explicit memory develops later, around age 4 or 5 (Bachevalier et al., 1993). This difference in maturation means that implicit memory is being stored from very early in life, which creates the basis for affective experiences including attachment relationships and bonding. Brain imaging of blood flow in the brain shows that the hippocampus and the prefrontal lobes are involved in explicit memory retrieval. During implicit memory retrieval, the hippocampus is not affected and there is reduced blood flow in the visual cortex. What this means is that persons may have damage to their hippocampus and have difficulty remembering conscious information, but might not have difficulty remembering information that was learned implicitly.

As stated earlier, researchers have found that the brain eliminates new information that does not fit with the individual's worldview. In other words, the brain operates to eliminate information that is different from stored information. This process is nonconscious and therefore a function of the implicit memory system. There is no awareness that information that does not fit has been eliminated. These implicit memories create rules and prototypes that exist independently from any conscious memory.

It is also probably true that implicit memory is responsible for emotional processes. These learned emotional memories form a type of bias that colors one's response to emotional stimulation so that one responds according to past prototypes. One behaves in familiar ways, even with new input, since he or she forces compliance and only accepts the part that fits into his/her established worldview.

Memory is stored in different parts of the brain and then is put together in a coherent piece when retrieved. Different pieces of the same experience may be stored in different regions of the brain. For example, the factual components of an experience are stored in one region and the emotional aspects in another part of the brain. Upon retrieval, the brain does an excellent job of putting the various parts together again as one coherent memory. Mistakes do happen and false memories can be created. While a memory may not be completely erased, it can be altered, either by adding new information that can be drawn into the memory, or by creating new experiences that weaken the memory. Brain imaging demonstrates that the same areas of the brain are involved in both true and false memories. A person not only believes that the false memory is true, but the brain also does not distinguish between them. False memories may be grafted to old memories as if they belong.

Researchers have found that some classes of drugs enhance memory if they are given within six hours after learning and others, such as benzodiazepines, impair the formation of memory (McGaugh, 2000). Both types of drugs affect the neurotransmitter GABA. Hormones can also have a powerful affect on memory. Emotional experiences are remembered in greater detail than neutral experiences are. For example, if a person senses danger, the hypothalamus sends a signal to the adrenal medulla, which responds by secreting epinephrine and norepinephrine into the blood stream. If the stress persists for more than a few seconds, the hypothalamus–pituitary adrenal (HPA) axis is activated. The hypothalamus secretes the hormone corticotrophin, releasing hormone (CRH), which causes the pituitary to release adrenocorticotropic hormone (ACTH), which causes the adrenal cortex to produce cortisol, generally referred to as the stress hormone. When a person has an emotional experience, this cycle of hormone release occurs and increases the impact on memory.

While emotional memories may form strong connections in the amygdala as a result of cortisol increasing memory formation, long-term exposure to cortisol has detrimental effects on learning and memory (Brown, Rush, & McEwen, 1999). Studies have found that long-term exposure to stress and increased cortisol production reduces the size of the hippocampus, thus affecting learning and memory. Long-term exposure to cortisol leads to neural death and cell atrophy. Researchers have found that adults diagnosed with posttraumatic stress disorder (PTSD) have smaller hippocampuses than normal subjects. On the other hand, researchers have not found the same result for children diagnosed with PTSD and conclude that the reduction in the size of the hippocampus in adults is due to repeated stressful experiences (Carrion, Weems, & Reiss, 2007).

In sum, recent findings support Hebb's (1949) proposition that structural changes in the brain, referred to as plasticity, are based on specific experiences in one's life related to bonding and regulation of emotional expression. Many mental disorders and relationship problems point to the inability of persons to regulate emotions, anxieties, fears, and stress. The amygdala is involved

32 • Handbook of Clinical Issues in Couple Therapy

in emotional learning and studies with animals have shown that long-term effects can be produced in the amygdala that cannot be altered substantially by explicit means.

Recent findings using brain imaging have concluded that learning alters the structure and functions of nerve cells and their connections resulting in anatomical changes in the brain (Kandel, 1999). Studies demonstrate changes in cortical thickness, size of synaptic contacts, number of dendritic spines, and dendritic branching. These processes constitute the mechanism by which psychotherapy facilitates changes in memory and emotional regulation. The next section relates more clearly the change mechanism that results in structural and functional changes in the brain.

Application of Brain Biology to Couple Therapy

Implicit memory is an enduring neural structure that regulates emotional responsiveness and attachment relationships. All interchanges with significant others have the potential of affecting this neural condition. Children are shaped by this affective interaction with caregivers. Early life is important because the infant has not learned self-regulation and is dependent on a caregiver to provide this function. This implicit way of learning relationships becomes the nonconscious basis for all relationships and provides the rules and prototypes for conscious experiences. Individuals process conscious experience through these implicit rules without any conscious knowledge of having done so.

From this perspective, implicit memory is what supports the establishment of pathology and provides a clear example of how persons may be completely unaware of and unable to change their behavior. These implicit rules take over and are guided by eliminating new experiences that do not fit in with these rules. This way of looking at problems is different from the traditional way of understanding problems. Problems are not related to rational ineptness at controlling the emotional aspects of one's life, or the attempt to understand the faulty beliefs that cognitive therapists attempt to eliminate. From this perspective, the very rules governing how one responds are beyond conscious control and, in fact, cannot be brought into consciousness or known by the conscious mind. What one deals with in consciousness is quite different from what may be actually taking place nonconsciously.

Brain biology suggests that traditional methods of therapy may need rethinking. For example, couple therapy generally involves a verbal interaction between the couple and the therapist. This view is certainly consistent with a top down emphasis of understanding brain processes, or the belief that emotions are generated from the rational or cognitive appraisal of experiences of mental processes. Brain research has demonstrated that emotional processes emanate from the ancient portions of the brain and develop and function independently from the neocortex. The problem in addressing therapy from a cognitive perspective is the inability to retrieve into conscious processes what was formed in memory implicitly (LeDoux, 1996). As a cognitive process, couple therapy attempts to change the relationship through conscious means, but does not focus attention on implicit or nonconscious processes. Implicit emotional experiences, such as attachment, were formed nonconsciously and cannot be accessed or changed consciously.

Some novel work exists in the literature to access the implicit memory of couples in therapy (Atkinson, 2005). Atkinson labels the approach Pragmatic/ Experiential Therapy for Couples (PET-C) which attempts to increase levels of neural integration by making implicit memory more accessible to consciousness. The idea behind this approach is that the therapist can see the implicit patterns that operate with each partner that are hidden to the client. By pointing out when these processes are in play, the couple can begin to understand their own implicit processes. This type of interpretive response is viewed as making memories more accessible for conscious awareness.

Perhaps some implicit memories can be understood and discussed in this manner and brought more into consciousness, but the question of how change is wrought remains to be answered. This author is suggesting that a fundamentally different starting point is needed. For example, the focus should be on how to change the implicit memory system of each of the partners *through implicit means*. The proof of the effectiveness of therapy is whether there is demonstrable change in the brain functioning in the form of nonconscious processes that create rules for behavior outside of awareness. While no markers exist for such change in the structure and functioning of the brain in the current literature, in the future we can expect to have markers that will exist for all types of problems. Brain imaging may be an accepted part of treatment in the future. Based on brain research, the author makes the following suggestions for couple therapy.

First, couple therapists should focus more on the internal emotional processes of each partner. Of particular focus should be the attachment style of each person. The therapist should assume that one of the underlying influences on the relationship quality is the autonomic response emanating from an emotional reservoir of each partner. When couples fail to understand each other, it can be assumed that their basic underlying attachment styles are in conflict. The couple's conscious attention at repairing that rift leads to greater misunderstanding and reproach.

Second, the model for therapeutic changes should be one in which re-attachment is experienced instead of verbally talked about. While emotion focused therapy (EFT) (Johnson, 1996) attempts to address attachment issues, the author believes that Johnson's procedure seems more attuned to attempting to change the attachment bonds by re-experiencing and making conscious connections to these past attachment patterns. In contrast, this author believes that the best way to address implicit learning that takes place in relationships nonconsciously is to foster a relationship with the couple that can alter the attachment styles of each partner. The therapeutic relationship is an attachment relationship in which the couple experiences a *nonconscious revision in their relationship patterns*. The therapeutic relationship is a curative factor and not a technique to elicit change. The focus is not the attachment bond as a repressed unconscious process, but as a nonconscious process that emanates from real emotional experiences with the client. It can be expected that clients reenact their implicit memories in their relationships with the therapist. As therapy progresses and the therapist assumes an attachment role, the implicit rules that govern the behavior of each partner will emerge (Amini et al., 1996). For example, forgotten concepts such as transference and projection, which are experienced directly in the therapeutic relationship, become evident. The author believes that experiencing attachment may be more curative than a conscious, cognitive, or even emotional discussion of issues such as attachment.

At the same time that attachment issues are experienced in the relationship with the therapist and the attachment styles shift, the therapist can motivate change by adopting a pattern of interactions that shifts modes of expression. The author believes that one of the roles of the therapist is to foster an atmosphere in which new learning can take place. The therapist must help couples change the mode of expression and use a wide range of responses so that the brains of each partner can receive new information and not filter it out because it does not fit his/her worldview. In addition, the therapist can present information that overloads the brain with inconsistencies so that the right brain can initiate change. This idea is similar to some of Minuchin's (1974) views that the therapist must unbalance or increase the stress in the system in order to produce change.

Changing the brain can come about through practice of new behaviors, trying new experiences, and repeated effort. Researchers have found that a form of implicit memory referred to as priming helps persons recognize or recall prior information that they were exposed to nonconsciously. Priming may be helpful in changing certain patterns nonconsciously. Brain researchers have found that new patterns have to be practiced until they become automatic (Kandel, 1999). In this way explicit and conscious behaviors can affect the formation and expression of implicit and nonconscious processes. However, as stated above, the brain turns off after repeated input of similar information, which means that priming is more effective through implicit means. It also suggests that attempting to make explicit input become part of the implicit memory system is very difficult and requires multiple types of presentations.

Third, this model takes the position that conscious insight is not needed for change. Clients improve, but they do not have conscious recall of how the change took place. This model proposes that even when therapists use verbal and interpretative responses and attempt to create insight into why clients improve, the real change comes about largely from nonconscious implicit changes. Researchers have demonstrated that when clients were asked to recall the most significant intervention in therapy, they remember very minor points and not the perceived significant interpretations made by the therapist (Lyons-Ruth, 1998). Clients recalled that the most therapeutic factor was the relationship with the therapist, and not the techniques or interventions used.

This model assumes that the most important information between client and therapist is shared *nonverbally*. The therapist listens with the third as it were and responds in like manner. While this notion seems common place and rudimentary to therapy, this author assumes that it is the underlying change factor. This aspect of the client/therapist relationship is what Stern (2004) calls "now moments," or specific times in the nonverbal communication in which there is potential for growth. Therapy is viewed as somewhat disjointed, with these moments occurring spontaneously.

The other important aspect of this process is the attunement of the therapist and client with regard to attachment in the development of the therapeutic relationship for a positive outcome in psychotherapy. Based on attunement research between parent and child (Siegel, 1999), Daniel Stern (2004) applied the idea of attunement to therapy. He frames the significance of "now moments" as flashes of interactions between the therapist and the client that are rich in potential for change and growth in both the client and therapist. Stern describes the process of therapy as moving along in a somewhat spontaneous, sometimes random manner until these moments occur.

A host of other types of nonverbal interventions have also been found to be effective in therapy. For example, therapy generally ignores the body, motor activity, and exercise. Brain research has shown how exercise is as helpful in reducing depression as is medication. Movement helps one learn more efficiently by increasing blood flow to the brain. A novel idea is to develop exercises that can be integrated into the therapy session. Homework assignments of developing and maintaining an exercise program should be standard in working with couples (Pederson & Saltin, 2006). Sharing physical activity together, such as taking long walks, could also provide an opportunity for more time together. The use of imagery, including visual, sound, and kinesthetic, can enhance learning because one gains practice while completing a task. Couples can be guided in visualizing the type of relationship they want.

In the past few years, researchers have found that the expressive arts have helped clients when verbal therapies were ineffective (Appleton, 2001; Rankin & Taucher, 2003). In some mental conditions, such as trauma, the nonverbal pieces of memory are more important for the continuation of the symptom than the verbal part (Van der Kolk, 2003). The importance of the expressive arts is that they integrate the left and right hemispheres of the brain.

The theory of psychotherapy using the expressive arts is that art expression affects the brain functioning of the artist. Different artistic expressions access different areas of the brain. For example, according to Lusebrink (2004), drama and dance activate the right and left hemispheres of the brain and the limbic system, while art and music use the sensory system to activate the implicit memory system. Researchers accessing brain damage have concluded that while the right brain may be more involved in creative activity, the role of the prefrontal cortex is central (Bogousslavsky, 2005). When involved in a creative activity, the whole brain is involved. If there are lesions to the prefrontal context and language and cognitive skills are drastically decreased, creative skills may be unaffected. Creativity may be unaffected even if there is irreparable damage to the neocortex. Other researchers have found that both hemispheres are integrated in art expression. This implies that both memories and emotions are accessed during art expression.

Fourth, emotions should be regarded as a prerequisite for rational thinking rather than as needing to be controlled by the neocortex. While the left prefrontal cortex has been found to dampen emotional expression through the amygdala (Davidson, 2001), focusing therapy on controlling emotional responses is not very helpful to clients (Amini et al., 1996). Successful therapy is one in which emotions are allowed to develop as a natural product of the attachment relationship. How rationality and emotionality work together should be a focal point of therapy. In other words, instead of attempting to control the emotional responses, it may be more helpful to clients to help them to understand what the rational brain needs from the emotional brain to make a decision. Blocking or controlling emotional content is detrimental to rational thinking. When one is overcome by emotional content, the question that should be asked is "What is this emotional content trying to convey to help create a rational decision?"

Fifth, therapists should attempt to activate the left prefrontal cortex because it dampens the negative emotional content from the amygdala. The use of humor (Lefcourt, 1996) and responding empathically to the partner (Atkinson, 2005) may help to activate the left prefrontal cortex. Research by Davidson (2001) has demonstrated that each person has a kind of flexible set point for emotional responding. Left hemisphere dominant persons are more positive than right hemisphere persons. While these set points can be changed, they take considerable effort. In activating the positive centers of the brain, humor is helpful in reducing depression and enhancing the immune system. Researchers have found that humor alters the response to stressful situations (Lefcourt). The processing of humor involves the whole brain. All parts of the brain are integrated rather than being processed in one area. For example, initially the left hemisphere is activated in processing words, followed by the frontal lobe, where emotions are processed, becoming active. As a joke is further processed, other parts of the brain are activated, including the right hemisphere. Before the person can laugh, the occipital lobe is activated. The brain wave patterns shift to delta waves as the person grasps the joke and laughs. Persons with right brain dominance need to increase the amount of humor in their lives. Therapists should give homework to increase the amount of humor, and depending on the circumstances, to see humor in their negative experiences.

Sixth, therapists should view therapy as a special consequence of memory work, particularly in reeducating the negative effects of memories. Emotional distress is caused by negative memory patterns, formed by both explicit and implicit memory. Helping people understand how memory is formed in the brain and changes over time without conscious recollection may help take the mystery out of their negative memories. Weakening emotional memories by adding pleasant content can alter their frightening characteristics.

Seventh, therapy should attempt to reduce stress levels. Researchers have found that one of the most effective methods of reducing stress is through exercise (Kramer, Colcombe, McAuley, Scalf, & Erickson, 2005). Neurogenesis of the hippocampus is facilitated by exercise. Exercise improves learning and enhances planning and reasoning. Recent research shows that the brain is changed by meditation (Kalb, 2004). Certain areas of the brain are activated in mediation that act as preventive measures for stress and threats to one's wellbeing. Mindfulness practices can help calm the amygdala and foster living more in the present by reducing the intrusion of past negative memories.

Eighth, couple therapy should pay more attention to love and romantic feelings between the partners. Love creates a nonconscious and implicit bond that initiated the relationship and without a feeling of romance and sexual desire, many couples would not want to continue the relationship. The sexual relationship acts as a metaphor for the overall health of the relationship. According to Helen Fisher (2005) romantic love stimulates the right caudate nucleus and right ventral tegmental area dopamine, increasing the level of dopamine, which is related to feelings of pleasure and satisfaction. Improving the sexual aspect of the relationship is a nonconscious and implicit way of re-attaching to the partner and increasing energy and feelings of satisfaction. When couples feel love for each other they are more likely to indulge in pleasing and satisfying behaviors and to reciprocate positive interactions.

Ninth, therapy should provide new experiences for the couple. New experiences can reduce old negative memories, provide practice for new desired behaviors, and increase bonding. New experiences create implicit learning situations that can change negative behaviors. Persons are not able to change by will or decision—they require new implicit memories, which develop from new experiences. The work of psychotherapy and affecting traumatic memories amounts to more than passive forgetting, rather it is a process involving new learning, new neural growth, and activation of key brain areas, such as the orbitofrontal cortex.

In conclusion, research in neuroscience is expected to continue to open new avenues of thought for application to couple and relationship therapy.

38 • Handbook of Clinical Issues in Couple Therapy

It is important to allow this research to forge new applications rather than using the research to merely bolster favorite therapeutic concepts. Neuroscience allows researchers and psychotherapists to truly think outside the box. Thinking outside the box will be met with critical analysis and change in established beliefs about the therapeutic value of cherished techniques will occur slowly. Nevertheless, psychotherapists are in an enviable position of being able to guide the direction of innovative and more effective interventions into relationship development and maintenance.

References

Amini, F., Lewis, T., Lannon, R., Louie, A., Baumbacher, G., McGuinness, T., et al. (1996). Affect, attachment, memory: Contributions toward psychobiologic integration. *Psychiatry, 59*, 213–239.

Andrews, M. W., & Rosenblum, L. A. (1994). The development of affiliative and agnostic social patterns in differentially reared monkeys. *Child Development, 65*(5), 1398–1404.

Appleton, V. (2001). An art therapy protocol for the medical trauma setting. *Art Therapy: Journal of the American Art therapy Association, 18*, 6–13.

Atkinson, B. (2005). *Emotional intelligence in couples therapy: Advances from neurobiology and the science of intimate relationships.* New York: W. W. Norton.

Bachevalier, J., Brickson, M., & Hagger, C. (1993). Limbic-dependent recognition memory in monkeys develops early in infancy. *Neuroreport, 4*, 77–80.

Baxter, R. L., Schwartz, J. M., & Phelps, M. E. (1989). Reduction of prefrontal cortex glucose metabolism common to three types of depression. *Archives of General Psychiatry, 46*, 243–250.

Bogousslavsky, J. (2005). Artistic creativity, style and brain disorder. *European Neurology, 54*, 103–111.

Bowen, M. (1978). *Family therapy in clinical practice.* New York: Jason Aronson.

Bowlby, J. (1969). *Attachment and loss. Vol. 1: Attachment.* New York: Basic Books.

Bowlby, J. (1984). *Secure attachments.* New York: Basic Books.

Brody, A. L., Saxena, S., & Stoessel, P. (2001). Regional brain metabolic changes in patients with major depression treated with either paroxetine or interpersonal therapy. *Archives of General Psychiatry, 58*, 631–640.

Brown, E. S., Rush, A. J., & McEwen, B. S. (1999). Hippocampal remodeling and damage by corticosteroids: Implications for mood disorders. *Neuropsychopharmacology, 21*(4), 474–484.

Carrion, V. G., Weems, C. F., & Reiss, A. L. (2007). Stress predicts brain changes in children: A pilot longitudinal study on youth stress, posttraumatic stress disorder, and the hippocampus. *Pediatrics, 119*(3), 509–516.

Cave, C. B., & Squire, L. R. (1992). Intact and long-lasting repetitive priming in amnesia. *Journal of Experimental Psychology: Learning, Memory, and Cognition, 18*(3), 509–520.

Cozolino, L. (2002). *The neuroscience of psychotherapy: Building and rebuilding the human brain.* New York: W. W. Norton.

Damasio, A. (1994). *Descartes' error: Emotion, reason and the human brain.* New York: Avon Books.

Davidson, R. J. (2001). Toward a biology of personality and emotion. *Annals of New York Academy of Science, 935*, 191–200.

Fisher, H. (2005). *The nature and chemistry of romantic love.* New York: Owl.

Freud, S. (1953). *The complete psychological works of Sigmund Freud* (vols. 4 and 5). London, U.K.: Hogarth.

Gottman, J. M., Murray, J. D., Swanson, C. C., Tyson, R., & Swanson, K. R. (2002). *The mathematics of marriage: Dynamic nonlinear approach.* Cambridge, MA: MIT Press.

Haydon, P. G. (2001). Glia: Listening and talking to the synapse. *Nature Reviews Neuroscience, 2,* 185–193.

Hebb, D. O. (1949). *The Organization of Behavior: A Neuropsychological Theory.* New York: Wiley.

Joffe, R., Segal, Z., & Singer, W. (1996). Change in thyroid hormone levels following response to cognitive therapy for major depression. *American Journal of Psychiatry, 153,* 411–413.

Johnson, S. (1996). *Creating connection.* New York: Brunner and Mazel.

Kalb, C. (2004). Buddha lesson: A technique called mindfulness teaches how to step back from pain and the worries of life. *Newsweek,* October 4, 2004, p. 52.

Kandel, E. C. (1998). A new intellectual framework for psychiatry. *American Journal of Psychiatry, 155,* 457–469.

Kandel, E. C. (1999). Biology and the future of psychoanalysis: A new intellectual framework for psychiatry revisited. *American Journal of Psychiatry, 156,* 505–524.

Kastin, A. J., Pan, W., Maness, L. M., & Banks, W. A. (1999). Peptides crossing the blood-brain barrier: Some unusual observations. *Brain Research, 848,* 96–100.

Kolb, B., & Whishaw, I. Q. (1998). Brain plasticity and behavior. *Annual Review Psychology, 49,* 43–64.

Kraemer, G. W. (1992). A psychobiological theory of attachment. *Behavioral and Brain Sciences, 15,* 493–541.

Kramer, A. F., Colcombe, S. J., McAuley, E., Scalf, P., & Erickson, K. I. (2005). Fitness, aging and neurocognitive function. *Neurobiology of Aging, 26,* 124–127.

Languis, M., Sanders, T., & Tipps, S. (1980). *The brain and learning: New directions in early childhood education.* NAEYC Annual Meeting, Washington, DC.

LeDoux, J. E. (1996). *The emotional brain: The mysterious underpinnings of emotional life.* New York: Simon & Schuster.

Lefcourt, H. M. (1996). Perspective-taking humor and authoritarianism as predictors of anthropocentrism. *Humor: International Journal of Humor Research, 9,* 61–75.

Liotti, M., & Panksepp, J. (2004). Imaging human emotions and affective feelings: Implications for biological psychiatry. In J. Panksepp (Ed.), *Textbook of biological psychiatry* (pp. 33–74). Hoboken, NJ: Wiley & Sons.

Lusebrink, V. B. (2004). Art therapy and the brain: An attempt to understand the underlying processes of art expression in therapy. *Art Therapy: Journal of the American Art Therapy Association, 23,* 136–142.

Lyons-Ruth, K. (1998). Implicit relational knowing: Its role in development and psychoanalytic treatment. *Infant Mental Health Journal, 19,* 282–289.

MacLean, P. D. (1990). *The triune brain evolution: Role of paleocerebral function.* New York: Plenum.

Mayberg, H. S. (2004). Depression: A neuropsychiatric perspective. In J. Panksepp (Ed.), *Textbook of biological psychiatry* (pp. 197–229). Hoboken, NJ: Wiley & Sons.

McGaugh, J. L. (2000). Memory: A century of consolidation. *Science, 287,* 248–251.

Minuchin, S. (1974). *Families and family therapy.* Cambridge, MA: Harvard University Press.

Panksepp, J. (1998). *Affective neuroscience: The foundations of human and animal emotions.* New York: Oxford University Press.

Panksepp, J. (Ed.). (2004). *Textbook of biological psychiatry.* Hoboken, NJ: Wiley & Sons.

40 • Handbook of Clinical Issues in Couple Therapy

Pederson, B. K., & Saltin, B. (2006). Evidence for prescribing exercise as therapy in chronic diseases. *Scandinavian Journal of Medicine and Science, 16*, 3.

Ramachandran, V. S., & Blakeslee, S. (1998). *Phantoms in the brain*. New York: William Morrow.

Rankin, A. B., & Taucher, L. C. (2003). A task oriented approach to art therapy treatment. *Art Therapy: Journal of the American Art Therapy Association, 20*, 138–147.

Ratey, J. J. (2001). *A user's guide to the brain*. New York: Pantheon.

Schacter, D. L. (2001). *The seven sins of memory: The brain, the mind, and the past*. Boston, MA: Houghton Mifflin.

Schwartz, J. M., Stoessel, P. W., Baxter, L. R., Martin, K. M., & Phelps, M. E. (1996). Systematic changes in cerebral glucose metabolic rate after successful behavior modification treatment of obsessive-compulsive disorders. *Archive of General Psychiatry, 53*, 109–114.

Shimura, H. R., Schlossmacher, M. G., Hattori, N., Frosch, M. P., Trockemacher, A., Schneider, R., et al. (2001). Ubiquitination of a new form of syncline by Parkin from human brain: Implications for Parkinson's disease. *Science, 293*, 263–269.

Siegel, D. J. (1999). *The developing mind: Toward a neurobiology of interpersonal experience*. New York: Guilford.

Stern, D. (2004). *The present moment in psychotherapy and everyday life*. New York: W. W. Norton.

Van der Kolk, B. A. (2003). *Frontiers in trauma treatment*. Presented at the R. Cassidy Seminars, St. Louis, MO, 2003.

Viinamaki, H., Kuikka, J., & Tiihonen, J. (1998). Change in monoamine transporter density related to clinical recovery: A case study. *Nordic Journal of Psychiatry, 52*, 39–44.

Zatorre, R. J., & Halpern, A. (2005). Mental concerts: Musical imagery and auditory cortex. *Nueron, 47*, 9–12.

3
Couple Therapy in the Presence of Mental Disorders

WAYNE H. DENTON and ANNA R. BRANDON

Contents

A General Framework for Systemic Couple Therapists	43
Symptoms as Communication	43
The Importance of an Accurate Diagnosis of Mental Disorder	44
A Medical Family Therapy Perspective on Mental Disorders	44
Current Medical Views of Mental Disorders	45
Emotion-Focused Therapy for Couples and Mental Disorders	45
Depressive Disorders	46
Research on the Association of Marital Discord and Depression	46
Research on the Treatment of Depression With Couple Therapy	46
A Systemic Approach to Depression	47
Bipolar Disorder	47
The Nature of Bipolar Disorder	47
Research on Couple Therapy in Bipolar Disorder	48
Considerations for the Systemic Couple Therapist	48
Anxiety Disorders	49
Anxiety Disorders and Relationship Satisfaction	49
Research on Couple Intervention With Anxiety Disorders	49
Couple Therapy and Panic Disorder With Agoraphobia	50
Posttraumatic Stress Disorder	50
Conclusions	51
References	51

Encountering mental disorders is unavoidable in the practice of couple therapy. Depression, anxiety, and other adult psychological problems are among the most frequent complaints presenting to marital and family therapists (Northey, 2002) and with good reason as marital dissatisfaction and mental disorders regularly co-occur or are "comorbid," in couples (Whisman, 1999). In a representative sample from the United States, the odds of a maritally distressed person having 1 of 11 mental disorders were significantly greater in every case except one (the exception being bipolar disorder where the odds were still greater but the diagnosis was infrequent resulting in low statistical power to detect differences) (Whisman & Uebelacker, 2003). In this research, maritally distressed persons were three times more likely to have a mood disorder, two and a half times more likely to have an anxiety disorder, and two times more likely to have a substance use disorder compared to individuals who were maritally satisfied (Whisman & Uebelacker). These results were replicated in a community survey of residents of Ontario, Canada (Whisman, Sheldon, & Goering, 2000).

Thus, if you are treating couples with relationship discord, it is inevitable that you will encounter couples where one or both partners have a mental disorder. Couple therapists have varying levels of comfort in treating mental disorders. In a random survey of members of the American Association for Marriage and Family Therapy, while nearly 100% of respondents reported feeling competent to treat anxiety, posttraumatic stress disorder and mood disorder, only 29% felt competent to treat severe mental illness (Northey, 2002).

In the past, some couple therapists may have received or perceived a message in their training that the construct of "mental disorders" was not valid or that they were disloyal to the practice of family systems-based couple therapy if they accepted the construct of "mental disorders." This was based in large part on the writings of some of the early family therapy theorists (e.g., Haley, 1976, 1980; Minuchin, 1974). Indeed, while a survey of marriage and family therapy program directors found that most reported providing some training in the *diagnosis* of mental disorders, they indicated that this was done primarily for pragmatic reasons (such as interacting with third party payers) rather than with the goal that such training would be clinically useful (Denton, Patterson, & Van Meir, 1997). Further, the extent to which the *treatment* of mental disorders via couple therapy is taught in marriage and family therapy graduate programs remains unknown. Family therapy has struggled with how to integrate concepts of individual mental disorders with family systems approaches (Denton, 1990).

Increasingly, however, as interest in medical family therapy has grown, marriage and family therapy training programs are developing innovative methods to incorporate training in the mental disorders into marriage and family therapy education (e.g., Patterson & Magulac, 1994; Patterson & Van Meir, 1996). Couple and family therapists are also increasingly training and working in medical settings where they are more likely to treat couples where a member has a mental disorder (Brucker et al., 2005; Edwards & Patterson, 2006; Edwards, Patterson, Grauf-Grounds, & Groban, 2001). Not only will couple and family therapists encounter mental disorders more frequently in these medical settings, but in collaborative treatment teams they will often be looked to as experts in mental disorders (McDaniel, Hepworth, & Doherty, 1992). Thus, the importance of being able to incorporate a consideration of mental disorders into couple therapy is great and is only likely to increase in the future.

Couple Therapy in the Presence of Mental Disorders • 43

The goal of this chapter is to provide some general clinical guidelines for couple therapists encountering mental disorders in their practice and to briefly review some of the more clinically pertinent research on couple therapy and mental disorders. While not entirely satisfactory, the term *mental disorders* will be used here for ease of communication in referring to the disturbances of mood and/or behavior that often bring clients to therapy. Additionally, although there are different paradigms that can underlie models of couple therapy, comments here are directed toward therapists that follow the family systems paradigm in some form (Watzlawick, Beavin, & Jackson, 1967).

Couple therapy is applicable to every mental disorder, yet there are only a few of the mental disorders for which couple therapy has been tested as a treatment in research studies. Even with these disorders, the amount of research has been small so that research provides relatively little guidance to the couple therapist treating mental disorders. There are too many disorders to specifically address each in this chapter so we begin by offering some general guidelines for couple therapists and then move on to discuss some of the mental disorders that the couple therapist is most likely to encounter. It is hoped that couple therapists will be able to usefully apply these general principles to the specific couples they treat.

A General Framework for Systemic Couple Therapists

Symptoms as Communication

Mental disorders, as defined in the *Diagnostic and Statistical Manual of Mental Disorders* (American Psychiatric Association, 2000), consist of collections of symptoms that are primarily internal experiences. Inevitably, however, these symptoms (e.g., low energy, lack of sexual desire, panic, obsessions, or hallucinations) are manifested in some way as behavior. For the systemically oriented couple therapist, these symptoms can be thought of as pieces of cybernetic information in the same manner that speech content, common nonverbal behavior, and so forth are conceptualized as information (Watzlawick et al., 1967). (Calls have been made to include a greater consideration of relationships in the developing *DSM-V* [Beach, Wamboldt, Kaslow, Heyman, & Reiss, 2006; Denton, 2007].)

Watzlawick et al. (1967) helped introduce the concept of "feedback" to the psychotherapeutic world and defined it with the example that

> A chain in which event *a* effects event *b*, and *b* then effects *c*, *c* in turn brings about *d*, etc. would have the properties of a deterministic linear system. If, however, *d* leads back to *a*, the system is circular... (pp. 30–31).

They went on to introduce the idea that all behavior is communication and explained that "Activity or inactivity, words or silence all have message value: they influence others and these others, in turn, cannot *not* respond to these

44 • Handbook of Clinical Issues in Couple Therapy

communications and are thus themselves communicating" (Watzlawick et al., p. 49). Similarly, symptoms of mental disorders all have communication value in a dyad. They are internal phenomenon of the index patient but have external manifestations that become communication to the partner. Importantly, the partner then "cannot not communicate" (Watzlawick et al., p. 48) and cannot help but provide feedback to the index patient in a circular and reciprocal manner.

The couple therapist skilled in the assessment and modification of systemic cycles of interaction can help couples coping with mental disorders by continuing to practice in a systemic way. Symptoms that clients experience and emit become information or communication that partners cannot help but respond to. The symptoms become part of a feedback loop couples may find themselves caught up in as with other feedback loops couples bring to therapy. Some examples with some specific mental disorders will be presented below.

The Importance of an Accurate Diagnosis of Mental Disorder

A mental disorder diagnosis can be a two-edged sword in couple therapy. On the one hand, a diagnosis may be useful to help "externalize" problems (White, 1984) and to provide the diagnosed person a framework with which to make sense of their experience. On the other hand, a diagnosis may be used by the non-diagnosed partner as proof that the diagnosed partner "is the cause of our problems." A diagnosis has also been known to become an unassailable excuse from responsibility—such as in "I didn't follow through on that because of my ADHD."

In knowing how to manage the implications of a diagnosis, one of the first challenges of the couple therapist is to know if the diagnosis as reported by the client is accurate. Clients may have received an erroneous diagnosis either through self-diagnosis or from a professional not skilled in making mental disorder diagnoses. Couple therapists may not, themselves, be skilled in making these diagnoses or may not wish to take the time away from the couple therapy necessary to establish a diagnosis. If other mental health professionals are part of the treatment team, then collaboration with these professionals and the sharing of information may be time-saving and useful to the course of the couple therapy. If a reported diagnosis has never been firmly established, then referral to a mental health professional skilled in diagnosis may be useful.

A Medical Family Therapy Perspective on Mental Disorders

Our perspective is not that mental disorders *are* systemic conditions but that they can be viewed from a systemic lens. Similarly, we would not say that mental disorders *are* biological conditions but that they can be examined with a biological lens as well. These lenses (and others) contribute valuable knowledge to our understanding of the conditions referred to as mental disorders and none are more "true" than another. A number of holistic models have

Couple Therapy in the Presence of Mental Disorders • 45

been proposed consistent with this view such as the popular biopsychosocial model (Engel, 1980). The biopsychosocial model draws upon general systems theory in proposing that cellular, physiological, relational, and social levels of organization are all in systemic interaction and reciprocally influence each other (Engel). This model has received some degree of acceptance in medical education and can provide a common systemic language for couple therapists and medical providers.

Current Medical Views of Mental Disorders

The predominant view of mental disorders in mental disorder research is of a "stress–diathesis" model (e.g., Corcoran et al., 2003; Nemeroff & Vale, 2005; Wood, 2004). That is, it is assumed that some type of environmental stress interacts with a particular diathesis or predisposition toward a particular mental disorder in an individual to produce illness (Post, 1992). While the focus of much medical research is on the "diathesis" or biological aspect of this model, the "stress" part is at least implicitly acknowledged. In fact, innovative studies are now beginning to explore and understand the relationship between stress and diathesis (e.g., Heim, Newport, Bonsall, Miller, & Nemeroff, 2001). The stress–diathesis model also provides the couple therapist another language that will be familiar to medical professionals.

Emotion-Focused Therapy for Couples and Mental Disorders

We have found emotion-focused therapy (EFT) (Johnson, 2004c; Johnson & Denton, 2002) particularly useful for couples where there is a mental disorder. It is a systems-based therapy that also incorporates a focus on internal experience. This blending allows for the phenomenon of the client's internal experience to be integrally linked in the feedback loop with their partner. Published accounts of the use of EFT with mental disorders include depression (Dessaulles, Johnson, & Denton, 2003), posttraumatic stress disorder (Johnson & Williams-Keeler, 1998), and low sexual desire (Macphee, Johnson, & Vanderveer, 1995).

Another attractive feature of EFT is its foundation in attachment theory (Johnson & Whiffen, 1999, 2003). Attachment theory proposes that we are "hardwired" to seek out relationships and that such attachments are key elements of healthy functioning for adults as well as children (Bowlby, 1980). Attachment theory is also discussed with regards to the mental disorders (e.g., Goodwin, 2003) and thus provides yet one more point of connection for couple therapists and medical providers.

In general, in working with couples where there is a mental disorder it will usually be necessary to go slower in the uncovering of underlying emotions and in the structuring of enactments than in couples with uncomplicated relationship distress (Johnson, 2002). EFT can be a powerful approach that is often necessary to unblock discordant couples with rigid negative

46 • Handbook of Clinical Issues in Couple Therapy

interactional cycles where there is no mental disorder. Where mental disorder is also present, however, one or both parties may be more fragile and subject to destabilization. Proceeding more slowly and conducting the therapy over a longer period of time can help couples change at a more comfortable pace.

Depressive Disorders

Research on the Association of Marital Discord and Depression

More research has been conducted on couples with depression than with any of the other mental disorders. Numerous studies have confirmed the findings that depression and dyadic discord have a significant association. This finding has now been verified in a meta-analysis of these studies (Whisman, 2001). In one of the most significant predictive studies, people experiencing marital discord at the time of an assessment were 2.7 times more likely to be experiencing a major depressive episode 12 months later than people without marital discord (Whisman & Bruce, 1999). About 30% of new cases of major depression in this study were associated with marital discord.

Research on the Treatment of Depression With Couple Therapy

There have now been several studies testing couple therapy as a treatment of depression. In general, it is found that couple intervention is as efficacious as individual therapy in treating depressive symptoms if there is also marital discord although the couple intervention has not been more successful than the individual treatment (Emanuels-Zuurveen & Emmelkamp, 1996, 1997; Foley, Rounsaville, Weissman, Sholomaskas, & Chevron, 1989; Jacobson, Fruzzetti, Dobson, Schmaling, & Salusky, 1991; O'Leary & Beach, 1990). Of potential significance, when compared to individual therapy, only the couple therapies improved relationship satisfaction scores in these studies. If this improvement in relationship quality led to fewer relapses of depression, then an argument might be made in favor of the couple therapy over individual therapy but none of these studies conducted such long-term follow-ups. The exact nature of the couple intervention in most of these studies is unclear with the exception of those studies that utilized behavioral marital therapy (Jacobson et al.; O'Leary & Beach).

There have been two studies comparing couple therapy with antidepressant medication. In one study an unspecified model of couple therapy was found to be equivalent to antidepressant medication in improving scores on the Hamilton depression rating scale (Hamilton, 1960) and was superior to medication in improving scores on the Beck Depression Inventory (BDI; Beck, Ward, Mendelson, Mock, & Erbaugh, 1961). This advantage of couple therapy over medication in improving BDI scores persisted at 2 years.

In another study comparing EFT for couples with antidepressant medication, both treatments were efficacious, and equally so, in improving depressive symptoms in women by the end of 4 months of treatment (at which time both treatments were terminated) (Dessaulles et al., 2003). At 6-month follow-up, the women who had received EFT had made additional improvement in their mood that was statistically significant while the women who had received medication had not (Dessaulles et al.).

A Systemic Approach to Depression

Where one or both members of a dyad suffer from depression the depressed mood is often integral to the systemic cycle that the couple presents with. As couple therapists track the couple's cycle they can explore how depressed mood fits into the cycle. Coyne (1976) described an interactional model of depression in which depression suppresses criticism from the spouse. The nondepressed spouse, however, has a buildup of resentments which "leak out" in various ways and lead to the depressed spouse feeling even more depressed and so on. Although this cycle may not occur universally, it does occur often enough that the couple therapist should be alert to it.

Sometimes the nondepressed partners worry that they may upset the depressed partners to the point of becoming suicidal (and, in fact, in some cases that has actually happened in their history). Therefore, they attempt to withhold their desires and feelings, which, again, lead to resentments. The expression of this resentment may be criticism of the depressed partner and negative criticism has been found to be associated with relapse of depression (Hooley & Teasdale, 1989). Carefully helping the couple to process unexpressed or unacknowledged emotions can help strengthen the bond between the couple and be a powerful buffer against the recurrence of depression.

Bipolar Disorder

The Nature of Bipolar Disorder

The bipolar disorders may involve depression but are distinguished from the depressive disorders by the presence of mania or hypomania. Bipolar disorder can be an overwhelming condition with great consequences on couple and family relations even when controlled by medication (Coryell et al., 1993; Gitlin, Swendsen, Heller, & Hammen, 1995).

Accurate diagnosis is especially important in regards to bipolar disorder as some people experience changes in mood that are not bipolar disorder but that result in a misdiagnosis of bipolar disorder (Hutto, 2001). The implications of having bipolar disorder are significant and need to be distinguished from less severe forms of mood lability. Bipolar Disorder tends to be recurrent, usually involves hospitalization at some point in the illness (Silverstone & Romans-Clarkson, 1989; Winokur et al., 1994), and is associated with work impairment (Silverstone & Romans-Clarkson). These are circumstances that a couple may need to prepare for and lend further importance to the accuracy of the diagnosis.

48 • Handbook of Clinical Issues in Couple Therapy

Research on Couple Therapy in Bipolar Disorder

There is a growing literature on the role of couple treatment in bipolar disorder (Clarkin, Carpenter, Hull, Wilner, & Glick, 1998; Croake & Kelly, 2002; Davenport, Ebert, Adland, & Goodwin, 1977). The treatments described have all been used in conjunction with medication. Among these, the greatest empirical support exists for the family-focused treatment model for bipolar disorder (Miklowitz & Goldstein, 1997). This model is gaining credibility and acceptance in the field of bipolar disorder treatment as it has superior outcomes when compared to "treatment as usual" in research studies (Miklowitz, Otto, Frank, Reilly-Harrington, Kogan, et al., 2007; Miklowitz, Otto, Frank, Reilly-Harrington, Wisniewski, et al., 2007; Miklowitz et al., 2000).

Although it is titled "family focused" the treatment manual clarifies that it can be used with couples as well and it lends itself readily to a couple format (Miklowitz & Goldstein, 1997). The model involves three treatment modules: family psychoeducation, communication enhancement training, and problem solving. The latter two sets of interventions will be familiar to most couple therapists who may primarily need to familiarize themselves with the psychosocial aspects of bipolar disorder for the psychoeducational module. The treatment manual for the model (Miklowitz & Goldstein) provides excellent information about bipolar disorder along with a description of the treatment approach.

Considerations for the Systemic Couple Therapist

Full mania is outside the realm of usual human experience and usually requires hospitalization. The aftermath of an episode of mania does not so much lend itself to a consideration of how it fit into a feedback loop as it does to a processing of the trauma that the couple has been through. Due to the short duration of inpatient hospital treatment in the current environment, the couple therapist seeing a couple soon after hospitalization must be alert to the probability that the person with bipolar disorder has not likely fully recovered yet. The emotional intensity of the session should not be pushed until the therapist has assessed the ability of the person with bipolar disorder (and perhaps the partner as well) to tolerate such intensity. Both partners will be able to assist the therapist in making this assessment. The family-focused treatment manual (Miklowitz & Goldstein, 1997) provides invaluable information and guidance pertaining to this early recovery stage.

It would not be uncommon that the partner without bipolar disorder had to have the partner with bipolar disorder committed involuntarily into the hospital. The partner who was hospitalized may continue to have resentments about this that may need to be processed in couple therapy. The couple can be led into discussing the motivations and intentions of the spouse who was forced to initiate the commitment. If there has had to be a hospitalization, it would be of benefit for the couple, at some point, to discuss a plan in the event that a relapse of serious mania or depression occurs. Details on how to do this can be found in Miklowitz and Goldstein (1997).

Of course, couples where one partner has bipolar disorder will have some of the same conflicts and challenges of other couples and these can profitably be addressed in couple therapy. There is evidence that life events and interpersonal relationships influence recurrences of bipolar disorder (reviewed in Alloy et al., 2005) so that helping to improve the supportiveness and decrease the conflict of the couple's relationship may be ameliorative in preventing or delaying future episodes of the bipolar disorder.

It is not uncommon in working with couples where there is bipolar disorder that the partner without bipolar disorder may view the only problem as being the bipolar disorder itself and may tend to be dismissive of any complaints that the partner with bipolar disorder has about the relationship. Sometimes the person with bipolar disorder did not voice these complaints until an episode of mania began which reinforces this view. The couple therapist may need to proceed carefully in helping the couple to untangle what can be "externalized" to the illness of bipolar disorder and what needs to be addressed as a legitimate and real concern about what is happening between them. Again, it cannot be emphasized enough that an understanding of bipolar disorder is invaluable in this process.

Anxiety Disorders

The dozen anxiety disorders described in the *DSM-IV* have widely varying presentations so that there may not seem to be much commonality between them. Complicating matters further, people diagnosed with one anxiety disorder tend to be diagnosed with several as the conditions tend to be comorbid (Noyes & Hoehn-Saric, 1998).

Anxiety Disorders and Relationship Satisfaction

Having a significant problem with anxiety (as evidenced by a diagnosable anxiety disorder) is a common experience in our society. In a randomized survey conducted in the United States (the National Comorbidity Survey), 24.9% of the sample of randomly selected individuals had met the criteria for at least one anxiety disorder sometime in their life (Kessler et al., 1994). Anxiety disorders tend to be associated with relationship distress although there has been somewhat less consistency in this finding than with depression. In the most thorough examination of this issue, Whisman (1999) analyzed data from the National Comorbidity Survey and found that having a diagnosis of an anxiety disorder was significantly associated with marital discord for both men and women although some of the sub-analyses presented a somewhat more complicated picture. Clearly, more research is needed in this area.

Research on Couple Intervention With Anxiety Disorders

Despite the common occurrence of anxiety disorders, there have been few clinical trials examining the efficaciousness of couple therapy in the treatment

50 • Handbook of Clinical Issues in Couple Therapy

of these conditions. One reason for this relative lack of attention may be that there exist highly efficacious individually delivered cognitive therapy interventions for panic disorder, agoraphobia, and obsessive-compulsive disorder (DeRubeis & Crits-Cristoph, 1998).

Where couple intervention has been studied with these conditions, the most common type of couple intervention has been "partner-assisted intervention" (Baucom, Shoham, Mueser, Daiuto, & Stickle, 1998, p. 62). As it is usually implemented, partner-assisted intervention is essentially individual cognitive therapy with the partner attending the session in order to function as a coach outside of the sessions (e.g., Cobb, Matthews, Childs-Clarke, & Blowers, 1984). Little attention is typically given to the systemic dynamics between the couple. Not surprisingly, partner-assisted versions of cognitive therapy have been found to be as efficacious as the individual formats. There has been more conflicting evidence as to whether partner-assisted versions are *more* effective than the individual treatment condition (e.g., Emmelkamp, de Haan, & Hoodguin, 1990; Emmelkamp & de Lange, 1983). Overall, it was concluded in one review that the potential benefits of having the partner attend the sessions is not great enough to recommend conjoint over the individually delivered versions (Baucom et al.). It has also been noted that a potential drawback to the partner-assisted approach is that one partner becomes labeled as the "identified patient" while the other partner has a "one up" position as the "well partner" (Baucom, Stanton, & Epstein, 2003, p. 68).

Couple Therapy and Panic Disorder With Agoraphobia

Agoraphobia (which typically occurs along with panic disorder) occasionally presents to the couple therapist. People with agoraphobia often develop a "safe person" with whom they can venture out into the world and, for people who are married, the safe person is usually the spouse. Recovery from agoraphobia thus can affect the homeostasis of what may have become a stable dyadic relationship. On the one hand, unaffected partners may be relieved that their partners can now be more independent. On the other hand, however, they may no longer feel needed by their spouse and there may be a deterioration of relationship quality (Arrindell, Emmelkamp, & Sanderman, 1986; Barlow, O'Brien, & Last, 1984). Couple therapy can be helpful in guiding the couple to renegotiate their relationship as the partner with agoraphobia has an increased level of independence. There is some evidence that inclusion of the spouse in treatment may prevent negative side effects from improvement in the agoraphobic symptoms (Emmelkamp et al., 1992).

Posttraumatic Stress Disorder

Posttraumatic stress disorder is one of the mental disorders most closely associated with relationship distress (Whisman, 1999) and has obvious relevance to the couple therapist (Sherman, Zanotti, & Jones, 2005). Trauma can impact

Couple Therapy in the Presence of Mental Disorders • 51

the ability to trust and impaired relationships are, in fact, one of the diagnostic criteria in the *DSM-IV* (2000). There has been much clinical writing about the role of couple therapy in posttraumatic stress disorder although there have been few clinical trials.

EFT for couples seems ideally suited to the treatment of posttraumatic stress disorder as EFT focuses on attachment and affect, both of which play key roles in the posttrauma experience (Johnson, 2002). Partners can be gently guided to face their fears as these fears occur in the present with each other and the bond between the couple can be a powerful antidote to the sequelae of past traumas (Beckerman, 2004). There has been much written about EFT for couples and trauma to guide the interested therapist (Johnson, 2002, 2004a,b; Johnson & Williams-Keeler, 1998).

Conclusions

Couple therapy has much to offer in the treatment of mental disorders by decreasing stress and increasing supportiveness as well as making a fundamental change in the symptomatic presentation through altering cybernetic cycles that include the presenting symptoms. Compared to the frequency and burden of mental disorders, there has been little research examining the ability of couple therapy to improve the symptomatic severity of the mental disorders or increase the amount of time people remain in remission from their symptoms. This is a cutting edge for couple therapy research and holds great promise for expanding the boundaries of the practice of couple therapy. In the meantime, couple therapists are skilled in altering negative interaction cycles and increasing the connection between relational partners and can be of great assistance in ameliorating suffering from the common human conditions sometimes known as mental disorders.

References

Alloy, L. B., Abramson, L. Y., Urosevic, S., Walshaw, P. D., Nusslock, R., & Neeren, A. M. (2005). The psychosocial context of bipolar disorder: Environmental, cognitive, and developmental risk factors. *Clinical Psychology Review, 25*, 1043–1075.

American Psychiatric Association. (2000). *Diagnostic and statistical manual of mental disorders* (4th ed., text revision). Washington, DC: Author.

Arrindell, W. A., Emmelkamp, P. M. G., & Sanderman, R. (1986). Marital quality and general life adjustment in relation to treatment outcome in agoraphobia. *Advances in Behavior Research and Therapy, 8*, 139–185.

Barlow, D. H., O'Brien, G. T., & Last, C. G. (1984). Couples treatment of agoraphobia. *Behavior Therapy, 15*, 41–58.

Baucom, D. H., Shoham, V., Mueser, K. T., Daiuto, A. D., & Stickle, T. R. (1998). Empirically supported couple and family interventions for marital distress and adult mental health problems. *Journal of Consulting and Clinical Psychology, 66*, 53–88.

Baucom, D. H., Stanton, S., & Epstein, N. (2003). Anxiety disorders. In D. K. Snyder & M. A. Whisman (Eds.), *Treating difficult couples* (pp. 57–87). New York: Guilford Press.

52 • Handbook of Clinical Issues in Couple Therapy

Beach, S. R. H., Wamboldt, M. Z., Kaslow, N. J., Heyman, R. E., & Reiss, D. (2006). Describing relationship problems in DSM-V: Toward better guidance for research and clinical practice. *Journal of Family Psychology, 20,* 359–368.

Beck, A. T., Ward, C. H., Mendelson, M., Mock, J., & Erbaugh, J. (1961). An inventory for measuring depression. *Archives of General Psychiatry, 4,* 561–571.

Beckerman, N. (2004). The impact of post-traumatic stress disorder on couples: A theoretical framework for assessment and intervention. *Family Therapy, 31,* 129–144.

Bowlby, J. (1980). *Attachment and loss. Volume 3: Loss: Sadness and depression.* New York: Basic Books.

Brucker, P. S., Faulkner, R. A., Baptist, J., Grames, H., Beckham, L. G., Walsh, S., et al. (2005). The internship training experiences in medical family therapy of doctoral-level marriage and family therapy students. *American Journal of Family Therapy, 33,* 131–146.

Clarkin, J. F., Carpenter, D., Hull, J., Wilner, P., & Glick, I. (1998). Effects of psychoeducational intervention for married patients with bipolar disorder and their spouses. *Psychiatric Services, 49,* 531–533.

Cobb, J. P., Matthews, A. M., Childs-Clarke, A., & Blowers, C. M. (1984). The spouse as co-therapist in the treatment of agoraphobia. *British Journal of Psychiatry, 144,* 282–287.

Corcoran, C., Walker, E., Huot, R., Mittal, V., Tessner, K., Kestler, L., et al. (2003). The stress cascade and schizophrenia: Etiology and onset. *Schizophrenia Bulletin, 29,* 671–692.

Coryell, W., Scheftner, W., Keller, M., Endicott, J., Maser, J., & Klerman, G. L. (1993). The enduring psychosocial consequences of mania and depression. *American Journal of Psychiatry, 150,* 720–727.

Coyne, J. C. (1976). Toward an interactional description of depression. *Psychiatry, 39,* 28–40.

Croake, J. W., & Kelly, F. (2002). Structured group couples therapy with schizophrenic and bipolar patients and their wives. *Journal of Individual Psychology, 58,* 76–86.

Davenport, Y. B., Ebert, M. H., Adland, M. L., & Goodwin, F. K. (1977). Couples group therapy as an adjunct to lithium maintenance of the manic patient. *American Journal of Orthopsychiatry, 47,* 495–502.

Denton, W. H. (1990). A family systems analysis of DSM-III-R. *Journal of Marital and Family Therapy, 16,* 113–125.

Denton, W. H. (2007). Issues for DSM-V: Relational diagnosis: An essential component of biopsychosocial assessment. *American Journal of Psychiatry, 164,* 1146–1147.

Denton, W. H., Patterson, J. E., & Van Meir, E. S. (1997). Use of the DSM in marriage and family therapy programs: Current practices and attitudes. *Journal of Marital and Family Therapy, 23,* 81–86.

DeRubeis, R. J., & Crits-Cristoph, P. (1998). Empirically supported individual and group psychological treatments for adult mental disorders. *Journal of Consulting and Clinical Psychology, 66,* 37–52.

Dessaulles, A., Johnson, S. M., & Denton, W. H. (2003). Emotion-focused therapy for couples in the treatment of depression: A pilot study. *American Journal of Family Therapy, 31,* 345–353.

Edwards, T. M., & Patterson, J. E. (2006). Supervising family therapy trainees in primary care medical settings: Context matters. *Journal of Marital and Family Therapy, 32,* 33–43.

Edwards, T. M., Patterson, J. E., Grauf-Grounds, C., & Groban, S. (2001). Psychiatry, MFT, & family medicine collaboration: The Sharp Behavioral Health Clinic. *Families, Systems, & Health, 19,* 25–35.

Emanuels-Zuurveen, L., & Emmelkamp, P. M. (1996). Individual behavioural-cognitive therapy v. marital therapy for depression in maritally distressed couples. *British Journal of Psychiatry, 169*, 181–188.

Emanuels-Zuurveen, L., & Emmelkamp, P. M. (1997). Spouse-aided therapy with depressed patients. *Behavior Modification, 21*, 62–77.

Emmelkamp, P. M., de Haan, E., & Hoodguin, C. A. L. (1990). Marital adjustment and obsessive compulsive disorder. *British Journal of Psychiatry, 156*, 55–60.

Emmelkamp, P. M., & de Lange, I. (1983). Spouse involvement in the treatment of obsessive compulsive patients. *Behavioural Research and Therapy, 21*, 341–346.

Emmelkamp, P. M., Van Dyck, R., Bitter, M., Heins, R., Onstein, E. J., & Eisen, B. (1992). Spouse-aided therapy with agoraphobics. *British Journal of Psychiatry, 160*, 51–56.

Engel, G. L. (1980). The clinical application of the biopsychosocial model. *American Journal of Psychiatry, 137*, 535–544.

Foley, S. H., Rounsaville, B. J., Weissman, M. M., Sholomaskas, D., & Chevron, E. (1989). Individual versus conjoint interpersonal therapy for depressed patients with marital disputes. *International Journal of Family Therapy, 10*, 29–42.

Gitlin, M. J., Swendsen, J., Heller, T. L., & Hammen, C. (1995). Relapse and impairment in bipolar disorder. *American Journal of Psychiatry, 152*, 1635–1640.

Goodwin, I. (2003). The relevance of attachment theory to the philosophy, organization, and practice of adult mental health care. *Clinical Psychology Review, 23*, 35–56.

Haley, J. (1976). *Problem solving therapy.* San Francisco, CA: Jossey-Bass Inc.

Haley, J. (1980). *Leaving home.* New York: McGraw-Hill.

Hamilton, M. (1960). A rating scale for depression. *Journal of Neurology, Neurosurgery, and Psychiatry, 23*, 56–62.

Heim, C., Newport, D. J., Bonsall, R., Miller, A. H., & Nemeroff, C. B. (2001). Altered pituitary-adrenal axis responses to provocative challenge tests in adult survivors of childhood abuse. *American Journal of Psychiatry, 158*, 575–581.

Hooley, J. M., & Teasdale, J. D. (1989). Predictors of relapse in unipolar depressives: Expressed emotion, marital distress, and perceived criticism. *Journal of Abnormal Psychology, 98*, 229–235.

Hutto, B. (2001). Potential overdiagnosis of bipolar disorder. *Psychiatric Services, 52*, 687–687.

Jacobson, N. S., Fruzzetti, A. E., Dobson, K., Schmaling, K. B., & Salusky, S. (1991). Marital therapy as a treatment for depression. *Journal of Consulting and Clinical Psychology, 59*, 547–557.

Johnson, S. M. (2002). *Emotionally focused couple therapy with trauma survivors: Strengthening attachment bonds.* New York: Guilford Press.

Johnson, S. M. (2004a). An antidote to post-traumatic stress disorder: The creation of secure attachment. In L. Atkinson & S. Goldberg (Eds.), *Attachment issues in psychopathology and intervention* (pp. 207–228). Mahwah, NJ: Lawrence Erlbaum Associates.

Johnson, S. M. (2004b). Facing the dragon together: Emotionally focused couples therapy with trauma survivors. In D. R. Catherall (Ed.), *Handbook of stress, trauma, and the family* (pp. 493–512). New York: Brunner-Routledge.

Johnson, S. M. (2004c). *The practice of emotionally focused couple therapy: Creating connection* (2nd ed.). New York: Brunner-Routledge.

Johnson, S. M., & Denton, W. (2002). Emotionally focused couple therapy: Creating secure connections. In A. S. Gurman & N. S. Jacobson (Eds.), *Clinical handbook of couple therapy* (3rd ed., pp. 221–250). New York: Guilford Press.

Johnson, S. M., & Whiffen, V. E. (1999). Made to measure: Adapting emotionally focused couple therapy to partners' attachment styles. *Clinical Psychology: Science and Practice, 6*, 366–381.

Johnson, S. M., & Whiffen, V. E. (2003). *Attachment processes in couple and family therapy*. New York: Guilford Press.

Johnson, S. M., & Williams-Keeler, L. (1998). Creating healing relationships for couples dealing with trauma: The use of emotionally focused marital therapy. *Journal of Marital and Family Therapy, 24*, 25–40.

Kessler, R. C., McGonagle, K. A., Zhao, S., Nelson, C. B., Hughes, M., Eshleman, S., et al. (1994). Lifetime and 12-month prevalence of DSM-III-R psychiatric disorders in the United States. Results from the National Comorbidity Survey. *Archives of General Psychiatry, 51*, 8–19.

Macphee, D. C., Johnson, S. M., & Vanderveer, M. M. C. (1995). Low sexual desire in women: The effects of marital therapy. *Journal of Sex & Marital Therapy, 21*, 159–182.

McDaniel, S. H., Hepworth, J., & Doherty, W. J. (1992). *Medical family therapy: A biopsychosocial approach to families with health problems*. New York: Basic Books.

Miklowitz, D. J., & Goldstein, M. J. (1997). *Bipolar disorder: A family-focused treatment approach*. New York: Guilford Press.

Miklowitz, D. J., Otto, M. W., Frank, E., Reilly-Harrington, N. A., Kogan, J. N., Sachs, G. S., et al. (2007). Intensive psychosocial intervention enhances functioning in patients with bipolar depression: Results from a 9-month Randomized controlled trial. *American Journal of Psychiatry, 164*, 1340–1347.

Miklowitz, D. J., Otto, M. W., Frank, E., Reilly-Harrington, N. A., Wisniewski, S. R., Kogan, J. N., et al. (2007). Psychosocial treatments for bipolar depression: A 1-year randomized trial from the systematic treatment enhancement program. *Archives of General Psychiatry, 64*, 419–427.

Miklowitz, D. J., Simoneau, T. L., George, E. L., Richards, J. A., Kalbag, A., Sachs-Ericsson, N., et al. (2000). Family-focused treatment of bipolar disorder: 1-year effects of a psychoeducational program in conjunction with pharmacotherapy. *Biological Psychiatry, 48*, 582–592.

Minuchin, S. (1974). *Families and family therapy*. Cambridge, MA: Harvard University Press.

Nemeroff, C. B., & Vale, W. W. (2005). The neurobiology of depression: Inroads to treatment and new drug discovery. *Journal of Clinical Psychiatry, 66*(Suppl. 7), 5–13.

Northey, W. F. (2002). Characteristics and clinical practices of marriage and family therapists: A national survey. *Journal of Marital and Family Therapy, 28*, 487–494.

Noyes, R., Jr., & Hoehn-Saric, R. (1998). *The anxiety disorders*. Cambridge, U.K.: Cambridge University Press.

O'Leary, K. D., & Beach, S. R. (1990). Marital therapy: A viable treatment for depression and marital discord. *American Journal of Psychiatry, 147*, 183–186.

Patterson, J. E., & Magulac, M. (1994). The family therapist's guide to psychopharmacology: A graduate level course. *Journal of Marital and Family Therapy, 20*, 151–173.

Patterson, J. E., & Van Meir, E. (1996). Using patient narratives to teach psychopathology. *Journal of Marital and Family Therapy, 22*, 59–68.

Post, R. M. (1992). Transduction of psychosocial stress into the neurobiology of recurrent affective disorder. *American Journal of Psychiatry, 149*, 999–1010.

Sherman, M. D., Zanotti, D. K., & Jones, D. E. (2005). Key elements in couples therapy with veterans with combat-related posttraumatic stress disorder. *Professional Psychology: Research and Practice, 36*, 626–633.

Silverstone, T., & Romans-Clarkson, S. (1989). Bipolar affective disorder: Causes and prevention of relapse. *British Journal of Psychiatry, 154*, 321–335.

Watzlawick, P., Beavin, J. H., & Jackson, D. D. (1967). *Pragmatics of human communication*. New York: John Wiley.

Whisman, M. A. (1999). Marital dissatisfaction and psychiatric disorders: Results from the National Comorbidity Survey. *Journal of Abnormal Psychology, 108*, 701–706.

Whisman, M. A. (2001). The association between depression and marital dissatisfaction. In S. R. H. Beach (Ed.), *Marital and family processes in depression: A scientific foundation for clinical practice* (pp. 3–24). Washington, DC: American Psychological Association.

Whisman, M. A., & Bruce, M. L. (1999). Marital dissatisfaction and incidence of major depressive episode in a community sample. *Journal of Abnormal Psychology, 108*, 674–678.

Whisman, M. A., Sheldon, C. T., & Goering, P. (2000). Psychiatric disorders and dissatisfaction with social relationships: Does type of relationship matter? *Journal of Abnormal Psychology, 109*, 803–808.

Whisman, M. A., & Uebelacker, L. A. (2003). Comorbidity of relationship distress and mental and physical health problems. In D. K. Snyder & M. A. Whisman (Eds.), *Treating difficult couples: Helping clients with coexisting mental and relationship disorders* (pp. 3–26). New York: Guilford Press.

White, M. (1984). Pseudoencopresis: From avalanche to victory, from vicious to virtuous cycles. *Family Systems Medicine, 2*, 150–160.

Winokur, G., Coryell, W., Akiskal, H. S., Endicott, J., Keller, M., & Mueller, T. (1994). Manic-depressive (bipolar) disorder: The course in light of a prospective 10-year follow-up of 131 patients. *Acta Psychiatrica Scandinavica, 89*, 102–110.

Wood, R. L. (2004). Understanding the 'miserable minority': A diathesis-stress paradigm for post-concussional syndrome. *Brain Injury, 18*, 1135–1153.

4
What's Love Got to Do With It?
Couples, Illness, and MFT

SHOBHA PAIS and MARY E. DANKOSKI

Contents

Research on Couples and Health	58
Mechanisms of Action: How Does Couple Interaction Influence Health?	60
Reciprocal Influences: Psychosocial Demands of Illness on Couples	61
From Partner to Patient	61
Partner as Caregiver	63
Couples-Based Intervention Studies	64
Breast Cancer: A Disease-Specific Example	65
Body Image and Sexuality	65
Emotional Distress, Depression, and Anxiety	66
Long-Term Adjustment	67
Breast Cancer and Life Cycle Transitions	67
Implications for Couples Therapy	68
Conclusion	69
References	70

Medical family therapy offers a new practice niche within marriage and family therapy (MFT). The term *medical family therapy* was introduced by McDaniel, Hepworth, and Doherty (1992) to refer to a comprehensive treatment approach for individuals and families dealing with medical problems. This approach is based on the biopsychosocial model of health, an integration of social and psychological issues with biomedical issues (Engel, 1977), counteracting traditional medical training, which tends to neglect such influences on health. Similarly, medical family therapy was introduced to counteract traditional couple and family therapy training, which emphasizes systemic and psychological bases for pathology to the neglect of the biological or physiological. A cornerstone of medical family therapy is that "all human problems are biopsychosocial systems problems: there are no psychosocial problems without biological features and no biomedical problems without psychosocial features" (McDaniel et al., p. 26).

In this chapter, we review research conducted on couples and health, the reciprocal impact of medical problems on couples, couples-based

58 • Handbook of Clinical Issues in Couple Therapy

interventions, and models for understanding mechanisms of action. The impact of breast cancer on couples' life cycle changes and functioning is discussed as a disease-specific example, and we also offer some clinical implications for marriage and family therapists. Our review of the literature is limited to a broad overview of biomedical health issues; many health issues such as infertility, cancer, or genetic screening could be explored much more in depth as separate topics. Additionally, much of the research has been conducted on married heterosexual couples, largely Caucasian and middle class, which limits the generalizability of the information.

Research on Couples and Health

Statistically speaking, married persons generally have better health status than their unmarried counterparts, but just how much so varies strongly by gender. Unmarried men have a 250% higher mortality rate than married men, and unmarried women have a 50% higher mortality rate compared to married women (Ross, Mirowsky, & Goldsteen, 1990). Associations between couple-related variables and health variables have been studied in a variety of ways. Multiple measures of couple dynamics have been employed, including self-reported marital satisfaction, cohesion, expressed emotion and negativity/hostility, overall quality, and observed and recalled marital conflict and interaction. Health-related variables have included objective physiological findings, self-perceived health status, the number of medical visits, pain, disability, survival rates, and recovery from life-threatening medical events, for example. Such measurement and methodological differences make comparisons across studies more challenging. However, one consistent finding is that gender differences commonly emerge and tend to be most robust and consistent in studies using objective physiological findings (Kiecolt-Glaser & Newton, 2001).

Many studies have found relationships between marital interaction and the functioning of the immune, endocrine, and cardiovascular systems (Kiecolt-Glaser & Newton, 2001; Robles & Kiecolt-Glaser, 2003). Marital conflict clearly alters physiological functioning, with hostility greatly increasing physiological reactivity (Kiecolt-Glaser & Newton, 2001). For example, hostility during a marital problem-solving task produced clinically significant increases in blood pressure among patients with hypertension; for women, hostile interactions and marital dissatisfaction accounted for 50% of the variance in their blood pressure readings (Ewart, Taylor, Kraemer, & Agras, 1991). Such physiological changes can be seen in both the early and the later years of marriage. In a study of newlyweds, marital conflict predicted changes in serum levels of epinephrine, norepinephrine, ACTH, growth hormone, and prolactin (Malarky, Kiecolt-Glaser, Pearl, & Glaser, 1994). This study was later replicated with couples married an average of 42 years. In this sample, husbands' endocrine data were not related to marital constructs; however, for wives, 16%–21% of the variance in hormone levels was accounted for by marital adjustment and negative behavior during conflict (Kiecolt-Glaser et al., 1997). Similarly, in patients with chronic low back pain, lumbar muscular reactivity increased during a marital conflict discussion, but not during a neutral topic (Flor, Breitenstein, Birbaumer, & Furst, 1995). Indeed, simply remembering a conflict can be enough to produce physiological change. One study by Carels, Sherwood, and Blumenthal (1998) showed that for women with lower marital satisfaction scores, blood pressure readings and heart rate responses were elevated by simply recalling marital conflict.

In addition to the impact of conflict, other links have been found between marital constructs and objective physiological measures and survival/recovery rates. For example, in early hypertensive men and women, elevated blood pressure was predicted by low cohesion (Baker et al., 1999). Women, with rheumatoid arthritis, who reported more positive marital interaction and less criticism from their spouse, had less disease activity over the course of a prospective study (Zautra et al., 1998). In a study of patients during the first year following a heart attack, Helgeson (1991) found that men who reported higher levels of disclosure to their wives were less likely to be rehospitalized or die within the year, than were men who reported low disclosure. Similarly, marital quality has been found to predict survival from congestive heart failure, especially for women (Coyne et al., 2001), and dyadic negativity predicted worse survival rates for women undergoing dialysis for end-stage renal disease (Kimmel et al., 2000). In a study examining medical records over 15 years, Hibbard and Pope (1993) found that for women, a lower risk for death was associated with higher levels of companionship and shared decision making with their spouses.

Gender differences in studies using self-reported health status tend to be less conclusive than when physiological outcomes are used (Kiecolt-Glaser & Newton, 2001). For example, married women who reported higher marital satisfaction reported better sleep and fewer visits to the doctor (Prigerson, Maciejewski, & Rosenheck, 1999), and reported better overall health and fewer medical symptoms (Barnett, Davidson & Marshall, 1991; Thomas, 1995). However, these samples were of women only, which limits the conclusions we can draw. Yet, similar associations have been found in some studies that included both men and women (Ganong & Coleman, 1991; Ren, 1997). Among partners in long-term marriages, Levenson, Carstensen, and Gottman (1993) found no differences in health status between husbands and wives in satisfied marriages; yet in dissatisfied marriages, women reported more mental and physical health problems than their husbands. Dissatisfaction in marriage also predicted greater disability and self-reported pain in women (but not men) with chronic low back pain (Saarijarvi, Rytokoski, & Karppi, 1990). Such associations between satisfaction levels and health may last over time. In a longitudinal study, participants with higher marital quality reported fewer physical symptoms at time one and continuing over a 4-year study period (Wickrama, Lorenz, & Conger, 1997).

60 • Handbook of Clinical Issues in Couple Therapy

Mechanisms of Action: How Does Couple Interaction Influence Health?

The Endocrine System as Gateway   One theory for understanding this phenomenon involves the endocrine system as an important "gateway" (Kiecolt-Glaser & Newton, 2001; Robles & Kiecolt-Glaser, 2003). Stress provokes the release of hormones, which impact immunological and cardiovascular functioning (Glaser & Kiecolt-Glaser, 1994). When a marriage becomes strained, couples often hold distress-maintaining cognitions (Gottman, 1994), become involved in absorbing states of negative affect (Johnson, 1999), and experience a great degree of "contagion" of tensions (Margolin, Christensen, & John, 1996). Partners who become entrenched in such a downward negative spiral are likely to have greater risks for health problems over time (Kiecolt-Glaser & Newton, 2001; Robles & Kiecolt-Glaser, 2003). This implies that the elderly in long-term dissatisfied, conflictual marital relationships may be at greatest risk, both because of the impact of chronic marriage-related stress, and because we become more physically vulnerable as we age (Kiecolt-Glaser & Newton, 2001).

Health Habits   Couple relationships can also influence health indirectly through health habits and coping. For example, in men followed longitudinally, positive marital interaction lowered the probability of unhealthy eating, poor sleep, and substance use (Wickrama, Conger, & Lorenz, 1995). Higher marital satisfaction predicts better adherence to medication regimens (at least with blood pressure patients; Trevino, Young, Groff, & Jono, 1990) and greater satisfaction with treatment and less illness-related stress in diabetic patients (Trief, Wade, Britton, & Weinstock, 2002). It is widely understood that smoking takes an enormous toll on health; and, since smokers are likely to marry other smokers (Venters, Jacobs, Luepker, Maiman, & Gillum, 1984), it is logical that spousal support is highly predictive of successful smoking cessation (Park, Schultz, Tudiver, Campbell, & Becker, 2002).

Gender Roles   In their comprehensive review of the literature, Kiecolt-Glaser and Newton (2001) theorized that the consistent gender differences may be related to differences between men's and women's self-representations and amount of role strain. The self-schemas of women tend to be more relational and interdependent than those of men, implying that women's thoughts and feelings in marriage will not only be impacted by their own experiences but also be reciprocally influenced by their partner's behavior, thoughts, and feelings. Thus, women may pay greater attention to the emotional quality of their relationships, and may pay a greater physiological consequence. Additionally, many women carry the lion's share of household and childcare tasks, often while working outside the home, placing them at greater risk for role strain and increasing their exposure to chronic stress, which ultimately may impact their immune and endocrine systems. In one study using saliva sampling and blood pressure readings throughout a workday, those with high marital role concerns had significant differences in cortisol levels, higher blood pressure readings, and reported greater stress (Barnett, Steptoe, & Gareis, 2005). Additionally, in one study of working women, those with the highest aggregate 24-hr blood pressure levels were those who had obtained a college degree and also reported the highest levels of family responsibility (i.e., increased amounts of domestic chores, having younger and more children at home; Brisson et al., 1999).

One such role for many women is as the caregiver, providing direct care to family members with medical problems, scheduling and transporting to doctor's visits, dispensing medications, staying home with ill children, etc. Many women perform this role not only for children, but for their spouses as well. This direct caregiving may be one of the reasons why married men generally have better health, and also why recently divorced and widowed men have increased mortality rates (Ross et al., 1990), because they no longer have someone to perform these tasks for them. The impact of caregiving on couples is further discussed in the following text.

Reciprocal Influences: Psychosocial Demands of Illness on Couples

From Partner to Patient

Much of the research reviewed earlier explores the impact of couple dynamics on health outcomes. However, it is also important to consider the reciprocal impact that an illness may have on the psychosocial functioning of a patient and his or her relationships. When the demands of illness become significant, either because of the changes in health status of the partner or due to the chronic nature of illness, the healthy partner may experience the cumulative effects of strain and over time, this may impact his or her own health. There are an innumerable amount of conditions and psychosocial correlates; far too many to mention here. Additionally, medications for any condition are likely to have a variety of side effects that may impact psychosocial functioning.

One helpful framework for understanding the psychosocial demands of health conditions is the psychosocial typology of illnesses, developed by Rolland (1994). This model maintains that all illnesses can be characterized by their onset (acute or gradual), their course (progressive, constant, or relapsing), the expected outcome (the extent to which a condition is likely to bring about death or shorten one's life), and the degree of incapacitation (on one's cognitions, sensations, movement, energy production, or appearance, i.e., through disfigurement). Conditions with an acute onset (such as a stroke or traumatic disabling accident) require couples to rapidly mobilize their resources and shift into crisis management mode, making emotional and practical changes in a short amount of time. On the other hand, gradual onset conditions such as Parkinson's disease allow for more time to adjust, but patients and their families often experience a time of ambiguity and anxiety when their symptoms are not yet fully understood. Illnesses with progressively

62 • Handbook of Clinical Issues in Couple Therapy

worsening courses (such as Alzheimer's disease) require continual adaptation and role changes, with increasing caregiving demands. Constant course conditions (such as a traumatic brain injury or a congenital problem) require an initial time of recovery and change, but eventually allow for some stability and predictability. In contrast, diseases with a relapsing course (such as inflammatory bowel diseases) require couples to have two *modes* of operation, one when the illness is in remission and one during an exacerbation. Variations in the degree to which a condition may shorten one's life has implications for ambiguous loss and anticipatory grief, and the type and severity of incapacitation clearly has implications for patients' functioning and caregiving demands on others, often the spouse.

Couples who face illness experience changes both as individuals and as a couple or dyad. These changes require the couple to evaluate and redefine roles within the relationship as well as outside it as individuals. The effect of illness—whether acute, chronic, or terminal—is not just on the physical body; it will also affect roles and responsibilities, create distressing emotional states, and present unpredictable futures for the couple (Turk, 2000). The change in roles can occur with the changes in the stages of illness, which include diagnosis, active treatment, adaptation to the illness, recovery, and end of life when illness becomes terminal. Each individual whether the patient or their partner will require a different set of skills to move through these stages. Sometimes these skills are complementary between partners, but sometimes they can conflict, such as when the patient needs more assistance in activities of daily living but the partner needs to work outside the home to maintain a household income. Often, the individuals in the relationship may not be able to accept the impact and concurrent responsibilities of chronic illness (Warren, 1992). During illness role confusion and conflict over roles is a common issue within couples. According to McDaniel and Cole-Kelly (2003), it is usually the spouse or intimate partner who helps the sick partner to identify symptoms and seek treatment. As treatment begins, expectations for the couple to abide by traditional gender roles when one partner is ill can come into play even for non-traditional couples.

Sometimes couples may find that when a partner becomes a patient, the relationship feels more like parent and child rather than equals. Finding ways to adapt to a new model of partnership can ensure fulfillment in the relationship. It is important for both individuals to feel a sense of independence and autonomy, and continue to communicate at an adult level to maintain a sense of equality within the relationship.

In addition to structure, assigned roles, and modes of interaction, couples also have a life cycle that changes over time, and marriage and family therapists should keep in mind that sudden serious illness or disability can be a major shock in the life cycle of a couple. For example, a serious illness that affects reproductive health will have different implications for a couple who desire children and are earlier in their adult years than it may for a couple who have already had children or who had decided not to. Some couples describe and compare the impact of illness to bereavement—with feelings of shock, anger, denial, regret, guilt, sadness, and loss. Often individuals in the relationship may feel they have to deal with the relationship by themselves, and may become isolated and angry. On the other hand, when couples are able to communicate more openly to each other about their feelings, it can also become a time when they grow closer and can provide support to each other.

When an illness is diagnosed as terminal, the remaining time together for the couple can be one of bittersweet moments. There can be a sense of urgency to make the most of every moment. Sometimes couples can find themselves slipping back to earlier feelings of intense connection, but for others, there can be a distressing feeling of growing separateness. In some couples, the knowledge that they may soon be without their partner creates the need to begin psychological and emotional distancing. This is usually completely unconscious and a natural response to try to soften the blow of an inevitable ending.

Further, what is considered supportive is highly contextual. It would be simplistic to believe that intimate relationships always provide a protective factor for illness. Not all support is positive even though it may be well intended, and not all people need or want the same type of support when ill. Support needs change over the course of illness and in response to the changing treatment regimens, pain, disability, and other symptoms.

Partner as Caregiver

Caregiving has both negative and positive consequences and couples respond differently. Partners sometimes feel significant responsibility and their involvement in caregiving can have an enormous impact on their quality of life. Research shows a tendency for the partner's quality of life to be worse than that of the patient. Kornblith, Herr, Ofman, Scher, and Holland (1994) found that wives of patients with prostate cancer reported greater psychological distress than did their husbands. Cancer-related distress was very common and significantly more severe in partners than in patients. Weitzenkamp, Gerhart, Charlifue, Whiteneck, and Savic (1997) found that spouses of patients with spinal cord injuries had higher levels of depression, than did patients. The manifestations of depression were both somatic (appetite loss, sleeplessness) and affective (feeling *blue*, crying). Research on cancer patients in palliative home care settings found that anxiety and depression were more common among partners, and that many partners attempted to disguise their feelings (Axelson & Sjoden, 1998; Hinton, 1994). A study on caregivers of rheumatoid arthritis patients has found lower health status scores compared to healthy controls on emotional, mental health, and general health status scales. The level of morbidity in caregivers was found to be only slightly less than individuals with major depression (Das Chagas Medeiros, Ferraz, & Quaresma, 2000).

64 • Handbook of Clinical Issues in Couple Therapy

Partners who provide care can face a number of difficulties including social isolation and struggles to combine the caregiving role with other responsibilities such as looking after the family. Especially in low-income families, caregiving can have significant financial implications, as one or both partners may be forced to give up work or major alterations to the home may be needed. Spouses of patients with Alzheimer's disease describe a feeling of limbo— not widowed but not married either (Guerriero Austrom & Hendrie, 1992). Gallagher-Thompson, Dal Canto, Jacob, and Thompson (2001) in their study of marital interaction patterns between couples in which the husbands either did or did not have Alzheimer's disease found that compared with their counterparts, caregiving wives reported higher levels of depression and stress, but similar shared values and closeness. When stroke patients become physically dependent, have psychological symptoms, and cognitive and communication deficits, the caregiving spouse often feels as though she or he is "not the same person." Partners described a decrease in their marital satisfaction although, by contrast, most patients claimed they had no marital difficulties (Bethoux, Calmels, Gautheron, & Minaire, 1996).

Caregiving literature has focused primarily on the negative consequences of caregiving, such as strain and burden. Although the nature of the relationship between caregiver and care recipient is considered a relevant factor, the nature of the marital relationship has received relatively little attention. The impact on aspects of the marital relationship, such as reduced shared activities, loss of emotional support from spouse, and a decrease in the quality of verbal communication between the couple, may have negative consequences for the morale of caregiving spouses and their perception of changes in marital intimacy and marital satisfaction.

Couples-Based Intervention Studies

Research has shown that when couples with illness learn to adjust to new roles and create a new identity, they are better able to accept the new responsibilities, respond to their partner's basic needs, exchange a sense of mutual satisfaction, and then separate into their individual identity states (Warren, 1992). In the past, most intervention has focused on the partner with illness. Research on various chronic illnesses suggests that interventions can improve the quality of the intimate relationship and provide ways of individual and couple coping.

Rankin-Esquer, Deteer, and Taylor (2000) reported that couples intervention with coronary heart disease has the potential to improve both psychological and physical recovery and strongly recommend consistent involvement of both members of the couple. With HIV, research with serodiscordant (when one spouse is HIV positive and the other spouse is negative) heterosexual couples, a psychoeducation group intervention for couples was found to be effective in reducing depression and anxiety and in increasing marital satisfaction (Pomeroy, Green, & Laningham, 2002). Integrative behavioral couples therapy, which includes behavioral changes and acceptance strategies, has been considered a viable intervention with couples with chronic pain (Cordova & Jacobson, 1993). While there is no research on couples' interventions with chronic respiratory conditions (such as asthma, chronic obstructive pulmonary disease, and cystic fibrosis), couples' treatment can be beneficial toward skill-building for enhanced emotional regulation and decreased emotional arousal (Schmaling & Afari, 2000). With rheumatic diseases, multimodal techniques involving family members are being studied. Keefe et al. (1996, 1999) found that with osteoarthritis, a spouse-assisted pain-coping skills training program showed the best outcomes. In couples facing fertility problems, experts in the field believe that both members of the couples should be included in the treatment due to the dyadic nature of infertility (Daniluk, 1997). Research on women with cancer has found that couples-based interventions that promote knowledge about treatment, effective decision making, enhancing mutual support, active coping skills, and preventing sexual problems is effective and superior to just individual treatment for women patients (Halford, Scott, & Smythe, 2000), indicating the importance of the role of intimate partner support in coping with cancer.

Breast Cancer: A Disease-Specific Example

Cancers are second to heart disease as the major cause of death in American men and women (Murphy, Lawrence, & Lenhard, 1995). Survival rates for cancer are associated with disease staging and grade, as well as diagnostic sites. The three common forms of cancer treatments include surgery, radiation therapy, and medical oncology, which involve systemic forms of treatment such as chemotherapy and the biologic response modifiers that are intended to enhance the response of the person to the tumor and disrupt the tumor–host relationship (Murphy et al.).

Body Image and Sexuality

A woman with breast cancer may have a very different view of her body after diagnosis and treatment. Often, breast cancer leaves visible reminders of the experience of cancer, either temporary or permanent, such as surgery scars, changes to the skin after radiotherapy, hair loss during chemotherapy or regrowth afterward. There may also be change in weight because of treatments. Since a woman can feel unsure of herself and how others view or respond to her, it may impact her self-esteem.

Body image changes and self-esteem can affect sexuality. Women often struggle with questions such as "what will happen to my body, how will my body look, will my partner find me attractive or will he or she be repulsed, and what will this change mean to my sexual life?" These questions are not always addressed when the focus is heavily on treatment and dealing with the disease. Yet, breast cancer can greatly impact sexuality and intimacy, and, of

66 • Handbook of Clinical Issues in Couple Therapy

course, each person's intimate and sexual relationship will be unique to him or her. Resuming sexual activity is a gradual process that must be at one's own pace, and the pace of each partner may not be the same. The healthy partner may face a time of readjustment to his or her spouse's diagnosis and treatment. Partners who are overprotective and trying to avoid further distress at all costs may not initiate sex for fear of upsetting or hurting their spouse. Some partners simply need time to accept what has happened. Others cannot come to terms with their partner's breast cancer and may emotionally push them away or even reject them, temporarily or permanently. Breast cancer can have significant psychosocial effects on a couple's sexual life: The possibility of a recurrence can increase anxiety within a relationship, while depression and grief and loss issues for both the woman with cancer and her spouse can impact how they relate to each other emotionally and sexually. Supportive communication between the couple has been found to be helpful (Halford et al., 2000), and couples need to communicate specifically about sexuality and intimacy.

Additionally, sexual dysfunction is common with cancer and cancer therapies. Sexual dysfunction after various cancer treatments has ranged from 40% to 100% post treatment (Derogatis & Kourlesis, 1981). About 50% of women who have had breast cancer experience long-term sexual dysfunction (Ganz, Rowland, Desmond, Meyerowitz, & Wyatt, 1998). The causes of sexual dysfunction are often both physiological and psychological. The most common sexual problems for women with cancer are loss of desire for sexual activity. Women may experience changes in genital sensations due to pain or a loss of sensation and numbness, as well as a decreased ability to reach orgasm. Loss of sensation can be as distressing as painful sensation for some women (Weijmar Schultz, Van de Wiel, Hahn, & van Driel, 1992). Unlike many other physiological side effects of cancer treatment, sexual problems do not tend to resolve within the first year or two of disease-free survival (Schover, Montague, & Lakin, 1997), rather, they may remain constant and severe. Intervention and follow-up are therefore important for optimizing the quality of life and intimacy for both partners.

Emotional Distress, Depression, and Anxiety

The initial diagnosis and treatment of cancer has a major psychological impact on individuals. There may be reactions of shock, emotional numbness, increased levels of depression, and anxiety (Anderson, Anderson, & de Prosse, 1989). Depression is often an underlying factor for many patients experiencing a loss of sexual desire or inability to feel sexual pleasure. But depression can have other far-reaching consequences as well. Often, depression is temporary and accompanies the understandable emotional trauma of a cancer diagnosis and its treatment. Emotional distress, depression, anxiety, and sexual difficulties are also frequently present in partners of women diagnosed with cancer (Ptacek, Pierce, Dodge, & Ptacek, 1997). Research indicates that partners of patients coping poorly also tend to cope poorly (Northhouse, Templin, Mood, & Oberst, 1998).

Spouses are more likely to be depressed if they are older, less well educated, more recently married, report heightened fears over their wife's well-being, worried about their job performance, are more uncertain about their future, or are in less well-adjusted marriages (Lewis, Fletcher, Cochrane, & Fann, 2008).

Long-Term Adjustment

Like many other chronic illnesses, despite improvement in mood, social support, and other psychosocial outcomes, many quality-of-life domains such as problems with body image, sexual functioning, and intimate relationships can remain impaired (Andersen et al., 1989). Depending on the treatment and stage of recovery, learning to engage in supportive communication, coping skills, effective partner support, and external social support has been found to be helpful in better adjustments to cancer for the patient as well as better adjustments for the partner (Halford et al., 2000).

Breast Cancer and Life Cycle Transitions

As couples transition through life cycle stages, there is an expectation to develop and master skills within each stage. For couples with illness such as breast cancer, some of the greatest challenges in managing the illness may come with family and individual life cycle transitions. Such challenges necessitate an awareness of life cycle development, open discussions of issues related to the illness and possible losses, and flexibility to manage the transitions well. From a life cycle perspective, the decision to have children is one that impacts individual development, the identity of the family, and the marital relationship. The introduction of a child into the family results in a major change in roles for the couple. Each parent has three distinct and demanding roles: as an individual, a spouse, and a parent. For new parents, individual identities will shift along with identity as a couple. In addition to the life cycle stage of becoming parents, when a couple has to deal with an illness such as breast cancer, the demands on the couple to realign the marital relationship become even greater. For example, a younger couple with breast cancer who want to have children would need to reflect cognitively and emotionally on issues that surround child bearing from a family life cycle stage as well as from a medical feasibility perspective. Questions that must be addressed include options for treatment and preserving fertility, when to consider pregnancy and how to best decide the timing; if chemotherapy is being started, the possibility of premature menopause and infertility become critical. On the other hand, depending on the stage of the cancer, the couple may need to consider the possibility that the mother may not be able to support and raise the child into adulthood. If a couple is in the next phase of the life cycle of raising school-age children, the challenges are somewhat different. After the initial phase of letting the children know about cancer and how it may impact life for the family, the couple may struggle with time for normal tasks of managing busy school and activity schedules of their children, especially during chemotherapy treatment when physical exhaustion is significant.

With children in their teenage years, the couple may face new challenges of helping children transition into complex roles and behaviors, and sometimes there is minimal focus on nurturing a marriage and the relationship between the couple. However, in the face of breast cancer, if the couple is engaged around the task of decision making and managing the illness, teenagers may feel left out and ignored. If the couple with breast cancer were at a different life cycle stage such as having young adult children, then the transitions for the couple would be to support them into becoming independent, and being an integral part of their individual milestones such as graduating from school, college, marriage, etc. Conversations about how cancer can impact the family would be more related to the mother with cancer "making it through" the milestones and being present for key events in her family's individual life cycle changes. Clearly, breast cancer, like most chronic or serious illnesses, can impact the entire family system.

Implications for Couples Therapy

The literature reviewed earlier contains several important implications for clinical assessment and intervention with couples. At the most basic level, marriage and family therapists should routinely ask about whether either member of a couple has any health conditions and is taking any medications. Genograms can and should include medical problems that run in the family. When a marriage and family therapist finds himself or herself working with a client with a medical condition, the marriage and family therapist should learn about some basic characteristics of that condition, such as the usual psychosocial implications of the disease, and its typical onset, course, and prognosis. Further, it will be important for the marriage and family therapist to understand where the patient and partner are in the timeline of the disease, from early diagnosis, to active treatment, remission, terminal phase, etc. The couple may be able to educate the marriage and family therapist about the condition (which is also a good indicator of the couple's understanding of the illness), and many health-related websites are also now readily accessible. Moreover, it is frequently important for the marriage and family therapist to establish a collaborative relationship with his or her client's primary care physician to best integrate care.

McDaniel et al. (1992) stated that the goals of medical family therapy include promoting agency or empowerment and communion. Specific to couples, several domains of individual and relationship functioning should be assessed for their impact on the medical problem and, reciprocally, for the impact of the medical problem on the couple, including conflict and hostility, communication and decision making, cohesion and intimacy (emotional and sexual), and body image and self-esteem. Additionally, marriage and family therapists should also carefully assess patterns of role flexibility and strain, particularly as they relate to gender role patterns, and also specifically in reference to caregiving. Sources of support for both the partner with the health condition and the caregiving partner will need to be assessed, and support networks external to the couple should be encouraged for both. Overall levels of anxiety and depression should also be assessed in both the patient and the partner. Of course, these domains of couple functioning are not only areas for assessment, but for psychoeducation and intervention as well, because improvement in these domains may also result in improved overall health status.

Further, knowing that chronic stress can cause changes in endocrine and immune functioning, it is also important for marriage and family therapists to discuss basic stress management and health habits. It is well within the domain of a marriage and family therapist to discuss issues such as healthy patterns of eating, exercise, and sleep, as well as smoking, alcohol, and other drug use. Specific relaxation techniques, such as progressive muscle relaxation, may be important for clients to use on a routine basis. Not only could such practices benefit their general health status, but they could also reduce overall levels of tension and conflict, which may help their overall individual and couple-level wellness.

Conclusion

When a marriage and family therapist ignores the biomedical components of a client's health, it is similar to when a physician ignores the relational, social, and psychological components of a patient's context. The whole picture is not captured. Since many marriage and family therapists have not been trained to integrate the biomedical into their thinking, it will take deliberate attention to these areas until they become a routine part of a thorough assessment. It will also take greater attention to these issues in marriage and family therapy training programs and supervision, implying that faculty development may be needed in this area.

The more we learn about mind/body interactions, the more it makes sense that couple interaction would impact health and vice versa. The marital relationship is the key for adult health—both mentally and physically—no other relationship has been found to be as influential on overall health for adults (Campbell, 2003). The two individual members of a couple have prior histories, experiences, and unique personalities and genetic backgrounds, which make the study of couples, their characteristics, and their patterns of interaction complex and dynamic. This complexity implies the need for sophisticated systemic conceptualization, yet, much of this research is conducted by nonsystemically trained researchers. We need more marriage and family therapists conducting research on how health problems impact couples, and how couple dynamics impact health. Further, we need more marriage and family therapists specializing in medical couple and family therapy to advance

70 • Handbook of Clinical Issues in Couple Therapy

clinical interventions. marriage and family therapists are well suited to this work; the biopsychosocial model of health is a systemic one, which fits well with the foundational tenets of couple and family therapy.

References

Andersen, B. L., Andersen, B., & de Prosse, C. (1989). Controlled prospective longitudinal study of women with cancer: Psychological outcomes. *Journal of Consulting and Clinical Psychology, 57*, 692–697.

Axelson, B., & Sjoden, P. (1998). Quality of life of cancer patients and their spouses in palliative home care. *Palliative Medicine, 12*, 29–39.

Baker, B., Helmers, K., O'Kelly, B., Sakinofsky, I., Abelsohn, A., & Tobe, S. (1999). Marital cohesion and ambulatory blood pressure in early hypertension. *American Journal of Hypertension, 12*, 227–230.

Barnett, R. C., Davidson, H., & Marshall, N. L. (1991). Physical symptoms and the interplay of work and family roles. *Health Psychology, 10*, 94–101.

Barnett, R. C., Steptoe, A., & Gareis, K. C. (2005). Marital role quality and stress-related psychobiological indicators. *Annals of Behavioral Medicine, 30*(1), 36–43.

Bethoux, F., Calmels, P., Gautheron, V., & Minaire, P. (1996). Quality of life of the spouses of stroke patients: A preliminary study. *International Journal of Rehabilitation Research, 19*, 291–299.

Brisson, C., Laflamme, N., Moisan, J., Milot, A., Masse, B., & Vezina, M. (1999). Impact of family responsibilities and job strain on ambulatory blood pressure among white collar women. *Psychosomatic Medicine, 61*, 205–213.

Campbell, T. L. (2003). The effectiveness of family interventions for physical disorders. *Journal of Marital and Family Therapy, 29*(2), 263–281.

Carels, R. A., Sherwood, A., & Blumenthal, J. A. (1998). Psychosocial influences on blood pressure during daily life. *International Journal of Psychophysiology, 28*, 117–129.

Connell, G. M., & Connell, L. C. (1995). In-hospital consultation: Systemic interventions during medical crisis. *Family Systems Medicine, 13*(1), 29–38.

Cordova, J. V., & Jacobson, N. S. (1993). Couple distress. In D. H. Barlow (Ed.), *Clinical handbook of psychological disorders* (pp. 481–512). New York: Guilford Press.

Coyne, J. C., Rohrbaugh, M. J., Shoham, V., Sonnega, J. S., Nicklas, J. M., & Cranford, J. A. (2001). Prognostic importance of marital quality for survival of congestive heart failure. *American Journal of Cardiology, 88*, 526–529.

Daniluk, J. (1997). Helping patients cope with infertility. *Clinical Obstetrics and Gynecology, 40*, 661–672.

Das Chagas Medeiros, M. M., Ferraz, M. B., & Quaresma, M. R. (2000). The effect of rheumatoid arthritis on the quality of life of primary caregivers. *Journal of Rheumatology, 27*, 76–83.

Derogatis, L. R., & Kourlesis, S. M. (1981). An approach to evaluation of sexual problems in the cancer patient. *CA: A Cancer Journal for Clinicians, 31*(1), 46–50.

Engel, G. L. (1977). The need for a new medical model: A challenge for biomedicine. *Science, 196*, 129–136.

Ewart, C. K., Taylor, C. B., Kraemer, H. C., & Agras, W. S. (1991). High blood pressure and marital discord: Not being nasty matters more than being nice. *Health Psychology, 10*, 155–163.

Flor, H., Breitenstein, C., Birbaumer, N., & Furst, M. (1995). A psycho-physiological analysis of spouse solicitousness towards pain behaviors, spouse interaction, and pain perception. *Behavior Therapy, 26*, 255–272.

Gallagher-Thompson, D., Dal Canto, P. G., Jacob, T., & Thompson, L. W. (2001). A comparison of marital interaction patterns between couples in which the husband does or does not have Alzheimer's disease. *The Journals of Gerontology Series B: Psychological Sciences and Social Sciences, 56,* 140–150.

Ganong, L. H., & Coleman, M. (1991). Remarriage and health. *Research in Nursing and Health, 14,* 205–211.

Ganz, P. A., Rowland, J. H., Desmond, K., Meyerowitz, B.E., & Wyatt, G.E. (1998). Life after breast cancer: Understanding women's health-related quality of life and sexual functioning. *Journal of Clinical Oncology, 16*(2), 501–514.

Glaser, R., & Kiecolt-Glaser, J. K. (Eds.). (1994). *Handbook of human stress and immunity.* San Diego, CA: Academic Press.

Gottman, J. (1994). *Why marriages succeed or fail.* New York: Simon & Schuster.

Guerriero Austrom, M., & Hendrie, H. C. (1992). Quality of life: The family and Alzheimer's disease. *Journal of Palliative Care, 8,* 56–60.

Halford, W. K., Scott, J. L., & Smythe, J. (2000). Couples and coping with cancer: Helping each other through the night. In K. B. Schmaling & T. G. Sher (Eds.), *The psychology of couples and illness: Theory, research and practice* (pp. 135–170). Washington, DC: American Psychological Association.

Helgeson, V. S. (1991). The effects of masculinity and social support on recovery from myocardial infarction. *Psychosomatic Medicine, 53,* 621–633.

Hibbard, J. H., & Pope, C. R. (1993). The quality of social roles as predictors of morbidity and mortality. *Social science and Medicine, 36,* 217–225.

Hinton, J. (1994) Can home care maintain an acceptable quality of life for patients with terminal cancer and their relatives? *Palliative Medicine, 8,* 183–196.

Johnson, S. M. (1999). Emotionally focused couple therapy: Straight to the heart. In J. M. Donovan (Ed.), *Short-term couple therapy* (pp. 13–42). New York: Guilford.

Keefe, F. J., Caldwell, D. S., Baucom, D., Salley, A., Robinson, E., Timmons, K., et al. (1996). Spouse-assisted coping skills training in the management of osteoarthritic knee pain. *Arthritis Care and Research, 9,* 279–291.

Keefe, F. J., Caldwell, D. S., Baucom, D., Salley, A., Robinson, E., Timmons, K., et al. (1999). Spouse-assisted coping skills training in the management of osteoarthritic knee pain: Long-term follow up results. *Arthritis Care and Research, 12,* 101–111.

Kiecolt-Glaser, J. K., Glaser, R., Cacioppo, J. T., MacCallum, R. C., Snydersmith, M., Kim, C., et al. (1997). Marital conflict in older adults: Endocrinological and immunological correlates. *Psychosomatic Medicine, 59,* 339–349.

Kiecolt-Glaser, J. K., & Newton, T. L. (2001). Marriage and health: His and hers. *Psychological Bulletin, 127*(4), 472–503.

Kimmel, P. L., Peterson, R. A., Weihs, K. L., Shidler, N., Simmens, S. J., Alleyne, S., et al. (2000). Dyadic relationship conflict, gender, and mortality in urban hemodialysis patients. *Journal of the American Society of Nephrology, 11,* 1518–1525.

Kornblith, A. B., Herr, H. W., Ofman, U. S., Scher, H. I., & Holland, J. C. (1994). Quality of life of patients with prostate cancer and their spouses. *Cancer, 73,* 2791–2802.

Levenson, R. W., Carstensen, L. L., & Gottman, J. M. (1993). Long-term marriage: Age, gender, and satisfaction. *Psychology and Aging, 2,* 301–313.

Lewis, F. M., Fletcher, K. A., Cochrane, B. B., & Fann, J. R. (2008). Predictors of depressed mood in spouses of women with breast cancer. *Journal of Clinical Oncology, 26,* 1289–1295.

Malarky, W., Kiecolt-Glaser, J. K., Pearl, D., & Glaser, R. (1994). Hostile behavior during marital conflict alters pituitary and adrenal hormones. *Psychosomatic Medicine, 56,* 41–51.

Margolin, G., Christensen, A., & John, R. S. (1996). The continuance and spillover of everyday tensions in distressed and nondistressed families. *Journal of Family Psychology, 10,* 304–321.

McDaniel, S. H., & Cole-Kelly, K. (2003). Gender, couples, and illness: A feminist analysis of medical family therapy. In L. B. Silverstein (Ed.), *Feminist family therapy: Empowerment in social context, Psychology of women book series* (pp. 267–280). Washington, DC: American Psychological Association.

McDaniel, S. H., Hepworth, J., & Doherty, W. J. (1992). *Medical family therapy: A biopsychosocial approach to families with health problems.* New York: Basic Books.

Murphy, G. P., Lawrence, W., & Lenhard, R. E. (1995). *American Cancer Society textbook of clinical oncology* (2nd ed.). Atlanta, GA: American Cancer Society.

Northhouse, L. L., Templin, T., Mood, D., & Oberst, M. (1998). Couple's adjustment to breast cancer and benign disease: A longitudinal analysis. *Psycho-oncology, 7,* 37–48.

Park, E. W., Schultz, J. K., Tudiver, F., Campbell, T., & Becker, L. (2002). Enhancing partner support to improve smoking cessation. *Cochrane Database of Systematic Reviews (Issue 2)* [computer software]. The Cochrane Library.

Pomeroy, E. C., Green, D. L., & Laningham, L. V. (2002). Couples who care: The effectiveness of psychoeducational group intervention for HIV serodiscordant couples. *Research on Social Work Practice, 12*(2), 238–252.

Prigerson, H. G., Maciejewski, P. K., & Rosenheck, R. A. (1999). The effects of marital dissolution and marital quality on health and health services use among women. *Medical Care, 37,* 858–873.

Ptacek, J. T., Pierce, G. R., Dodge, K. L., & Ptacek, J. J. (1997). Social support in spouses of cancer patients: What do they get and to what end? *Personal Relationships, 4,* 431–449.

Rankin-Esquer, L., Deeter, A., & Taylor, C. (2000). Coronary heart disease and couples. In K. Schmaling (Ed.), *The psychology of couples and illness: Theory, research, and practice* (pp. 43–70). Washington, DC: American Psychological Association.

Ren, X. S. (1997). Marital status and quality of relationships: The impact on health perception. *Social Science and Medicine, 44,* 241–249.

Robles, T. F., & Kiecolt-Glaser, J. K. (2003). The physiology of marriage: Pathways to health. *Physiology & Behavior, 79*(3), 409–416.

Rolland, J. S. (1994). The psychosocial typology of illness. In J. S. Rolland (Ed.), *Families, illness, & disability: An integrative treatment model* (pp. 19–42). New York: Basic Books.

Ross, C. E., Mirowsky, J., & Goldsteen, K. (1990). The impact of the family on health: The decade in review. *Journal of Marriage and Family, 52,* 1059–1078.

Saarijarvi, S., Rytokoski, U., & Karppi, S. L. (1990). Marital satisfaction and distress in chronic low back pain patients and their spouses. *Clinical Journal of Pain, 6,* 148–152.

Schmaling, K. B., & Afari, N. (2000). Couples coping with respiratory disorders. In K. B. Schmaling & T. G. Sher (Eds.), *The psychology of couples and illness: Theory, research and practice* (pp. 71–104). Washington, DC: American Psychological Association.

Schover, L. R., Montague, D. K., & Lakin, M. M. (1997). Sexual problems. In V. T. DeVita Jr., S. Hellman, & S. A. Rosenberg (Eds.), *Cancer: Principles and practice of oncology* (5th ed., pp. 2857–2872). Philadelphia: Lippincott-Raven.

Thomas, S. P. (1995). Psychosocial correlates of women's health in middle adulthood. *Issues in Mental Health Nursing, 16,* 285–314.

Trevino, D. B., Young, E. H., Groff, J., & Jono, R. T. (1990). The association between marital adjustment and compliance with antihypertension regimens. *Journal of the American Board of Family Practice, 3*, 17–25.

Trief, P. M., Wade, M. J., Britton, K. D., & Weinstock, R. S. (2002). A prospective analysis of marital relationship factors and quality of life in diabetes. *Diabetes Care, 25*(7), 1154–1158.

Turk, D. C. (2000). Foreword. In K. B. Schmaling & T. G. Sher (Eds.), *The psychology of couples and illness: Theory, research, and practice* (pp. xi–xvi). Washington, DC: American Psychological Association.

Venters, M. H., Jacobs, D. R., Jr., Luepker, R. V., Maiman, L. A., & Gillum, R. F. (1984). Spouse concordance of smoking patterns: The Minnesota Heart Survey. *American Journal of Epidemiology, 120*, 608–616.

Warren, M. T. (1992). Maintaining identity in elderly couples with chronic illness. *Journal of Psychosocial Nursing and Mental Health Services, 10*, 8–10.

Weijmar Schultz, W. C., Van de Wiel, H. B., Hahn, D. E., & van Driel, M. (1992). Sexuality and cancer in women. *Annual Review of Sex Research, 3*, 151–200.

Weitzenkamp, D. A., Gerhart, K. A., Charlifue, S. W., Whiteneck, G. G., & Savic, G. (1997). Spouses of spinal cord injury survivors: The added impact of caregiving. *Archives of Physical Medicine and Rehabilitation, 78*, 822–827.

Wickrama, K. A. S., Conger, R. D., & Lorenz, F. O. (1995). Work, marriage, lifestyle, and changes in men's physical health. *Journal of Behavioral Medicine, 18*, 97–111.

Wickrama, K. A. S., Lorenz, F. O., & Conger, R. D. (1997). Marital quality and physical illness: A latent growth curve analysis. *Journal of Marriage and the Family, 59*, 143–155.

Zautra, A. J., Hoffman, J. M., Matt, K. S., Yocum, D., Potter, P. T., Castro, W. L., & Roth, S. (1998). An examination of individual differences in the relationship between interpersonal stress and disease activity among women with rheumatoid arthritis. *Arthritis Care and Research, 11*(4), 271–279.

5
Couples Therapy and Addictions

THORANA S. NELSON and NEAL J. SULLIVAN

Contents

Alcohol Abuse	76
Initiation of Treatment	76
Primary Treatment	78
Treatment Maintenance	80
Substance Abuse	81
Sexual Compulsivity/Addiction	82
Pathological Gambling	83
Eating Disorders	84
Summary	84
Systemic Couples Therapy for Substance-Abusing Women	85
Conclusion	88
References	89

Alcoholism, substance abuse, and other addictions that include gambling, eating disorders, and sex are traditionally treated as habits or emotional disorders requiring attention to characteristics of individuals that focus on their behaviors, thoughts, and emotions. Treatment frequently consists of attending 12-step meetings such as Alcoholics Anonymous, various outpatient counseling programs that use primarily psychoeducation and behavioral interventions, and inpatient detoxification and other treatments. All of these kinds of programs tend to target problems inside the abusing person rather than a person within a system or the system itself. When a person's context is included as part of the conceptualization of treatment, interventions often focus on ways the individual can cope with or respond differently to the environment. Given varying success with treatments, much of it dismal, recent treatments also have been developed that locate the problems within systems of people—for example, couples and families—and that benefit from systemic interventions. These might include using partners and other people in ancillary treatment, including them in various treatments that target the index person, including them as conceptualized as part of the system as a whole needing or benefiting from treatment, or a combination of all of these different perspectives.

    Whether the locus or cause of the abuse or addiction is seen as arising from disease processes, systemic dynamics, or other mechanisms that lead to unfortunate habits and behaviors, utilizing the individual's partner or family in therapy has become known as an important part of successful treatment. Partners and families have been seen variously as victims, reinforcers or enablers, and causes of addictions. Regardless of the relationship to the abuser or the abuse, it has become more and more clear that when partners are included in treatment, success is more likely. This chapter first reviews models of treatment for addictions that include intimate partners and research using them, and then presents a systemic couples treatment model that demonstrated some success with women substance abusers. No distinctions are made in this article between misuse, abuse, or addiction. In addition, the literature does not make these distinctions (yet) in terms of treatment.

Alcohol Abuse

In 1995, Edwards and Steinglass reviewed what they considered to be 21 of the most extensive articles on the effectiveness of various family-involved alcohol abuse treatments published between 1972 and 1993. Included within these studies were several treatments utilizing non-alcoholic spouses or partners as the focus of intervention (e.g., unilateral family therapy) or that engaged both the alcoholics and their partners in conjoint sessions (e.g., cognitive behavioral therapy [CBT]). A more recent review of marriage and family therapy outcomes for alcohol abuse (O'Farrell & Fals-Stewart, 2002) included several more couple-involved treatments. This section will review couples therapy outcomes following the outline used by Edwards and Steinglass, which included three phases of treatment: initiation, primary, and maintenance.

Initiation of Treatment

Alcohol abusers frequently are reluctant to enter treatment on their own. The Johnson Institute intervention (V. E. Johnson, 1986) addresses reluctance by involving the family or caring others of the alcoholic in a series of sessions that prepares them as a group to confront the resistant alcoholic. Miller, Meyers, and Tonigan (1999) showed that only 30% of the family or caring others were successful at engaging the alcoholic in treatment when using the Johnson Institute intervention.

Community reinforcement training, CRT (Azrin, 1976; Azrin, Naster, & Jones, 1973; Hunt & Azrin, 1973), or community reinforcement approach, CRA (Smith, Meyers, & Miller, 2001), is typically a cognitive-behavioral program. One goal of the program is to educate caring others about ways to engage their reluctant alcoholic partners in treatment when the alcoholic expresses some motivation to change. Additional goals of CRT are to reduce dependency on an alcoholic relationship through other activities and to facilitate sobriety in the alcoholic spouses (Edwards & Steinglass, 1995; O'Farrell & Fals-Stewart, 2002), or, in other words, to create an environment that rewards sobriety (Smith et al., 2001). Sisson and Azrin (1986) found that six of seven alcoholics entered treatment when their female spouses were in CRT, whereas none of the five alcoholics whose female partners were assigned to a traditional program entered treatment. Not only has the approach been shown to be useful in initiating treatment, but it also has been found to successfully help alcoholic clients in other stages of treatment. Three meta-analytical reviews placed CRT as one of the top five most effective approaches for treating alcohol abuse (Smith et al., 2001).

Similar to CRT, the community reinforcement and family training program (CRAFT) adds Unilateral family therapy (UFT) components (Stanton, 2004), which will be discussed in the next paragraph. A large, controlled study of CRAFT treatment compared to the Johnson intervention and a traditional Al-Anon program (Miller et al., 1999) supported CRAFT's effectiveness in engaging couples in treatment. Sixty-four percent of the CRAFT participants entered treatment within 6 months while only 30% of the Johnson intervention participants entered treatment.

UFT is a treatment approach born out of CRT that focuses on helping the nonalcoholic spouse to assist the alcoholic spouse into treatment (Thomas, 1989). Through the course of UFT treatment, nonalcoholic spouses learn about alcohol abuse, its effects on family dynamics, and how to initiate confrontations with spouses aimed at easing them into treatment one step at a time (Edwards & Steinglass, 1995; O'Farrell & Fals-Stewart, 2002; Stanton, 2004). The alcoholic spouses are not included in this treatment; its sole purpose is to help the nonalcoholic spouses engage the alcoholics in treatment.

Two studies of UFT indicated both statistically and clinically significant findings. In a study of 25 spouses (24 male and 1 female alcoholics), 61% of the alcoholics whose spouses had UFT entered treatment, decreased their drinking, or both, and their spouses reported more affection, higher sexual satisfaction, and less emotional distress after treatment (Thomas, Santa, Bronson, & Oyserman, 1987). A second study (Thomas, Yoshioka, Ager, & Adams, 1993, cited in Edwards & Steinglass, 1995) that included 69 spouses (65 male and 4 female alcoholics) had similar results. More alcoholics entered treatment and reduced drinking when their spouses received UFT treatment. UFT was related to decreases in alcohol-enabling and control behaviors in spouses and increases in marital satisfaction.

Another approach, based on both CRT and UFT, prepares non-alcoholic spouses to apply increasing levels of pressure to their alcoholic spouses who are resistant to entering therapy in a briefer period of time than CRT and UFT: the pressure to change approach, PTC (Barber & Crisp, 1995). The PTC approach sometimes leads to the Johnson intervention, in which case, 4–6 weeks are added to weekly treatments (Stanton, 2004). In three studies to date, PTC was found to move alcoholics toward significant change, defined as "the drinker either (a) seeking treatment, (b) ceasing drinking, or (c) reducing drinking to a level acceptable to the partner and maintaining this change for at least 2 weeks" (O'Farrell & Fals-Stewart, 2002, p. 129).

78 • Handbook of Clinical Issues in Couple Therapy

Studies of the differences in outcomes between the Johnson Institute intervention and the other three treatments (UFT, CRAFT, and PTC) would be a welcome addition to the collection of growing studies on couple therapy in the initiation phase of treatment.

Primary Treatment

Behavioral Couple Therapies Behavioral couples therapy (BCT) typically focuses on aspects of couple interaction such as communication skills training, problem-solving skills, and caring exchanges (e.g., Jacobson & Margolin, 1979). BCT and interactional therapy (IT; McCrady, Paolino, Longabaugh, & Rosi, 1979) were compared with standard individual treatment for alcoholics who were released from inpatient rehabilitation or detoxification programs (O'Farrell, Cutter, & Floyd, 1985). Ten couples were randomly assigned to the BCT group and showed an increase in the number of abstinent days between pre- and post-treatment (43% and 99%, respectively). IT emphasizes the importance of teamwork, support, caring, problem-solving, and sharing feelings within families with alcoholics. The 12 couples assigned to the IT group showed improvement from 46% days of abstinence at pretreatment to 83% at post-treatment. Couples in both BCT and IT showed improved marital functioning; however, improvements found at 6 month post-treatment were not maintained at the 24-month follow-up. In 6-month and 24-month follow-ups, days of abstinence had decreased for all three groups with the greatest drop occurring in the standard treatment group (O'Farrell, Cutter, Choquette, Floyd, & Bayog, 1992).

BCT for treatment of alcoholics has evolved into what is now known as alcohol behavioral couple therapy, ABCT (Epstein & McCrady, 2002). Two forms of ABCT exist: One form was developed to work alone as a treatment for alcoholic couples (Epstein & McCrady); the other was developed by O'Farrell and Fals-Stewart (2000) to be used in association with or after more traditional BCT. Epstein and McCrady's version (ABCT) is an integration of three major treatments: CBT, UFT, and BCT. Therapy using BCT as described by O'Farrell and Fals-Stewart (2002) "sees the alcoholic patient together with the spouse or cohabitating partner to build support for abstinence and to improve relationship functioning" (p. 131). It includes a behavioral contract component through which the alcoholic agrees to commit to abstinence each day, attend after-care treatment, or take disulfiram.

In one study, 33 male and 12 female alcoholics and their non-alcoholic spouses were randomly assigned to ABCT, alcohol-focused spouse involvement (AFSI), or minimal spouse involvement (MSI) groups (McCrady, Noel, & Abrams, 1986). Although the MSI treatment included the spouse, interventions were aimed at helping the alcoholic learn behavioral techniques that promote abstinence (such as refusing drinks), and assertiveness and relaxation training. The AFSI treatment added several components to MSI treatment: training the non-alcoholic spouse to facilitate sobriety, assertively expressing feelings

Couples Therapy and Addictions • **79**

related to drinking behaviors, relaxation, and drink refusal through role play. ABCT included all the skills taught in MSI and AFSI plus specific behavioral marital interventions such as communication, problem-solving training, or shared activities. At a 6-month follow-up, all three treatment groups showed similar results in terms of percent of abstinent subjects (ABCT = 37%, AFSI = 42%, MSI = 36%). Edwards and Steinglass (1995) concluded that this study suggested that couple involvement in therapy is beneficial, but it is unclear as to how involved couples need to be, given that each of the groups showed similar outcomes.

Having become one of the most empirically supported treatments for alcohol abuse, ABCT usually yields decreases in alcohol use and increases in couple functioning (McCrady, Epstein, & Hirsch, 1999; McCrady et al., 1986; McCrady, Noel, Stout, Abrams, & Nelson, 1991; McCrady, Stout, Noel, Abrams, & Nelson, 1991; McKay, Longabaugh, Beattie, Maisto, & Noel, 1993; O'Farrell & Birchler, 1987; O'Farrell, Choquette, & Birchler, 1991; O'Farrell, Choquette, & Cutter, 1998; O'Farrell, Choquette, Cutter, & Birchler, 1997; O'Farrell, Choquette, Cutter, Brown, & McCourt, 1993; O'Farrell et al., 1985, 1992; O'Farrell & Fals-Stewart, 2000; O'Farrell, Van Hutton, & Murphy, 1999). In addition, one study revealed positive outcomes for the children of couples who were involved in BCT (Kelley & Fals-Stewart, 2002) and others showed decreases in social costs (O'Farrell et al., 1996; O'Farrell, Choquette, Cutter, Floyd, et al., 1996).

Couple Group Therapy   Four family systems-oriented studies were reviewed by Edwards and Steinglass (1995). Outcomes from Corder, Corder, and Laidlaw's (1972) study of a couple treatment (CT) component included in a traditional inpatient program (TIP) were both statistically and clinically significant. Their study included 39 male alcoholics and their wives assigned to either a TIP or CT group. In addition to the alcoholics' traditional treatment, couples in the CT group attended two sessions of multiple couple therapy, learned medical and psychological aspects of alcoholism together, and participated in Al-Anon or AA meetings. Fifty-eight percent of the participants in the CT group and 15% of the TIP group were abstinent at a 6-month follow-up.

Cadogan (1973) used a couple group therapy approach in a study of 35 male and 5 female alcoholics and their spouses. Results showed that treatment in the couple group therapy yielded 45% abstinence as compared with 10% abstinence for a wait-list control group. Cadogan's study was similar to Corder et al.'s (1972) in that it involved couple groups. However, Cadogan's treatment focused more on improving emotional expression, communication, and problem-solving skills.

McCrady et al. (1979) found that couples assigned to either a couple involvement (CI) or joint admission (JA) treatment showed greater clinically significant levels of abstinence (83% and 61%, respectively) after treatment than their counterparts in individual treatment (43% abstinence). Although there were no statistically significant differences among the groups, the study did show that couple therapy is helpful.

The CI groups were involved in multiple couple group therapy and individual group therapy for the alcoholics and their spouses. These sessions addressed relational, alcohol, sobriety, and coping issues. In the JA group, both partners in the couples were admitted to an inpatient ward and participated in all activities of the CI group plus all of the team meetings and ward activities. In a 4-year follow-up study (McCrady, Moreau, & Paolino, 1982), there still were no statistically significant differences among the three treatment groups. However, abstinence rates fell below the clinically significant baseline (50%), suggesting that the effectiveness of treatment for all three groups greatly diminished over time. Although all treatments were effective short-term, none was more statistically effective than the others and none produced long-term effectiveness across multiple measures of alcohol use, marital status, or other measures of functioning.

Family systems therapy (FST) was reviewed by O'Farrell and Fals-Stewart (2002) as therapy that could be used with families or couples. In its generic form, FST uses several family systems concepts and is administered in several forms (e.g., brief strategic family therapy, Milan family therapy, experiential systemic couple therapy). In their review of several studies, O'Farrell and Fals-Stewart reported that although FST effected greater reduction in drinking, greater "overall condition" (p. 144), and positive outcomes in marital/family relationship measures, treatment group results did not differ significantly from those of the control groups, which used individual or group therapy. One study found that couples who were classified as having a demand-withdraw relationship fared better in FST than in CBT although there were no differences in retention outcomes (Shoham, Rohrbaugh, Stickle, & Jacob, 1998).

Treatment Maintenance

Few studies have investigated the involvement of couples in the maintenance phase of the treatment of alcohol abuse. In one study of BCT with a relapse prevention additive, O'Farrell et al. (1993) found that after 1 year post-treatment, participants maintained 94% days of abstinence while those who received BCT only maintained 82% days of abstinence.

McCrady et al. (1999) studied the effects of a relapse prevention (RP) component on ABCT treatment outcomes. Randomly assigning 90 male alcoholics and their female partners to ABCT alone, ABCT plus RP, or ABCT plus Al-Anon treatment, McCrady et al. found that all groups increased abstinence, decreased heavy drinking, and showed general improvement. In addition, if subjects participated in post-treatment as planned in the ABCT plus RP and ABCT plus Al-Anon models, "they were more likely to be abstinent than those who did not" (O'Farrell & Fals-Stewart, 2002, p. 139).

Couples Therapy and Addictions • **81**

Whether in the initiation, primary, or maintenance phase of treatment, different models of couple therapy often yield more improvements than traditional inpatient, outpatient, and individual treatments. Moreover, Edwards and Steinglass's (1995) call for more research on the effectiveness of couple treatments in the treatment maintenance phase, with nontraditional alcoholic couples, and with female alcoholics still stands.

Substance Abuse

Few models of couple therapy for adult substance abuse exist. However, several researchers have maintained that the more plentiful research done on treatments for adult alcohol abuse hold promise for similar positive outcomes for substance abuse clients (Rowe & Liddle, 2002; Stanton & Shadish, 1997). In addition, outcomes related to adult substance abuse recovery often match outcomes for adolescents, especially in terms of family functioning and cost effectiveness (Rowe & Liddle, 2002).

In terms of initiating treatment, CRT was the treatment of choice in one study (Kirby, Marlowe, Festinger, Garvey, & LaMonaca, 1999), which was patterned after Sisson and Azrin's (1986) work. Thirty-two family members or significant others were randomly assigned to CRT or a 12-step self-help group. After 10 weeks of treatment, family and significant others in the CRT group were found to have higher treatment retention rates and their substance abusing others were more apt to enter treatment; however, there were no statistically significant differences in levels of social and emotional functioning for the family or significant other.

A more recent study (Meyers, Miller, Smith, & Tonigan, 2002) compared CRAFT alone and CRAFT with an aftercare option for spouses with Al-Anon and Nar-Anon groups. Ninety adult drug abusers and their caring others participated, with results showing that of the three groups studied, the two CRAFT groups were able to engage 67% of the abusers in treatment.

BCT has been the most recently and repeatedly studied couple therapy for drug abusers. Rowe and Liddle (2002) reviewed the effectiveness of substance abuse treatments in marriage and family therapy and offered a comprehensive outline of several of the studies that reported effectiveness of BCT. For example, the initial study of BCT with 80 substance abusing males and their spouses showed that

> [C]ouples who received BCT (individual, group, and couples sessions) had better relationship outcomes and husbands had fewer days of drug use, longer periods of abstinence, and fewer drug-related arrests and hospitalizations up to 1-year follow-up than those in individual therapy (involving cognitive and behavioral coping skills training)

> **(Rowe & Liddle, p. 73)**

82 • Handbook of Clinical Issues in Couple Therapy

Similar to BCT studies of alcoholics, Rowe and Liddle's reviewed studies showed decreases in domestic violence (Fals-Stewart, Kashdan, O'Farrell, & Birchler, 2002), better cost outcomes (Fals-Stewart, O'Farrell, & Birchler, 1997), behavioral improvement in the children of the substance abuser (Kelley & Fals-Stewart, 2002), and greater medical treatment compliance among substance abusers (Fals-Stewart, O'Farrell, & Birchler, 2001; Fals-Stewart, O'Farrell, & Martin, 2002). In addition, one study replicated positive outcomes in both relationship and abstinence measures for 75 female substance abusers (Winters, Fals-Stewart, O'Farrell, Birchler, & Kelley, 2002).

McCollum, Lewis, Nelson, Trepper, and Wetchler (2003) and McCollum, Nelson, Lewis, and Trepper (2005) tested a model of systemic couple treatment for substance abusing women. Details of this study are reported in the "Systemic Couples Treatment for Substance-Abusing Women" section of this chapter.

Sexual Compulsivity/Addiction

Searches for literature on treatment of sexual compulsivity or addiction yielded a scarcity of research using couple therapy models. However, Sprenkle (1987) suggested that marital sex therapy could be used to treat sexual addiction. Sprenkle's approach included six steps: joining, defining and specifying the problem, mapping the couple (an assessment focusing on couple boundaries and other structural concepts), reframing, restructuring, and terminating. No studies to date have reported research using this particular treatment. However, acknowledgment of other sex therapy concepts (e.g., that sexual compulsivity/addiction is triggered by several events, is often a result of family-of-origin issues, and is generally associated with other addictions) was discussed in McCarthy's work (2002). McCarthy approached recovery from a systems standpoint and emphasized the role of the wife in facilitating recovery of sex-addicted men. He promoted the practice of conjoint therapy, which included discussion of the couple's sexual style, relapse prevention, the forming of an abstinence contract, honest and open communication about sexual issues, and education of sexual triggers. Note that this program is not dissimilar from couples' programs for treating alcohol or substance abuse.

Adams and Robinson (2001) explained that successful treatment of sexual addictions includes at least three areas: reduction of shame, affect regulation, and sexual boundaries. Nerenberg (2000) and Line and Cooper (2002) add that group psychotherapy continues to be a vital part of recovery due to its interpersonal nature and several other therapeutic factors not present in individual-focused treatments. Also, disclosure seems to be an important element of recovery, but if, when, what, and to whom to disclose is currently debatable (Corley & Schneider, 2002). Based on these elements for successful treatment of sexual addictions, models such as BCT, emotionally focused therapy (EFT; Greenburg & Johnson, 1988), and other couple therapies seem well equipped to help couples struggling with this issue.

Although little research has been conducted in terms of how effective specific couple therapy models are in helping pornography and sex addictions, Zitzman (2004) interviewed six married couples after they had completed marital therapy for pornography addiction. The couples were treated conjointly with either cognitive-behavioral, emotionally focused, or an eclectic blend of systemic therapy (Zitzman & Butler, 2005). The outcome of Zitzman's research points to a few salient concepts, which, when added to what we already know about addictions, should promote research and development in what is becoming a critical area of study for marriage and family therapists. Zitzman found that when couples understood each others' roles in addiction and recovery processes, they were more satisfied in their marriages, could better identify interventions to employ in the recovery process, trusted each other, and were softer toward each other. From a systemic standpoint, it would seem that this research suggests confirmation of a recursive process in couples regarding unhappiness, distressing behaviors, couples treatment, rapprochement of the couple, increased satisfaction, and decreased addictive behaviors. This hypothesized process needs further study with multiple kinds of addictions, multiple methods of systemic therapy, and cultural sensitivity in terms of definitions of problems, couple interaction, and suitable interventions.

Pathological Gambling

As with sexual addiction, pathological gambling research is a relatively new field of study. We mention it here because of the similarities in addictive processes and potential for similarities in couple therapy approaches to treatment. In Petry and Armentano's (1999) update on the prevalence, assessment, and treatment of gambling addicts, two marital therapies were reviewed. The first involved 90 pathological gamblers and their spouses, who were self-assigned to participate in Gamblers Anonymous (GA), Gam-Anon ($n = 44$), or to the regular GA group ($n = 46$). Those gamblers whose spouses participated in Gam-Anon were more likely to abstain from gambling, but the differences were not statistically significant (E. E. Johnson & Nora, 1992). The second study (Tepperman, 1985) compared abstinence and marital measures among 10 GA members and their wives who were involved in a 12-step recovery program together and 10 married GA members who did not enter couple treatment. At the end of the study, couples in the treatment group were more aware of their relationship issues and maintained their resistance to depression; however, treatment group outcomes were not statistically significantly different from those of the control group. In a meta-analytical review of 22 studies (Pallesen, Mitsem, Kvale, Johnsen, & Molde, 2005), behavioral and cognitive-behavioral approaches constituted the majority of treatments, but modalities remained mostly individually focused. Studies such as these show promise and suggest further investigation of systemic treatments in addition to mere spousal involvement in traditional treatment.

Eating Disorders

Most research in the area of family-based treatments for eating disorders has focused on outcomes for children and adolescents (Lock, Le Grange, & Forsberg, 2007). Relatively few studies have focused on treatment for adult eating disorders (Peake, Limbert, & Whitehead, 2005) and fewer still have examined couple-based treatments. It is hoped that results from studies done on children, adolescents, and their families will prove replicable in the treatment of adult couples.

One study involving 105 adult men with eating disorders (bulimia, anorexia nervosa, and eating disorders not otherwise specified) in a residential treatment setting showed that using a multimodal approach, including family therapy, was effective in reducing the severity of eating disorder symptoms and increasing weight (Weltzin, Weisensel, Cornella-Carlson, & Bean, 2007).

Though inpatient treatment is usually recommended for severe eating disorders, one study indicated little difference between patients treated in residential and outpatient settings (Peake et al., 2005). One such outpatient model of treatment is the Maudsley model of family-based treatment for anorexia nervosa (Rhodes, Gosbee, Madden, & Brown, 2005). Developed over 20 years ago, this model of treatment for adolescents has its origin in the United Kingdom and has been manualized, subjected to random clinical trials, and shown effective in the United States (Rhodes & Madden, 2005; Rhodes et al.). Rhodes and his colleagues commented that narrative therapy (White & Epston, 1990) has been used to augment the Maudsley model with some success.

Some research has been conducted on the effects of spouse involvement in treatment for bulimia or binge eating disorders. One study of 94 overweight, binge-eating women who were randomly assigned to either a CBT group, CBT group with spouse involvement, or a wait-list control group found that both CBT groups showed improvement in measures of binge eating, weight, and psychological measures in a 6-month follow-up study (Gorin, Le Grange, & Stone, 2003).

Results from family-based and spouse-involved treatments for eating disorders provide some indication that developing a model to specifically address the needs of adults with eating disorders and their spouses may be worthwhile.

Summary

Consistent findings suggest that spousal involvement alone or spousal involvement in systemic therapies in conjunction with traditional treatments are not harmful and, in some cases, are more helpful than control group treatments. Controlled studies alone are insufficient, however, to tell us much about how well different therapies work with what kinds of participants under what kinds of conditions. Effectiveness or "real world" research is necessary to tease out the multitude of variables that are likely to affect the processes of abuse or addiction as well as the processes of treatment. It is possible that spousal involvement in treatment, whether the treatment consists of traditional components that focus on the abuser's issues, or systemic treatments that focus on couple dynamics, is variably effective, depending on other factors. That is, some clients may do better in individual treatments of one sort or another while other clients may do better in couple-oriented treatments. In addition, it is possible (and some would say probable) that treatments designed for one segment of the population of interest would not be effective for other segments. Finally, none of the studies reviewed focused on culturally-specific dynamics or contexts. The treatment model described next, systemic couples therapy (SCT; Nelson, McCollum, Wetchler, & Trepper, 1996; Wetchler, McCollum, Nelson, Trepper, & Lewis, 1993; Wetchler, Nelson, McCollum, & Trepper, 1994), was based on the hypothesis that women's pathways into treatment are different from men's, that women's issues in treatment (e.g., need for daycare for their children) are different, and that the meaning of women's involvement in substance abuse (oriented more toward relationships) are different from men's (oriented more toward effects of the substance). The following section describes this treatment and the results of research conducted that used SCT.

Systemic Couples Therapy for Substance-Abusing Women

Women's experiences in the context of substance abuse are reportedly different from men's experiences. Women reportedly are frequently introduced to drugs by men and are maintained in abuse by men (Anglin, Kao, Harlow, & Peters, 1987), especially when women are involved in intimate relationships with male addicts. Women often cite problems with spouses or cohabiting male partners as strongly associated with alcohol and drug abuse (Williams & Klerman, 1984). These factors affect the pathways for women into alcohol and drug abuse, treatment, maintenance, and relapse (Kauffman, Dore, & Nelson-Zlupko, 1995; Lewis, Haller, Branch, & Ingersoll, 1996). McCollum and Trepper (1995), in a qualitative study that queried women in a treatment program for drug-abusing women, found a number of factors that seemed to affect the women differently than men as barriers they experienced to effective treatment. These included transportation (not having access to the family vehicle), child care (not wanting to leave their children with previous caregivers who also were substance abusers), and non-supportive partners. Stanton (1997) suggested that women are reluctant to attend treatment in opposition to their partners' wishes because of the disruption that this caused in the home, which sometimes included violence. Finally, Connors, Maisto, and Zywiak (1998) suggested that partner issues increased the probability of treatment relapse. Thus, it appears that for women, the entry into abuse, the entry into and ability to stay in treatment, and the ability to maintain gains made in treatment are affected by relationships with intimate partners.

86 • Handbook of Clinical Issues in Couple Therapy

Including intimate partners in substance abuse treatment was hypothesized by McCollum et al. (2003) to positively affect outcomes in two ways. First, it was believed that when partners were involved in treatment, there would be less disruption in the couple dynamics, thus enhancing the probability that the woman would stay in treatment. A review of Stanton's (1997) work suggests that family therapy approaches in drug treatment increases women's retention in treatment by nearly twofold. Second, O'Farrell (1991) suggested from his work that recovery is longer lasting when intimate partners are involved. Further, Collins (1990) suggested that gains are made in non-drinking areas such as communication and parenting. Given these factors, it is not surprising that women who are involved in systemic treatments report higher rates of treatment success than do men. Without support, women do not enter treatment, leave sooner, do not benefit as much, and relapse more.

McCollum et al.'s (2003) hypothesis was that women who received substance abuse treatment that involved their intimate partners in some way would have better outcomes than women whose partners were not involved. A model for addressing relationship issues that impact women's substance use was developed as an add-on for standard psychoeducational treatment and was tested with three groups: women whose partners participated in conjoint therapy; women whose partners did not participate in conjoint therapy, but whose therapy included a focus on relationship issues; and women who participated in a standard treatment only. One hundred twenty-two women were randomly assigned to one of the three groups and they and their partners participated in extensive research testing that included self-report substance use measures, urinalysis assessment, individual measures, and couple measures. Women and their partners participated in research testing before treatment, at the end of treatment, and at 3, 6, and 12 months post-treatment. Participants were paid nominal sums for the testing time. Participants were relatively young and poor, and tended to abuse drugs more than alcohol (McCollum et al.).

Therapy was conducted at two outpatient agencies in a large Southwestern city. One agency used a predominantly psychoeducational model plus a few available individual counseling sessions. The second agency employed methadone treatment for heroin addiction. In addition to the treatment as usual from each agency (TAU), added couple treatment consisted of up to 12 therapy sessions with a therapist who had been trained in marriage and family therapy as their foundational education and were additionally trained in the research treatment model. After initial training in the model, therapists participated in live and phone supervision on a weekly basis and occasional re-training to ensure adherence to the treatment model. Supervision was conducted by the developers of the model.

The treatment model included components of structural (Minuchin, 1974), strategic (Bowen, 1978; Watzlawick, Weakland, & Fisch, 1974),

Couples Therapy and Addictions • **87**

behavioral (primarily communication training; Jacobson & Margolin, 1979), and solution-focused (e.g., de Shazer, 1982) therapies. Assessment included understanding relationship dynamics in the intimate relationship; family of origin dynamics, including dynamics around substance use; domestic violence; prior sexual abuse that was currently affecting the woman severely; mental status; and goals for treatment. Women who were diagnosed with severe dual diagnoses, in current abusive relationships, or who were dealing with severe symptoms of sexual abuse (e.g., flashbacks) were referred for primary treatment elsewhere.

TAU groups (one third of the women) included 12 sessions of psychoeducation in mixed-sex groups. Participants were required to attend at least one AA meeting, but were not required to attend after that if they did not find the meetings helpful. Systemic couple therapy (SCT; Nelson et al., 1996) used the systemic treatment model with the women participants and their partners together. Systemic individual therapy (SIT), did not include the women's partners in conjoint sessions, but treatment focused on intimate and family of origin relationship dynamics. Because all of the women were receiving primary substance abuse treatment, SCT and SIT did not focus on substance use except as the women named these issues in their goals for treatment and as they were explored in the family of origin interviews. It was hypothesized that strengthened couple relationships would lead to changes in the women's contexts and treatment for substance use that would enhance rather than hinder retention in treatment and positive results.

Briefly, structural family therapy components of the model addressed power and boundary issues in the couple's dynamics. Strategic therapy intervened in dysfunctional interactional patterns (paradoxical interventions were not used). Bowen Family Therapy principles were used to understand dynamics of managing anxiety from families of origin and for connecting relationship patterns from the past as they were repeated or mirrored in current intimate relationships. Behavioral interventions consisted of communication skills training and solution-focused interventions were used to mark and enhance gains made in therapy. Therapy was feminist-informed (Nelson et al., 1996) and sensitive to potential intimate violence.

Multiple measures for testing individual functioning, couple functioning, and substance use were employed in a repeated measures design with testing before treatment, at the end of treatment, and at 3, 6, and 12 months posttreatment. Results of substance use changes among the groups based on the Addiction Severity Index, ASI (McLellan, Luborsky, Woody, & O'Brien, 1980) were reported by McCollum et al. (2003).

At the 3-month phase of testing, women who participated in SCT or SIT scored higher (higher severity) for alcohol use on the ASI than those in TAU. At all other times, no differences appeared among the groups. McCollum et al. (2003) did not speculate on these results. In contrast to results for alcohol

88 • Handbook of Clinical Issues in Couple Therapy

use, McCollum and colleagues' results for changes in drug abuse suggested a decrease in ASI scores for all three groups. Women in SIT and SCT fared better than those in TAU at 6 months and 1 year post-treatment. Results for SIT and SCT did not differ from each other. In addition, scores for the participants' need for treatment, as assessed by the ASI, decreased at 6 months and 1 year for women in the systemic couples treatment groups. The authors concluded that providing women substance abusers with treatment that includes attention to intimate relationships in addition to standard drug treatment enhances treatment outcomes and, more particularly, helped the women in the study to better maintain gains than women in the standard treatment alone.

A second analysis of data from the study (McCollum et al., 2005), comparing effects of participants' and partners' perspectives of relationship quality on women's use of treatment, yielded apparently confusing results. Women whose partners perceived high marital quality as measured by the Dyadic Quality Inventory (originally known as the Dyadic Formation Inventory; Lewis, 1973) did not fare as well in the systemic substance abuse treatment. These women reported more days of substance use at post-test and were less likely to complete treatment. The authors conjectured that partners who were satisfied with the quality of their relationships did not find drug use a problem and thus were not as likely to be supportive of less use or abstinence. Laudet, Magura, Furst, Kumar, and Whitney (1999) interviewed 62 male partners of crack-addicted women and found that their partners' drug use was a problem for them only when it interfered with traditional gender-related activities. McCollum et al. found that women most at risk of continued drug use and dropping out of treatment were those who rated their relationship quality as low while their partners rated quality as high. These women seemed particularly susceptible to their partners' lack of treatment support. The authors suggested that results suggest that it might be important to include women's partners in treatment so that their attitudes can be assessed and their cooperation enlisted more directly. McCollum et al. did not analyze the data by treatment group; thus, no reports are available on the relative merits of SCT versus SIT, which might reveal interesting patterns.

Conclusion

This chapter suggests that couple therapy for addictions is a mixed bag. It appears that definitions of what constitutes couple therapy may affect outcomes. For example, it appears that unilateral treatment of non-abusing spouses and partners may assist abusers entering treatment. Specifics of including partners during treatment are not clear. Conjoint treatments that merely included partners in the same treatment as the abusers seem to enhance treatment outcomes as do treatments that are based on systemic or recursive relationship dynamics principles. Reviews do not reveal the differences among treatment models or modalities, differences when applied to abusers with differing characteristics, differences among different kinds of addictions, differences among ethnic populations, or differences on different levels of abuse (misuse, abuse, addiction). One study (McCollum et al., 2003), however, that utilized systemic family therapy principles with substance abusing women found that, for the women in the study, attention to relationship issues and dynamics helped women to reduce their drug use and, more specifically, to maintain the gains they had made in treatment. When partners of these women perceived the relationship quality to be high, however, the women did less well in treatment and tended more to drop out of treatment. To the current authors, these results suggest that more work needs to be done to tease out specific factors that affect treatment outcomes so that treatments can be developed that optimize positive results, treating abusers (and, perhaps, their partners) based on identifiable characteristics rather than using single models for all abusers.

References

Adams, K. M., & Robinson, D. W. (2001). Shame reduction, affect regulation, and sexual boundary development: Essential building blocks of sexual addiction treatment. *Sexual Addiction and Compulsivity, 8*, 23–44.

Anglin, M. D., Kao, C., Harlow, L. L., & Peters, K. (1987). Similarity of behavior within addict couples: I. Methodology and narcotics patterns. *International Journal of the Addictions, 22*, 497–524.

Azrin, N. H. (1976). Improvements in the community-reinforcement approach to alcoholism. *Behaviour Research and Therapy, 14*, 339–348.

Azrin, N. H., Naster, B. J., & Jones, R. (1973). Reciprocity counseling: A rapid-learning based procedure for marital counseling. *Behaviour Research and Therapy, 11*, 365–382.

Barber, J. G., & Crisp, B. R. (1995). The "pressure to change" approach to working with the partners of heavy drinkers. *Addiction, 90*, 269–276.

Bowen, M. (1978). *Family therapy in clinical practice*. New York: Jason Aaronson.

Cadogan, D. A. (1973). Marital group therapy in the treatment of alcoholism. *Quarterly Journal of the Study of Alcohol, 34*, 1187–1194.

Collins, R. L. (1990). Family treatment of alcohol abuse: Behavioral and systems perspectives. In R. L. Collins, K. E. Leonard, & J. S. Searles (Eds.), *Alcohol and the family* (pp. 285–308). New York: Guilford.

Connors, G. J., Maisto, S. A., & Zywiak, W. H. (1998). Male and female alcoholics' attributions regarding the onset and termination of relapses and the maintenance of abstinence. *Journal of Substance Abuse, 10*, 27–42.

Corder, B. F., Corder, R. F., & Laidlaw, N. C. (1972). An intensive treatment program for alcoholics and their wives. *Quarterly Journal of the Study of Alcohol, 33*, 1144–1146.

Corley, M. D., & Schneider, J. P. (2002). Disclosing secrets: Guidelines for therapists working with sex addicts and co-addicts. *Sexual Addiction and Compulsivity, 9*, 43–67.

Edwards, M. E., & Steinglass, P. (1995). Family therapy treatment outcomes for alcoholism. *Journal of Marital and Family Therapy, 21*, 475–509.

Epstein, E. E., & McCrady, B. S. (2002). Couple therapy in the treatment of alcohol problems. In A. S. Gurman & N. S. Jacobson (Eds.), *Clinical handbook of couple therapy* (3rd ed., pp. 597–628). New York: Guilford.

Fals-Stewart, W., Kashdan, T. B., O'Farrell, T. J., & Birchler, G. R. (2002). Behavioral couples therapy for male drug abusing patients and their partners: The effect on interpartner violence. *Journal of Substance Abuse Treatment, 22*, 1–10.

Fals-Stewart, W., O'Farrell, T. J., & Birchler, G. R. (1997). Behavior couples therapy for male methadone maintenance patients: Effects on drug-using behavior and relationship adjustment. *Behavior Therapy, 32*, 391–411.

Fals-Stewart, W., O'Farrell, T. J., & Birchler, G. R. (2001). Behavioral couples therapy for male substance abusing patients: A cost outcomes analysis. *Journal of Consulting and Clinical Psychology, 65*, 789–802.

Fals-Stewart, W., O'Farrell, T. J., & Martin, J. (2002, March). Using behavioral family counseling to enhance HIV-medication compliance among HIV-infected male drug abusing patients. Paper presented at *Treating addictions in special populations conference*, Binghamton, NY.

Gorin, A. A., Le Grange, D., & Stone, A. A. (2003). Effectiveness of spouse involvement in cognitive behavioral therapy for binge eating disorder. *International Journal of Eating Disorders, 33*(4), 421–433.

Greenburg, L. S., & Johnson, S. M. (1988). *Emotionally focused therapy for couples.* New York: Guilford Press.

Hunt, G. M., & Azrin, N. H. (1973). A community reinforcement approach to alcoholism. *Behavior Research and Therapy, 11*, 91–104.

Jacobson, N. S., & Margolin, G. (1979). *Marital therapy: Strategies based on social learning and behavior exchange principles.* New York: Brunner/Mazel.

Johnson, E. E., & Nora, R. M. (1992). Does spousal participation in Gamblers Anonymous benefit compulsive gamblers? *Psychological Reports, 71*, 914.

Johnson, V. E. (1986). *Intervention: How to help someone who doesn't want help.* Minneapolis, MN: Johnson Institute Books.

Kauffman, E., Dore, M. M., & Nelson-Zlupko, L. (1995). The role of women's therapy groups in the treatment of chemical dependence. *American Journal of Orthopsychiatry, 65*, 355–363.

Kelley, M. L., & Fals-Stewart, W. (2002). Couples versus individual-based therapy for alcoholism and drug abuse: Effects on children's psychosocial functioning. *Journal of Consulting and Clinical Psychology, 70*, 417–427.

Kirby, K. C., Marlowe, D. B., Festinger, D. S., Garvey, K. A., & LaMonaca, V. (1999). Community reinforcement training for family and significant others of drug abusers: A unilateral intervention to increase treatment entry of drug users. *Drug and Alcohol Dependence, 56*, 85–96.

Laudet, A., Magura, S., Furst, R. T., Kumar, N., & Whitney, S. (1999). Male partners of substance-abusing women in treatment: An exploratory study. *American Journal of Drug and Alcohol Abuse, 25*, 607–627.

Lewis, R. A. (1973). The dyadic formation inventory: An instrument for measuring heterosexual couple development. *Journal of Sociology of the Family, 23*, 207–216.

Lewis, R. A., Haller, D. L., Branch, D., & Ingersoll, K. S. (1996). Retention issues involving drug-abusing women in treatment research. In E. R. Rahdert (Ed.), *Treatment for drug-exposed women and children: Advances in research methodology—NIDA Research Monograph 165* (pp. 110–122). Rockville, MD: National Institute on Drug Abuse.

Line, B. Y., & Cooper, A. (2002). Group therapy: Essential component for success with sexually acting out problems among men. *Sexual Addiction & Compulsivity, 9*, 15–32.

Lock, J., Le Grange, D., & Forsberg, S. (2007). Is family therapy effective in children with anorexia nervosa? *Brown University Child and Adolescent Behavior Letter, 23*(1), 3.

McCarthy, B. W. (2002). The wife's role in facilitating recovery from male compulsive sexual behavior. *Sexual Addiction & Compulsivity, 9,* 275–284.

McCollum, E. E., Lewis, R. A., Nelson, T. S., Trepper, T. S., & Wetchler, J. L. (2003). Couple treatment for drug abusing women: Effects on drug use and need for treatment. *Journal of Couple and Relationship Therapy, 2*(4), 1–18.

McCollum, E. E., Nelson, T. S., Lewis, R. A., & Trepper, T. S. (2005). Partner relationship quality and drug use as predictors of women's substance abuse treatment outcome. *The American Journal of Drug and Alcohol Abuse, 1,* 111–127.

McCollum, E. E., & Trepper, T. S. (1995). "Little by little, pulling me through." Women's perception of successful drug treatment: A qualitative inquiry. *Journal of Family Psychotherapy, 6*(1), 63–82.

McCrady, B. S., Epstein, E. E., & Hirsch, L. S. (1999). Maintaining change after conjoint behavioral alcohol treatment for men: Outcomes at 6 months. *Addiction, 94,* 1381–1396.

McCrady, B. S., Moreau, J., & Paolino, T. J. (1982). Joint hospitalization and couples therapy for alcoholism: A four-year follow-up. *Journal of Studies on Alcohol, 43,* 1244–1250.

McCrady, B. S., Noel, N. E., & Abrams, D. B. (1986). Comparative effectiveness of three types of spouse involvement in outpatient behavioral alcoholism treatment. *Journal of Studies on Alcohol, 47,* 459–467.

McCrady, B. S., Noel, N. E., Abrams, D. B., Stout, R. L., Nelson, H. F., & Hay, W. M. (1986). Comparative effectiveness of three types of spouse involvement in outpatient behavioral alcoholism treatment. *Journal of Studies on Alcohol, 47,* 459–467.

McCrady, B. S., Noel, N. E., Stout, R. L., Abrams, D. B., & Nelson, H. F. (1991). Comparative effectiveness of three types of spouse-involved behavioral alcoholism treatment: Outcome 18 months after treatment. *British Journal of Addictions, 86,* 1415–1424.

McCrady, B. S., Paolino, T. F., Longabaugh, R., & Rosi, J. (1979). Effects of joint hospital admission and couples treatment for hospitalized alcoholics: A pilot study. *Addictive Behaviors, 4,* 155–165.

McCrady, B. S., Stout, R., Noel, N., Abrams, D., & Nelson, H. F. (1991). Effectiveness of three types of spouse-involved behavioral alcoholism treatment. *British Journal of Addiction, 86,* 1415–1424.

McKay, J. R., Longabaugh, R., Beattie, M. C., Maisto, S. A., & Noel, N. E. (1993). Does adding conjoint therapy to individually focused alcoholism treatment lead to better family functioning? *Journal of Substance Abuse, 5,* 45–59.

McLellan, A. T., Luborsky, L., Woody, G. E., & O'Brien, C. P. (1980). An improved diagnostic evaluation instrument for substance abuse patients: The Addiction Severity Index. *Journal of Nervous and Mental Disease, 168,* 26–33.

Meyers, R. J., Miller, W. R., Smith, J. E., & Tonigan, J. S. (2002). A randomized trial of two methods for engaging treatment refusing drug users through concerned significant others. *Journal of Consulting and Clinical Psychology, 70,* 1182–1185.

Miller, W. R., Meyers, R. J., & Tonigan, J. S. (1999). Engaging the unmotivated in treatment for alcohol problems: A comparison of three strategies for intervention through family members. *Journal of Consulting and Clinical Psychology, 67,* 688–697.

Minuchin, S. (1974). *Families and family therapy.* Cambridge, MA: Harvard University Press.

Nelson, T. S., McCollum, E. E., Wetchler, J. L., & Trepper, T. S. (1996). Therapy with women substance abusers: A systemic couples approach. *Journal of Feminist Family Therapy, 8,* 5–27.

92 • Handbook of Clinical Issues in Couple Therapy

Nerenberg, A. (2000). The value of group psychotherapy for sexual addicts in a residential setting. *Sexual Addiction and Compulsivity*, 7, 197–209.

O'Farrell, T. J. (1991, August). Using couples therapy in treatment of alcoholism. Paper presented at the *Annual Convention of the American Psychological Association*, San Francisco, CA.

O'Farrell, T. J., & Birchler, G. R. (1987). Marital relationships of alcoholic, conflicted, and nonconflicted couples. *Journal of Marital and Family Therapy*, 13, 259–274.

O'Farrell, T. J., Choquette, K. A., & Birchler, G. R. (1991). Sexual satisfaction and dissatisfaction in the marital relationships of male alcoholics seeking marital therapy. *Journal of Studies on Alcohol*, 52, 441–447.

O'Farrell, T. J., Choquette, K. A., & Cutter, H. S. G. (1998). Couples relapse prevention sessions after behavioral marital therapy for alcoholics and their wives: Outcomes during three years after starting treatment. *Journal of Studies on Alcohol*, 59, 357–370.

O'Farrell, T. J., Choquette, K. A., Cutter, H. S. G., & Birchler, G. R. (1997). Sexual satisfaction and dysfunction in marriages of male alcoholics: Comparison with nonalcoholic maritally conflicted and nonconflicted couples. *Journal of Studies on Alcohol*, 58(1), 91–99.

O'Farrell, T. J., Choquette, K. A., Cutter, H. S. G., Brown, E. D., Bayog, R., McCourt, W., et al. (1996). Cost-benefit and cost-effectiveness analyses of behavioral marital therapy with and without relapse prevention sessions for alcoholics and their spouses. *Behavior Therapy*, 27, 7–24.

O'Farrell, T. J., Choquette, K. A., Cutter, H. S. G., Brown, E. D., & McCourt, W. (1993). Behavioral marital therapy with and without additional couples relapse prevention sessions for alcoholics and their wives. *Journal of Studies on Alcohol*, 54, 652–666.

O'Farrell, T. J., Choquette, K. A., Cutter, H. S. G., Floyd, F. J., Bayog, R. D., Brown, E. D., et al. (1996). Cost-benefit and cost-effectiveness analyses of behavioral marital therapy as an addition to outpatient alcoholism treatment. *Journal of Substance Abuse*, 8, 145–166.

O'Farrell, T. J., Cutter, H. S. G., Choquette, K. A., Floyd, F. J., & Bayog, R. D. (1992). Behavioral marital therapy for male alcoholics: Marital and drinking adjustment during the two years after treatment. *Behavior Therapy*, 23, 529–549.

O'Farrell, T. J., Cutter, H. S. G., & Floyd, F. J. (1985). Evaluating behavioral marital therapy for male alcoholics: Effects of marital adjustment and communication from before to after treatment. *Behavior Therapy*, 16, 147–167.

O'Farrell, T. J., & Fals-Stewart, W. (2000). Behavioral couples therapy for alcoholism and drug abuse. *Journal of Substance Abuse Treatment*, 18, 51–54.

O'Farrell, T. J., & Fals-Stewart, W. (2002). Alcohol abuse. In D. H. Sprenkle (Ed.), *Effectiveness research in marriage and family therapy* (pp. 123–161). Alexandria, VA: American Association for Marriage and Family Therapy.

O'Farrell, T. J., Van Hutton, V., & Murphy, C. M. (1999). Domestic violence before and after alcoholism treatment: A two-year longitudinal study. *Journal of Studies on Alcohol*, 60, 317–321.

Pallesen, S., Mitsem, M., Kvale, G., Johnsen, B., & Molde, H. (2005). Outcome of psychological treatments of pathological gambling: A review and meta-analysis. *Addiction*, 100, 1412–1422.

Peake, K. J., Limbert, C., & Whitehead, L. (2005). An evaluation of the Oxford adult eating disorders service between 1994 and 2002. *European Eating Disorders Review*, 13, 427–435.

Petry, N. M., & Armentano, C. (1999). Prevalence, assessment, and treatment of pathological gambling: A review. *Psychiatric Services*, 50(8), 1021–1027.

Rhodes, P., Gosbee, M., Madden, S., & Brown, J. (2005). 'Communities of concern' in the family-based treatment of anorexia nervosa: Towards a consensus in the Maudsley model. *European Eating Disorders Review, 13*, 392–398.

Rhodes, P., & Madden, S. (2005). Scientist-practitioner family therapists, postmodern medical practitioners and expert parents: Second-order change in the eating disorders program at the children's hospital at Westmead. *Journal of Family Therapy, 27*, 171–182.

Rowe, C. L., & Liddle, H. A. (2002). Substance abuse. In D. H. Sprenkle (Ed.), *Effectiveness research in marriage and family therapy* (pp. 53–88). Alexandria, VA: American Association for Marriage and Family Therapy.

de Shazer, S. (1982). *Patterns of brief family therapy: An ecosystemic approach.* New York: Guilford.

Shoham, V., Rohrbaugh, M. J., Stickle, T. R., & Jacob, T. (1998). Demand-withdraw couple interaction moderates retention in cognitive behavioral versus family-systems treatments for alcoholism. *Journal of Family Psychology, 12*, 557–577.

Sisson, R. W., & Azrin, N. H. (1986). Family-member involvement to initiate and promote treatment of problem drinkers. *Journal of Behavior Therapy and Experimental Psychiatry, 17*, 15–21.

Smith, J. E., Meyers, R. J., & Miller, W. R. (2001). The community reinforcement approach to the treatment of substance use disorders. *American Journal on Addictions, 10*, 51–59.

Sprenkle, D. H. (1987). Treating a sex addict through marital sex therapy. *Family Relations, 36*, 11–14.

Stanton, M. D. (1997). The role of family and significant others in the engagement and retention of drug-dependent individuals. In L. S. Onken, J. D. Blain, & J. J. Boren (Eds.), *Beyond the therapeutic alliance: Keeping the drug-dependent individual in treatment—NIDA Research Monograph 165* (pp. 157–160). Rockville, MD: National Institute on Drug Abuse.

Stanton, M. D. (2004). Getting reluctant substance abusers to engage in treatment/self-help: A review of outcomes and clinical options. *Journal of Marital and Family Therapy, 30*(2), 165–182.

Stanton, M. D., & Shadish, W. R. (1997). Outcome, attrition, and family-couples treatment for drug abuse: A meta-analysis and review of the controlled, comparative studies. *Psychological Bulletin, 122*(2), 170–191.

Tepperman, J. H. (1985). The effectiveness of short-term group therapy upon the pathological gambler and wife. *Journal of Gambling Behavior, 1*, 119–130.

Thomas, E. J. (1989). Unilateral family therapy to reach the uncooperative alcohol abuser. In B. A. Thyer (Ed.), *Behavioral family therapy*. Springfield, IL: Charles C. Thomas.

Thomas, E. J., Santa, C. A., Bronson, D., & Oyserman, D. (1987). Unilateral family therapy with spouses of alcoholics. *Journal of Social Service Research, 10*, 145–162.

Thomas, E. J., Yoshioka, M., Ager, R., & Adams, K. B. (1993). Reaching the uncooperative alcohol abuser through a cooperative spouse. Paper presented at the *Fifth congress of the International Society for Bio-Medical Research on Alcoholism*, Toronto, Ontario, Canada.

Watzlawick, P., Weakland, J., & Fisch, R. (1974). *Change: Principles of problem formation and problem resolution.* New York: Norton.

Weltzin, T. E., Weisensel, N., Cornella-Carlson, T., & Bean, P. (2007). Improvements in the severity of eating disorder symptoms and weight changes in a large population of males undergoing treatment for eating disorders. *Best Practices in Mental Health, 3*(1), 52–65.

94 • Handbook of Clinical Issues in Couple Therapy

Wetchler, J. L., McCollum, E. E., Nelson, T. S., Trepper, T. S., & Lewis, R. A. (1993). Systemic couples therapy for alcohol-abusing women. In T. J. O'Farrell (Ed.), *Marital and family therapy: Alcoholism treatment* (pp. 236–260). New York: Guilford.

Wetchler, J. L., Nelson, T. S., McCollum, E. E., & Trepper, T. S. (1994). Couple focused therapy for drug abusing women. In J. Lewis (Ed.), *Addictions: Concepts and strategies for treatment* (pp. 236–260). Rockville, MD: Aspen.

White, M., & Epston, D. (1990). *Narrative means to therapeutic ends.* New York: Norton.

Williams, C. N., & Klerman, L. V. (1984). Female alcohol abuse: Its effects on the family. In S. C. Wilsnack & L. J. Beckman (Eds.), *Alcohol problems in women: Antecedents, consequences, and interventions* (pp. 280–312). New York: Guilford.

Winters, J., Fals-Stewart, W., O'Farrell, T. J., Birchler, G. R., & Kelley, M. L. (2002). Behavioral couples therapy for female substance-abusing patients: Effects on substance use and relationship adjustment. *Journal of Consulting and Clinical Psychology, 70*(2), 344–455.

Zitzman, S. T. (2004). *Couples sharing recovery from a husband's addiction to pornography: A qualitative study.* Retrieved December 17, 2005 from http://contentdm.lib.byu.edu/ETD/image/etd448.pdf

Zitzman, S. T., & Butler, M. H. (2005). Attachment, addiction, and recovery: Conjoint marital therapy for recovery from a sexual addiction. *Sexual Addiction and Compulsivity, 12,* 311–337.

6

Current State of Sexuality Theory and Therapy

JOAN D. ATWOOD and EMILY KLUCINEC

Contents

Paradigm 1: The Early Years—From Religious to Medical to Psychiatric and Clinical Explanations	96
The Judeo-Christian Religion	96
The Rise of the Medical Professions	96
The Rise of Psychology: The Freudian Paradigm	97
Paradigm 2: The Middle Years—The Researchers, the Therapists, and the Shift to Normal	98
Alfred Kinsey	99
Masters and Johnson	100
Helen Singer Kaplan	101
Systems Theory	102
Paradigm 3: The Shift to the Social	104
Gagnon and Simon	104
Paradigm 4: Adding the Historical to the Social	105
Foucault	105
Paradigm 5: The Feminist Influence	106
Paradigm 6: The Current Paradigm—Postmodern Views	107
Summary	109
References	110

The Wuli Masters know that 'science and religion are only dances, and that those who follow them are dancers. The dancers may claim to follow 'truth' or claim to seek 'reality', but the Wuli Masters know better. They know that the true love of all dancers is dancing.'

(Zukav, 1979, p. 111)

Inquiries into the areas of human sexuality that we would now recognize as having some academic/scientific merit began approximately 70–80 years ago. Interestingly, while other areas of social and psychological exploration and practice have amassed an impressive and diverse body of knowledge, research and theory underlying the clinical enterprise of sex knowledge and therapy, for the most part, has remained comparatively sparse. In spite of this, the field has experienced several important paradigm shifts (Kuhn, 1970) which constitute the main focus of this chapter. In order to understand the present state of sexuality theory and therapy, it is helpful to explore the sociohistorical roots of these theoretical stances. The chapter presents the sociohistorical background of sexuality theory and therapy, tracing the movement from the religious foundations, to the medical explanations, to the melding of psychological into the social theories of sexual behavior. Next, it explores the basic assumptions underlying various sex therapy approaches from a focus on the "dysfunction in sexuality" and anecdotal cases of "perversion," to the exploration of "normality in sexualities." The final sections of this chapter end with a discussion of the current state of sexuality theory and therapy in light of the role of postmodernism and its influence on this field of inquiry.

Historically, sexual conduct was largely explained in biological, medical, psychological, or clinical terms. Explanations for behavior in general have moved historically from the mystical to the scientific. This is true also for the explanations for sexual conduct. For example, there has been a historical transition from Judeo-Christian explanations to more medically based explanations for sexuality to more psychological descriptions and interpretations. In addition, often interest focused on what might be called deviations from normal or functional sexuality without any consideration of what "normal" or functional might be. Yet each theory is fully loaded with implicit and explicit assumptions that define "normal" functioning.

Paradigm 1: The Early Years—From Religious to Medical to Psychiatric and Clinical Explanations

The Judeo-Christian Religion

Initially, definitions of sexuality were based in the Judeo-Christian religion which characterized the attitudes and values in Western society. In this view, sex was seen solely as a reproductive act and any sex for non-reproductive purposes, that is, masturbatory behavior or sex simply for pleasure, was considered a sin. These beliefs and attitudes dictated that sex for any other reason was a wasting of energy and/or seed (semen) and severe punishments would ensue. Punishments for "sins of the flesh" involved moral shame and degradation and often invoked the devil and damnation. This punitive-based ideology fastened within the confines of fear and morality was the primary one in Western society from approximately the Middle Ages until around the 1600s.

The Rise of the Medical Professions

During the 1600s and up until the late 1800s, with the rise of the medical professions, physicians became an increasingly important secular source of values, beliefs, education, and guidance (i.e., often prescriptive of how to behave sexually and otherwise). Sexuality still tinged with morality, albeit less so, was now entrenched in explanations of health and sickness. This shift in emphasis from religious bases to one of a matter of health and disease carried its own classification, organization, and propriety. The judgments of evil in the definitions of deviant sexual conduct that characterized the earlier religious tradition were now replaced with new expanding typologies of disease by physicians practicing the "science of desire" or as it is called today, sexology. Early sexologists such as Kraft-Ebing (1965), Havelock Ellis (1936), Magnus Hirshfeld (1935), and many others played an integral role in expanding our knowledge of sexual behaviors while paradoxically confining this domain. In their search for the "true" meaning of sexuality and the categorization of sexual perversities, these early pioneers contributed to the codification of a "sexual tradition," a more or less coherent body of assumptions, beliefs, prejudices, rules, methods of investigation, and forms of moral regulation, which still in many ways shape the way we live our sexualities (Weeks, 2003).

Overlap existed between the medical profession and the religious institutions concerning the negative consequences of sex for non-reproductive purposes. The focus remained not on the sex act itself, but transferred "the deficiency" to the object (Weeks, 2003). As the paradigm shifted, the reasoning and consequences were modified accordingly. The religious domain maintained that those who engaged in sex for non-procreative purposes were morally infirm; now the same baton was passed to the medical profession who touted that it was biologically unnatural, an imminent cause for disease. A clear example is masturbation (a sex act for non-reproductive purposes). The medical doctors of the day believed that masturbation could lead to all sorts of physical disorders, such as hysteria, epilepsy, and venereal diseases; whereas, according to the clergy, it would lead to the soul's eternal damnation. It is important to note that moral uniformity surrounding sexuality discourse and preoccupation with whom one has sex with to this day remain legacies from this era.

The Rise of Psychology: The Freudian Paradigm

The medical tradition and its explanations for behavior rooted in health and disease was the dominant conceptual framework up until the early 1900s. With the rise of Freudian psychology in the early 1900s, once again the lens changed as the paradigm shifted. The Freudian point of view became the principle tradition in psychology with regard to sexuality (Rosen & Weinstein, 1988) and best characterizes the psychological paradigm during the early to mid-twentieth century (Comer, 1995). Psychoanalysis has made a critical contribution to the theorization of sex during this century, though its impact has often been ambiguous and contradictory (Weeks, 2003), making Freud's work a treasure trove for interpretation. Freud (1905) believed that sexuality was related to psychosexual development and that the psychologically mature end behavior was monogamous heterosexual intercourse. The term "perversion" had a precise technical meaning and was an inescapable aspect in the lives of all.

98 • Handbook of Clinical Issues in Couple Therapy

It was problematic only when it became an end in itself and blocked the path to mature sexuality (Freud).

Freud (1905) believed that sexual behavior was shaped by a combined development of biological and environmental factors. He stressed the importance of biological drives while also analyzing how those biological energies were channeled by family dynamics. In particular, he focused on conflicts over problematic attachments and tension in relation to one's parents. Central to Freud's thesis was his repression hypothesis. Freud (1905) believed that civilization was founded on the suppression of instincts. He theorized that it was the tragic destiny of humankind to necessarily forego the infinite range of desires in order to ensure survival of the species. Simply interpreted: each individual had to accomplish the "tyranny of genital organization" because the culture demanded it (Freud, p. 279).

The typical therapies for sexual problems that have evolved from this tradition were dyadic. Their aim was not to focus on the sexual symptom; but rather, to achieve a more complete understanding of the person's mental life. Psychoanalytic approaches were based on the underlying assumption that current sexual dysfunction was a manifestation of intrapsychic conflicts from unresolved issues in the individual's personal history (Kaplan, 1974, 1979). The first implication of the psychoanalytic view of sexual dysfunction is that the dysfunction itself is not the problem. It is only a symptom of a deeper, underlying pathology. The second implication is that sexual problems are symptomatic of an underlying, deeper personality conflict that requires intense psychiatric therapeutic intervention and resolution.

In this view, the therapeutic goal is not just to relieve the symptom, but to resolve its infrastructure—the underlying conflict. Insight, understanding, mastery, and psychological growth are highly valued therapeutic goals. Importantly, the true etiological factors were seen as unconscious (or at least subconscious), and hence associations had to be reconstructed between current problems in sexual functioning and earlier issues. The means of symptom removal used by this approach were "transference cures" or "suggestion," likely to be followed by symptom substitution. This psychodynamic or psychoanalytically based treatment approach requires a lengthy treatment often with questionable outcomes (Atwood, 2006).

Paradigm 2: The Middle Years—The Researchers, the Therapists, and the Shift to Normal

During the middle years of the twentieth century, there was a shift from a discussion of clinical cases to survey research and laboratory research, aiming at discovering "normal" sexual behavior. As a result, the more recently accumulated body of data tended to be more systematically gathered than that of the past and overwhelmingly supported the assertion that the story of sex is definitely not limited to reproduction. Armed with data, Kinsey (1948, 1953) resoundingly proclaimed, biologists and psychologists who have accepted the doctrine that the only natural function of sex is reproduction have simply ignored the existence of sexual activity which is not reproductive ... the vast majority of erotic interaction that which we deem heterosexual does not lead to procreation.

Alfred Kinsey

Kinsey's publications of *Sexual Behavior in the Human Male* (1948) and *Sexual Behavior in the Human Female* (1953) were explorations into the "normal" sex lives of American men and women. Kinsey probably influenced the American public more than any other since Freud. Both vast volumes have noted criticisms of methodological problems, insufficiently represented samples, and his unconscious biases, but the thousands (his team interviewed over 10,000 American men and women) of subjects he and his colleagues interviewed provided an unparalleled insight into American sexual life (Hertlein et al., 2008). Categorizing people according to certain social dimensions such as social class, level of education, occupation, religious affiliation, and place of residence and comparing these social groups in sexual behavior, Kinsey's (1948, 1953) research posed the question of whether or not a single pattern of sexual behavior exists, yet simultaneously his research magnified the range of variation in human sexual behavior even within the previously mentioned categories. So that we must remember that any study exploring what is "normal" is by definition defining what is not.

The New Research: Kinsey Updated   Also exploring normal sexual behavior, researchers Laumann, Gagnon, Michael, and Michaels (1994) conducted interviews in 1992 of a random probability sample of 3,432 men and women in the United States between the ages of 18 and 59. Despite substantial political opposition (that included attacks by Senator Jesse Helm on the Senate floor) culminating in the eventual withdrawal of all federal funding, the research team completed the most comprehensive survey of sexual behavior ever attempted in the United States. It resulted in the publication of two books: *The Social Organization of Sexuality* (1994), a book for academics, and *Sex in America* (1994), a more popular book.

Building on the previous works of Kinsey (1948, 1953) as well as adding their own expertise in terms of the factors that influence sexual practices, the authors prefaced their work by contending that such research is both academically valid and socially valuable because the results can often undermine the widely held myths about what people do sexually, while urging caution about interpretation and implications of their findings. The book examines incidences and frequencies of masturbation, sexually transmitted diseases, cohabitation and marriage, fertility, and homosexuality.

The aspect that has met with the most controversy is the authors' assertion (based on the scripting perspective) that what many of us imagine to be our most intimate behavior, driven by our most private fantasies, is actually determined by social factors that are just as regular, and therefore just as measurable, as are rates of birth, death, and suicide. Once the facts about Americans' sexual practices are obtained (Laumann et al., 1994), the authors believe that one can then see that sex is just another social phenomenon that conforms to the same kind of laws that make social scientific research possible in the first place. It seems as if the authors encourage reflexivity, which at some level allows one to see that her/his questions are about knowledge and self just as much as they are about sex, thus demonstrating this theorized paradox that informs the way we live.

It appears at this point that evidence has mounted supporting the idea that anatomy was not destiny. As Margaret Mead stated when speaking of the female orgasm, "There seems therefore to be a reasonable basis for assuming that the human female's capacity for orgasm is to be viewed much more as a potentiality that may or may not be developed by a given culture" (Mead, 1949, p. 217). Although old theories die hard, the point is, of course, that the prevailing view now is that sexual behavior is social behavior.

Masters and Johnson

W. H. Masters and Johnson (1966) did laboratory observations of sexual behavior, focusing on sexual anatomy and physiology, presenting the human sexual response cycle: excitement, arousal, orgasm, and resolution. In so doing, they laid the foundation for the human sexual response cycle and with the publication of the second book in 1970, *Human Sexual Inadequacy*, the foundations for modern day sex therapy. Now the exploration shifted from Kinsey's survey analysis of normal sexual behavior to the laboratory as these researchers explored and documented the "normal" human sexual response. In their second publication, *Human Sexual Inadequacy* (1970), there was an emphasis on cognitive-behavioral methods of treatment and one that appeared to be an effective treatment approach of much shorter therapeutic duration than the analytic one of the past. This new approach challenged the earlier psychoanalytic attitudes and suggested a radically different method for therapeutically approaching sexual problems. It emphasized the non-biological factors in sexual development. In this view sexual dysfunctions were defined as learned disorders rather than symptoms of underlying personality problems. The dysfunctional man or the woman with an orgasmic disorder was viewed as a person who was exposed to an environment that taught him/her to be anxious in a particular sexual situation. In addition, while the psychoanalytic view saw the man's sexual problem, his interpersonal relationships, and his attitudes toward his parents as understandable in terms of one single underlying conflict, the cognitive behavioral view suggested that each aspect of the man's functioning might be caused by separate variables.

As stated, the W. Masters and Johnson (1970) approach differed greatly from the earlier psychoanalytic approaches additionally in that they made the couple as the unit of analysis and therapy rather than the individual. The concerns of each partner were considered without placing blame for the dysfunction. They believed that the psychological mechanisms of dysfunction were largely related to current rather than past influences. Their focus was on eliminating the symptom of the sexual issue. They emphasized brief, intensive treatment of the symptoms regardless of their origins. They believed that male and female co-therapy teams were uniquely suited to fostering communication and mutual understanding between the spouses and they felt the therapy team was also more effective in identifying and dealing with the high frequency of serious interpersonal problems. Correction of misinformation and imparting of knowledge were some of their main goals. The rapid acceptance of the new form of therapy by both the lay and the professional public testified to the inadequacy of psychoanalytic tradition to deal with the widespread presence of sexual problems.

As stated earlier, before these researchers (Kinsey, 1948, 1953; Laumann et al., 1994; W. H. Masters and Johnson, 1966), there were very little data on human sexuality practices utilizing good methodology with generalizable samples. There was even less exploration into effective treatment approaches. W. H. Masters and Johnson's and W. Masters and Johnson (1970) data represented the first study examining the human sexual response cycle and sexual functioning and dysfunctioning. Even though their model did not go without criticism primarily from Zilbergeld and Evans (1980), the Masters and Johnson Treatment Model still forms the basis of most sex therapy programs today.

Helen Singer Kaplan

Helen Singer Kaplan (1979) in *The New Sex Therapy* blended the theory and procedures of the psychodynamic theory with the cognitive behavioral perspectives of Masters and Johnson. In so doing, she attempted to modify the antecedents to a couple's sexual difficulty, with recognition that it could have deeper roots. In this hypothesis, W. Masters and Johnson's (1970) learning theory principles were brought into the process of identifying the mechanisms by which transactions are maintained and reinforced in order to provide appropriate behavioral modifications. The symptoms were considered the disorder rather than the underlying cause. For the most part, the relationship, not the individuals, was seen as the problem. This approach involved the couple but Kaplan (1974) believed that if one of the partners could not tolerate the anxiety or change that this treatment was based on, the behavioral principles would not work. The goal here was more limited than traditional psychodynamic therapies in that the focus was on alleviating symptom distress rather than personality overhaul.

In terms of the human sexual response cycle, originally Helen Singer Kaplan (1974) proposed a biphasic model of human sexuality. The first phase involved vasocongestion of the genitals and the second phase consisted of the reflective muscular contractions of orgasm. Later Kaplan's (1979) biphasic model evolved into a triphasic one consisting of a desire phase, an excitement phase, and a resolution phase. She also believed that the sexual dysfunctions could fall into one of these categories and that these categories are separate and distinct, that is, one phase can function well even if the individual was having problems with the other. Adding the desire phase to the human sexual response cycle was an important contribution since in many cases sexual desire is not always present. This phase basically expanded the Masters and Johnson's model and has since been incorporated into their basic paradigm.

Systems Theory

Systems theorists generally see sexuality only as a symptom or a metaphor in order that the couple might avoid dealing with the more essential couple issues. Similarly, there are a variety of ways in which sexual issues may be viewed by systems theorists, depending on the context of the relationship. This viewpoint stressed that sexual dysfunctions do not exist in a vacuum but that they were often related to problems in the couple's emotional relationship, such as poor communication, hostility and competitiveness, or sex role problems. Even in those cases where the sexual dysfunction was not related to relationship problems, the couple's emotional relationship was often damaged by the sexual problem, feelings of guilt, inadequacy, and frustration that usually accompany sexual dysfunction (see J. D. Atwood, 2001).

In this view, sexual problems had a cyclical position in the couple's interaction. One's demands may be the result of his or her sexual frustration and feelings of rejection. The other's anxiety may be a combination of sexual conflict, self-doubt about sexuality, and/or fear of failure to please the partner. Thus, the important features of systems therapy included interrupting whatever cycle had been developed. Therapy from this perspective tended to focus on the couple's interactions and the system dynamics that maintained the problematic sexual patterns.

Sex therapy in the 1970s was an outgrowth of an earlier cultural shift (post Kinsey and those coming of age in the 1960s) toward greater focus on increased sexual gratification and discussion of sexual issues (Wiederman, 1989). The rapid acceptance of the new form of therapy by both the lay and the professional public testified to the inadequacy of psychoanalytic tradition to accommodate a growing public interest, which during this period consisted of many of whom simply needed to overcome ignorance and negative sexual attitudes (LoPiccolo, 1994).

Current State of Sexuality Theory and Therapy • **103**

During the 1980s and 1990s, a noticeable increase in an "informed" public arose due to endless mainstream discourse of "normal" sexuality that saturated all forms of media, especially the widespread self help literature aimed at optimizing sexual functioning in adults. Those whose sexual difficulties could be addressed successfully from a direct, educational approach no longer sought sex therapists as the needed assistance was forthcoming from the mass media (LoPiccolo, 1994). Consequently, the types of cases commonly seen in sex-therapy clinics have changed dramatically from the earliest days of contemporary sex therapy (S. R. Leiblum & Rosen, 1995; Rosen & Leiblum, 1995). Interestingly, as the proportion of clients who simply needed education and direction dwindled, the proportion of clients with more pervasive and chronic sexual problems increased. Correspondingly, the therapeutic approaches have changed as well. With increasing frequency, systemic approaches have been used to treat the more complex, relationship-bound sexual problems presented to sex therapists (e.g., J. Atwood, 1993; S. R. Leiblum & Rosen, 1991).

So the major approaches to sex therapy at this point in history can be separated into two camps. On the one hand using the W. Masters and Johnson (1970) and the newer sex therapies' model (1974), sexual dysfunction was treated seriously and the sexual issue presented was the problem to be worked on. On the other hand, using the psychoanalytic and the more systemically based therapies, sexual dysfunction is seen as a manifestation of some underlying unconscious conflict or as a metaphor or a symptom of a problematic relationship. These two major divisions with few exceptions continue to represent the division between the fields of sex therapy and couples therapy today. The few dissenting voices are represented by: Sager (1976) who believed that the marriage and family therapists need to be versed in sex therapy and be ready to shift focus when necessary rather than refer clients to a "sex therapist." Lief (1982) also believed it is impossible to do sex therapy without exploring the quality of the couple's relationship. A strong proponent of a more integrated sex therapy approach, J. Weeks (1986) and G. R. Weeks (2005), G. Weeks and Gambescia (2000), G. R. Weeks and Hof (1987), and J. D. Atwood and Weinstein (1989) suggest that it is time that the two fields are brought together. At this point also, J. D. Atwood and Dershowitz (1992) pointed out that a major problem in the field was that sex therapy for the most part had not been grounded or related to systems theory. What this meant was that sex continued to be treated as a special area both theoretically and clinically with the couples therapy field. In other words, there was little effort to elaborate the conceptual connections between the couple theories and theories of sexual behavior.

Encouraging a combined approach, Atwood, Klucinec, and Neave (2006) posit that in the late 1990s, emphasis has shifted to the role of biomedical and organic factors utilizing medical and surgical interventions in the etiology of sexual dysfunction, de-emphasizing the quality of the overall couple

104 • Handbook of Clinical Issues in Couple Therapy

relationship. However, by using only a medical approach, these authors contend that the couple is left with balancing the positive and negative facets of a considerably different relationship with sex now in their lives and their relationship. They encourage a combined approach urging couples therapists to have a familiarity of the medical conditions associated with sexual problems along with applicable medical interventions, as well as sex therapy theory and therapy techniques. They also state that a working knowledge of appropriate medical processes and terminology and the comfort in discussing various sexual terms with couples are also essential components.

It is also important to keep in mind that the above approaches assume that sex is a primary way of exchanging pleasure, that it is a natural activity, that both partners are equally involved, that people should be educated about sexuality and that communication is a necessary factor in sexual relationships. However, culture also has a great influence on sexual attitudes, sexual scripts, and behavior.

Paradigm 3: The Shift to the Social

Gagnon and Simon

Gagnon and Simon (1973, 2005), in a pioneering effort, led the way for social constructionism. Predictive of future trends, they rejected the importance of biology and instead adopted a social interpretation of sexual behavior. They sought to replace biological theories of sexual behavior with a social theory of sexual scripts (Gagnon, 1990). They focused on the individual's scripting of sexual behaviors through a three-way dialectic of cultural symbolic systems, an individual's fantasy life, and social interactional norms.

In their book *Sexual Conduct* (Gagnon and Simon, 1973, 2005), they introduced a social constructionist approach to sexuality. Entrenched in the symbolic interactionism of the Chicago School with the Meadian emphasis on role taking, which refers to the ability of social actors to anticipate the situationally specific behaviors of their partners in action, which in turn contributes to the actor's synthesis of his or her own reflexive sense of self, they sought to replace biological and psychoanalytic theories of sexual behavior with a social theory of sexual scripts. They argued that individuals use their interactional skills, fantasy materials, and cultural myths to develop scripts that they then use as a means for organizing their sexual behavior. According to them, there are three distinct levels of scripting: cultural scenarios provide instruction on the narrative requirements of broad social roles, interpersonal scripts which are institutionalized patterns in everyday interaction, and intrapsychic scripts which are the details that an individual uses in his or her internal dialogue with cultural and social behavioral expectations (Simon & Gagnon, 1986). Thus, they posited an in depth social interpretation of sexual behavior.

In opposition to the Freudian position, then, Gagnon and Simon (1973) were more concerned with the social origin of sexual development. The implication was that sexual behavior, along with all other forms of behavior, was acquired in and determined by the social and cultural milieu. This idea related to the belief that social and cultural forces shape the acquisition and expression of sexual behavior. They suggested that men and women construct or invent the capacity for sexual behavior, learning how to be aroused and learning how to be responsive (Gagnon & Simon, 1973, 2005). Thus any differences found in sexual behavior in terms of incidences and frequencies occur not because of differential sexual energy allotment but rather because of differential learning environments. Men learn to be more genitally oriented; females learn more romantic orientations and therefore are more heterosocial in their psychosocial development. Any differences in the expression of sexual behavior, they contended, were related to the differential socially legitimate or acceptable avenues of sexual expression existing for men and women. Their theory of sexual development and conduct is the most substantive theory of sexuality at this time (see also Gagnon, 1990; Gagnon, Rosen, & Lieblum, 1982).

Paradigm 4: Adding the Historical to the Social

Foucault

With the publication of Michel Foucault's (1990) *History of Sexuality*, a sweeping sociohistorical interpretation of Western sexuality was presented. His theoretical framework also countered the psychoanalytic explanation of sexual development. Foucault argued that the self is socially constructed and that the coordination and symbolic interaction of social subjects shape sexuality.

Foucault (1990) like Gagnon and Simon (1973, 2005) saw the discourse of sexual repression as an "integral part of the bourgeois order" designed to chronicle sex and its trials into a ceremonial history of the modes of production (p. 5). He explained how an externally enforced belief/value system came to be internalized by the masses. He pointed to the small but increasingly influential middle class who made the sexual hygiene of marital reproduction the cornerstone of its personal individuality and class identity, stigmatizing the sexual practices of aristocrats, peasants, and the working class as moral and medical pathologies. Foucault questioned, "Why do we say with so much passion and so much resentment against our most recent past, and against ourselves, that we are repressed?" (pp. 8–9). For Foucault, the central issue was to account for the fact that sex is spoken about, then to discover who did the speaking, to explore the positions and view points from which they spoke, and the institutions which prompted people to speak about it and which stored and distributed things which are said. What he examined is the overall discursive fact, the way in which sex is put into discourse (p. 11). Thus for him, sexual conduct was shaped not only by repressive mechanisms as Freud and others believed but also by a process of discursive construction. Sexuality was not an essential characteristic of human nature or gender, but a thoroughly social-historical construction.

106 • Handbook of Clinical Issues in Couple Therapy

To Foucault (1990), sexuality was fundamentally about power. Sexuality was not simply a distinction between male and female; sexuality extended into a realm of discourses and interpretations. Discourses on women's bodies, marriage, family structure, and children's sexuality were all important aspects of the broad definition of sexuality. Sexuality carried many connotations having to do with medical approaches to interpreting the body, gender issues, and so on. He believed that sex was not merely an act; rather, it was the way in which we spoke, wrote, and discussed matters dealing with sex. Our discourses then affect society, resulting in an intricate web of power relations concerning sexuality.

Foucault (1990) listed some institutions where systems of power were present. These institutions included the medical field where sex was often defined as a pathological issue and "perverse" sexualities were studied in an attempt to "cure" them; pedagogy in which children were sent to boarding schools in order to form a healthy body and mind and to incur proper discipline; and the state where matters of population control brought sexuality into the dominion of the government. Thus, sexuality was shaped by a process of discursive construction. It was not an essential characteristic of human nature as Freud and the earlier theorists had suggested; but rather, a social historical construction.

Paradigm 5: The Feminist Influence

The purpose of science is to debunk myths. Perhaps nowhere in science are biases more evident that in the study of sexuality, especially in discussions regarding female sexuality. As Mednick (1978) states, "Women have always been studied as a reflection of man, from a masculine point of view and in the service of man's world" (p. 79). Even in terms of the frequency of studies, the sexual behavior of men has been studied more often that the sexual behavior of women. Thus, there is more knowledge accumulated about male sexuality than about female sexuality. Implicit in this focus is the obvious assumption that male sexuality is more important than female sexuality. Also implicit is that the results of the studies involving men could be generalized to women. It seems that the results of the studies done on men can be generalized to everyone while the results of the studies done with women can be generalized only to women. Moreover, even if the studies do manage to include women, the researchers whether men or women—for both genders have absorbed the cultural attitudes about the value of the male—tend to view male sexuality as the norm. This creates a situation whereby the sex differences between the genders are always examined in terms of men and the variations between the genders are then labeled as problematic for women.

More recently, researchers (Laumann et al., 1994) have reported a leveling of the gender differences with regard to sexual behavior. As the studies have become more recent, sexual behavior among women has been seen as approaching that of men. Higher frequencies of all types of sexual behavior have been reported as positive, a result of more effective birth control (no more fears about pregnancy), or the liberal female (women are now free to express themselves). While this may be an accurate reflection of the more current sexual experiences of women, implicit in this type of logic is that women's behavior (sexual or otherwise) is now approaching that of men and this is considered to be positive. Male sexuality is somehow better than female sexuality. Women everywhere applaud the latest female sexual expression, yet what they are applauding is but one more instance of bias for they are assuming that the pattern of male sexual expression is better and that it should be the desired goal for women.

The feminist critique of sex therapy has been that sex therapy is too genital and goal oriented (basically the male response); that sex therapy relies on sexist sex research, language, and theory; that the definition of the sex problem is sexist; that sex therapy neglects gender-related power differentials; that sex therapy sacrifices pleasure for performance; that sex therapy is oblivious to subjective sexual meaning and ignorance of cultural variations; that sex therapy unintentionally or not has reinforced patriarchal interests and sexual double standards; that it has supported heterosexuality; and that sex therapy has historically ignored social causes and solutions of sexual problems. According to the feminists (Goodrich, 1991; Goodrich, Rampage, Ellman, & Halstead, 1988), in terms of sexuality, its expression and meanings, the norm is heterosexual male, middle to upper class, Caucasian, not too young, not too old, college educated, religious (when necessary), procreative (when convenient), romantic, passionate, intimate and in control of his "healthy" sexual appetite, and having the ability to give "healthy" penetrative orgasmic sexual pleasure to a doting monogamous sexual partner.

Paradigm 6: The Current Paradigm—Postmodern Views

> Reality is what we take to be true. What we take to be
> true is what we believe. What we believe is based
> upon our perceptions. What we perceive depends
> upon what we look for. What we look for depends
> upon what we perceive. What we perceive determines
> what we believe. What we believe determines what
> we take to be true. What we take to be true is our
> reality

(Zukav, 1989, p. 324)

With Einstein's (Capra, 1982; Zukav, 1989) notions of relativity and Heisenberg's (1958) uncertainty principle, the predictable, reductionistic universe was pulled out from under us. The finding that human observations at the quantum level could actually change what was being observed moved us

108 • Handbook of Clinical Issues in Couple Therapy

into a new way of understanding "seeing." The resulting paradigm shift (Kuhn, 1970) infiltrated the social sciences in the 1960s and now, made its way into the couple and sex therapy literature as social constructionism, the new epistemology, holding profound implications not only for sexuality theory (and other social science theory) but also for sexual therapy practice. Social constructionism places emphasis on social interpretation and the intersubjective influences of language, family, and culture. As K. Gergen (1985) states, "From the constructional position the process of understanding is not automatically driven by the forces of nature or the drive of empirical science, but is the result of an active, cooperative enterprise of persons in relationship" (p. 267). Thus, social construction theory proposes that there is an evolving set of meanings that continually emerge from social interactions. These meanings are part of a general flow of constantly changing narratives.

White and Epston (1990) took Foucault's (1990) notions to the arena of a postmodern psychotherapy, and began to search for episodes in the client's past which contradicted the dominant story which has become "problem saturated" (i.e., the dominant story empowers the problem). Just as Foucault searched for documents which could not exist if the usual story were the only one which could be told, so White and Epston invited their clients to search for memories of alternative narratives.

Their point was not so much to tell the "real story," so much as to make us wonder if there ever is a "real story" that can be fixed other than by an appeal to the needs and desires of some person or group. So White and Epston (1990) took this idea of stories having a life of their own, and presented the problematic ones as externalized entities (e.g., "the voice of anorexia") which coach people toward certain ways of life; but these "demons," they believe, are capable of being deconstructed, and as they are deconstructed space is opened for alternative and client preferred narratives to emerge.

Recently, postmodern approaches have begun to explore sex therapy with couples. For a description of one such postmodern approach, please see J. Atwood (1993). Atwood, combining Gagnon's (1973, 2005) socially based sexual scripting theory with the assumptions of White and Epston (1990), developed a model of social constructionist sex therapy. She believes that the sexual meanings that sexual incidents, behaviors, and encounters have for individuals are determined by their sociocultural environment. The sociocultural environment equips them with methods and ways of understanding and making judgments about aspects of sexuality, ranging from how they feel about their bodies to sexual values. These ways of making sense of experiences are embedded in a sexual meaning system which is accepted as reality by the social group and in the sexual scripts that are a part of the individual's worldview. The dialectical relationship between individual realities and the socially constructed sexual meanings is the recurring focus of this therapy.

Using the above as a background for constructing a sex therapy frame, she divides couple therapy around sexual issues into three different stories: the couple's story about their families of origin (how the sexual meanings and sexual scripts developed in the first place), their story about their relationship (how the sexual meanings are maintained and an exploration of the couple's sexual script), and their story about what they see for their future (how their sexual meanings and their sexual script can change). Knowledge of each of these three stories helps the therapist to understand the couple's frame of the sexual problem. The telling of these stories helps the couple learn about their frame of the problem. Hoffman (1990) states that,

> Problems are stories people have agreed to tell themselves (p. 3), then we have to persuade them to tell themselves a different, more empowering story, have conversations with them, though the awareness that the findings of their conversations have no other reality than that bestowed by mutual consent (p. 4).

Thus, clients are asked about what sexual problems mean to them in their given sociocultural contexts. Sexuality is treated as a symbol invested with meaning by society, as all symbols are. The approach to the sexual problem is thus a matter of symbolic analysis and interpretation. The sexual problem is seen as emanating from various forms of action or practice within the person's sexual life.

A note for therapists: All of us have ideas about sexuality that are infused with our own value system based on the sociocultural milieu. Therapists carry with them their own sexual scripts and because the therapy itself is grounded in the cultural environment it is crucial for the therapist to keep in mind that clients have their own ideas about the meaning of their sexuality, what role gender plays, and what a good sexual relationship is for them. They also have ideas about what constitutes the sexual dysfunctions, what causes them, what the role of a good therapist is, and what the goals of the therapy should be. The therapist needs to be respectful of what the clients bring in to therapy in terms of their own definitions and meanings and also the therapist should explore his or her own biases, assumptions, and legacies.

Summary

This chapter explored the current state of sexuality theory and therapy. It did so within a context of shifting paradigms. They were as follows: (a) moving from mystical to the scientific explanations for behavior, (b) shifting from examining abnormal to normal sexual behaviors, (c) the movement from biological to social interpretations, (d) adding the historical to the social, (e) pointing out the feminist influence, and (f) exploring sex therapy from a postmodern stance.

110 • Handbook of Clinical Issues in Couple Therapy

As we can see, the field of sexuality theory and therapy has experienced several important paradigm shifts (Kuhn, 1970) or revolutions where one conceptual worldview was replaced by another—where the remnants of the obsolete theories of the past become usurped by the new. Kuhn posited that scientific revolutions are forced upon us by mounting evidence that is contradictory to the prevailing theory. As we saw in this chapter, the meanings and interpretations of sexual behavior shifted from the mystical to the scientific, and shifted once again from the sacred cows of empiricism to postmodernism, one must ponder if we have not come full circle in our study of knowledge. The rationality and predictability of empiricism are dead, as is the independent observer, replaced by chaos, probability, and uncertainty. As we have learned from quantum physics, all of the parts of the universe are connected in an intimate and immediate way—all (including us) part of one all-encompassing pattern. In the past, this view has only been the claim of the mystics and other scientifically objectionable people.

> Since everything is but an apparition
> Perfect in being what it is,
> Having nothing to do with good or bad,
> Acceptance or rejection,
> One may well burst out in laughter.

(Longehenpa, in Zukav, 1979, p. 297)

References

Atwood, J. (1993). Social construction couple therapy. *The Family Journal: Counseling and Therapy for Couples and Families: 1, 2,* 116–130.

Atwood, J., Klucinec, E., & Neaver, E. (2006). A combined-constructionist therapeutic approach to couples experiencing erectile dysfunction: Part I. *Contemporary Family Therapy: An International Journal, 28*(4), 393–402. doi:10.1007/s10591-006-9017-8.

Atwood, J. D. (2001). Sexual dysfunctions and sex therapy. In J. Wecksler (Ed.), *An introduction to marriage and family therapy.* New York: The Haworth Press.

Atwood, J. D., & Dershowitz, S. (1992). Constructing a sex and marital therapy frame: Ways to help couples deconstruct sexual problems. *Journal of Sex and Marital Therapy, 18*(3), 196–218.

Atwood, J. D., & Weinstein, E. (1989). The couple relationship as the focus of sex therapy: The integration of sex therapy ideas and techniques with marital and family therapy. *The Australian and New Zealand Journal of Family Therapy, 10*(3), 161–168.

Capra, F. (1982). *The tao of physics.* New York: Bantam.

Comer, R. J. (1995). *Abnormal psychology* (2nd ed.). New York: W. H. Freeman.

Ellis, H. (1936). *Studies in the psychology of sex* (Vol. I). New York: Random House.

Epston, D., & White, M. (1990). Consulting your consultants: The documentation of alternative knowledges. *Dulwich Centre Newsletter, 4.*

Epston, D., & White, M. (1992). *Experience, contradiction, narrative & imagination: Selected papers of David Epston & Michael White 1989–1991* (2nd ed.). Adelaide, South Australia: Dulwich Centre Publications.

Foucault, M. (1990). *The history of sexuality*. Toronto: Doubleday.

Freud, S. (1905). *Three essays on sexuality. Vol. VII., Complete psychological works*, London: Hogarth Press.

Gagnon, J. H. (1990). The explicit and implicit use of the scripting perspective in sex research. *Annual Review of Sex Research, 1*, 1–43.

Gagnon, J. H., Rosen, R. C., & Leiblum, S. R. (1982). Cognitive and social aspects of sexual dysfunction: Sexual scripts in sex therapy. *Journal of Sex & Marital Therapy, 8*, 44–56.

Gagnon, J. H., & Simon, W. (1973). *Sexual conduct: The social sources of human sexuality*. Chicago: Aldine.

Gagnon, J., & Simon, W. (1973, 2005). *Sexual conduct: The social sources of human sexuality*. New Brunswick, NJ: Aldine Transaction Publishers.

Gergen, K. (1985). The social constructionist movement in modern psychology. *American Psychologist, 40*, 266–275.

Goodrich, T. J. (Ed.). (1991). *Women and power*. New York: W.W. Norton & Company.

Goodrich, T. J., Rampage, C., Ellman, B., & Halstead, K. (1988). *Feminist family therapy*. New York: W. W. Norton & Company.

Heisenberg, W. (1958). *Physics and philosophy*. New York: Harper Torchbooks.

Hertlein, K., Weeks, G., & Gambescia, N. (2008). *Systemic sex therapy*. London, U.K.: Routledge.

Hirshfield, M. (1917). *Sexualpathologie*. Bonn, Germany: A. Marcus & E. Webers.

Hirshfeld, M. (1935). *Sex in human relationships*. London: John Lane The Bodley Head; translated from the French volume of Rodker, J. (1935). *L'Ame et l'amour, psychologie sexologique*. Paris: Gallimard.

Hoffman, L. (1981). *Foundations of family therapy: A conceptual framework for systems change*. New York: Basic Books.

Kaplan, H. (1974). *The new sex therapy*. New York: Brunner Mazel.

Kaplan, H. (1979). *Disorders of desire*. New York: Brunner Mazel.

Kinsey, A. C., Pomeroy, W. B., & Martin, C. E. (1948). *Sexual behavior in the human male*. Philadelphia: Saunders.

Kinsey, A. C., Pomeroy, W. B., & Martin, C. E. (1953). *Sexual behavior in the human female*. Philadelphia: Saunders.

Kraft-Ebing, R. (1965). Psychopathia sexualis. *British Journal of Psychiatry, 122*, 211–218.

Kuhn, T. (1970). *The structure of scientific revolutions* (2nd ed.). Chicago: Chicago University Press.

Laumann, E. O., Gagnon, J. G., Michael, R. T., & Michaels, S. (1994). *The social organization of sexuality: Sexuality practices in the United States*. Chicago: University of Chicago Press.

Leiblum, S. R., & Rosen, R. C. (1991). Couples therapy for erectile disorder: Conceptual and clinical considerations. *Journal of Sex & Marital Therapy, 17*, 147–159.

Leiblum, S. R., & Rosen, R. C. (1995). The changing focus of sex therapy. In R. C. Rosen & S. R. Leiblum (Eds.), *Case studies in sex therapy* (pp. 3–17). New York: Guilford.

Lief, H. I. (Ed.). (1982). *Sexual problems in medical practice*. Chicago: AMA.

LoPiccolo, J. (1994). *The assessment of sexual dysfunction within a marital systems theory approach*. J. LoPiccolo Publisher.

Masters, W., & Johnson, V. (1970). *Human sexual inadequacy*. Boston: Little, Brown and Co.

Masters, W. H., & Johnson, V. E. (1966). *Human sexual response*. Boston: Little, Brown and Co.

Mead, M. (1949). *Male and female: A study of the sexes in a changing world*. Oxford, England: William Morrow. Retrieved from PsycINFO database.

Mednick, S. A. (1978). Gender differences in creativity. *Journal of Creative Behavior, 34*, 65.

Rosen, R., & Leiblum, S. (1995). *Case studies in sex therapy*. New York: Guildford Press.

Rosen, E., & Weinstein, E. (1988). Introduction: Sexuality counseling. In E. Weinstein & E. Rosen (Eds.), *Sexuality counseling: Issues & complications* (pp. 1–15). Pacific Grove, CA: Brooks/Cole.

Sager, C. J. (1976). The role of sex therapy in marital therapy. *Am J Psychiatry, 133*, 555–559.

Simon, W., & Gagnon, J. H. (1986). Sexual scripts: Permanence and change. *Archives of Sexual Behavior, 15*, 97–120.

Simon, W., & Gagnon, J. H. (1987). A sexual scripts approach. In J. H. Greer & W. T. O'Donohue (Eds.), *Theories of human sexuality* (pp. 363–383). New York: Plenum Press.

Weeks, G., & Gambescia, N. (2000). *Erectile dysfunction: Integrating couple therapy, sex therapy, and medical treatment*. New York: W. W. Norton.

Weeks, G., Gambesia, N., & Jenkins, L. (2003). *Treating infidelity: Therapeutic dilemmas and effective strategies*. New York: W. W. Norton.

Weeks, G. R. (2005). The emergence of a new paradigm in sex therapy: Integration. *Sexual and Relationship Therapy, 20*(1), 89–103.

Weeks, G. R., & Hof, L. (1987). *Integrating sex and marital therapy: A clinical guide*. New York: Bruner Mazel, Inc.

Weeks, J. (1986). *Sexuality*. London, U.K.: Routledge.

White, M., & Epston, D. (1990). *Narrative means to therapeutic ends*. New York: W. W. Norton.

Wiederman, M. W., & Sansone, R. A. (1999). Sexuality training for professional psychologists: A national survey of training directors in doctoral programs and predoctoral internships. *Professional Psychology: Research and Practice, 30*, 312–317.

Zilbergeld, B., & Evans, M. (1980). The inadequacy of Masters and Johnson. *Psychology Today, 14*, 29–43.

Zukav, G. (1979). *The dancing Wuli masters*. New York: William Morrow.

Zukav, G. (1989). *The seat of the soul*. New York: Simon & Schuster.

II
Traumatic Issues

7

Conjoint Couples Treatment and Intimate Partner Violence
Best Practices

ERIC E. McCOLLUM and SANDRA M. STITH

Contents

Is There a Place for Couples Treatment?	117
Research on Conjoint Treatment for IPV	119
IPV and Behavioral Couples Treatment for Substance Abuse	119
Neidig, O'Leary, and Heyman Models	120
Domestic Violence–Focused Couples Treatment	121
The Navy Study	122
Best Practices	122
A Clinical Specialty	123
Coordinated Community Response	123
Careful Screening for Conjoint Treatment	124
Modifying Treatment Structure to Provide Safety	124
Ongoing Assessment and Contingency Plans for Increased Risk	125
Conclusion	125
References	125

Intimate partner violence (IPV) is a serious public health issue whose effects are felt not only by the adults involved but also by their children. In the United States, 24.4% of married couples commit some violence against one another and in 10.7% of marriages the violence is severe (Dutton, 1995). While this obviously puts partners at risk for both emotional and physical injury, when IPV occurs in couples with children, it has been linked to profound and long-lasting emotional and behavioral harm for the children who witness it (Jaffe & Suderman, 1995). Unfortunately, IPV is often overlooked by marriage and family therapists who often tell us that they only rarely see couples who have been violent. Careful assessment of couples presenting for marital therapy, however, suggests that as many as 50%–60% of troubled couples have experienced at least some violence (Holtzworth-Munroe et al., 1992; O'Leary, Vivian, & Malone, 1992). Frequently these couples do not raise the issue of violence themselves with their therapists and, if the therapist does not ask carefully about it, it may go completely unaddressed. Thus, as marriage and family therapy (MFTs), we need to

116 • Handbook of Clinical Issues in Couple Therapy

be aware of IPV, be able to assess for it competently, and know when it is appropriate to proceed with conjoint treatment once violence is identified.

Historically, treatment for IPV has occurred in separate-gender "tracks" based on the assumption that men are the perpetrators of violence and women are the victims. In this approach, men are typically ordered into treatment after police and court intervention and are treated in male-only psychoeducational groups designed to change their violent behavior as well as their patriarchal attitudes. They may remain under the supervision of the probation service and thus accountable to the court throughout. Women are offered an array of victim support services that can include support groups, access to an advocate to help with legal issues, and refuge at a battered women's shelter. Despite the fact that this strategy is treatment as usual in much of the country, in general such interventions have a minimal impact on reducing recidivism beyond the effect of being arrested (Babcock, Green, & Robie, 2004). All-male battering intervention groups tend to have at least a 50% dropout rate (O'Leary, 2002), unless they adopt supportive, adjunctive measures to increase retention and even these procedures only result in modest gains (e.g., Taft, Murphy, Elliot, & Morrel, 2001). Male-only treatment may also elicit negative male bonding (Hart, 1988) that can support the violence. For example, one man in Edelson and Tolman's (1992) study told his female partner that she should stop complaining because the other men in the group beat their wives much more severely than he beat her. As noted above, male batterer treatment is typically paired with legal sanctions. However, despite declarations that arrest followed by court-ordered treatment offers "great hope and potential for breaking the destructive cycle of violence" (*U.S. Attorney General's Task Force on Family Violence*, 1984, p. 48), there is little empirical evidence that treatment is effective in reducing recidivism of family violence to any meaningful degree. In a recent meta-analysis of battering intervention programs, the effects due to treatment were in the small range, meaning that the current interventions have a minimal impact on reducing recidivism beyond the effect of being arrested (Babcock et al., 2004). While many men certainly make important changes as a result of batterer intervention programs, and we are not suggesting that male psychoeducation groups have no utility whatsoever, it does appear that there is room for something other than a "one-size-fits-all" approach to treating this difficult problem. We propose that conjoint couples treatment offers a useful approach for a carefully selected group of couples who have been violent.

Despite growing evidence of its effectiveness, as well as increasing clinical use, conjoint couples treatment when there has been IPV remains controversial. Critics of couples treatment fear that it will result in further injury to female victims as well as that it implies at least partial responsibility on the woman's part for her own abuse since to treat the couple together suggests that both need to change. Adams (1988) argued against couples therapy, commenting that "many battered women report that past family therapy sessions were followed by violent episodes" (p. 187). Such arguments assume that disclosures or confrontations in the conjoint session that make the man feel disparaged will result in retaliation against the woman once the session is over. Others fear that women will be more likely to make such disclosures because the fact that the couple has come to treatment may give them a false sense of security and lead them to think that "putting everything out on the table" is what needs to happen in therapy.

At a broader level, other critics attack the very assumptions of systemic therapies as inappropriate when there has been IPV. Bograd (1992) feared that "systems formulations still either implicate the battered woman or diffuse responsibility for male violence" (p. 246). Looking at violence in an interpersonal context, critics assert, leaves the woman at least partially responsible for helping to control her male partner's violence if both are urged to change the relationship. Further, the man may evade responsibility for his violent acts in the midst of examining interactional patterns, learning conflict resolution skills, or addressing attachment wounds through conjoint couple therapy.

The critiques of conjoint treatment remain influential. In the face of the assertion that conjoint treatment will both endanger victims and implicate them in their own abuse, many policy makers and clinicians continue to opt for gender-specific groups for male batterers and female victims—reputedly a safer approach. Maiuro and Eberle (2008) analyzed state standards for batterer intervention programs and found that 68% of states with such standards (currently 44) expressly prohibit couples treatment until gender-specific treatment has been completed—sometimes as long as 52 weeks. This represents an increase in the percentage of states proscribing couples treatment since Maiuro and colleagues' 2001 survey (Maiuro, Hager, Lin, & Olson, 2001).

Is There a Place for Couples Treatment?

No one dealing with IPV would be wise to minimize the risks involved in conjoint treatment or to assume that men or women will automatically be safe when engaged in such treatment. Indeed, safety must be taken very seriously. However, evidence in the professional literature is clear that couples therapy focusing on eliminating domestic violence has been successful with many couples where there have been assaults and has helped many of those couples end violence. Clearly, we believe there is a place for conjoint treatment in the wake of IPV. What arguments do we make for such an approach? There are several.

First, it has become increasingly clear that not all couples experience violence in the same way. In contrast to earlier models that claimed all violence was the same—motivated by male efforts to completely dominate a female partner—Johnson (1995) proposed two types of IPV. *Patriarchal terrorism* (now called *intimate terrorism*) is the pervasive effort to dominate and control one's partner and all aspects of her life, with violence being the basic, but not necessarily only, control tactic used. A terrorized victim and dominating abuser are characteristic of this type of violence. Feminist analyses have focused on intimate terrorism and most pro-feminist approaches to batterer intervention are aimed at stopping this type of violence (for instance, see Pence & Paymar, 1993). *Common couple violence* (now called *situational violence*), on the other hand, is violence in intimate relationships that occurs in an effort to exert control in specific situations and not as part of an overarching control agenda. There is no *pervasive* fear on the part of one partner. Situational violence is often part of an escalating pattern of conflict that gets out of hand with one or both partners using physical aggression. While serious injury, or even death, can occur in either situation, Johnson and Leone (2005) reported that situational violence is less likely to escalate over time, is less likely to involve severe violence, is not as likely to involve unilateral male-to-female violence, and has a lower frequency of violent episodes. What do typologies such as Johnson's suggest about conjoint couples treatment for IPV? First, they suggest that men and women who experience violence in their relationships are a varied group and that a one-size-fits-all approach to intervention (gender-specific, pro-feminist psycho-education) may leave important issues unattended for at least some couples. Johnson's assertion that some IPV results from relationship conflict suggests that conjoint treatment may be a valuable approach for a carefully selected subset of couples—namely those who experience situational violence.

While male-only batterer intervention is often proposed as the treatment of choice for IPV, as we described above the research evidence for its effectiveness is hardly convincing. Indeed, we see some dangers in male-only treatment in cases of situational violence. First, it may ignore the impact of women's aggression. While in intimate terrorism, women's assaults are likely to be defensive, men and women in relationships where situational violence occurs tend to assault each other at nearly the same rate as part of specific conflicts that get out of control (Johnson, 1995). In addition, women's assaults of their male partners are associated with higher injury for the women (Feld & Straus, 1989; Gondolf, 1998) and make it less likely that violence in the relationship will cease since cessation of violence by one partner is dependent on cessation by the other (Feld & Straus; Gelles & Straus, 1988).

A second reason to consider conjoint treatment in addressing situational violence concerns the role that marital discord plays in IPV. Pan, Neidig, and O'Leary (1994) reported that for every 20% increase in marital discord, the odds of mild partner assault increase by 102% while the odds of severe assault increase 183%. Gender-specific treatment for the man only cannot attend to marital discord and the resulting risk for continued assault.

Finally, many couples remain together after violence has occurred. Feazelle, Mayers, and Deschner (1984) found that between 50% and 70% of women remain with their male partner after an assault, or return soon after a brief separation. Such couples then face the problems of managing violence along

Conjoint Couples Treatment and Intimate Partner Violence • **119**

with the myriad of other issues arising from couple relationships including raising children, supporting a family, and running a household. In such cases, conjoint treatment may help ameliorate such stresses and remains one of the services often requested by couples in the wake of IPV.

Research on Conjoint Treatment for IPV

To date, four broad streams of controlled outcome research have addressed the efficacy of conjoint treatment for IPV. In each study, the couples treatment condition performed at least as well as, and did not appear to endanger women more than, the comparison conditions. We will briefly review this body of research since it provides a basis for suggesting best practices.

IPV and Behavioral Couples Treatment for Substance Abuse

A series of studies conducted at the Families and Addictions Program at Harvard Medical School (O'Farrell, Fals-Stewart, Murphy, Stephan, & Murphy, 2004; O'Farrell & Murphy, 1995) and at the Research Institute on Addictions at SUNY Buffalo (Fals-Stewart, Kashdan, O'Farrell, & Bircher, 2002; Fals-Stewart, O'Farrell, & Bircher, 2004) have demonstrated an impressive effect of behavioral couples therapy (BCT) in reducing IPV when used to treat co-occurring addictions. This is important work because IPV and substance abuse and misuse frequently co-occur (e.g., Bennett, Tolman, Rogalski, & Srinivasaraghavan, 1994; Gondolf & Foster, 1991).

BCT, as the name implies, is a cognitive–behavioral approach, typically delivered to outpatients in 15–20 sessions over several months. The goal is to change interactional patterns around substance abuse and early on, at least, violence was not directly addressed. Several studies have examined the impact of this treatment model on IPV. Inclusion criteria for the studies varied but generally were that the relationship had to be stable and of 1 year's duration, the man had to meet criteria for substance abuse or dependence, and the couple had to agree to abstain from use during the study and to not seek other treatment aside from self-help groups. Couples were excluded if the woman met criteria for a substance abuse disorder, either partner was psychotic or organically impaired and if either was participating in methadone maintenance. Since the original work, both the Harvard and Buffalo groups have begun to exclude couples where significant injuries or intimidation are reported as a result of IPV and when the participants refuse to agree to sign a no-violence pledge.

The results of these programs of research have been consistent. All of the published studies demonstrate the efficacy of BCT in reducing IPV in substance abusing couples. As one example, O'Farrell, Van Hutton, and Murphy (1999) found that male alcoholics treated with BCT had higher rates of IPV than a comparable nonalcoholic group of men prior to treatment. In the treated group, the number of families experiencing any act of violence was reduced from

120 • Handbook of Clinical Issues in Couple Therapy

61.3% prior to treatment to 22.7% in the first year posttreatment and 18.7% 2 years after treatment. In addition, after treatment, the rate of occurrence of IPV did not significantly differ from the nonalcoholic comparison group.

Fals-Stewart and Kennedy (2005) believed that couples-based intervention, particularly BCT, is the treatment of choice when couples report a history of IPV during substance abuse treatment. They report five IPV-related exclusion criteria for conjoint treatment: Fear on either partner's part of injury, death or physical retaliation, severe violence resulting in injury or hospitalization, use of a weapon in the past, fear on the part of either partner of participating in couples treatment, and either partner wishing to leave the relationship because of the severity of partner aggression. While these criteria may seem restrictive, Fals-Stewart and Kennedy report that they have excluded only about 5% of the couple they have screened.

Neidig, O'Leary, and Heyman Models

Neidig (1985) first developed the Domestic Conflict Containment Program (DCCP). DCCP is a highly structured skills-based program whose goal is to teach couples conflict containment skills. It was first delivered in a multi-couple group format to six to eight couples at a time over 10 weeks. Neidig first tested DCCP in the military and found that 8 out of 10 participants remained violence-free at 4-month follow-up. The structure of the military with closer monitoring and more definite consequences for both missing sessions and repeat offense made it difficult to know how well DCCP would migrate to the civilian community. There have been two major modifications to Neidig's original model. Brannen and Rubin (1996) added separate orientations and periodic checks for female partners to buttress their safety while in the program. Heyman and Neidig (1997) added other psychoeducational components designed to improve relationship quality including such things as communication skills, fair fighting tactics, and dealing with gender differences, sex, and jealousy. They called their adaptation of this model Physical Aggression Couples Treatment (PACT). Exclusion criteria are similar to those for BCT, most notable fear of participating or of her partner on the woman's part and a history of injury from partner aggression.

Since Neidig (1985) developed DCCP and tested it in the military, adaptations of this model have also been tested with court-ordered civilians (Brannen & Rubin, 1996) and voluntary civilian couples (O'Leary, Heyman, & Neidig, 1999). Each of these studies shows DCCP (or PACT) to be effective in helping men reduce their level of violence. With one exception, no significant difference between DCCP and comparison conditions (i.e., male-only batterer treatment) has been found in either dropout rates or violent recidivism. Only Brannen and Rubin found that in their court-ordered population, the couples condition was more effective in reducing violence than was a gender-specific treatment for participants with a history of alcohol abuse.

Domestic Violence–Focused Couples Treatment

Stith, McCollum, and Rosen at Virginia Tech developed a solution-focused model of couples treatment—Domestic Violence–Focused Couples Treatment (DVFCT: see Stith, McCollum, Rosen, & Locke, 2002; Stith, McCollum, Rosen, Locke, & Goldberg, 2005). The primary goal of DVFCT is to end violence with the additional goal of helping couples improve the quality of their relationships. The program is currently 18 weeks in duration and can be delivered in either individual or multi-couple group format. DVFCT begins with a 6-week period of largely gender-separate treatment during which assessment for the suitability of the couple for conjoint treatment continues and psychoeducational material is provided to both partners. When conjoint sessions begin, the session structure supports ongoing assessment of safety. Each conjoint session begins with separate meetings with each partner to inquire about violence or conflict since the last session, assess safety and decide whether it is safe to continue into the conjoint session. At the end of the conjoint session, separate meetings are again held to "decompress" from the session and ascertain if the couple is safe to go home together. Aside from these modifications to address safety, the conjoint portion of DVFCT uses the solution-focused framework (e.g., Pichot & Dolan, 2003) much like it would be used with other couples. However, should the threat of violence arise, the therapists depart from the solution-focused framework in order to assure safety, returning to solution-focused work only when, and if, both partners again are safe from violent acts.

Couples are excluded from DVFCT if either partner has injured the other to the extent that medical care is needed, if the couple refuses to remove guns and weapon knives from their home, if they cannot understand English well enough to meaningfully participate and if they have untreated psychopathology that would prevent them from participating. Couples must also clearly state that each is voluntarily seeking conjoint treatment and that they intend to remain in the relationship (although ending the relationship without violence is certainly an acceptable goal for DVFCT if so decided by the couple).

To test DVFCT, Stith, Rosen, McCollum, and Thomsen (2004) randomly assigned couples to either individual or multi-couple group formats of DVFCT. Nine couples who completed all pretest and follow-up assessments but could not start treatment for reasons unrelated to violence (e.g., scheduling problems) served as a comparison group. Three domains were assessed to determine outcome—aggression, attitudes toward violence, and relationship satisfaction. Stith et al. found that participants in the multi-couple group improved in all three areas at posttest compared to either the individual or the comparison conditions. Further, based on female reports, men who participated in either of the two couples conditions were less likely than the comparison group men to recidivate by either 6-month or 2-year posttreatment follow-up.

122 • Handbook of Clinical Issues in Couple Therapy

The Navy Study

Dunford (2000) conducted the only experimental study to date with a randomly assigned no-treatment control group. He randomly assigned over 800 Navy couples to one of four conditions—a 26-week cognitive–behavioral men's group followed by monthly follow-up for 6 months, a 26-week cognitive–behavioral multi-couple group, a "rigorously monitored" group, and a group that got no formal intervention aside from a contact of the woman by the military authorities soon after the assault to determine her immediate safety. The rigorously monitored group consisted of monthly individual sessions with the male offender for 12 months, monthly contact with the female partner to determine if violence had recurred and regular records checks to see if the man had been arrested again. Commanding officers were regularly apprised of the perpetrators' status.

Seventy-one percent of the participants were determined by military authorities to have successfully completed treatment. No significant differences in victim reports of being injured, hit or pushed, or of feeling endangered were found between the four conditions at either 6- or 12-month follow-up.

As with Neidig's earlier study, the stricter structure and monitoring of perpetrators in the military, as well as the consequences of re-offense, may limit the generalizability of the Dunford's work to civilian settings. In addition, wives were not mandated to attend the multi-couple group and the number attending was rather low—two women for every five men. Rather than being a systemic couples intervention, then, this model was more like a men's group with women as partial participants or observers. However, the study does suggest that women are not more likely to be endangered by participating in their partners' treatment.

Best Practices

In addition to the research literature on couples treatment of IPV, many clinical papers have been written on this topic as well. Almeida and Durkin (1999), for example, described a comprehensive community-centered approach to treating IPV that involves couples therapy as one of several components. The Ackerman Institute program (Goldner, 1998) integrates feminist, individual and systemic models to fashion an outpatient treatment of IPV where both partners are seen. Finally, Lipchik and Kubicki (1996) engaged in typical solution-focused couples therapy only after careful screening to make sure that couples being seen present with minimal risk for recurrence of violence.

While we cannot describe these or other clinically derived approaches in detail here, they do help us examine the current state of practice and, along with the research literature, help us propose current best practices. We believe that these practices provide a sound foundation for conjoint couples therapy in the context of IPV regardless of the theoretical couples treatment model used.

A Clinical Specialty

Treating couples who have experienced IPV poses a variety of challenges to the therapist. First, therapists who work in this area must be skilled in both couples treatment and in IPV. Working with these couples demands both a thorough knowledge of couple dynamics as well as an understanding of the dynamics of violence and abuse. Therapists must be able to intervene actively to manage and contain session escalation, join with, and effectively support, two people in conflict with one another, and manage their own countertransference issues (Strawderman, Rosen, & Coleman, 1997). In addition, therapists must understand IPV so they can keep responsibility for their actions squarely in the lap of the participants and not let personal responsibility slip away as the system is explored. They must also be able to identify and act decisively in response to signs of potential escalation. They must be aware of ethical and legal issues regarding when to break confidentiality if they are concerned about the potential for escalating violence and must know their state regulations regarding mandatory reporting. Therapists working with violent couples must be familiar with safety planning, the use of timeout to control escalation, and must know how to conduct psychoeducational sessions. The treatments discussed here are not traditional marriage counseling; rather they are specifically informed by knowledge of IPV and designed to prevent its occurrence. In our view, therapists who intend to work with violent couples need specialized training and supervisory support to do so effectively. They also need to be connected with their community's domestic violence resources.

Coordinated Community Response

Treatment of violent couples cannot occur in isolation. It is important that couples therapists be aware of, and ready to use, the full range of community resources. In some situations, legal sanctions for offenders and shelter services and restraining orders to protect victims are appropriate interventions to help preserve safety. The coordinated community response to IPV may include victim advocates, support groups, more traditional batterer intervention services, substance abuse treatment programs, as well as services for children who witness their parents' violence. Couple therapists need to help clients tailor an appropriate complement of these services and also need to work closely with other services providers. Vetere and Cooper (2001) provided a rich description of how couples therapists can fruitfully collaborate with community agencies to provide a net of both safety and accountability for couples struggling to end IPV. They ask the referral source to be "the stable third in our therapeutic triangle, sharing and managing the risks of doing this work" (p. 385). They do not accept self-referred clients and they use their partnership with the referring agency to establish a network of both protection and accountability for the family. If therapy proceeds, the representatives of the referring agency come to each sixth session to assess progress and

124 • Handbook of Clinical Issues in Couple Therapy

risk, and renew the community safety net surrounding the family. This type of community partnership ensures that couples therapists are not operating in a vacuum and that necessary supports are in place to enhance the likelihood of successful treatment.

Careful Screening for Conjoint Treatment

We have found consistently in the literature—both research and clinical— that couples therapists who work with violent couples carefully screen them before beginning conjoint work. Screening must include separate interviews with both partners to determine the level of violence and the willingness of victims, in particular, to participate in couples work voluntarily. Separate interviews assure that partners are free to speak openly and will not endanger themselves by revealing more than the other partner might prefer. In addition, screening tools like the Revised Conflict Tactics Scales (Straus, Hamby, Boney-McCoy, & Sugarman, 1996) can be used to assure more than a cursory assessment of violence. In our own work, we have found that using multiple sources of data (e.g., written questionnaires, direct questioning and partners' reports) to screen for the presence of violence provides the richest and most comprehensive understanding.

Throughout this chapter, we have tried to describe the inclusion and exclusion criteria used by each of the programs. In general, exclusion criteria include a history of violence resulting in injury, use of, or threats to use, weapons, fear of the other on the part of either partner, fear of retaliation for things said in conjoint sessions, a history of violence outside the family on the part of the perpetrator, and serious mental illness that may interfere with treatment. In addition, it is important that both partners express a clear wish to work on the relationship and that neither feels coerced into conjoint treatment. None of the programs described above advocate for conjoint treatment as the only appropriate treatment for IPV. Assessment and thoughtful matching of clients to treatment—as best we can accomplish it—are the foundation of conjoint treatment.

Modifying Treatment Structure to Provide Safety

While no therapist can guarantee the safety of participants when working with IPV, efforts must be made to assure safety as much as possible. In many cases, this will mean deviating from the structure one might use with a nonviolent couple in conjoint treatment. For instance, in Stith et al.'s (2002) model, separate meetings with each partner are a routine part of treatment rather than a response to exceptional circumstances. Not only does this increase the therapist's ability to assess for violence, it also makes individual meetings the norm rather than the exception that might raise suspicions on the part of either partner if they are held only when violence is suspected or reported. Some kind of regular individual communication with both partners seems to be common in the models we have reviewed. Thus, therapists who tell couples they will keep no secrets in regular marital therapy need to rethink this position when revealing an individual communication may endanger one of the partners. Therapists may also need to be more directive and structure sessions more tightly than they would do with a nonviolent couple.

Ongoing Assessment and Contingency Plans for Increased Risk

Assessment is always a process rather than an event. This is even truer in couples treatment for IPV. As noted above, regular, separate check-ins with each partner are part of most of the programs reviewed here. Check-ins may be either verbal or written but they must afford the couple the opportunity to communicate their concerns about safety and any recurrence of violence. In addition, it may take the therapist some time to truly appreciate the potential for violence a couple faces since a stronger therapeutic relationship may lead to more disclosure. Issues such as the level of substance abuse in either partner or the degree to which depression or PTSD play a part in the couple relationship may also take time to ascertain. As assessment proceeds, the therapist must be willing to abandon—either temporarily or for good—the conjoint process in the service of safety and providing needed services to both partners. Clear protocols for managing increased risk or recurrence of violence are helpful as is access to consultation.

Conclusion

A growing body of evidence suggests that couples therapy that is specifically focused on ending IPV can be a safe and effective way to end violence in relationships for a carefully selected group of couples. Best practices drawn from this research, as well as the growing literature on clinical practice in this area, suggest that therapists who choose to work with this group need specialized training and supervision; they need to work within the community to provide a coordinated response to IPV; clients need to be carefully screened to determine if this type of treatment is appropriate; the structure of traditional couples therapy needs to be adapted to enhance safety; and therapists need to ensure that assessment is ongoing throughout the work and that contingency plans are in place if they become aware of evidence of increased risk. With these practices in place, couples therapists can appropriately offer a needed resource to many couples who suffer in the throes of a violent relationship.

References

Adams, D. (1988). Treatment models of men who batter: A pro-feminist analysis. In K. Yllo & M. Bograd (Eds.), *Feminist perspectives on wife abuse* (pp. 176–199). Newbury Park, CA: Sage.

Almeida, R. V., & Durkin, T. (1999). The cultural context model: Therapy for couples with domestic violence. *Journal of Marital and Family Therapy, 25*, 313–324.

Babcock, J. C., Green, C. E., & Robie, C. (2004). Does batterers' treatment work? A meta-analytic review of domestic violence treatment. *Clinical Psychology Review, 23*, 1023–1053.

126 • Handbook of Clinical Issues in Couple Therapy

Bennett, W., Tolman, R. M., Rogalski, C. J., & Srinivasaraghavan, J. (1994). Domestic abuse by male alcohol and drug addicts. *Violence and Victims, 9,* 359–368.

Bograd, M. (1992). Values in conflict: Challenges to family therapists' thinking. *Journal of Marital and Family Therapy, 18,* 245–256.

Brannen, S. J., & Rubin, A. (1996). Comparing the effectiveness of gender-specific and couples groups in a court-mandated spouse abuse treatment program. *Research on Social Work Practice, 6,* 405–424.

Dunford, F. W. (2000). The San Diego Navy experiment: An assessment of interventions for men who assault their wives. *Journal of Consulting and Clinical Psychology, 68*(3), 468–476.

Dutton, D. G. (1995). *The batterer: A psychological profile.* New York: Basic Books.

Edleson, J., & Tolman, R. (1992). *Intervention for men who batter: An ecological approach.* Newbury Park, CA: Sage.

Fals-Stewart, W., Kashdan, T. B., O'Farrell, T. J., & Bircher, G. R. (2002). Behavioral couples therapy for drug abusing patients: Effects on partner violence. *Journal of Substance Abuse Treatment, 22,* 87–96.

Fals-Stewart, W., & Kennedy, C. (2005). Addressing intimate partner violence in substance abuse treatment: Overview, options, and recommendations. *Journal of Substance Abuse Treatment, 29,* 5–17.

Fals-Stewart, W., O'Farrell, T. J., & Bircher, G. R. (2004). Behavioral couple therapy as a treatment for substance abuse: Rationale, methods, and findings. *Science and Practice Perspectives, 2,* 30–41.

Feazelle, C. S., Mayers, R. S., & Deschner, J. P. (1984). Services for men who batter: Implications for programs and policies. *Family Relations, 33,* 217–223.

Feld, S. L., & Straus, M. A. (1989). Escalation and desistence of wife assault in marriage. *Criminology, 27,* 141–159

Gelles, R. J., & Straus, M. A. (1988). *Intimate violence.* New York: Simon & Schuster.

Goldner, V. (1998). The treatment of violence and victimization in intimate relationships. *Family Process, 37,* 263–286.

Gondolf, E. W. (1998). The victims of court-ordered batterers: Their victimization, help-seeking, and perceptions. *Violence Against Women, 4,* 659–676.

Gondolf, E. W., & Foster, R. A. (1991). Wife assault among VA alcohol rehabilitation patients. *Hospital and Community Psychiatry, 42,* 74–79.

Hart, B. (1988). *Safety for women: Monitoring batters' programs* (manual). Harrisburg, PA: Pennsylvania Coalition Against Domestic Violence.

Hart, W. L., Ashcroft, J., Burgess, A., Flanagan, N., Meese, U., Milton, C., Narramore, C., Ortega, R., & Seward. F. (1984). *Attorney General's task force on family violence.* Washington, DC: U.S. Department of Justice.

Heyman, R. E., & Neidig, P. H. (1997). Physical aggression couples treatment. In W. K. Halford & H. J. Markman (Eds.), *Clinical handbook of marriage and couples interventions.* New York: John Wiley & Sons.

Holtzworth-Munroe, A., Waltz, J., Jacobson, N. S., Monaco, V., Fehrenbach, P. A., & Gottman, J. M. (1992). Recruiting non-violent couples as control subjects for research on marital violence: How easily can it be done? *Violence and Victims, 7,* 79–88.

Jaffe, P. G., & Sudermann, M. (1995). Child witnesses of woman abuse: Research and community responses. In S. Stith & M. A. Straus (Eds.), *Understanding partner violence: Prevalence, causes, consequences, and solutions.* Minneapolis, MN: National Council on Family Relations.

Johnson, M. P. (1995). Patriarchal terrorism and common couple violence: Two forms of violence against women. *Journal of Marriage and the Family, 57,* 283–294.

Conjoint Couples Treatment and Intimate Partner Violence • **127**

Johnson, M. P., & Leone, J. M. (2005). The differential effects of intimate terrorism and situational couple violence. *Journal of Family Issues, 26*, 322–349.

Lipchik, E., & Kubicki, B. (1996). Solution-focused domestic violence views: Bridges toward a new reality in couples therapy. In S. D. Miller, M. A. Hubble, & B. L. Duncan (Eds.), *Handbook of solution-focused brief therapy* (pp. 65–97). San Francisco: Jossey-Bass.

Maiuro, R. D., & Eberle, J. A. (2008). State standards for domestic violence perpetrator treatment: Current status, trends, and recommendations. *Violence and Victims, 23*, 133–155.

Maiuro, R. D., Hager, T., Lin, H., & Olson, N. (2001). Are existing state standards for the treatment of perpetrators of domestic violence adequately informed by research? A question of questions. *Journal of Aggression, Maltreatment and Trauma, 5*, 21–44.

Neidig, P. H. (1985). Domestic conflict containment: A spouse abuse treatment program. *Social Casework: The Journal of Contemporary Social Work, 66*, 195–204.

O'Farrell, T. J., Fals-Stewart, W., Murphy, C. M., Stephan, S. H., & Murphy, M. (2004). Partner violence before and after couples-based alcoholism treatment for male alcoholic patients: The role of treatment involvement and abstinence. *Journal of Consulting and Clinical Psychology, 72*, 202–217.

O'Farrell, T. J., & Murphy, C. M. (1995). Marital violence before and after alcoholism treatment. *Journal of Consulting and Clinical Psychology, 63*, 256–262.

O'Farrell, T. J., Van Hutton, V. M., & Murphy, C. M. (1999). Domestic violence before and after alcoholism treatment: A two-year longitudinal study. *Journal of Studies on Alcohol, 60*, 317–321.

O'Leary, K. D. (2002). Conjoint therapy for partners who engage in physically aggressive behavior: Rationale and research. Special issue: Domestic violence offenders: Current interventions, research, and implications for policies and standards. *Journal of Aggression, Maltreatment & Trauma, 5*, 145–164.

O'Leary, K. D., Heyman, R. E., & Neidig, P. H. (1999). Treatment of wife abuse: A comparison of gender-specific and conjoint approaches. *Behavior Therapy, 30*, 475–505.

O'Leary, K. D., Vivian, D., & Malone, J. (1992). Assessment of physical aggression against women in marriage: The need for multimodal assessment. *Behavioral Assessment, 14*, 5–14.

Pan, H. S., Neidig, P. H., & O'Leary, K. D. (1994). Predicting mild and severe husband-to-wife physical aggression. *Journal of Consulting and Clinical Psychology, 62*, 975–981.

Pence, E., & Paymar, M. (1993). *Education groups for men who batter: The Duluth model.* New York: Springer.

Pichot, T., & Dolan, Y. (2003). *Solution-focused brief therapy: Its effective use in agency settings.* New York: Haworth Press.

Stith, S. M., McCollum, E. E., Rosen, K. H., & Locke, L. (2002). Multicouple group treatment for domestic violence. In F. Kaslow (Ed.), *Comprehensive textbook of psychotherapy* (vol. 4, pp. 499–520). New York: John Wiley & Sons.

Stith, S. M., McCollum, E. E., Rosen, K. H., Locke, L., & Goldberg, P. (2005). Domestic violence focused couples treatment. In J. Lebow (Ed.), *Handbook of clinical family therapy* (pp. 406–430). New York: John Wiley & Sons.

Stith, S. M., Rosen, K. H., McCollum, E. E., & Thomsen, C. J. (2004). Treating intimate partner violence within intact couple relationships: Outcomes of multi-couple versus individual couple therapy. *Journal of Marital and Family Therapy, 30*(3), 305–318.

128 • Handbook of Clinical Issues in Couple Therapy

Straus, M. A., Hamby, S. L., Boney-McCoy, S., & Sugarman, D. B. (1996). The Revised Conflict Tactics Scale (CTS2): Development and preliminary psychometric data. *Journal of Family Issues, 17*, 283–316.

Strawderman, E. T., Rosen, K. H., & Coleman, J. (1997). Therapist heal thyself: Countertransference and the treatment of a battered woman. *Journal of Family Psychotherapy, 8*(3), 35–50.

Taft, C. T., Murphy, C. M., Elliot, J. D., & Morrel, T. M. (2001). Attendance enhancing procedures in group counseling for domestic abusers. *Journal of Counseling Psychology, 48*, 51–60.

Vetere, A., & Cooper, J. (2001). Working systemically with family violence: Risk, responsibility and collaboration. *Journal of Family Therapy, 23*, 378–396.

8
Trauma and Recovery in Couple Therapy

LORNA HECKER

Contents

Traumas and Responses to Traumas	130
Posttraumatic Stress Disorder	131
Couples and Trauma	131
Relational Ramifications of Childhood Maltreatment	132
Reduced Relational Intimacy	132
Increased Relational Conflict	133
Difficulty Sharing the Grief of Trauma	133
"Couples-Ship" Strains	133
Boundary Issues	134
Communication Difficulties	134
Sexual Anxiety and Sexual Disorders	134
Hypervigilance and Related Trust Issues	135
Depression and Risk of Suicide	135
Cognitive Distortions	135
Anxiety	136
Tension Reducing Activities	136
Anger	136
Spiritual Issues	136
Clinical Intervention	136
Creating a Safe Environment	137
Provide Psychoeducation	137
Tailor Care and Understanding	138
Giving Voice to the Couple	138
Encouraging Self and Other Care	139
When Appropriate, Aid the Couple in Accessing Social Support	139
Learning From Successful Mastery of Past Traumas	139
Fortify the Couple Foundation	139
Understanding and Utilizing Primary Emotions	140
Teach the Spouse to Be a "Container" for Trauma	140
Use of EMDR	140
Touch Techniques	141

130 • Handbook of Clinical Issues in Couple Therapy

Nuts and Bolts	141
Creating Shared Meaning Around the Trauma	141
Summary	141
References	142

At the moment of trauma, the victim is rendered helpless by overwhelming force. When the force is that of nature, we speak of disasters. When the force is that of other human beings, we speak of atrocities. Traumatic events overwhelm the ordinary systems of care that give people a sense of control, connection and meaning.

(Judith Herman, 1997, p. 33)

Trauma typically harms the body, self, and/or spirit (Whitfield, 1998), often altering one's ability to connect with a significant other. There may be a single trauma (only one partner reports a trauma history) or a dual trauma (both partners report a trauma history). When traumatic events affect connection and one's sense of control, the couple relationship is certain to be a mediating variable in recovering from the trauma. Likewise, the couple relationship can be damaged or strengthened as a result of a trauma. The single most common reaction after a trauma is resilience (Mills, 2001; NSW Institute of Psychiatry and Centre for Mental Health, 2000). Most people recover from a major trauma in 12–24 months (Freedy & Kilpatrick, 1999). Some traumas bring a re-prioritization of values, and positive changes in life, termed *posttraumatic growth* (NSW Institute of Psychiatry and Centre for Mental Health, 2000). All traumas, past and present, have the ability to severely affect the couple relationship, for better or for worse.

Traumas and Responses to Traumas

Traumas occur when an individual experiences an abnormal event that renders the individual helpless and overwhelmed. The individual may feel a threat to his or her life, body, or mind (Pearlman & Saakvitne, 1995). The person can have great difficulty integrating the experience because it does not fit his or her life schema in a way was previously experienced or possibly even imagined. The following are extreme stressors that constitute trauma:

- Witnessing a traumatic event
- Sudden, unexpected death of a loved one
- Sudden, unexpected abandonment by a loved one
- Child sexual abuse, physical abuse, intense emotional abuse, or severe neglect
- Being held hostage or imprisoned, tortured, or displaced
- Combat exposure
- A serious accident or natural disaster
- Terrorism or mass violence (Foa, Davidson, & Frances, 1999, p. 34).

Immediate responses to trauma vary. Shock and denial are typically the earliest responses to trauma. Within the first month following a trauma, a person may develop acute stress disorder, which is similar to posttraumatic stress disorder (PTSD), with heightened emphasis on dissociative symptoms, lasting only 4 weeks. Acute stress disorder must be diagnosed within 4 weeks after the occurrence of the traumatic event (Gibson, 2006). Others who are traumatized go on to develop PTSD, which may severely impair the individual and potentially disable the couple.

Within the couple relationship, unless both experience the traumatic event, there is a "primary victim," or the person who experienced the event, and "secondary victims"—in this case, the spouse of the victim who experiences grief or other responses to the catastrophic incident. The responses include emotional, physical, and cognitive features. Emotional responses can include shock, anger, irritability, and helplessness or a feeling of loss of control. Physical reactions may include fatigue, sleep disturbances, hyperarousal, and somatic complaints. Cognitive effects may include concentration and memory difficulties, worry, and intrusive thoughts (NSW Institute of Psychiatry and Centre for Mental Health, 2000, p. 23).

Posttraumatic Stress Disorder

PTSD responses vary according to individual and cultural meanings placed on the event (Marsella, Friedman, Gerrity, & Scurfield, 1996). There are, however, three main responses within PTSD, with several symptoms within each category (Foa et al., 1999, p. 34).

Reexperiencing of the Traumatic Event The reexperiencing occurs through flashbacks, nightmares, exaggerated startle response, or intrusive recollections of the event. In addition, there may be exaggerated emotional and physical reactions to triggers that remind the person of the past event.

Avoidance and Emotional Numbing This includes intense avoidance of activities, places, thoughts, feelings or conversations related to the trauma, loss of interest, feeling detached from others, and restricted emotions.

Increased Arousal These symptoms include difficulty sleeping, irritability or outbursts of anger, hypervigilance, and/or an exaggerated startle response.

Couples and Trauma

An intimate connection can guard against mental and physical illness (Seligman, 2000) in the face of stress and trauma. Most relationships return to their prior level of intimacy after a traumatic experience (Mills, 2001); as stated previously, the overwhelming response to trauma is resilience. Some couples, however, may struggle in responding to the traumatic stressor and

132 • Handbook of Clinical Issues in Couple Therapy

struggle with the symptoms of PTSD. While there are no universal reactions to traumatic events, the following struggles may be seen in couples who face recovering from a myriad of traumatic stressors.

While interpersonal traumas are more likely to have more profound effects than impersonal ones (Van der kolk, 1996), probably the most insidious of trauma issues that affect couple relationships is that of adults who have survived childhood maltreatment. Childhood trauma of physical or emotional abuse or neglect, and/or sexual abuse can have developmental consequences that can drastically alter how one forms and maintains attachments both in childhood and in adulthood. Childhood abuse is the most common cause of PTSD for women in the United States at about 10% prevalence compared to 5% for men (Kessler, Sonnenga, Bromet, Hughes, & Nelson, 1995). Because of the greater likelihood of therapist treating couples where one or both were maltreated as children, the aftermath of childhood trauma on the couple relationship will be the focus of this chapter. While most people's response to trauma results in growth, the following responses may occur in the struggles in healing the traumatic wounds.

Relational Ramifications of Childhood Maltreatment

While the individual ramifications of childhood maltreatment are many, there are many relational ramifications to be described as follows.

Reduced Relational Intimacy

Child abuse disturbs the acquisition of interpersonal skills (Fairbank, Putnam, & Harris, 2007). This affects intimacy in varying ways. Secrecy may occur when the survivor does not want to share the abuse with his or her partner, which can happen for a myriad of reasons (he or she may know the perpetrator, he or she has not fully dealt with the issue internally, he or she fears being looked down upon or seen as "dirty," and so on). The secrecy of an untold or repressed event can unwittingly erode intimacy.

Likewise, the dread that can besiege a survivor as he or she awaits a flashback or other response to the trauma can be crippling. Withdrawal is a normal response to deal with this dread as an attempt to quiet the emotion. Depending upon the type of trauma, the survivor may even cringe at being touched, often leaving the partner feeling rejected or angry, and not understanding the drive behind the rejection. The partners may avoid the topic of the incident and slowly slide away from a shared intimacy due to numbing and distancing reactions common with PTSD (NSW Institute of Psychiatry and Centre for Mental Health, 2000). Van der kolk (1996) noted that traumatized individuals must deal with the PTSD symptom of hyperarousal and to compensate, they often shut down. In addition, anger is a common emotion after trauma, and can damage interpersonal intimacy if not managed well (Mills, 2001). For adults physically abused as children, they may fear hurting their partner if they do not distance when emotions rise to the surface. Their emotions may also be frightening, unfamiliar, and/or unacceptable to themselves and they may be hesitant to share them for fear of being rejected.

Increased Relational Conflict

One of the effects of childhood maltreatment is the survivor experiences decreased capacity for emotional regulation (Fairbank et al., 2007). The survivor's partner may vacillate between wanting comfort from his or her partner to wanting to be left alone so feelings of any sort are not triggered, for fear a "domino effect" of feelings will occur. This leaves the partner feeling unsure of whether to pursue or distance; they may want to assure the partner he or she is available, yet not agitate the partner in the process. In addition, the survivor's irritability may precipitate fights that have little to do with the couple relationship. Alienating behaviors (e.g., picking fights) or dysfunctional tension reducing behaviors (e.g., drugs or alcohol) may leave the partner feeling angry or at a loss for how to relate to the survivor. Distance-/closeness-regulating mechanisms may be strained. The constant strain of the "flight or fight" mechanism brought into play relationally by the survivor's hyperarousal or PTSD may create for a roller-coaster relationship.

Difficulty Sharing the Grief of Trauma

Many couples have difficulty sharing the overwhelming feelings of grief that can accompany trauma. The trauma survivor may be reticent to share grief for a myriad of reasons. When working with trauma survivors, Mills (2001) reported survivors gave a myriad of reasons for their reticence, including fears of not feeling listened to, not getting a sympathetic response, being seen in a lesser light, overburdening the partner, losing the partner if they know the full story of their past, the partner sharing the information with others, and loss of respect. In addition, survivors felt anxiety about critical comments their partner might make about their coping strategies, and feared the partner could not manage the intensity of the affect accompanying the survivor's experience. Finally, survivors feared "contaminating" their relationships by sharing the event, they feared their partner would not let them forget the trauma when they wanted to forget it, and they feared the partner would use the perceived weakness to gain power in the relationship.

"Couples-Ship" Strains

As the survivor deals with the trauma, there is a tendency to withdraw into one's self, leaving the partner at a loss as to how to be a couple. The interests once shared may no longer have meaning or appeal to the survivor. The survivor may fear that friends cannot understand the gravity of his or her experience, or he or she does not want to burden them with the weight of his or her feelings.

134 • Handbook of Clinical Issues in Couple Therapy

Boundary Issues

Because personal boundaries are violated in virtually any type of abuse, child maltreatment survivors often surface with boundary issues. Excessive dependence or isolation may occur (Van der kolk, 1996), leading to boundaries that can be highly enmeshed or rigid. Survivors may have difficulties setting boundaries with their significant other. The therapist should closely watch couples for signs of abuse as individuals who felt trapped in original traumas where they were felt unable to escape may have difficulty navigating out of relationships that are destructive for them. Likewise, some may have also learned abusive patterns and potentially become perpetrators of abuse.

Communication Difficulties

One not uncommon characteristic of trauma survivors is difficulty talking about the trauma experience itself, especially around the affective experience related to the trauma. Typically, the non-victimized partner picks up on this, and not wanting to upset his or her partner, also does not discuss the trauma. It often sits, night after night, like an uninvited guest, affecting their lives, but remains a topic silently deemed off-limits. When the survivor does try to talk about it, he or she often finds himself or herself at a loss for words. The survivor may literally not be able to get words out of his or her mouth about the experience of the trauma. The partner may interpret this as a cue that the survivor does not want to talk about the trauma. This may not be the case. In a study by Rauch et al. (1996) when survivors were shown stimuli similar to their original trauma, there is a decrease in oxygen utilization in Broca's area (as cited in Van der kolk, 1996). Broca's area is "the region in the left frontal cortex responsible for generating words to attach to internal experience" (Van der kolk, 1996, p. 193). Indeed, the survivor may be trying to communicate his or her experience to the spouse but literally may not be able to. Educating the couple regarding the physiological difficulties related to speaking about the incident(s) that a survivor can encounter and providing alternatives can lead to enhanced intimacy and to revisit and remold the notion that the trauma is off-limits.

Sexual Anxiety and Sexual Disorders

Especially for those who experienced child sexual abuse, survivors may experience arousal disorders, vaginismus, dyspareunia, erectile disorders, or compulsive sexual behaviors (Gil, 1988; Maltz, 2003). In a national study by Laumann, Paik, and Rosen (1999) it was found women who were ever sexually abused or raped were more than twice as likely to have arousal disorders. These researchers also found male victims of sexual abuse to be three times as likely to experience erectile dysfunction. Thus, retreat from sexual activities is not uncommon. Anxiety can be heightened when the survivor is fearful of a flashback if engaging in sexual behavior. At times a cutoff from affect can allow a sexual abuse survivor to sexualize both themselves and others, leading

Trauma and Recovery in Couple Therapy • **135**

to a cadre of potentially troublesome behaviors. Alternatively, some trauma survivors wish to cut off all affect due to the enormity of pain they experience, rendering them unable to engage in an intimate experience. Overall sexual satisfaction may be decreased. Maltz wrote (2003, p. iii): "Sexual symptoms can be viewed as trauma reactions of hypersensitivity, withdrawal, dissociation, and avoidance."

Hypervigilance and Related Trust Issues

In survivors of childhood trauma the hypothalamic–pituitary–adrenal (HPA) axis, and the sympathetic nervous system may become hyperactive, causing hypervigilance (Fairbank et al., 2007). Hypervigilance resulting from the original trauma and an increased sense of one's vulnerability can increase trust issues within and outside of the couple relationship. A sense of foreboding and scanning the environment for threats of harm can disrupt intimate connection. In addition, due to the attachment issues that arise when one was abused as a child, there is a tendency for adult survivors to anticipate future potential abandonment (i.e., "waiting for the other shoe to drop") in their emotional landscape. Thus any distancing on the part of their partner, imagined or real, can quickly lead the survivor into a strong offensive, or alternatively defensive, emotional position. They may evidence concerns of abandonment, while at the same time seemingly holding their partner at bay, or creating the very conditions that might cause their partner to want to distance from them or abandon them. When their partners pull away, they may have a profound sense of injustice with little sense of how their actions contributed to the situation.

Depression and Risk of Suicide

Of potential significant threat to the couple is that of depression and suicide. Major depression is the most common risk for someone who was abused as a child (Dinwiddle et al., 2000; Nelson, Heaht, Madden, Copper, & Dinwiddle, 2002; Paoluccui, Genuis, & Violato, 2001). Suicide risk is also significantly raised (Felitti et al., 1998). The wear and tear on the partner of being in the position of "sentry" can try a relationship as well. Conversely, the dependence of the survivor may keep them from fully functioning as an adult.

Cognitive Distortions

Cognitive distortions include helplessness or hopelessness, as well as inaccurate attributions about fault. Self-esteem of the survivors is often impaired; guilt is common. Survivors will ascribe self-blame for the trauma. Survivors also have the tendency to attribute bad events occurring in their lives to internal factors, whereas ascribing good events occurring in their lives to external factors (Briere & Elliott, 1994; Corby, 2000). They may also see their inability to "move past" the trauma as a moral defect (American Psychiatric Association, 2004).

136 • Handbook of Clinical Issues in Couple Therapy

Anxiety

Survivors of childhood maltreatment are more likely than non-abused individuals to meet the criteria for generalized anxiety disorders, phobias, panic disorder, and obsessive–compulsive disorder (Saunders, Villeponteaux, Lipovsky, Kilpatrick, & Veronen, 1992; Van der kolk, 1996).

Tension Reducing Activities

Survivors may be besieged by eating disorders such as bulimia, anorexia, or obesity (Chandy, Blum, & Resnick, 1996), or non-suicidal self-injurious behavior. Self-medicating, alcohol, substance abuse, and acting out are also common in the wake of trauma or abuse (NSW Institute of Psychiatry and Centre for Mental Health, 2000; Van der kolk, 1996). Self-destructive behaviors can stress any relationship, especially when the spouse does not understand their origin and/or must always be on the lookout for danger.

Anger

While some survivors of interpersonal traumas self-blame, others are angry at their perpetrators. This anger can hinder a relationship when it is unharnessed anger (i.e., rage), or when it is so overwhelming it affects everyday living.

Spiritual Issues

Spirituality may be truncated due to the numbing that can come with trauma. If a couple is religious, trauma can affect the couple's relationship with God, and/or their religious institution, which in turn can affect their ability to access spirituality or their faith community as a healing resource. Conversely, religion or faith may help alleviate feelings of guilt and shame. If the survivor's faith is shaken by the trauma, the division in faith may be difficult for the couple to navigate.

Clinical Intervention

While there are many types of trauma, there are some similarities in how trauma is treated which can be integrated into couple's therapy. Couple therapy is not a panacea for trauma treatment, and empirical evidence is lacking (Welch & Rothbaum, 2007), but relationships can be central to healing from trauma. Johnson (2002, p. 7) noted the importance of including a partner or significant other in treatment: "if a person's connection with a significant others is not part of the coping and healing process, then, inevitably, it becomes part of the problem and even a source of retraumatization." The therapist must screen couples for their suitability for couple therapy. It is assumed that the survivor will be in concurrent individual therapy or has had sufficient individual therapy such that his or her therapist concurs that couples therapy may commence. When PTSD is evident, couples therapy should be considered an adjunct to more established therapy for PTSD (Riggs, 2000;

Welch & Rothbaum, 2007). Chronic PTSD that is accompanied with an incapacitating mental illness may benefit more from case management and psychosocial rehabilitation than psychotherapy or psychopharmacology (Foa, Keane, & Friedman, 2004).

Other contraindications may include active violence in the relationship, current extreme dissociative experiences, or the survivor does not yet trust the experience with the therapist and/or with the spouse. The survivor must be ready and able to consent to couple therapy. Both partners may need individual therapy to lay the foundation for couple work. For example, the survivor may need relaxation training and to first share information with the couples therapist before sharing it with a spouse. Likewise, individual sessions with a spouse can be used to assess his or her ability to be supportive, and to prepare him or her for conjoint sessions.

Macrosystemic context should also be assessed and integrated in couple's therapy. Culture, race, religion, gender, sexual orientation issues, and so on will all influence how someone responds to trauma because they particularly interact with power and privilege. Abuse always follows power lines. Thus, macrosystemic variables will intertwine with abuse and should be assessed for and integrated in therapy. In addition, couple relationship variables related to power and privilege should not be overlooked. Finally, culture may provide avenues for healing rituals that may be important to the couple that could prove valuable to therapy.

All therapy should be conducted in conjunction and approval of the survivor's involved individual therapist, and any treating psychiatrist. This being said, it is also recognized that there are various types and levels of traumas, and although there are chronic PTSD cases, there are also people who suffer traumas that do not rise to the levels of acute stress disorder or PTSD and may not need all types of treating clinicians. What follows are suggestions for treatment specific to trauma survivors and their spouses in couple therapy.

Creating a Safe Environment

The couple therapist should strive to "create a safe and contained environment in which the couple can share thoughts and feelings honestly and openly with an attitude of respect and compassion, to attain a level of mutual empathy" (Mills, 2001, p. 199). Setting rules for emotional safety is important (Johnson, 2002). The trauma survivors should feel that she or he has a feeling of *choice* at all times throughout therapy. These conditions best allow for the creation or enhancement of a secure attachment that can support the needs of both partners.

Provide Psychoeducation

Education about trauma and its effects can provide tremendous relief for a couple. Education about PTSD and secondary trauma can help to "normalize

138 • Handbook of Clinical Issues in Couple Therapy

an abnormal event." Information about acute and chronic reactions to trauma should be provided, and has been shown to be a protective factor against PTSD (NSW Institute of Psychiatry and Centre for Mental Health, 2000). It is important that psychoeducation includes the therapist normalizing symptoms, lest the couple believe their relationship to be inadequate (Mills, 2001). Many couples do not realize that their current difficulties are a natural consequence of the trauma that was experienced. Learning about PTSD and how it affects the individual, and as importantly how it impacts the couple can greatly lessen stress for the pair. The partner may need to know how to respond to panic attacks, dissociation, or other ramifications of the trauma. In addition, given the risk for suicide and suicide attempts (American Psychiatric Association, 2004), the non-victimized partner should be trained about basic suicide assessment and intervention. In some cases, there may be risk of other harm from the victim as well. High-risk cases should be carefully assessed for the advisability of commencing couples treatment. Finally, the couple should know that in addition to psychoeducation about trauma and its sequelae, psychopharmacology and psychotherapy are other effective treatments that should be pursued and maintained (American Psychiatric Association, 2004).

Tailor Care and Understanding

Learning about the needs of the trauma survivor and teaching his or her partner to respond appropriately can be helpful to both partners. Often the traumatized individual wishes to be cared for but has a hard time verbalizing what he or she wants or needs from his or her partner. The partner may feel trepidation, wanting to comfort, while at the same time not wanting to evoke painful feelings or be rejected in the process. Care and understanding, however, are major protective factors from PTS, or PTSD (NSW Institute of Psychiatry and Centre for Mental Health, 2000). Likewise, the caretaker needs to learn to express his or her needs so that burnout does not occur, and so that there is a sense of give and take in the relationship.

Giving Voice to the Couple

Because communication can be so taxing for the trauma survivor, it is recommended the therapist aids the couple in finding alternative methods of giving voice to the trauma experience as well as stories of the couple's triumphs over it. As the survivor decides to share his or her story, the survivor may decide the medium with which he or she wishes to disclose with the help of his or her therapist. The survivor should always be in control of the process in order to increase his or her sense of empowerment. The therapist may be able to coach the spouse in ways that he or she can be supportive. The trauma story is not likely to be disclosed all at once, both because of survivor comfort, and because the survivor may not remember it all at once. The survivor may find that letter writing, journaling, or drawings may be alternatives to vocalizations that can help survivors and their spouses to "give voice" to the experiences at hand. Even e-mails with measured "doses" of the trauma and supportive messages back from the spouse may be a way to take a "slow and steady" course to managing the trauma and build intimacy on the road to healing. Writing about emotional experiences has been found to be therapeutic (Pennebaker, 1997) and may also increase intimacy when shared with one's partner.

Encouraging Self and Other Care

While the couple therapist will undoubtedly work to increase avenues to intimacy for the couple as they traverse trauma, the spouse cannot always be the one providing comfort. The therapist must teach both partners that self-care is imperative in the recovery process, and find specific ways that each partner can restore and rejuvenate himself or herself in the midst of recovery. The non-victimized other will need to be educated that his or her spouse will at times be ambivalent about his or her individual therapy and that this is typically a part of the healing process. The intense feelings a survivor must face in trauma recovery make that ambivalence part and parcel of recovery. Nurturing the partner during this time, but also gently nudging him or her through the process is important. The spouse can play an important role of enhancing treatment adherence; therapists can provide surveillance to ensure this is a productive process for the client.

When Appropriate, Aid the Couple in Accessing Social Support

Deriving comfort from social support is an important coping skill (Van der kolk, 1996). The survivor may find recovery groups helpful. The therapist can determine if there are local support groups for recovery from the specific trauma. Encouraging couples to access child care to have alone time may even provide a modicum of needed stress relief. "Couple care" should be encouraged in addition to self care.

Learning From Successful Mastery of Past Traumas

All couples have had to navigate previous traumas of some nature. Recalling and examining these traumas for the recovery efforts made and consequent gained strengths can bolster the couple in the face of their present dilemmas. Family of origin resiliencies may also be explored and utilized. Successful mastery of past traumas has also been evidenced to be a protective factor against PTS or PTSD (NSW Institute of Psychiatry and Centre for Mental Health, 2000).

Fortify the Couple Foundation

Gottman (1999) has found that the stability of marriages or other couple relationships depends upon positive interactions outweighing negatives with a ratio of at least five positives to one negative interchange. Because trauma is generally considered a negative event, and can pose great challenges to the relationship, increasing positive interchanges within the relationship can buttress the couple for the hardships that the trauma may bring to their relationship. Mills (2001, p. 200) wrote: "An infusion of playfulness, spontaneity, relaxation and mutual enjoyment would lighten the load for many traumatized couples."

Understanding and Utilizing Primary Emotions

Trauma survivors can have intense primary emotional experiences from the abuse that are triggered by here-and-now issues due to the isomorphism of the relationship dynamic. For example, present situations that render the survivor feeling helpless may leave the survivor with unkempt fear or rage, out of proportion with the here-and-how event. Understanding the original source of the primary emotions, as well as the here-and-now triggers can be extremely helpful to healing both for the individual and the couple. Linking once useful survival mechanisms to present relationship blocks can be useful. For example, when a client becomes furious when his or her spouse does not come home on time, exploring primary emotions may move therapists to learn the client's terror is caused by the fact that when the client was a child, his or her sister did not come home one night, and it was also learned that she died in an automobile crash. These types of revelations that put unusual emotional responses in context aid the spouse in responding to the traumatized partner in a nurturing manner. Emotionally focused therapy itself can be a staple of couple therapy for trauma survivors (Johnson & Williams-Keeler, 1998).

Teach the Spouse to Be a "Container" for Trauma

Spouses inevitably are privy to the material of the original trauma. Therapists can teach them how to respond in such a way that it is therapeutic and loving for the affected spouse. Many partners tend to want to "fix" the situation, thereby making things worse and causing the survivor to not feel listened to, and the spouse to feel frustrated in his or her attempts at fixing. Therapists can teach the spouse to simply listen to the traumatic material while keeping his or her spouse safe. They can teach the spouse to listen with simple responses such as "tell me more," "that must have been very difficult for you," "I'm here for you". The responses should be kept very simple so that the spouse does not get overwhelmed. The spouse should be given specific education on PTSD and how to respond to flashbacks. These include grounding techniques such as asking the survivor his or her name, what year it is, what month it is, what day it is, what they can see, taste, feel, smell. Other techniques include asking the survivor to breathe deeply, blow his or her nose, take a drink, describe items in the room, etc.

Use of EMDR

Use of eye movement desensitization and reprocessing (EMDR) has been found to be effective in treating clients suffering from reactions to trauma

(Shapiro, 1995). EMDR has been found to be as effective as exposure therapy and other cognitive behavioral treatments (Bradley, Greene, Russ, Dutra, & Westen, 2005; Davidson & Parker, 2001; Seidler & Wagner, 2006). Protinsky, Flemke, and Sparks (2001) advocated the use of EMDR with emotionally oriented couple therapy.

Touch Techniques

Clients who have undergone traumatic experiences may need to relearn the safety of touch with their partners. Therapists may need to organize this through sensate-focus exercises, gentle massage techniques, or relearning touch techniques advocated by Maltz (1995, 2001).

Nuts and Bolts

Couples also need to work out with each other how to navigate traumatic experiences on a day-to-day basis. How are flashbacks to be managed around children? What do they tell the in-laws? If he or she dissociates at work, how does it need to be managed? Who does he or she tell prior in order to survive the experience with dignity? How can he or she set up his or her work experience to minimize the chances of a flashback?

Creating Shared Meaning Around the Trauma

The experience of trauma can create a chasm as the couple experiences the trauma quite differently from each other. The therapist can aid the couple in creating a shared meaning of the trauma by exploring their feelings, beliefs, frames of references, and perceptions about the event. In this process, the partner is encouraged to create an environment of acceptance so that the survivor can tell his or her story. As the survivor is able to tell and retell his or her story, the couple is able to create new meaning around various aspects of the story. The victim becomes a survivor, and the couple becomes a successful vehicle for healing.

Creating a shared meaning may also mean exonerating the offender to the extent that as the couple creates a survivor story, they give less energy to the trauma, and have less couple identity tied into the abusive event.

Summary

There has been significant progress on both treatments for individual psychotherapy and pharmacological treatments for PTSD and trauma-related disorders (Welch & Rothbaum, 2007). However, the field of marriage and family therapy has yet to yield empirical evidence on the validity of treatment in this area. Nevertheless, couples risk potential estrangement when trauma affects their life, and to ignore couple relationships when trauma is involved does not behoove survivors and their mates. The information provided in this chapter are guidelines based on anecdotal clinical evidence and the existing literature;

142 • Handbook of Clinical Issues in Couple Therapy

much work needs to be done to expand our clinical repertoire in trauma treatment in couple therapy.

While couples face a myriad of stressors when trauma occurs, the overwhelming response to trauma is growth and resilience. A therapist can aid a couple who have survived a trauma by providing a safe environment, utilizing psychoeducation, helping them access social support, learning from successful mastery of past traumas, and utilizing primary emotions to enhance emotional intimacy. Spouses can be taught to be "containers" for processing of trauma, and self- and other care can be tailored to best meet the needs of the couple. Alternative forms of communication are encouraged to be able to "give voice" to the couple. Allowing couples to respond to a trauma together, with guidance and support, can allow them to create a shared meaning around the trauma that results in a stronger couple, with a new, more resilient view of themselves as survivors of life's adversities.

References

American Psychiatric Association. (2000). *Diagnostic and Statistical Manual of Mental Disorders DSM-IV-TR* (4th ed.) [Text Revision]. Arlington, VA: Author.

American Psychiatric Association. (2004). *Practice guideline for the treatment of patients with acute stress disorder and posttraumatic stress disorder*. Arlington, VA: Author.

Bradley, R., Greene, J., Russ, E., Dutra, L., & Westen, D. (2005). A multidimensional meta-analysis of psychotherapy for PTSD. *American Journal of Psychiatry, 162*(2), 214–227.

Briere, J. N., & Elliott, D. M. (1994). Immediate and long-term impacts of child sexual abuse. *The Future of Children, Summer/Fall*, 54–69.

Chandy, J. M., Blum, R. W. M., & Resnick, M. D. (1996), Gender-specific outcomes for sexually abused adolescents. *Child Abuse & Neglect, 20*, 1219–1231.

Corby, B. (2000). *Child abuse: Towards a knowledge base* (2nd ed.), Buckingham, Philadelphia, PA: Open University Press.

Davidson, P. R., & Parker, K. C. H. (2001). Eye movement desensitization and reprocessing (EMDR): A meta-analysis. *Journal of Consulting and Clinical Psychology, 69*, 305–316.

Dinwiddle, S., Heath, C., Dunne, M., Bucholz, K., Madden, P., Slutske, W., Bierut, L., Statham, D., & Martin, N. (2000). Early sexual abuse and lifetime psychopathology: A cotwin-controlled study. *Psychological Medicine, 30*, 41–52.

Fairbank, J. A., Putnam, F. W., & Harris, W. W. (2007). In M. J. Friedman, T. M. Keane, & P. A. Resick (Eds.), *Handbook of PTSD: Science and practice* (pp. 469–496). New York: Guildford Press.

Felitti, V. R., Anda, D., Nordenberg, D., Williamson, A., Spitz, V., Edwards, M., Koss, M., & Marks, J. (1998). Relationship of childhood abuse and household dysfunction to many of the leading causes of death in adults. *American Journal of Preventative Medicine, 14*, 245–258.

Foa, E., Keane, T., & Friedman, M. (2004). Introduction. In E. Foa, T. Keane, & M. Friedman (Eds.), *Effective treatments for PTSD* (pp. 1–17). New York: Guilford Publications.

Foa, E. B., Davidson, J. R. T., & Frances, A. (Eds.). (1999). Expert consensus guidelines series: Treatment of posttraumatic stress disorder. *Journal of Clinical Psychiatry*, (Suppl. 16), 1–79.

Freedy, J. R., & Kilpatrick, D. G. (1999). Everything you ever wanted to know about natural disasters and mental health. *National Center for PTSD Clinical Quarterly, 4*, 6–8.

Gibson, L. E. (2007). *Acute stress disorder: A National Center for PTSD fact sheet.* Retrieved October 12, 2010, from the National Center for Post Traumatic Stress Disorder Web site: http://www.ptsd.va.gov/professional/pages/acute-stress-disorder.asp

Gil, E. (1988). *Treatment of adult survivors of childhood abuse.* Rockville, MD: Launch Press.

Gottman, J. M. (1999). *The marriage clinic: A scientifically-based marital therapy.* New York: W. W. Norton & Company.

Herman, J. (1997). *Trauma and recovery: The aftermath of violence—From domestic abuse to political terror.* New York: Basic books.

Johnson, S. (2002). *Emotionally focused couple therapy with trauma survivors: Strengthening attachment bonds.* New York: The Guilford Press.

Johnson, S., & Williams-Keeler, L. (1998). Creating healing relationships for couples dealing with trauma: The use of emotionally focused marital therapy. *Journal of Marital and Family Therapy, 24*, 25–20.

Kessler, R. C., Sonnenga, A., Bromet, E., Hughes, M., & Nelson, C. B. (1995). Posttraumatic stress disorder in the national comorbidity survey. *Archives of General Psychiatry, 52*, 1-45-1060.

Maltz, W. (1995). Relearning touch: Healing techniques for couples [video]. Eugene, OR: InterVision.

Maltz, W. (2001). *The sexual healing journey: A guide for survivors of sexual abuse.* New York: Harper Collins.

Maltz, W. (2003). Treating the sexual intimacy concerns of sexual abuse survivors. *Contemporary Sexuality, 37*(7), i–vii.

Marsella, A. J., Friedman, M. J., Gerrity, E. T., & Scurfield, R. M. (1996). *Ethnocultural aspect of post traumatic stress disorder: Issues, research, and clinical applications.* Washington, DC: American Psychological Association.

Mills, B. (2001). Impact of trauma on sexuality and relationships. *Sexual and Relationship Therapy, 16*(3), 197–205.

Nelson, E., Heaht, C., Madden, P., Copper, M., & Dinwiddle, S. (2002). Association between self-reports of childhood sexual abuse and adverse psychosocial outcomes: Results from a twin study. *Archives of General Psychiatry, 59*, 139–145.

NSW Institute of Psychiatry and Centre for Mental Health. (2000). *Disaster mental health response handbook.* North Sydney, Australia: NSW Health.

Paolucci, E., Genuis, M., & Violato, C. (2001). A meta-analysis of the published research on the effects of child sexual abuse. *Journal of Psychology, 135*, 17–36.

Pearlman, L. A., & Saakvitne, K. W. (1995). *Trauma and the therapist.* New York: Norton.

Pennebaker, J. W. (1997). Writing about emotional experiences as a therapeutic process. *American Psychological Society, 8*(3), 162–166.

Protinsky, H., Flemke, K., & Sparks, J. (2001). EMDR and emotionally oriented couples therapy. *Contemporary Family Therapy, 23*(2), 153–168.

Rauch, S., van der Kolk, B. A., Fisler, R., Alpert, N., Orr, S., Savage, C., Jenike, M., & Pitman, R. (1996). A symptom provocation study of posttraumatic stress disorder using position emission tomography and script-driven imagery. *Archives of General Psychiatry, 53*, 380–387.

Riggs, D. S. (2000). Marital and family therapy. In E. B. Foa, T. M. Keane, & M. J. Friedman (Eds.), *Effective treatment for PTSD: Practice guidelines for the International Society for Traumatic Stress Studies* (pp. 354–355). New York: Guildford Press.

144 • Handbook of Clinical Issues in Couple Therapy

Saunders, B. E., Villeponteaux, L. A., Lipovsky, J. A., Kilpatrick, D. G., & Veronen, L. J. (1992). Child sexual assault as a risk factor for mental disorders among women: A community survey. *Journal of Interpersonal Violence, 7,* 189–204.

Seidler, G. H., & Wagner, F. E. (2006). Comparing the efficacy of EMDR and trauma-focused cognitive-behavioral therapy in the treatment of PTSD: A meta–analytic study. *Psychological Medicine, 36,* 1515–1522.

Seligman, M. (2000). Positive psychology. *American Psychologist, 55,* 5–14.

Shapiro, F. (1995). *Eye movement desensitization and reprocessing: Basic principles, protocols, and procedures.* New York: Guilford Press.

Van der kolk, B. A. (1996). The complexity of adaptation to trauma: Self-regulation, stimulus discrimination, and characterological development (pp. 182–213). In *Traumatic stress.* New York: The Guilford Press.

Welch, S. S., & Rothbaum, B. G. (2007). Emerging treatments for PTSD. In. M. J. Friedman, T. M. Keane, & P. A. Resick (Eds.), *Handbook of PTSD: Science and practice* (pp. 469–496). New York: Guildford Press.

Whitfield, C. L. (1998). Adverse childhood experiences and trauma. *American Journal of Preventative Medicine, 14*(4), 361–364.

9
The Field of Infidelity
Past, Present, and Future

KATHERINE M. HERTLEIN and GERALD R. WEEKS

Contents

Introduction	145
Issues	146
Definitions	146
Typologies	147
Development of Infidelity Within a Relationship	147
Larger Systemic/Multigenerational Characteristics	148
Theories	149
Therapeutic Issues	150
Research	151
Techniques and Frameworks	152
Internet Infidelity	156
Research	156
Treatment	156
Future Directions	158
References	158

Introduction

The American poet Robert Frost once described two roads diverging in a wood, telling of their beauty and their differences. The field of infidelity is strikingly similar: There appear to be two paths, one road followed by researchers and another followed by therapists working with couples seeking treatment for infidelity. While research in infidelity focuses on predisposing factors, justifications, demographics, and permissiveness values, there are a wide variety of treatment models, and typologies, none of which have been empirically validated. In addition to the wide scope of the research, the emotions, betrayal, secrecy, and complicated picture presented by couples experiencing infidelity are a complex issue for couples and for marital therapists. The consequences can be far-reaching and potentially disastrous for couples experiencing its

145

146 • Handbook of Clinical Issues in Couple Therapy

effects. Just a handful of the effects for the uninvolved[1] partner include hurt, grief, anger, and betrayal, and consequences for the involved partner include feeling shameful, guilty, and may endure mourning the ended affair (Spring, 1996; G. R. Weeks, Gambescia, & Jenkins, 2003). The purpose of this chapter is to review current treatment models, research, and present ideas on bridging the clinician–researcher gap for this topic.

Issues

Definitions

The definition of infidelity has been a topic of discussion in the scholarly literature since at least the early 1990s. Researchers such as A. Thompson (1984) and Brown (1991) defined infidelity as exclusively sexual, limiting its definition to any physical contact/coitus with an individual other than one's partner. In spite of this specific definition, there are still vague elements to it (G. R. Weeks et al., 2003). Thompson contends that "genital sexual involvement" (p. 36) is a component of infidelity. Though this act is certainly considered infidelity by many, relying solely on this item eliminates the possibility of other behaviors being included, such as kissing, petting, or a close emotional relationship to the exclusion of the primary partner. Thompson's criterion restricting infidelity to occurring solely within the context of a marital relationship is also limiting for couples and therapists (G. R. Weeks et al.). Certainly, dating and same sex couples experience events within their relationship that they would define as infidelity (see, e.g., Bettinger, 2005; Drigotas, Safstrom, & Gentilia, 1999; Hansen, 1987).

As a result of these arguments (and potentially the postmodern movement in family therapy), researchers, therapists, and couples acknowledge a broadened definition of infidelity, one that comprises emotions and/or behaviors. Pittman (1989), for example, defines an affair as "a breach of trust, a betrayal of a relationship, a breaking of an agreement" (p. 20); Spring (1996) states infidelity occurs when an agreement established between two partners is broken, either emotionally or physically. The crux for several infidelity scholars is component of secrecy (D. Lusterman, 1998); this component is crucial to the definition (Glass, personal communication, 2003). Our definition (G. R. Weeks et al., 2003) can be applied to a variety of couple situations and relationship organization and is a "violation of the couple's assumed or stated contract regarding emotional and/or sexual exclusivity." (p. xvii). This definition encompasses issues of emotional infidelity and does not restrict itself to heterosexual relationships. It also allows the therapist to respect the couple's definition of infidelity

---

[1] For consistency, the term *uninvolved partner* refers to the betrayed partner; the term *involved partner* refers to the partner who engaged in the infidelity.

and to determine for themselves whether there was a breach in trust rather than having the therapist define it, a consistent theme in infidelity treatment (Hertlein, 2004).

Typologies

In addition to the variety of definitions that have been published to the definition of infidelity, a wide variety of treatment typologies have also been published. In a recent review of such types, G. R. Weeks et al. (2003) catalog eight separate typology-based models of infidelity including Brown (1991, 2005), Charney (1992), Drigotas et al. (1999), Lawson (1988), Levine (1998), D. D. Lusterman (1995), Pittman (1989), and Strean (1976).

Though the typologies are comprehensive, they are also problematic for researchers and therapists for three reasons: (a) they tend to be vastly different, (b) were developed in isolation of one another, and (c) are largely based on opinion and clinical observation rather than research. As a result, the utility of such typologies is significantly limited in the clinical setting. The only typologies that appear to be empirically validating are those proposed by Drigotas et al. (1999): emotional (one invests a significant amount of energy, time, and intimacy to an outside relationship to the exclusion of his or her primary partner), physical (physically sexual relationship with a person outside of the primary relationship), and composite (combined elements of physical and emotional). It is using these three types that researchers have explored gender differences in infidelity as well as the intensity of extradyadic relationships.

Development of Infidelity Within a Relationship

The origin of a particular couple's problem can frequently be difficult to unravel, given the dynamics of each individual, the couple, and the context in which they are embedded. Because of these interacting factors, the cause of the presence of infidelity within a relationship is not well understood. The body of literature and the research in this area primarily examine the characteristics of individuals engaging in infidelity and the characteristics of the relationship of couples who experience infidelity.

Individual Characteristics Individual characteristics under investigation in terms of their contribution to the development of infidelity within a relationship include gender of the involved partner (Oliver & Hyde, 1993; Treas & Giesen, 2000; Weiderman, 1997), age (D. C. Atkins, Baucom, & Jacobson, 2001), geography (A. P. Thompson, 1983), education (Reiss, Anderson, & Sponaugle, 1980), religion (Treas & Giesen), sexual permissiveness (Roscoe, Cavanaugh, & Kennedy, 1988; Treas & Giesen), and individual psychopathology (Weeks, Jenkins, & Gambescia, 2003). However, this body of research is plagued with inconsistencies in their findings. Such inconsistencies are likely

148 • Handbook of Clinical Issues in Couple Therapy

related to the complex interplay of individual characteristics and attitudes (Blow & Hartnett, 2005). Examples include

- D. Atkins, Yi, Baucom, and Christensen (2005) note that men who were likely to cheat were also older and demonstrated increased substance use.
- Liu (2000) reported attending church was related to a lower likelihood of engaging in infidelity for men, but not for women.
- Although researchers have found people living closer to a city are more likely to engage in extradyadic relationships (Bell, Turner, & Rosen, 1975; A. P. Thompson), this may be a result of the different and more permissive sex values associated with a city more than geography (Treas & Giesen).
- Women and men may have different sexual permissiveness values, possibly leading to gender differences in infidelity behavior (Treas & Giesen); this was confirmed by Oliver and Hyde.
- Liu found that opportunity to engage in infidelity influenced likelihood of infidelity for men, but not for women.

It is also worth noting that the characteristics under investigation have primarily focused on those of the involved partner, with little to no emphasis on the individual characteristics of the uninvolved partner (Allen & Atkins, 2005).

Couple Characteristics   The couple characteristics that have been investigated in terms of their relationship to infidelity include the relational satisfaction of the individuals in the couple (D. C. Atkins et al., 2001; Buss & Shackelford, 1997), age at the beginning of relationship (Allen & Atkins, 2005), duration of the relationship (Liu, 2000), and other relationship dynamics. For example, Liu found a curvilinear relationship predicting when men are more likely to engage in infidelity based on the duration of the relationship. Allen and Atkins note that infidelity occurs more frequently in relationships where the couples have married at a young age, lived together prior to the marriage, and experience power imbalances within their relationship. Additionally, Mongeau, Hale, and Alles (1994) found that infidelity is sometimes motivated by revenge within a relationship.

Larger Systemic/Multigenerational Characteristics

Other authors have tied larger systemic concepts to the incidence of infidelity within a relationship. In diffuse intimacy conception, a person places all of his or her energies into providing for one's partner and neglecting personal needs (Reiss et al., 1980; Saunders & Edwards, 1984). Individuals with diffuse intimacy conception experience difficulties sharing personal and private feelings with their partner, spending their energy focusing on meeting the perceived needs of their partner, not providing for their own needs (Saunders & Edwards).

The Field of Infidelity • **149**

This is similar to fusion (Bowen, 1978). Individuals with high levels of fusion, or a high level of involvement with others, are characterized revolving their life around persons with whom they are fused. By neglecting their own needs and taking care of another person, or practicing diffuse intimacy conception, persons are engaging themselves in fusion. As a result, this partner may be more willing to accept infidelity because they are threatened by the loss of the relationship (Reiss et al.; Saunders & Edwards). Further, early research has found support for the claim that knowing someone who engaged in infidelity seems to be related to a higher likelihood of infidelity for women (i.e., B. Buunk, 1980; A. P. Thompson, 1983).

Theories

Many of the infidelity treatment frameworks are based on several theoretical models. From a functional family therapy (FFT) perspective, infidelity inherently creates emotional distance between two partners (Barton & Alexander, 1981; Moultrup, 1990; Pittman & Wagers, 1995) and brings attention to communication problems in the relationship (Moultrup; Taibbi, 1983). Through the lens of FFT, a classic symptom in couple relationships is infidelity because it provides a distancing function between partners in circumstances where developing intimacy is perceived as threatening. This is consistent with Bowen family systems theory (Friedman, 1991; Moultrup) where infidelity is perceived as a classic example of triangulation, different from the balanced, natural triangle where anxiety a couple experiences shifts to a third party, often viewed as a way to manage the anxiety. Other authors have discussed these affairs, which may be driven by fear of intimacy (i.e., Brown, 1991; G. R. Weeks et al., 2003). However, Weeks et al. highlight that affairs may serve many reasons/have many functions besides distancing.

In addition to FFT, other frameworks informing infidelity scholarship have been influenced by postmodern theories (specifically social constructionist theory and narrative theories) (e.g., Atwood & Seifer, 1997), and cognitive-behavioral theories (such as equity theory) (e.g., Walster, Traupmann, & Walster, 1978). Another result of the postmodern movement related to the treatment of infidelity is the context of infidelity as a narrative: Reissman (1989) and Atwood and Seifer, for example, have used the narrative as a powerful tool in working through infidelity with couples. Informed by cognitive-behaviorist, social equity theories (Shackelford, 1997; Treas & Giesen, 2000; Walster et al.) enable researchers to consider balance in relationships from a combined social and behavioral standpoint. Infidelity, according to these theories, is the result of a power equity imbalance. Implications for treatment are to work toward balancing equity in the relationship.

The gap with these theories in their application to infidelity is the lack of empirical evidence supporting the utility of these theories in clinical work. Most published evidence of these theories is found in the case examples

150 • Handbook of Clinical Issues in Couple Therapy

following the framework's description rather than through process-oriented research. Research in this area would be an example of bridging the clinician–researcher gap.

Therapeutic Issues

Society One important aspect for consideration in infidelity treatment is the social context of the couple. B. P. Buunk and Bakker (1995) report that uninvolved women familiar with involved women were more likely to engage in infidelity, citing the importance of social norms relating to infidelity behavior. Vaughan (2003) and Glass (2003) also discuss the influence of one's social context in infidelity, suggesting that the idea of a fairy-tale marriage, secrecy around issues related to sex, and role expectations contribute.

Multiple Dimensions of Infidelity G. R. Weeks et al. (2003) formulate a unique contribution to the infidelity literature with their presentation of multiple dimensions of infidelity, positing that not every case of infidelity is alike. In fact, they believe that typological models have limited utility and it is best to investigate the various dimensions of infidelity. As infidelity cases differ among several critical facets, therapists should consider these dimensions in treatment decisions. These dimensions are listed below:

- Duration of infidelity
- Frequency of communication (sexual contact between the affair partners; total number of transactions)
- Location of encounters
- Risk of discovery
- Degree of collusion by the betrayed partner
- Level of deception
- History of past infidelity
- Gender of the affair partner
- Type of infidelity
- Unilateral and bilateral infidelity
- Relationship of the affair partner to the spouse
- Perceived attractiveness of the affair partner
- Social context of infidelity

Forgiveness Forgiveness in infidelity treatment provides hope, helps the client to determine whether trust can be restored, and assists couples to determine a plan of action for healing (Case, 2005; G. R. Weeks et al., 2003). As a factor in treatment, the therapist needs to assess how the uninvolved partner conceptualizes forgiveness. In infidelity treatment, it is imperative that therapists distinguish between forgiveness and accepting or making accommodations for one's behavior. G. R. Weeks et al. propose that the therapist facilitates the development of empathy, humility, commitment, and hope. The therapist also directs the unfaithful partner to provide a sincere apology and a commitment to change, the purpose of which is to make an attempt to repair the relationship. Gordon and Baucom (1998, 1999) present an integrative model of forgiveness in infidelity cases. Specifically, they believe forgiveness is composed of three stages and focus on the affective, behavioral, and cognitive components of each stage. Like Glass (2002), this framework also discusses the overlap between the infidelity treatment process and a trauma reaction. Gordon and Baucom (1999) also developed a model based partially on relational ethics concepts (Boszormenyi-Nagy, Grunebaum, & Ulrich, 1991), focusing on the cognitive, emotional, and behavioral tasks. Case's process includes helping the uninvolved partner to stop seeking revenge or demanding justice, reducing his or her feelings of anger and resentment, wishing the other person well, and moving toward restoration of trust in the primary relationship.

Self-of-the-Therapist Equally as important to treatment are the therapists' values and beliefs. Moultrup (1990) states therapists should remain as neutral as possible in the treatment of infidelity cases. Just as therapist may need to remain neutral during the sessions, yet it is also important they are aware of any countertransference issues that may be occurring during treatment (G. R. Weeks et al., 2003). The therapist should be aware of his or her own limitations and be clear about his or her values when working with infidelity cases (Hurlbert, 1992; Taibbi, 1983). Some of the reactions that therapists need to be sensitive to include making projections, engaging in reaction formation, and overidentifying with one of the partners to the point where therapy becomes nonproductive. Taibbi advises that supervision is helpful in reducing the likelihood of these effects. G. R. Weeks et al. provide greater details on the issues facing therapists working with these couples, such as countertransference issues and other resulting ethical issues.

Research

Much of the research in the field of infidelity has sought to uncover factors precluding one to engage in infidelity. Two major literature syntheses have been conducted to identify the influence of interpersonal and intrapersonal factors mediating one's involvement in infidelity: Allen et al. (2005) and Blow and Hartnett (2005). Allen et al. synthesize the infidelity literature through organization in several dimensions. In the temporal dimension, characterizing infidelity as a process, Allen et al. also discuss the predisposing factors to infidelity, the approach factors, precipitating factors, maintenance factors, disclosure factors, and response factors. Each of these factors is composed of examining the involved partner's factors, the uninvolved partner's factors, the factors in the marriage, and the contextual factors.

Though Blow and Harnett (2005) disclosed several important findings, only two main points are summarized here. First, they found that demographics

152 • Handbook of Clinical Issues in Couple Therapy

such as age, level of education, religions, etc., were found to impact the likelihood of one engaging in infidelity, but their effect depended on mediating variables. For example, ethnicity might be an important mediating variable in terms of determining one's sexual satisfaction with his or her primary relationship and the likelihood of them engaging in infidelity, and educational levels and likelihood of engaging in infidelity appear to be influenced by the educational dynamics of the partners in the relationship and the couple's history of divorce. Second, much of the research in infidelity is, at best, inconsistent. For example, while some research indicates that religion or education plays a part in likelihood of infidelity (i.e., Treas & Giesen, 2000), others have drawn vastly different conclusions about how likelihood of engaging in infidelity is impacted.

As much research as there is, there are also areas where the research could be improved. Suggestions include improving the reliability and validity concerns, reducing overstated inference, reducing the use of analogue studies in infidelity research, and addressing sampling problems (specifically nonprobability sampling) (Hertlein, 2004). For example, some studies (D. C. Atkins et al., 2001; Liu, 2000) have found that one's likelihood of engaging in infidelity varies depending on one's age or years married, which varies over time. G. R. Weeks et al. (2003) also identify some of the weaknesses in infidelity research as its lack of empirical investigation into the effect of transgenerational influences on infidelity instances, a heavy reliance on correlational investigations, and inconsistent definitions of infidelity across studies, thereby limiting its generalization.

Techniques and Frameworks

Glass (2002) noted: "The extramarital literature has failed to provide a coherent conceptual framework or consistent treatment approach" (p. 488). Like the typologies, the published approaches are generated by individual scholars with little or no research support. In Elbaum's (1981) framework, each partner is to be seen individually for the first few sessions. The therapist should ask the involved spouse to break off the extramarital relationship while therapy is continuing, then work with the hurt and anger generated from the revelation of the affair. The therapist then should shift the focus to the involved partner and encourage him or her to take responsibility for his or her actions.

Westfall (1989) describes several matters for consideration when treating infidelity. One task is to assess the extent of the infidelity, specifically focusing on the degree of secrecy around the affair, degree of involvement with the third party, the permissiveness values of the couple, etc. Another task for the therapist is to ensure he or she is reacting to the crisis of the infidelity and connecting the infidelity to the larger processes of the couple's interaction. The therapist then moves to assist the couple with rebuilding their relationship.

Pittman and Wagers (1995) detail an eight-step model. In the first step, the therapist must determine the affair type: Was this a one-time event,

The Field of Infidelity • **153**

throughout the marriage, or contain a romantic element? Further, the therapist should manage the responses after the revelation of the affair. Typically, this might involve normalizing feelings. The therapist works to bring everyone together and helps the couple define the problem. How has this affected the couple relationship? Does the couple have a problem not being able to trust one another? Do they have difficulties communicating? The therapist is also responsible for managing anxiety through providing a safe environment and reducing chaos. After understanding what the issues are between the couple and being able to manage the anxiety and emotional reactivity of the individuals involved, the therapist's task is to find a solution. Often, a proposed solution might be to negotiate any resistance encountered by the family with the proposed solutions. Finally, once the therapist has worked through resistance to solutions and have implemented the solutions, the couple can terminate sessions.

In Spring's (1996) model, the therapist normalizes feelings, establishes with the couple whether they want to commit to the relationship or end it, and then facilitate rebuilding the relationship should the couple decide to continue. Like Spring, D. Lusterman (1998) also has three phases in recovery of infidelity. Phase One is characterized by two steps: building trust and honesty into the relationship. Phase Two builds on trust and honesty with a focus on reviewing the marriage. The couple must then determine ground rules for their marriage, work on conflict resolution, and identify where things went wrong. Protecting the affair partner is also a component of this phase. Finally, in Phase The, the couple should determine if they would be happier remaining married or separating. Some couples decide they do not want to continue in the relationship, whereas others want to commit again. The therapist helps the couple to determine outcome through facilitating understanding and acknowledgment of their options, and to move toward a "good divorce" if they choose not to recommit to the relationship.

Gordon and Baucom's (1999) model encourages the therapist to manage the impact of the affair on all partners, explore the context of the relationship, and build on the relationship. In the impact phase, the therapist assesses and sets boundaries for the couple. It is also important for the therapist to implement self-care guidelines, allow the couple time out to vent, talk about the impact of the affair, and help them cope with flashbacks. The second phase is characterized by exploring factors related to infidelity. Problem solving is the next step, followed by cognitive restructuring. The last phase is moving on, accomplished by understanding the story of the affair. It is important in this stage that the couple has a conversation about what it would take to forgive. The therapist also helps the couple to explore commitment in relationships and factors related to commitment.

Brown (1999) focuses her treatment in part on helping individuals engaging in infidelity to fully consider the risks and benefits of telling their partner

154 • Handbook of Clinical Issues in Couple Therapy

about an affair. Once the affair is disclosed, he or she encourages the uninvolved partner to allow himself or herself to experience his or her emotions. Brown advises couples to disclose the full picture of the affair, hold off on making large decisions, gain support, and use the opportunity to better the relationship. Consistently in this treatment, Brown normalizes feeling for each member of the couple. In terms of rebuilding the marriage, trust and honesty are of utmost importance. Couples are encouraged to pay close attention to their emotions throughout this process, develop reasonable expectations for their relationship, and to start taking responsibility, which can take the form of working on one's self individually, healing past or childhood wounds.

Glass (2001, 2002) presents a model of infidelity treatment akin to post-traumatic stress disorder (PTSD) treatment, specifically with the components of flashbacks and obsessive rumination. In this model, the therapist can provide crisis intervention strategies. Glass (2002) noted weekly and bi-weekly sessions might be necessary to help the individuals deal with the PTSD symptoms. The therapist should also be helpful in assisting the couple in navigating times in which there will be flashbacks and other reminders of infidelity, establish safety and hope, foster care and good will, and be able to manage affect as well as post-traumatic symptoms. Also critical is the story of the affair, which needs to be told. The therapist then facilitates understanding vulnerabilities in the context of the affair, and to provide meaning to the couple in order to terminate. D. Lusterman (2005) has a similar framework in his recent approach to treating infidelity where he considers the delayed trauma reaction of those marital dyads experiencing this event and organizes treatment around the delayed trauma reaction.

G. R. Weeks et al. (2003) provide a model based on the intersystem approach to working with infidelity cases. The intersystem approach has five different components: individual physiological perspective, individual's psychological makeup, the couple's relationship, family of origin, and the environment (G. Weeks, 2004). In the initial phases of their treatment, therapists are to adequately assess partner's commitment level to one another and whether a therapeutic separation or individual sessions would be warranted. Emotions about the affair partner are to be processed as well as the motivations for engaging in extramarital behavior. One last important stage in this early part of treatment is to be able to rebuild trust within the relationship. In the next phase of treatment, the therapist explores the systemic properties influencing the relationship. This includes looking at individual risk factors in infidelity behavior (such as infidelity being a consequence of personality disorders or Axis I diagnoses), relational issues (such as infidelity as the result of relationship conflict), intergenerational factors (i.e., using the anger genogram developed by DeMaria, Weeks, & Hof, 1999), and appropriate reframing. A major component of the treatment is to facilitate forgiveness based on recent research in social psychology. The final state involves

The Field of Infidelity • **155**

restructuring the relationship so that the factors that contributed to the affair are removed and the couple is functioning well. In looking at these factors, Weeks et al. operate from an intimacy-based approach though exploring the ways in which the couple fits with Sternberg's (1986) triangle, identifying the commitment level in the couple toward each other and toward treatment, and addressing intimacy fears within the couple.

Gordon, Baucom, and Snyder (2004, 2005) present a three-stage integrative model for treatment of infidelity cases. Stage 1 is the impact stage where couples are struggling to know what happened. The goals of therapy in this stage are to contain the damage done by the affair and help the couple to begin processing the affair. In Stage 2, the couple begins the recovery process, whose goals are to encourage partners to develop empathy to one another, understanding of how each operates and responds to stressors. Stage 3 is the "move on" phase. The uninvolved partner should develop a realistic view of the relationship, be released from feeling negative emotions, and step away from his or her right to punish the other partner. It is in this phase that there is a concerted effort to forgive.

Johnson (2005) views infidelity as one example of an attachment injury, or a violation of trust resulting from the betrayal (the infidelity event) or from abandonment (moving toward another partner and away from the primary partner). Treatment revolves around encouraging the attachment bond between partners. As couples describe the extramarital involvement and the impact it has on their lives and their relationship, the therapist encourages the couple to use the vocabulary of attachment. Johnson outlines the key stages of treatment as (a) uninvolved partner describes the event, such as when the affair was discovered or when the betrayal occurred; (b) the couple discusses its impact and significance; (c) involved partner acknowledges uninvolved partner's pain; (d) uninvolved partner organizes the injury in a clear manner; (e) the involved partner takes responsibility; (f) uninvolved partner asks for caring that was not available at the time of the infidelity; and (g) involved spouse responds in a caring manner. Johnson's treatment is consistent with research detailing a link between attachment and extradyadic relationship style (Allen & Baucom, 2004).

Blow's (2005) framework encourages couples to face the infidelity issues directly to use the crisis of infidelity as a way to draw the couple closer together. Blow emphasizes that the involved partner should be apologetic toward the uninvolved partner, detailing specific actions the involved partner should include in the apology. Specifically, the involved partner is advised to have a long-term (life-long) apologetic stance around the infidelity, accompanied by validation, addressing security needs, and understanding. The therapist encourages the uninvolved partner to shift from critical attitudes and embrace a realistic stance around the involved partner's apology.

Overall, these treatment frameworks serve as a guideline for assisting therapists in the various treatment of infidelity. But like the theories informing the frameworks, few of the frameworks have been researched specifically to

156 • Handbook of Clinical Issues in Couple Therapy

determine the effects with couples experiencing infidelity. To date, there have been two studies examining the impact of infidelity treatment on couples. D. Atkins et al. (2005) demonstrated that behavioral interventions in infidelity treatment can be effective. Similarly, Gordon et al. (2004) tested a multitheoretical approach and found it to be effective. Both studies, however, utilized relatively small sample sizes, and results should be interpreted with caution.

Hertlein (2004) identified common factors present across frameworks for the treatment of Internet infidelity, discovering that most therapists operate from a *deficit model,* or identifying a missing element from a couple's relationship and finding ways to incorporate that in the current relationship. Scheinkman (2005) also noted that "most family therapists writing about infidelity assume that an affair is a symptom of problems in a marriage" (p. 229). Similar research should be conducted with traditional infidelity cases as a way to identify the manner in which therapists typically conceptualize and treat these cases.

Another criticism of the body of literature in infidelity treatment is the lack of treatment models appropriate for couples from diverse backgrounds. While many authors note that the therapist should be aware of cultural differences, few models have addressed this issue specifically. One notable exception is the work of Martell and Prince (2005) who outline a treatment strategy for infidelity within same-sex couple relationships. Specifically, the authors outline the application of Integrative Behavioral Couple Therapy to the treatment of infidelity while also providing a list of "dos and don'ts" for therapists working with this population. Above all, the authors emphasize the needs for therapists to tailor the treatment to the specific context in which the client system is embedded.

Internet Infidelity

Research

Though there is a wealth of research on the topic of Internet sexuality, there are few studies that are strictly devoted to Internet infidelity, and even fewer which examine behavior rather than attitudes. Attitudinal studies such as Henline and Lamke (2003) and Whitty (2003) continues to focus on issues that are related to what behaviors are perceived as infidelity. To date, Hertlein's (2004) investigation is the only study exploring the theories therapists use when treating infidelity cases, Internet or otherwise. In this study, therapists were asked about their treatment of Internet infidelity cases. Results indicated there were differences in how therapists would treat these cases depended to some degree on the social background characteristics of the therapist and their clients. The treatment strategies therapists reported using included solution-focused, transgenerational theories, and emotionally focused therapy.

Treatment

One treatment model presenting factors influencing Internet infidelity is the Shaw (1997) model based on reducing vulnerability factors for Internet

The Field of Infidelity • **157**

infidelity. Examples of vulnerability factors include a lack of connection with partners or a lack of ability to discuss problems with one's partners, resulting in searching for something else, and one's readiness to be in an emotional relationship with someone, and the fear of being oneself. In an Internet relationship, people can be whomever they present themselves to others (Shaw). Shaw suggests therapists examine secrets between the partners in a relationship, emphasize a maturing process, and build integrity and trust between the partners. Similarly, Young, Griffin-Shelley, Cooper, O'Mara, and Buchanan (2000) discuss factors leading to cybersex addiction (anonymity, convenience, and escape), and suggest that these factors provide a context for understanding the phenomenon of Internet infidelity. This framework includes improving communication between the spouses, rebuilding trust, and addressing underlying issues within the marriage.

Other treatment frameworks focus on transgenerational theory. Maheu and Subotnik (2001) provide strategies for dealing with Internet affairs in their book on Internet infidelity based on Cooper's (2000, 2002) "Triple A engine"—anonymity, accessibility, and affordability. The interventions include both common couple interventions, followed by interventions with elements of transgenerational theory, such as having the couple explore family-of-origin issues, expressing empathy, and accepting responsibility. Atwood and Schwartz (2002) identify factors associated with Internet infidelity involvement include projection, differentiation of self, anonymity, intimacy issues, and communication difficulties, mid-life crisis, and Internet addiction. They encourage therapists to assess the Internet user's accessibility to the Internet as well as the activities in which the user is engaged when online, consider social networks, and address underlying issues. Gonyea (2004) also emphasizes differentiation and where treatment is characterized by the establishment of boundaries, making the therapy room safe, exploring relationship secrets and their functions, and acceptance of responsibility. Finally, Whitty and Carr (2005) suggest therapists adapt Klein's object relations model for conceptualizing and treating Internet infidelity cases.

What is problematic about these treatment frameworks is that they partially are informed by a Bowenian stance. In an attempt to generate framework consistent with Bowen theory, Hertlein and Piercy (2005) prescribe an assessment phase where the couple defines its idiosyncratic rules for their relationship. This is followed by a Bowenian-informed treatment phase where the therapist examines the behavior around Internet infidelity, specifically focusing on anxiety, differentiation, and triangulation, then planning interventions which support detriangulation (e.g., getting the couple and/or third person out of the emotional system) and individuation (e.g., supporting both closeness and distance through direct, clear communication [Bowen, 1978]).

158 • Handbook of Clinical Issues in Couple Therapy

Future Directions

Though Frost selected the road less traveled, infidelity treatment would be the most effective if the roads eventually converge, making one solid pathway with the strengths of both. In this situation, research would inform treatment, thereby informing future research, etc. We believe that this integration of research and practice will propel infidelity knowledge farther. As an intricate and multifaceted problem, those experiencing the effects of infidelity have a difficulty journey ahead of them as they navigate their recovery. We look forward to when clinicians and researchers work closely together on empirically validating treatment frameworks and resolving the inconsistencies that plague this body of knowledge.

References

Allen, E. S., & Atkins, D. C. (2005). The multidimensional and developmental nature of infidelity: Practical applications. *Journal of Clinical Psychology, 61*(11), 1371–1382.

Allen, E. S., Atkins, D. C., Baucom, D. H., Snyder, D. K., Gordon, K. C., & Glass, S. P. (2005). Intrapersonal, interpersonal, and contextual factors in engaging in and responding to extramarital involvement. *Clinical Psychology, 12*(2), 101–143.

Allen, E. S., & Baucom, D. H. (2004). Adult attachment and patterns of extradyadic involvement. *Family Process, 43*(4), 467–488.

Atkins, D., Yi, J., Baucom, D., & Christensen, A. (2005). Infidelity in couples seeking marital therapy. *Journal of Family Psychology, 19*(3), 470–473.

Atkins, D. C., Baucom, D. H., & Jacobson, N. S. (2001). Understanding infidelity: Correlates in a national random sample. *Journal of Family Psychology, 15*(4), 735–749.

Atwood, J. D., & Schwartz, L. (2002). Cybersex: The new affair treatment considerations. *Journal of Couple and Relationship Therapy, 1*(3), 37–56.

Atwood, J. D., & Seifer, M. (1997). Extramarital affairs and constructed meanings: A social constructionist approach. *American Journal of Family Therapy, 25*(1), 55–75.

Barton, C., & Alexander, J. F. (1981). Functional family therapy. In A. S. Gurman & D. P. Kniskern (Eds.), *Handbook of family therapy* (Vol. 1, pp. 403–443). Bristol, PA: Brunner/Mazel.

Bell, R. R., Turner, S., & Rosen, L. (1975). A multivariate analysis of female extramarital coitus. *Journal of Marriage and the Family, 37*, 375–384.

Bettinger, M. (2005). A family systems approach to working with sexuality open gay male couples. *Journal of Couple and Relationship Therapy, 4*(2/3), 149–160.

Blow, A. (2005). Face it head on: Helping a couple move through the painful and pernicious effects of infidelity. *Journal of Couple & Relationship Therapy, 4*(2/3), 91–102.

Blow, A., & Hartnett, K. (2005). Infidelity in long-term committed relationships I: A methodological review. *Journal of Marital and Family Therapy, 31*(2), 183–216.

Boszormenyi-Nagy, L., Grunebaum, J., & Ulrich, D. (1991). Contextual therapy. In A. S. Gurman & D. P. Kniskern (Eds.), *Handbook of family therapy* (Vol. 2, pp. 200–238). New York: Brunner/Mazel.

Bowen, M. (1978). *Family therapy in clinical practice.* Northvale, NJ: Jason Aronson.

Brown, E. M. (1991). *Patterns of infidelity and their treatment.* New York: Brunner/Mazel.

Brown, E. M. (1999). *Affairs: A guide to working through the repercussions of infidelity.* San Francisco: Jossey-Bass, Inc.

The Field of Infidelity • **159**

Brown, E. M. (2005). Split self affairs and their treatment. *Journal of Couple and Relationship Therapy*, 4(2/3), 55–70.

Buss, D. M., & Shackelford, T. K. (1997). Susceptibility to infidelity in the first year of marriage. *Journal of Research in Personality*, 31, 193–221.

Buunk, B. (1980). Extramarital sex in the Netherlands: Motivation in social and marital context. *Alternative Lifestyles*, 3, 11–39.

Buunk, B. P., & Bakker, A. B. (1995). Extradyadic sex: The role of descriptive and injunctive norms. *Journal of Sex Research*, 32(4), 313–318.

Case, B. (2005). Healing the wounds of infidelity through the healing power of apology and forgiveness. *Journal of Couple and Relationship Therapy*, 4(2/3), 41–54.

Charney, I. (1992). Catering and not catering affairs: The proper and improper pursuit of extramarital relationships. In I. Charney (Ed.), *Existential/dialectical marital therapy* (pp. 220–244). New York: Brunner/Mazel.

Cooper, A. (2000). *Cybersex: The dark side of the force*. New York: Brunner-Routledge.

Cooper, A. (2002). *Sex and the internet: A guidebook for clinicians*. New York: Brunner-Routledge.

DeMaria, R., Weeks, G., & Hof, L. (1999). *Focused genograms: Intergenerational assessment of individuals, couples, and families*. Philadelphia: Brunner/Mazel.

Drigotas, S. M., Safstrom, C. A., & Gentilia, T. (1999). An investment model prediction of dating infidelity. *Journal of Personality and Social Psychology*, 77(3), 509–524.

Elbaum, P. (1981). The dynamics, implications, and treatment of extramarital sexual relationships for the family therapist. *Journal of Marital and Family Therapy*, 7(4), 489–495.

Friedman, E. H. (1991). Bowen theory and therapy. In A. S. Gurman & D. P. Kniskern (Eds.), *Handbook of family therapy* (Vol. 2). New York: Brunner/Mazel.

Glass, S. P. (2001, October). The trauma of infidelity: Research-based treatment. Paper presented at the *Annual meeting of the American Association for Marriage and Family Therapy*, Nashville, TN.

Glass, S. P. (2002). Couple therapy after the trauma of infidelity. In A. Gurman & N. Jacobson (Eds.), *Clinical handbook of couple therapy* (3rd ed.). New York: Guilford Press.

Glass, S. P. (2003). *Not "just friends."* New York: Free Press.

Gonyea, J. L. (2004). Internet sexuality: Clinical implications for couples. *American Journal of Family Therapy*, 32, 375–390.

Gordon, K. C., & Baucom, D. H. (1998). Understanding betrayals in marriage: A synthesized model of forgiveness. *Family Process*, 37, 425–449.

Gordon, K. C., & Baucom, D. H. (1999). A multitheoretical intervention for promoting recovery from extramarital affairs. *Clinical Psychology: Science and Practice*, 6(4), 382–399.

Gordon, K. C., Baucom, D. H., & Snyder, D. K. (2004). An integrative intervention for promoting recovery from extramarital affairs. *Journal of Marital and Family Therapy*, 30(2), 213–231.

Gordon, K. C., Baucom, D. H., & Snyder, D. K. (2005). Treating couples recovering from infidelity: An integrative approach. *JCLP/In Session*, 61(11), 1393–1405.

Hansen, G. L. (1987). Extradyadic relations during courtship. *Journal of Sex Research*, 23, 382–390.

Henline, B. H., & Lamke, L. K. (2003). The experience of sexual and emotional online infidelity. Poster presented at the *65th Annual Conference of the National Council on Family Relations*, Vancouver, British Columbia, Canada, November 19–22, 2003.

Hertlein, K. M. (2004). Internet infidelity: An examination of family therapist treatment decisions and gender biases. Unpublished doctoral dissertation, Virginia Polytechnic Institute and State University, Blacksburg.

160 • Handbook of Clinical Issues in Couple Therapy

Hertlein, K. M., & Piercy, F. P. (2005). A theoretical framework for defining, understanding, and treating Internet infidelity. *Journal of Couple and Relationship Therapy*, *4*(1), 79–91.

Hurlbert, D. F. (1992). Factors influencing a woman's decision to end an extramarital sexual relationship. *Journal of Sex and Marital Therapy*, *18*(2), 104–113.

Johnson, S. M. (2005). Broken bonds: An emotionally focused approach to infidelity. *Journal of Couple and Relationship Therapy*, *4*(2/3), 17–29.

Lawson, A. (1988). *Adultery*. New York: Basic Books.

Levine, S. B. (1998). Extramarital sexual affairs. *Journal of Sex and Marital Therapy*, *24*(3), 207–216.

Liu, C. (2000). A theory on marital sexual life. *Journal of Marriage and the Family*, *62*(2), 363–374.

Lusterman, D. (1998). *Infidelity: A survival guide*. New York: MJF Books.

Lusterman, D. (2005). Helping children and adults cope with parental infidelity. *Journal of Clinical Psychology*, *61*(11), 1439–1451.

Lusterman, D. D. (1995). Treating marital infidelity. In R. Mikesey, D. D. Lusterman, & S. H. McDaniel (Eds.), *Integrating family therapy: Handbook of family psychology and systems theory* (pp. 561–569). Washington, DC: American Psychological Association.

Maheu, M. M., & Subotnik, R. B. (2001). *Infidelity on the internet*. Naperville, IL: Sourcebooks, Inc.

Martell, C. R., & Prince, S. E. (2005). Treating infidelity in same-sex couples. *Journal of Clinical Psychology*, *61*(11), 1429–1438.

Mongeau, P. A., Hale, J. L., & Alles, M. (1994). An experimental investigation of accounts and attributions following sexual infidelity. *Communication Monographs*, *61*, 326–344.

Moultrup, D. J. (1990). *Husbands, wives, and lovers: The emotional system of the extramarital affair*. New York: Guilford Press.

Oliver, M. B., & Hyde, J. S. (1993). Gender differences in sexuality: A meta-analysis. *Psychological Bulletin*, *114*(1), 29–51.

Pittman, F. (1989). *Private lies: Infidelity and the betrayal of intimacy*. New York: W. W. Norton & Co.

Pittman, F., & Wagers, T. P. (1995). Crises of infidelity. In N. S. Jacobson and A. S. Gurman (Eds.), *Clinical handbook of couple therapy* (pp. 295–316). New York: Guilford Press.

Reiss, I. L., Anderson, R. E., & Sponaugle, G. C. (1980). A multivariate model of the determinants of extramarital sexual permissiveness. *Journal of Marriage and the Family*, *42*(2), 395–411.

Reissman, C. K. (1989). Life events, meaning and narrative: The case of infidelity and divorce. *Social Science Medicine*, *29*(6), 743–751.

Roscoe, B., Cavanaugh, L. E., & Kennedy, D. R. (1988). Dating infidelity: Behaviors, reasons, and consequences. *Adolescence*, *23*(89), 35–43.

Saunders, J. M., & Edwards, J. N. (1984). Extramarital sexuality: A predictive model of permissive attitudes. *Journal of Marriage and the Family*, *46*(4), 825–835.

Scheinkman, M. (2005). Beyond the trauma of betrayal: Reconsidering affairs in couples therapy. *Family Process*, *44*(2), 227–244.

Shackelford, T. K. (1997). Cues to infidelity. *Personality and Social Psychology Bulletin*, *23*(10), 1034–1046.

Shaw, J. (1997). Treatment rationale for Internet infidelity. *Journal of Sex Education and Therapy*, *22*(1), 29–34.

Spring, J. A. (1996). *After the affair: Healing the pain and rebuilding the trust when a partner has been unfaithful.* New York: HarperCollins.

Sternberg, R. (1986). A triangular theory of love. *Psychological Review, 93*, 119–135.

Strean, H. (1976). The extramarital affair: A psychoanalytic view. *Psychoanalytic Review, 63*(1), 101–113.

Taibbi, R. (1983). Handling extramarital affairs in clinical treatment. *Social Casework: The Journal of Contemporary Social Work, 64*(4), 200–204.

Thompson, A. (1984). Extramarital sexual crisis: Common themes and therapy implications. *Journal of Sex and Marital Therapy, 10*(4), 239–253.

Thompson, A. P. (1983). Extramarital sex: A review of the research literature. *Journal of Sex Research, 19*(1), 1–22.

Treas, J., & Giesen, D. (2000). Sexual infidelity among married and cohabitating Americans. *Journal of Marriage and the Family, 62*, 48–60.

Vaughan, P. (2003). *The monogamy myth: A personal handbook for dealing with affairs* (3rd ed.). New York: Newmarket Press.

Walster, E., Traupmann, J., & Walster, G. W. (1978). Equity and extramarital sexuality. *Archives of Sexual Behavior, 7*(2), 127–141.

Weeks, G. (2004). The emergence of a new paradigm in sex therapy: Integration. *Sexual and Relationship Therapy, 20*(1), 89–103.

Weeks, G. R., Gambescia, N., & Jenkins, R. E. (2003). *Treating infidelity: Therapeutic dilemmas and effective strategies.* New York: W. W. Norton & Co.

Weiderman, M. L. (1997). Extramarital sex: Prevalence and correlates in a national survey. *Journal of Sex Research, 34*, 167–174.

Westfall, A. (1989). Extramarital sex: The treatment of the couple. In G. Weeks (Ed.), *Treating couples: The intersystem model of the Marriage Council of Philadelphia* (pp. 163–190). Philadelphia: Brunnel/Mazel.

Whitty, M. T. (2003). Pushing the wrong buttons: Men's and women's attitudes toward online and offline infidelity. *CyberPsychology and Behavior, 6*(6), 569–579.

Whitty, M. T., & Carr, A. N. (2005). Taking the good with the bad: Applying Klein's work to further our understandings of cyber-cheating. *Journal of Couple and Relationship Therapy, 4*(2/3), 103–116.

Young, K. S., Griffin-Shelley, E., Cooper, A., O'Mara, J., & Buchanan, J. (2000). Online infidelity: A new dimension in couple relationships with implications for evaluation and treatment. *Sexual Addiction and Compulsivity, 7*, 59–74.

III
Divorce and Remarital Issues

10
Divorce Therapy

JEROME F. ADAMS

Contents

Deciding to Divorce: Helping Couples Weighing the Alternatives	166
Why Couples Divorce	167
Emotional Disaffection	168
Emergence of Conflict	169
Divorce Theory	170
Impact of Divorce	171
Impact of Divorce on Partners	171
Impact of Divorce on Children	175
Surviving Divorce	178
A Perspective for Marital Therapists	180
References	182

We may hope that the field has moved past the association of divorce with pathology and the belief that divorce therapy is "antifamily" or "anti-marriage"

(Sprenkle, 1985, p. 5)

The difference between marital therapy and divorce therapy is not as easy to define as it might first appear. A great deal of marital therapy is conducted with couples in which at least one partner is seriously considering divorce. At the same time, divorce therapy clients are often ambiguous about uncoupling. Moreover, there is little that is strategically or technically unique to divorce therapy (Gurman & Kniskern, 1981). What does distinguish the two therapies are their goals. In its strictest sense, marital therapy can be defined as relationship treatment that focuses on strengthening the marital bond. Divorce therapy can be defined as relationship treatment that focuses on decreasing the marital bond, with the eventual goal of dissolving it. Rarely, however, is such a clear-cut dichotomy found in clinical practice. Marital and divorce therapies are not so much distinct clinical entities as they are segments of a continuum (Sprenkle, 1996). Partners may shift their objectives during the course of treatment, motivated in varying degrees to continue or end their marriage. The therapist continually assesses such motivation and shifts the focus of treatment accordingly.

166 • Handbook of Clinical Issues in Couple Therapy

Practitioners recognize that divorce is not a single event but a process that involves a series of stages or steps. A number of models of marital dissolution have been proposed, each emphasizing different aspects or stages of this process (e.g., Baxter, 1984; Kaslow, 1995; Kessler, 1975; Lee, 1984). Anthropologist Paul Bohannan (1970) developed one of the most influential psychological models to describe the divorce process. (For a discussion of other models, see Guttman [1993].) Bohannan views divorce as consisting of six "stations" (processes) or "divorces": (1) emotional, (2) legal, (3) economic, (4) co-parental, (5) community, and (6) psychic. As people divorce, they undergo these divorces with varying levels of intensity though not necessarily in a particular order or simultaneously.

Other scholars conceptualize transitional frameworks. Developed from her longitudinal research on divorcing families, Ahrons (1994, 2005) identifies five overlapping transitions each with distinct role changes and tasks. The first three transitions (decision, announcement, separation) form the core of an emotional separation process. The last two (reorganization, aftermath) form the family reorganization process. Salts (1985) and Sprenkle (1989, 1996) favor a three-stage model consisting of (1) pre-divorce decision making, (2) divorce restructuring, and (3) post-divorce recovery. Sprenkle notes these stages are more heuristic than descriptive of all divorces, since divorces vary widely. Some individuals have no time or even the option to think about the decision to divorce because they are abruptly abandoned. Others, far into the second stage, reevaluate their decision and reconcile (Sprenkle, 1989, p. 175).

These models have many theoretical limitations (Rollie & Duck, 2006). Nevertheless, they do help clinicians better understand the challenges divorcing couples face by describing the complex and painful emotions involved. They also offer guidance for clinicians on assessment strategies, goals, and interventions at each transition to facilitate constructive outcomes for all family members (for recommendations on relevant clinical resources, see Sprenkle [1996]).

Deciding to Divorce: Helping Couples Weighing the Alternatives

Understanding the decision-making phase of the divorce process is important for two reasons. First, a substantial part of marital therapy is conducted with couples hovering on the brink of breakup, where at least one partner is thinking about divorce as an option. Therapists are entrusted with the responsibility of helping clients make a fully informed decision—one that has considered the possible outcome of each alternative, so that the best or fairest solution can be achieved. Second, therapists are doing this against the backdrop of a renewed values debate on the "divorce problem." Policy makers have proposed changes in state divorce laws so that divorces would be more difficult to get. An assumption behind this movement is that tougher divorce laws would foster a renewed "culture of marriage" (Council on Families in America, 1996).

"Pro-marriage" therapists have been pushing back against what they feel is a divorce culture out of control and advocate an ethos in which therapists encourage clients to take their marriage more seriously. Doherty (2002, 2006), for example, believes so strongly that marital therapists value individual interests over moral obligations to the marriage and responsibility to its stakeholders (especially children), that he has set up a national registry of marriage-friendly therapists who endorse a pro-marriage position. Doherty equates value-neutral marital counseling as the equivalent of "undermining the marital relationship" (Doherty, 2002, p. 10).

Pro-marriage advocates "quote liberally and publicly from what they call 'definitive' research" on the damaging effects of broken marriages on children (Lebow, 2006, p. 83). There is also an implicit assumption, based on recent marital-interaction research, that if therapists worked harder to improve communication and conflict management, marital satisfaction will increase and couples will divorce less. We will examine these assertions in more detail later, but a review of the evidence warrants caution. Family science research indicates that divorce is not always or necessarily bad for children, and the effectiveness of marital conflict/communication programs in preventing divorce is virtually unknown (Belluck, 2000; Lebow). Whether they view divorce as a problem or a solution, therapists have a responsibility to present a dispassionate review of the facts so that couples whose relationship is tracking toward dissolution have an informed choice about their alternatives.

Why Couples Divorce

Why do some marriages succeed and others fail? In order to understand why a relationship fails, it is necessary to understand the conditions under which it was initiated (Berscheid, 2006). Of prime importance are the partners' expectations of the benefits they are likely to receive from the relationship because the relationship becomes more vulnerable to divorce when those expectations are violated. These expectations and the nature of marriage itself have changed over the past 30 years. Couples increasingly see marriage less as an institution of economic benefit and more as a close relationship. Today's marriages are contracted and endure on the basis of the partners' emotional ties such as love, affection, and companionship.

Marriage has changed in another way. Structural changes such as increased economic inequality, work–family conflict, and cultural changes regarding gender roles have made marriage a more difficult arrangement (Van Laningham, Johnson, & Amato, 2001). Normative roles for husbands and wives are no longer taken for granted and require more negotiation, more work, and involve more stress. Marital conversation today is "more struggle and less chitchat" (p. 418) (Lamanna & Riedmann, 2009).

Historically, family sociology has not been very accurate in coming up with a relationship profile that predicts divorce. This has not deterred commentators

168 • Handbook of Clinical Issues in Couple Therapy

on marriage from citing an array of "warning signs" and recommending policy. Yet, when examined more closely, the picture often turns out to be more complex. Here are two brief examples. Premarital sex and cohabitation are widely cited as increasing the likelihood of divorce. True, but only when these take place with someone *other* than your future marital partner (Heaton, 2002; Teachman, 2003) and even then it is not well understood why this is so. Researchers are also uncertain as to the impact of women's employment on divorce rates. There is some evidence that employment may give unhappily married women more financial independence and the economic option to divorce (Schoen, Astone, Rothert, Standish, & Kim, 2002; South, 2001), thus leading to higher divorce rates. On the other hand, there is research that suggests women's employment has no direct effect on marital stability (L. Sayer & Bianchi, 2000). Moreover, there is an income effect to women's employment. That is, among low-income couples, a wife's earnings may actually help to hold the marriage together by counteracting the negative effects of poverty (Heckert, Nowak, & Snyder, 1998; Ono, 1998).

Emotional Disaffection

Many married couples struggle to sustain love in their relationships. In fact, it seems much easier to fall into love than to stay in love. Separated and divorced individuals indicate that lack of love is one of the top two reasons for marital breakdown, second either to an extramarital affair (De Munck & Korotayev, 1999) or communication difficulties (Gottman & Notarius, 2002). In fact, intimacy and love have been identified as strong indicators of whether couples plan to continue or terminate their relationships (Riehl-Emde, Volker, & Willie, 2003). These affective variables were more important than factors such as exchange of resources, conflict resolution, and self-disclosure.

Kayser and Rao (2006) describe the process of emotional disaffection as moving through an initial phase of disappointments, then escalating anger and hurt and eventual apathy and indifference. The ink is barely dry on the marriage license when doubts and disillusionment about partners begin to set in. When asked about their first doubts about their marriage, approximately 40% of the individuals indicated that marital doubts occurred during the first 6 months of their marriage. Another 20% reported doubts between 6 months and 1 year. Thus, more than half (60%) of the couples they studied were having serious doubts about their marriages during the first year. For the remaining 40% of the respondents, disaffection started to set in later in their marriage (Kayser & Rao). The events that contribute to their doubts are not necessarily major crises but rather crystallizing events after an accumulation of seemingly minor events. In this respect, marital disaffection may be the result of the pileup effect of stressors (Boss, 2002; McCubbin & Patterson, 1983). Frequently mentioned are a partner's controlling behavior (e.g., unilateral decisions made that disregard a spouse's input and opinions), irresponsibility (e.g., breaking trust, leaving children unattended), and lack of emotional support (e.g., no care or concern during the birth of a child or an illness). This early onset of dissatisfaction corresponds with longitudinal studies in which marital adjustment declines significantly during the first 2 years of marriage and conflict increases (Huston & Houts, 1998; L. A. Kurdek, 1999; Leonard & Roberts, 1998; Lindahl, Clements, & Markman, 1998).

Why this occurs is less clear. Some studies indicate that partners behave differently after marriage (e.g., they work less to secure their partner's love on a daily basis). More likely, what has changed is the meaning given to a partner's behavior. Traits previously identified as positive are now relabeled as negative. What is initially viewed as "spontaneous," for example, is later seen as irresponsibly "impulsive." A third explanation is that new couples are naively upbeat and view each other through "rose-colored glasses," minimizing shortcomings until after the wedding. Glenn (1991) takes a benign view of such illusions. He remarks: "the institution of marriage may be as healthy as it is only because of the unrealistic optimism of many persons who marry" (p. 269). Fowers and his colleagues (Fowers, Lyons, Montel, & Shaked, 2001) provide evidence that positive illusions are an integral component of healthy marriages. It is necessary for spouses to exaggerate the positive qualities of their mates and their marriages in order to sustain long-term satisfying relationships. Couples who no longer are able to do so are on the road to disenchantment.

Emergence of Conflict

The longitudinal studies of marital interaction over the last decade, most notably those on couple communication, have greatly improved our understanding of marital satisfaction. Precisely which communication behaviors promote sustained relationship quality are somewhat inconsistent across studies and remain a matter of controversy among researchers (Stanley, Bradbury, & Markman, 2000). Gottman and his colleagues (Gottman, 1994; Gottman & Levenson, 2000) focus on conflict management behaviors and find that the extent to which couples argue is unrelated to divorce. It is the way they argue that matters. Gottman's team found that the presence in marital interaction of what they term the "five horsemen" (criticism, defensiveness, contempt, stonewalling, and belligerence) were problematic and strong predictors of dissatisfaction and eventual divorce. These patterns of arguing tend to produce a cascade effect—a downward spiral of increasingly toxic behavior by both spouses which eroded marital satisfaction and increased the probability of divorce. Newer research is examining the emotional tone of communication. The ability of spouses to regulate negative affect (accept or tolerate anger and criticism) and remain supportively engaged predicts high relationship satisfaction and may be mediated by attachment styles (Davila & Bradbury, 2001; Pasch & Bradbury, 1998).

170 • Handbook of Clinical Issues in Couple Therapy

Berscheid (1998) is critical of studies of marital interaction because they focus their attention on the relationship interior and overlook the environmental context in which it exists. Conflict researchers, in her view, assume that a conflict is a conflict. "How the conflict is 'handled' is considered critical to satisfaction and stability, whereas the dimensions of the conflict- its roots, its magnitude, its inherent 'resolvability'- receive little attention" (Berscheid, p. 448). It is easy to agree that partners equipped with better communication skills are better able to resolve their difference than those not so equipped. Some couples, however, are more likely than others to encounter more difficult problems, more often, and over a longer period of time. Warren's research on the economic problems of two income families speaks directly to this point. As of 2003, more children from middle class families will live through their parents' bankruptcy than their parents' divorce (Warren & Tyagi, 2003). Newer models of marital dissolution are beginning to address the effects of such environmental impacts (Stanley et al., 2000).

Another assumption of marital interaction research is that relationship satisfaction is the key determinant of its stability. Improving communication and conflict-resolution skills will decrease conflict and negative affect, thereby increasing relationship satisfaction, which should promote marital stability. This has special appeal to therapists because such skills are amenable to change. But the stability of a marriage is not necessarily related to the quality of its contents. We know little about how couples succeed in preventing divorce (or at least try to) in cases where it is predictable but does not actually occur (Rollie & Duck, 2006). Many couples stay in "non-voluntary" relationships in which they feel compelled to remain even if they would prefer not to. Obligation and resignation hold many of these marriages together, along with the lifestyle they have built and the history they have shared. Spouses in 80% of these marriages report pervasive unhappiness, conflict, or dissatisfaction in many facets of their relationship (Cuber & Harroff, 1965; Olson & Olson, 2000).

Divorce Theory

The social exchange theory (interdependence theory) of Thibaut and Kelley (1959) has been widely used by scholars interested in studying how individuals decide to continue or terminate relationships (e.g., Levinger, 1976; Spanier & Lewis, 1980). Levinger's cohesion model focuses primarily on factors that influence relational stability and dissolution, and asserts that cohesiveness in a relationship is a function of relational attractiveness, barriers to leaving, and alternative attractions. Relational attractiveness is based on rewards and costs. The extent to which the relationship provides more rewards than costs is associated with the degree of attraction or desire to stay in the relationship. Factors that make a relationship rewarding include income, status, affection, and companionship. These factors hold the marriage together. Cohesiveness is also influenced by perceptions of barriers to leaving the relationship. Barriers are relevant only insofar as one of the members desires to discontinue the relationship (Rollie & Duck, 2006). Barriers actively restrain individuals from leaving the relationship and include elements such as religious values, pressure from friends or the community to remain married, consideration of children's interests, impact on the spouse, or a sense of obligation to the marriage. Finally, cohesiveness is influenced by individuals' perception of alternative attractions. Regardless of the degree of relationship attractions and the presence of barriers, individuals are unlikely to leave a relationship unless alternatives to the relationship appear more attractive. These attractions may include a more satisfying single life or the possibility of remarriage.

Impact of Divorce

Not everyone who thinks about divorce actually gets one. As individuals wrestle with the divorce decision, the ambivalence and anguish they experience is reflected in the questions they ask. L. C. Sayer, England, and Allison (2005) refer to this as an evaluation of whether one would be better off divorced. Therapists rely on family research to inform the insights and perspectives they offer their clients. What conclusions can we draw about the emotional and economic impact of divorce on adults and on the health and welfare of their children?

Impact of Divorce on Partners

P. R. Amato (2000) notes that the polemical quality of divorce scholarship has profoundly shaped research on the effects of divorce, such that the greatest body of research focuses on the negative effects of divorce on children and (secondarily) on parents, with little emphasis on either positive effects for children or adults or the experiences of adult divorcees apart from their role as parents. When clients ask "would I be happier?" clinicians have inconsistent and mostly negative research to guide their answers. There is evidence that married couples are happier than their divorced counterparts (Waite & Gallagher, 2000). Married people also have better physical and emotional health, but only if they are happily married. People without a partner are likely to be depressed—but those in unhappy relationships are likely to be even more depressed (Elias, 2004; Ross, 1995). The determination as to whether one would be happier in the long run trying to improve a relationship rather than divorcing needs to be informed by more research (there is very little) about less than satisfactory but continuing marriages. With a greater awareness of the heightened psychological distress associated with staying in an unsatisfactory marriage for adults (Williams, 2003) and for children (Rodgers & Pryor, 1998), information about "good-enough marriages" (p. 18) is particularly useful now, at a time when states and the federal government are promoting marital preparation, covenant marriage, and legislation designed to make marital dissolution more difficult (Kitson, 2006).

172 • Handbook of Clinical Issues in Couple Therapy

Tashiro, Frazier, and Berman (2006) describe potential positive outcomes of divorce (coexisting with negative ones) as stress-related growth. These researchers distinguish two pathways by which adults' post-divorce outcomes might be better relative to their pre-divorce functioning. They call the first the *crisis-growth* pathway. In this model, the divorce is a painful or even traumatic and worldview-shattering experience with long-term effects. Nevertheless, some people are able to capitalize on the growth opportunity presented by this stressful event to become stronger, better people in various ways. They call the second the *stress-relief pathway*. In contrast to the previous model, in this pathway the divorce is not conceptualized primarily as a stressful event. Instead, the divorce represents the end of a miserable or abusive partnership and the beginning of a clearly better life alone or with another partner. Divorce, for at least half of all adults who experience it, is very unlike most other stressful experiences (and also unlike the experiences of the divorcing partners' children) in that it is a *deliberately chosen* event. If partners who choose to divorce did not anticipate deriving some important benefit from divorcing, it is difficult to understand why they would undertake the costly and difficult process of uncoupling from a spouse. Partners' anticipation of benefits from the divorce process may be more or less carefully considered and more or less accurate, but partners who believe that divorce offers no benefits likely do not choose to end their marriages (Tashiro et al.).

How common are positive outcomes of divorce? According to Tashiro et al. (2006), although rarely assessed (Ahrons, 1994; P. R. Amato, 2000), they are frequently reported when divorcees are asked specifically about them. For example, Hetherington (1993) found 2 years after the divorce, 75% of the women in the Virginia Longitudinal Study of Divorce and Re-marriage reported being happier in their present situations than in the final year of the marriage. In a later follow-up, roughly 30% of the divorced adults were classified as either Enhancers—people who, by 10 years post-divorce, had become more successful and resilient in many areas of their lives, and were currently involved in a satisfying remarriage—or Competent Loners, individuals who were enhanced in most areas of their lives post-divorce, but did not remarry and often did not wish to (Hetherington & Kelly, 2002). Freedom and independence are commonly reported benefits of divorce. In two studies, 19%–38% of women described increased freedom and independence as positive changes resulting from the divorce, as did 16%–25% of the men (Colburn, Lin, & Moore, 1992; Stewart, Copeland, Chester, Malley, & Barenbaum, 1997). In Reissman's (1990) study, freedom was among the most common themes mentioned by participants in her interviews; for women, the freedom generally was from subordination and their husbands' control, whereas men more commonly described it as freedom from obligation to their wives and families. Increased freedom post-divorce may be an especially important benefit for members of groups whose freedom often is curtailed by oppression

Divorce Therapy • **173**

or discrimination. Kitson (1992) found that 42% of non-White participants (compared with 33% of White participants) mentioned more freedom as a benefit of divorce. Increased freedom and independence may be one area where divorcees may actually be better off than their married counterparts. Goldsmith (1980) reported that by 1 year post-divorce, the vast majority (95%) of divorcees reported positive feelings toward their ex-spouse. One third chose to maintain regular contact with their divorced partner for the purposes of maintaining a friendship. What is clear from the existing research on positive outcomes following divorce, whether conceptualized as growth or as stress relief, is that it is at least as common to experience positive outcomes following divorce as negative ones, and that positive outcomes can coexist with even substantial psychological pain and stress (Tashiro et al.).

Predicting who is likely to report positive outcomes depends, in part, on who initiates the divorce. Initiating the divorce process ought to be associated with better adjustment and increased benefits from a divorce for a variety of reasons, including initiators' presumably greater sense of dissatisfaction with the marriage and greater sense of personal control over the divorce process (Pettit & Bloom, 1984; Vaughan, 1986). However, the research findings regarding the impact of initiator status on positive outcomes following divorce have been mixed. Two studies have reported few differences between initiators and non-initiators in post-divorce adjustment (Buehler, Hogan, Robinson, & Levy, 1986; Spanier & Thompson, 1984), whereas another found that differences in overall adjustment immediately following divorce had largely disappeared 18 months later (Pettit & Bloom). However, initiators, particularly if they were women, did report increasing benefits from divorce over time. Similarly, in a study by Wang and Amato (2000), initiators were more likely than non-initiators to view the divorce process as a good idea. Timing may also be a factor. Initiators may mourn the loss of the marriage and experience much of the stress of divorce while still married, leaving them free to take advantage of benefits and opportunities for growth when the divorce becomes final, whereas non-initiators may begin the stress–growth process only when the marriage actually ends (P. R. Amato, 2000; Emery, 1994). Initiators and non-initiators may also travel different pathways to positive outcomes, with divorce serving as a stress reliever for initiators, but as a crisis with attendant opportunities for growth for non-initiators.

Men consistently report deriving fewer (or no) benefits from the divorce compared with women (Colburn et al., 1992; Kitson, 1992; Marks & Lambert, 1998; Reissman, 1990), although findings are mixed with regard to the overall adjustment of men and women divorcees. Why might men report fewer positives from the divorce experience? P. R. Amato and Previti (2003) found consistent gender differences in the appraisals individuals made about the divorce, such that women were about twice as likely as men to attribute the cause of the divorce to their partners. It is likely that this gender difference

174 • Handbook of Clinical Issues in Couple Therapy

reflects the greater likelihood of men to behave badly in the marriage. In terms of specific causes of divorce, women are more likely than men to mention infidelity, mental or physical abuse, and alcohol or drug use (generally by their husbands, not themselves) as causing the divorce, a finding that echoes similar results in other studies (Bloom, Niles, & Tatcher, 1985; Cleek & Pearson, 1985; Kitson). These transgressions on the part of men may partially explain why women are more likely to initiate divorce and they may also serve to explain why men derive fewer benefits from the divorce process.

When we talk about the economic impact of divorce on parents, research has historically focused on mothers since they are the custodial parent 80% of the time (U.S. Bureau of the Census, 2000). Almost all studies have shown that mothers tumble down the economic ladder after they divorce. Two remedies to this seemed obvious: get more income for women and collect more from dads for their children.

Considerable progress has been made on the first solution. Today's mothers embark on single life with better educations, better job training, better legal support, and bigger paychecks than any women in history. Since 1960, women's wages have grown 10 times faster than men's wages. They have not yet caught up with men but they are gaining fast. Despite this progress, divorced women are less secure financially than they were in the mid-1980s. Single mothers are now more likely than any other group to file for bankruptcy including minorities and the poor. Since the beginning of the 1990s, the number of single mothers going broke has increased by 62%. And single mothers who have been to college, have a good job, and own their own home are 60% more likely to end up bankrupt than financially less well off women (Warren & Tyagi, 2003).

The second solution is based, in part, on studies that typically report divorced men are financially better off relative to divorced women (L. C. Sayer, 2006). One of the more recent findings of this sort is by Bianchi, Subaiya, and Kahn (1999) who found that divorced mothers' economic well-being is only 56% of the matched fathers. Braver (2006) contends such findings are misleading because they do not account for taxes and visitation expenses paid by the noncustodial father. When these are included, post-divorce women and men are largely equal economically. Another problem with the "make dads pay more" solution is that they already are paying. Changes in state laws in the mid-1990s have substantially increased child support compliance rates. Among fathers who are steadily employed, 80% or more of their ex-wives report receiving full payment (Braver, 1998; Meyer & Bartfield, 1996). Many fathers couldn't pay more even if ordered to by the courts. One third cannot even maintain their own household and live with parents or extended family (Sorensen, 1997). The idea that dads can pay enough to stabilize the divorced family is an illusion.

Warren and Tyagi (2003) argue that the financial predicament of a divorced mother starts long before her husband moves out. Her financial circumstances

Divorce Therapy • **175**

have worsened because today's marriages are in worse financial shape before the couple splits up. Families now need to commit two incomes to afford a home in a safe neighborhood with good schools. Families a generation ago were able to achieve this on a single income. By committing both paychecks to cover monthly expenses (mortgage debt, cars, child care, education) two income families are more vulnerable to financial crisis (job loss by either partner, illness, disability) because they no longer have a second income as a safety net. Families worry about how to make ends meet: How we will support ourselves, educate (or feed) our children, get affordable healthcare, finance our old age. The United States provides fewer services to families than does any other industrialized nation. And it is getting worse. As state and federal governments enact policies and fund programs with the explicit goal of promoting marriage and maintaining two-parent families (e.g., 1996 federal welfare reform legislation, Oklahoma Marriage Initiative), they simultaneously press for policies that transfer more financial responsibility and the attendant risk onto families (e.g., privatization of social security, health-care savings accounts). This is occurring in a climate where good paying jobs are moving off shore, companies are defaulting on pension plans, and banks encourage couples to assume risky and largely unsustainable debt to enhance their corporate profits. Couples incur credit card debt trying to hold on. Credit card debt has increased 6000% in 25 years (Warren & Tyagi). When a single mother loses the income of her ex-spouse, she must still meet these financial commitments including legal responsibility for all marital debts.

Impact of Divorce on Children

There is considerable evidence that young children do serve as a barrier to divorce. Affection for their children and concern for their children's welfare discourage some parents from dissolving their marriage (Heaton, 2002). Their children's welfare is certainly a significant question for those contemplating divorce and evidence indicates divorce is a very difficult crisis in the lives of the vast majority of children who experience it. Most children grieve over the divorce and wish it were not happening. However, when we take the longer view, the kids are for the most part alright (Barber & Demo, 2006).

As is the case with research on the effects of divorce on partners, research on children of divorce is biased toward finding negative effects (Barber & Demo, 2006). Studies more often find negative than positive effects because they are designed to do so—they use measures of distress, clinical samples, and informants (such as teachers) who expect more negative outcomes among children from divorced families (Tashiro et al., 2006). Some of the most vocal professionals describing the negative impact of divorce on children include Judith Wallerstein and her colleagues (Wallerstein & Blakeslee, 2003; Wallerstein & Lewis, 2004). They conducted a longitudinal study on a small sample of families and concluded that divorce has a long-term negative impact

176 • Handbook of Clinical Issues in Couple Therapy

on children. Five to ten years after divorce, they found approximately one third of the children showed signs of moderate-to-severe depression and other emotional problems. She describes a sleeper effect to divorce that impaired children's love relationships into their adult lives. On the basis of her findings, Wallerstein currently recommends parents should stay in marriages if no partner pathology is present. These findings are frequently cited by policy makers to make a case for the damaging effects of divorce on all children.

Although several authors have noted the need to assess the positive as well as negative effects of divorce on children (e.g., Dreman, 2000; Stewart et al., 1997), like the research on adults, existing data are piecemeal and unsystematic. Because few studies have specifically asked about positive outcomes and there are no standard measures of growth outcomes for children of divorce, it is difficult to estimate the frequency with which children are enhanced in at least some area of their life as a result of a divorce (Tashiro et al., 2006). Nonetheless, studies do show that there is a great deal of diversity in how children are affected by a divorce, and that for some children divorce can be a growth-promoting experience.

In one study, L. Kurdek and Siesky (1979) asked a direct question about growth, and 84% of parents reported that their children had acquired strengths that could be due to the divorce. In another study, Stewart et al. (1997) asked parents a more neutral question about major changes in their children, and 39% of the mothers reported that their child's behavior or personality had improved. In that same study, two thirds of the children could think of something that was better after the separation. Interestingly, when Rosen (1977) asked children the extent to which they had been *adversely* affected by the divorce, 43% reported that they did not feel they had been negatively affected in any way and 24% felt they had benefited. Heatherington and Kelly (2002) found that between 75% and 80% of children were doing rather well 6 years after the divorce. Resiliency was much more prominent than pathology in the children Heatherington studied. The first year was difficult for most children but it got better in the second year with most of the children going on to do well in their careers and relationships. Another major study by Buchanan, Machoby, and Dornbusch (1996) found children from divorced families to be functioning rather well as adolescents. They had good relationships with both parents although contact with the non-custodial parent tended to drop off over time (Buchanan & Heiges, 2001).

What about the 25%–30% of children that do not cope well? High levels of conflict and hostility between parents both before and after divorce have consistently been related to poorer outcomes—anxiety, withdrawal, low self-esteem, depression, aggression, and lower social competence—in children and adolescents (Barber & Demo, 2006). Ahrons (2004) reports that one third of children of divorce she studied lived in pre-divorce families characterized by frequent fighting between their parents. Sometimes divorce can provide relief from that conflict. This appears to fit with the stress-relief pathway to growth proposed by Tashiro et al. (2006) with one notable difference. Unlike adults who initiate divorce because they anticipate some benefits, children do not generally have a choice in the matter. Nonetheless, children at times view divorce as involving relief of stress and can experience better adjustment than those who remain in high-conflict homes. For example, when asked about their initial reactions to the news of the divorce, 10% of the children in one study said they were relieved and 31% said they were glad their parents had divorced (Stewart et al., 1997). When children were interviewed 2 years later and asked about what was better, more than 25% noted the absence of conflict (implying a relief from stress). Similarly, when children were asked about some of the good things about the divorce, the most common answer (43%) in another study was that Mom and Dad don't fight (L. Kurdek & Siesky, 1980). This theme was also reported by college students whose parents had divorced (Harvey & Fine, 2004). Students described their parents' separation as the happiest time of their lives, said their home was more peaceful as a result, and that they were glad they didn't have to continue to live with constant fighting. In another study of college students, Laumann-Billings and Emery (2000) asked questions related to feelings about divorce. In two samples, 62%–81% of the participants agreed that divorce was the right thing for their parents, 62%–74% agreed that their parents seemed happier, and 46%–48% agreed that the divorce relieved a lot of tensions in their own lives. The notion of divorce as stress relief for children also is consistent with the finding that parental conflict has a more negative effect on children than does divorce (e.g., Doucet & Aseltine, 2003; Stewart et al.) and that, when parental conflict is high, divorce is associated with positive outcomes for children (P. Amato & Booth, 1997).

However, divorce does not always reduce conflict. Twenty-five percent of couples are still highly conflictual 6 years after the divorce (Hetherington & Kelly, 2002). A surprising finding is that in low-conflict burnout (devitalized) marriages where the divorce may have come as a complete surprise (about two thirds of marriages), there was more negative impact on children's emotional adjustment than in high-conflict marriages that ended in divorce (Thompson & Amato, 1999). This finding is somewhat difficult to interpret because we have no way of knowing how these children's lives would have progressed if their parents had stayed together (Lebow, 2006).

Even when viewed as a traumatic event Tashiro et al. (2006) found evidence of growth in many areas of children's lives. The most commonly reported positive change involved improved relationships with parents. In contrast to their relationships before the divorce, children whose parents have divorced reported being closer to and having better relationships with both their custodial (usually the mother) and non-custodial parent. They also feel that their parents are "nicer" and 25% of the children reported that their relationships with their siblings had improved following the divorce (Harvey & Fine, 2004;

178 • Handbook of Clinical Issues in Couple Therapy

Stewart et al., 1997). Increased responsibility and maturity have been described as positive changes stemming from the divorce by both parents and children. Although they regret having had to do so, children report they are proud of themselves for having mastered new responsibilities such as the care of younger children, especially when they are given tasks that are age appropriate and not overwhelming (Tashiro et al.).

Surviving Divorce

Just as the evaluation of relationship quality depends on what we expect of marriage, expectations color our perception of divorce. Is there such a thing as a "good divorce"? Some commentators view divorce as a catastrophe for most families and see few if any positive outcomes. Whitehead (1997), for example, proposes we stop celebrating family diversity and re-stigmatize divorce as a way to preserve the inherent benefits of the nuclear family. Against the assumption that divorce is a disaster that solidifies a lasting enmity between the partners, to the detriment of their children, one can instead find a different pattern whereby couples maintain civility and cooperative parenting. The Binuclear Family Study, led by sociologist Constance Ahrons (1994), interviewed 98 divorcing couples after their divorce. At the 1-year point, 50% of the ex-spouses had amicable relations while the other 50% did not. In half the cases, the divorce was a bad one, and harmful to family members; in the other half, the divorcing spouses had preserved family ties and provided children with two parents and healthy families.

Ahrons maintains that

> in a good divorce a family with children remains a family. The family undergoes dramatic and un-settling changes in structure and size, but its functions remain the same. The parents- as they did when they were married-continue to be responsible for the emotional, economic, and physical needs of their children.
>
> **(Ahrons, 1994, p. 3)**

The couples she studied represented a broad range of post-divorce relationships. In 12% of the cases, couples were what Ahrons termed *Perfect Pals*, friends who called each other often and brought their common children and new family ties together on holidays or for outings or other activities. This was a minority pattern among the "good divorces." More often (38%), the couples were *Cooperative Colleagues*, who worked well together as co-parents, but did not attempt to share holidays or be in constant touch—occasionally, they might share children's important occasions such as birthdays. Ex-spouses might talk about extended family, friends, or work. They still had areas of conflict but were able to compartmentalize them and keep them out of the collaboration that they wanted to maintain for their children (Ahrons). Family rituals play

Divorce Therapy • **179**

an important role for these families as they learn to adapt to changes in their family structure, routines, and relationships and gain a new sense of identity (Imber-Black, 2002).

Other divorcing couples were the *Angry Associates* (25%) or *Fiery Foes* (25%) that we often think of in conjunction with divorce. Ahrons's overall point is that the "good divorce" does not end a family but instead produces a binuclear family; two households, one family. She argues that we must "recognize families of divorce as legitimate." To encourage more "good divorces," it is important to dispel the "myth that only in a nuclear family can we raise healthy children" (p. 4). People often find what they expect, and social models of a functional post-divorce family have been lacking.

Ahrons (2004) recently re-interviewed 173 children from 89 of the original families in her Binuclear Family Study. Now averaging 31 years of age, 79% think that their parents' decision to divorce was a good one, and 78% feel that they are either better off than they would have been, or else not that affected. Twenty percent, however, did not do so well, with "emotional scars that didn't heal" (p. 44), a finding consistent with Hetherington and Kelly's (2002) research. Ahrons judges that the prime factor affecting outcomes was how the parents related to each other in terms of avoiding conflict. She concludes from her research that it is possible for families of divorce to still function as families. To do so, parents need to "accept that your child's family will expand to include non-biological kin" (p. 252). Divorce and the new relationships that follow can produce a divorce-extended family, a kinship system that is produced by links between ex-spouses and their new spouses and significant others and on beyond to their extended kin. Some post-divorce extended families find they can enjoy and benefit from connections to one another even when there had earlier been conflict, and tensions sometimes resurface (Kleinfield, 2003).

The U.S. family court system has initiated and sponsored a variety of interventions and services to help families cope with toxic conflict during the divorce transition. Mediation is the most widely known, but newer cooperative and parallel co-parenting education programs have been developed for high-conflict parents, especially those (about 10%) who pursue extended litigation, court hearings, and trials, as a way to resolve their hostility (Johnston, 2000). The goal of cooperative parenting is to enable parents to work together to resolve their disagreements. In contrast, parallel parenting encourages parents to disengage from each other at least initially until conflict subsides, rather than seeking cooperation too quickly (Blaisure & Geasler, 2006). Family therapists, in addition to providing individual and group counseling for partners recovering from divorce, are developing therapeutic models for high-conflict couples (e.g., Lebow & Rekart, 2007) and are increasingly offering their services in these emerging dispute resolution programs. The effectiveness of these court-connected programs is largely unknown at present. Parents consistently indicate they are receptive to mandatory programs, satisfied with them, and

180 • Handbook of Clinical Issues in Couple Therapy

report finding them useful in promoting positive interactions with their children, and reducing conflict with the other parent (Blaisure & Geasler). However, the extent to which the information provided is actively employed by parents in their relationship with each other or their child, or whether there is any change in the child's well-being has yet to be determined (Lamanna & Riedmann, 2009).

A Perspective for Marital Therapists

People appear to be deeply ambivalent about divorce (P. R. Amato & Irving, 2006). In their 2000 survey, Amato et al. (2003) found only a minority of people (17%) agreed with the statement, "It's okay for people to get married thinking that, if it does not work out, they can always get a divorce." However, the majority of people continue to believe that personal happiness is more important than remaining in an unhappy marriage. Similarly, 66% of people believed that children are better off in a divorced family than in "an unhappy marriage in which parents stay together mainly for the kids." At the same time, however, 64% of people believed that children always or frequently are harmed when parents get divorced (P. R. Amato & Irving). It appears that many people today hold contradictory, unresolved views on divorce.

Public confusion about divorce is reflected in debate among family scholars. Some scholars view the retreat from marriage and the corresponding spread of single-parent families as a cause for alarm (Waite & Gallagher, 2000; Whitehead, 1997). These scholars believe that American culture has become inordinately preoccupied with the pursuit of personal happiness. Other scholars view the rise in marital instability with less concern. They point out that divorce provides a second chance at happiness for adults and an escape from a dysfunctional and aversive home environment for many children. Moreover, because children are adaptable and can develop successfully in a variety of family structures, the spread of alternatives to mandatory lifelong marriage is, as we have previously noted, not necessarily destructive. Coontz (2000) believes that it is the increasing legitimization of these diverse family forms that drives most of the contemporary debate over values and policy.

In their historical review of divorce trends, P. R. Amato and Irving (2006) point out that divorce has always been controversial.

> During the Colonial era, sharp differences existed between New England and the southern colonies about whether divorce should be allowed at all. In the latter part of the 18th century, divorce became a matter of widespread and contentious debate in the media and among policy makers. After World War I, many observers (including many social scientists) believed that the family was in danger, with harmful consequences for children and society in general. During the last two decades of the 20th century, this debate emerged yet again among policymakers, the media,

the general public, and family scholars. Curiously, many of the arguments that are advanced today (both in favor of and against divorce) are similar, if not identical, to arguments made in previous centuries (p. 54).

P. R. Amato and Irving (2006) attribute differences in opinion about the meaning and implications of divorce to the de-institutionalization of marriage, a trend predicted by family sociologist Ernest Burgess in the first part of the twentieth century. Burgess argued that marriage was in a process of transition (due to industrialization and urbanization) from a social institution to a private arrangement based on companionship. In the old model, once married, spouses were expected to sacrifice their personal goals, if necessary, for the sake of the marriage, as well as the economic survival and security of the family. In the new model commitment is to the spouse, not the institution of marriage. Companionate marriage is held together not by bonds of social obligation but by ties of love, friendship, and common interest. People in the United States have always expected marriage to be a source of love and emotional support. However, the notion that marriage should be based primarily on mutual satisfaction began to gain widespread public acceptance only during the early decades of the twentieth century. Psychologists, educators, and social service providers applied these ideas in their professional practice, and it was in this context that marital therapy emerged as a discipline, with its goal being to help couples achieve emotional closeness and sexual satisfaction through improved communication and conflict management (P. R. Amato & Irving).

Amato (P. R. Amato & Irving, 2006) believes our love–hate relationship with divorce centers around two concerns. On the one hand, people value the freedom to leave unhappy unions, correct earlier mistakes, and find greater happiness with new partners. On the other hand, people are deeply concerned about social stability, tradition, and the overall impact of high levels of marital instability on the well-being of children. The clash between these two concerns reflects a fundamental contradiction within marriage itself; that is, marriage is designed to promote both institutional and personal goals. Happy and stable marriages meet both of these goals without friction. In contrast, when unhappy spouses wrestle with the decision to end their marriages, they are caught between their desire to further their own personal happiness and their sense of obligation to others, including their spouses, their children, their churches, and their communities.

In making the choice to practice marital therapy or divorce therapy, therapists confront these same contradictions. The goal of treatment can shift many times as the clients' position changes. It requires therapists to monitor their own values so the focus of treatment is determined by the client and not their own biases. This is particularly challenging in the current climate where being neutral to outcome (i.e., where divorce is a legitimate option) is viewed as anti-family (Doherty, 2006).

182 • Handbook of Clinical Issues in Couple Therapy

A frustration for many therapists trying to assess whether the focus of treatment should lean toward saving the marriage or helping it dissolve is that it might already be too late. At least one partner is too far down the disaffection track. For a marriage that is this emotionally bankrupt, selling couples on "staying together for the sake of the kids," honoring their vows no matter how miserable, or giving up the happiness they imagine having with another would likely be ethically unpalatable. What little research we have on the effects of remaining in such long-term marriages is not encouraging. In addition to highlighting the barriers to divorce, pro-marriage therapists promise (or at least imply) they will increase relationship attractions. If couples are willing to commit to "working" on the marriage (see Kipnis [2003] for a sobering analysis of marriage as work) the therapist can enrich their relationship so it is "good enough" (Doherty, 2006, p. 39). They don't offer guarantees of course, but it begs one of the most difficult questions both therapists and clients might ask—how good is that? (Kitson, 2006).

References

Ahrons, C. (1994). *The good divorce: Keeping your family together when your marriage comes apart*. New York: Harper Collins.

Ahrons, C. (2004). *We're still family*. New York: Harper Collins.

Ahrons, C. (2005). Divorce: An unscheduled family transition. In B. Carter & M. McGoldrick (Eds.), *The expanded family lifecycle: Individual, family, and social perspectives* (3rd Ed.). New York: Allyn & Bacon.

Amato, P., & Booth, A. (1997). *A generation at risk: Growing up in an era of family upheaval*. Cambridge, MA: Harvard University Press.

Amato, P. R. (2000). The consequences of divorce for adults and children. *Journal of Marriage and Family, 62*, 1269–1287.

Amato, P. R., Johnson, D., Booth, A., & Rogers, S. J. (2003). Continuity and change in marriage between 1980 and 2000. *Journal of Marriage and the Family, 65*, 1–22.

Amato, P. R., & Irving, S. (2006). Historical trends in divorce in the United States. In M. Fine & J. Harvey (Eds.), *Handbook of divorce and relationship dissolution* (pp. 41–57). New Jersey: Lawrence Erlbaum.

Amato, P. R., & Previti, D. (2003). People's reasons for divorcing: Gender, social class, the life course, and adjustment. *Journal of Family Issues, 24*, 602–626.

Barber, B., & Demo, D. (2006). The kids are alright (at least, most of them): Links between divorce and dissolution and child well-being. In M. Fine & J. Harvey (Eds.), *Handbook of divorce and relationship dissolution* (pp. 289–311). New Jersey: Lawrence Erlbaum.

Baxter, L. A. (1984). Trajectories of relationship disengagement. *Journal of Social and Personal Relationships, 1*, 29–48.

Belluck, P. (2000, April 21). States declare war on divorce rates before any "I dos's." *New York Times*. Retrieved from www.nytimes.com/2000/04/21/us/states-declare-war-on-divorce-rates-before-any-i-dos.html?scp=7&sq=&st=nyt

Berscheid, E. (1998). A social psychological view of marital dysfunction. In T. N. Bradbury (Ed.), *The developmental course of marital dysfunction*. Cambridge, England: Cambridge University Press.

Berscheid, E. (2006). The changing reasons for marriage and divorce. In M. Fine & J. Harvey (Eds.), *Handbook of divorce and relationship dissolution* (pp. 223–240). New Jersey: Lawrence Erlbaum.

Bianchi, S. M., Subaiya, L., & Kahn, J. R. (1999). The gender gap in the economic well-being of nonresidential fathers and custodial mothers. *Demography, 36*, 195–203.

Blaisure, K. R., & Geasler, M. J. (2006). Educational interventions for separating and divorcing parents and their children. In M. Fine & J. Harvey (Eds.), *Handbook of divorce and relationship dissolution* (pp. 575–602). New Jersey: Lawrence Erlbaum.

Bloom, B. L., Niles, R. L., & Tatcher, A. M. (1985). Sources of marital dissatisfaction among newly separated persons. *Journal of Family Issues, 6*, 359–373.

Bohannan, P. (1970). The six stations of divorce. In P. Bohannan (Ed.), *Divorce and after.* New York: Doubleday.

Boss, P. G. (2002). *Family stress management: A contextual approach.* Thousand Oaks, CA: Sage.

Braver, S. L. (1998). *Divorced dads.* New York: Tarcher/Putnam.

Braver, S. L. (2006). Consequences of divorce for parents. In M. Fine & J. Harvey (Eds.), *Handbook of divorce and relationship dissolution* (pp. 313–337). New Jersey: Lawrence Erlbaum.

Buchanan, C. M., & Heiges, K. L. (2001). When conflict continues after the marriage ends: Effects of post-divorce conflict in children. In J. H. Grych & F. D. Fincham (Eds.), *Interpersonal conflict and child development: Theory, research and applications.* New York: Cambridge University Press.

Buchanan, C. M., Machoby, E. E., & Dornbusch, S. M. (1996). *Adolescents after divorce.* Cambridge, MA: Harvard University Press.

Buehler, C., Hogan, M. J., Robinson, B., & Levy, R. (1986). The parental divorce transition: Divorce-related stressors and well-being. *Journal of Divorce, 9*, 61–81.

Cleek, M. G., & Pearson, T. A. (1985). Perceived causes of divorce: An analysis of interrelationships. *Journal of Marriage and the Family, 47*, 179–183.

Colburn, K., Lin, P. L., & Moore, M. C. (1992). Gender and divorce experience. *Journal of Divorce and Remarriage, 17*, 87–108.

Coontz, S. (2000). Historical perspectives on family diversity. In D. H. Demo, K. R. Allen, & M. A. Fine (Eds.), *Handbook of family diversity* (pp. 15–31). New York: Oxford University Press.

Council on Families in America. (1996). Marriage in America: A report on the nation. In D. Popenoe, J. B. Elshtain, & D. Blackenhorn (Eds.), *Promises to keep: Decline and renewal of marriage in America* (pp. 293–318). Lanham, MD: Rowman & Littlefield.

Cuber, J., & Harroff, H. (1965). *The significant Americans.* New York: Random House.

Davila, J., & Bradbury, T. (2001). Attachment insecurity and the distinction between unhappy spouses who do and do not divorce. *Journal of Family Psychology, 15*, 371–393.

De Munck, V. C., & Korotayev, A. (1999). Sexual equality and romantic love: A reanalysis of Rosenblatt's study on the function of romantic love. *Cross-Cultural Research: The Journal of Comparative Social Science, 33*, 265–277.

Doherty, W. J. (2002). How therapists harm marriages and what we can do about it. *Journal of Couple and Relationship Therapy, 1*(2), 1–17.

Doherty, W. J. (2006, March/April). Couples on the brink. *Psychotherapy Networker*, 30–39.

184 • Handbook of Clinical Issues in Couple Therapy

Doucet, J., & Aseltine, R. (2003). Childhood family adversity and the quality of marital relationships in young adulthood. *Journal of Social and Personal Relationships, 20,* 818–842.

Dreman, S. (2000). The influence of divorce on children. *Journal of Divorce and Remarriage, 32,* 41–71.

Elias, M. (2004, March 4). Marriage taken to heart. *USA Today,* Section D, p. 8.

Emery, R. E. (1994). *Renegotiating family relationships: Divorce, child custody, and mediation.* New York: Guilford.

Fowers, B. J., Lyons, E., Montel, K. H., & Shaked, N. (2001). Positive illusions about marriage among married and single individuals. *Journal of Family Psychology, 15,* 95–109.

Glenn, N. D. (1991). The recent trend in marital success in the United States. *Journal of Marriage and the Family, 53,* 261–270.

Goldsmith, J. (1980). Relationships between former spouses: Descriptive findings. *Journal of Divorce, 4,* 1–20.

Gottman, J. M. (1994). *What predicts divorce.* New Jersey: Lawrence Erlbaum Associates.

Gottman, J. M., & Levenson, R. W. (2000). The timing of divorce: Predicting when a couple will divorce over a 14-year period. *Journal of Marriage and the Family, 62,* 737–745.

Gottman, J. M., & Notarius, C. I. (2002). Marital research in the 20th century and a research agenda for the 21st century. *Family Process, 41,* 159–198.

Gurman, A. S., & Kniskern, O. P. (1981). Editor's note to "Divorce and divorce therapy." In A. S. Gurman & D. P. Kniskern (Eds.), *Handbook of family therapy.* New York: Brunner/Mazel.

Guttman, J. (1993). *Divorce in psychosocial perspective: Theory and research.* New Jersey: Lawrence Erlbaum.

Harvey, J., & Fine, M. (2004). *Children of divorce: Stories of loss and growth.* New Jersey: Lawrence Erlbaum Associates.

Heaton, T. B. (2002). Factors contributing to increasing marital stability in the United States. *Journal of Family Issues, 23*(3), 392–409.

Heckert, D. A., Nowak, T. C., & Snyder, K. A. (1998). The impact of husbands' and wives' relative earnings on marital disruptions. *Journal of Marriage and Family, 60*(3), 690–703.

Hetherington, E. M. (1993). An overview of the Virginia Longitudinal Study of Divorce and Remarriage with a focus on early adolescence. *Journal of Family Psychology, 7,* 39–56.

Hetherington, E. M., & Kelly, J. (2002). *For better or worse: Divorce reconsidered.* New York: W. W. Norton.

Huston, T. L., & Houts, R. M. (1998). The psychological infrastructure of courtship and marriage: The role of personality and compatibility in romantic relationships. In T. N. Bradbury (Ed.), *The developmental course of martial dysfunction* (pp. 114–151). Cambridge, England: Cambridge University Press.

Imber-Black, E. (2002). Family rituals-from research to the consulting room and back again: Comment on the special section. *Journal of Family Psychology, 16,* 445–446.

Johnston, J. R. (2000). Building multidisciplinary professional partnerships with the court on behalf of high-conflict families and their children: Who needs that kind of help? *University of Little Rock Law Review, 22,* 453–479.

Kaslow, F. W. (1995). The dynamics of divorce therapy. In R. H. Mikesell, D. Lusterman, & S. McDaniel (Eds.), *Integrating family therapy: Handbook of family psychology and systems theory.* Washington, DC: American Psychological Association.

Kayser, K., & Rao, S. S. (2006). Process of disaffection in relationship breakdown. In M. Fine & J. Harvey (Eds.), *Handbook of divorce and relationship dissolution* (pp. 201–221). Mahwah, NJ: Lawrence Erlbaum.

Kessler, S. (1975). *The American way of divorce: Prescriptions for change.* Chicago, IL: Nelson-Hall.

Kipnis, L. (2003). *Against love: A polemic.* New York: Random House.

Kitson, G. C. (1992). *Portrait of divorce: Adjustment to marital breakdown.* New York: Guilford.

Kitson, G. C. (2006). Divorce and relationship dissolution research: Then and now. In M. Fine & J. Harvey (Eds.), *Handbook of divorce and relationship dissolution* (pp. 15–40). Mahwah, NJ: Lawrence Erlbaum.

Kleinfield, N. R. (2003, December 24). Around tree, smiles even for wives no. 2 and 3. *New York Times.*

Kurdek, L., & Siesky, A., Jr. (1979). An interview study of parent's perceptions of their children's reactions and adjustments to divorce. *Journal of Divorce, 3,* 5–17.

Kurdek, L., & Siesky, A., Jr. (1980). Children's perceptions of their parent's divorce. *Journal of Divorce, 3,* 339–378.

Kurdek, L. A. (1999). The nature and predictors of the trajectory of change in marital quality for husbands and wives over the first 10 years of marriage. *Developmental Psychology, 35*(5), 1283–1296.

Lamanna, M., & Riedmann, A. (2009). *Marriages and families: Making choices in a diverse society* (10th ed.). Belmont, CA: Thomson Wadsworth.

Laumann-Billings, L., & Emery, R. (2000). Distress among young adults from divorced families. *Journal of Family Psychology, 14,* 671–687.

Lebow, J. (2006, March/April). The marriage preservation debate: Re-examining the research on divorce. *Psychotherapy Networker, 30*(2), 83–86.

Lebow, J., & Rekart, K. N. (2007). Integrated family therapy for high-conflict divorce with disputes over child custody and visitation. *Family Process, 46,* 79–91.

Lee, L. (1984). Sequences in separation: A framework for investigating the endings of personal relationships. *Journal of Social and Personal Relationships, 1,* 49–74.

Leonard, K. E., & Roberts, L. J. (1998). Martial aggression, quality, and stability in the first year of marriage: Findings from the Buffalo newlywed study. In T. N. Bradbury (Ed.), *The developmental course of martial dysfunction* (pp. 44–73). Cambridge, England: Cambridge University Press.

Levinger, G. (1976). A social psychological perspective on divorce. *Journal of Social Issues, 32,* 21–47.

Lindahl, K., Clements, M., & Markman, H. (1998). The development of marriage: A 9-year perspective. In T. N. Bradbury (Ed.), *The developmental course of martial dysfunction* (pp. 205–236). Cambridge, England: Cambridge University Press.

Marks, N. F., & Lambert, J. D. (1998). Marital Status continuity and change among young and midlife adults: Longitudinal effects on psychological well-being. *Journal of Family Issues, 19,* 652–686.

McCubbin, H. I., & Patterson, J. M. (1983). Family transitions: Adaptation to stress. In H. I. McCubbin & C. R. Figley (Eds.), *Stress and the family* (Vol. 1, pp. 5–25). New York: Brunner/Mazel.

Meyer, D. R., & Bartfield, J. (1996). Compliance with child support orders in divorce cases. *Journal of Marriage and Family, 58,* 201–212.

Olson, D. H., & Olson, A. K. (2000). *Empowering couples: Building on your strengths.* Minneapolis, MN: Life Innovations.

Ono, H. (1998). Husbands' and wives' resources and marital dissolution. *Journal of Marriage and Family, 60*(3), 674–689.

186 • Handbook of Clinical Issues in Couple Therapy

Pasch, L., & Bradbury, T. (1998). Social support, conflict and the development of marital dysfunction. *Journal of Consulting and Clinical Psychology, 66*, 219–230.

Pettit, E. J., & Bloom, B. L. (1984). Whose decision was it? The effects of initiator status on adjustment to marital disruption. *Journal of Marriage and the Family, 46*, 587–595.

Reissman, C. K. (1990). *Divorce talk: Men and women make sense of personal relationships*. New Brunswick, NJ: Rutgers University Press.

Riehl-Emde, A., Volker, T., & Willie, J. (2003). Love, an important dimension in marital research and therapy. *Family Process, 42*, 253–267.

Rodgers, B., & Pryor, J. (1998). *Divorce and separation: The outcomes of children*. York, U.K.: Rowntree Foundation.

Rollie, S., & Duck, S. (2006). Divorce and dissolution of romantic relationships: Stage models and their limitations. In M. Fine & J. Harvey (Eds.), *Handbook of divorce and relationship dissolution* (pp. 223–240). Mahwah, NJ: Lawrence Erlbaum.

Rosen, R. (1977). Children of divorce: What they feel about access and other aspects of the divorce experience. *Journal of Clinical Child Psychology, 6*, 24–27.

Ross, C. E. (1995). Re-conceptualizing marital status as a continuum of social attachment. *Journal of Marriage and Family, 57*, 129–140.

Salts, C. J. (1985). Divorce stage theory and therapy: Therapeutic implication throughout the divorcing process. In D. H. Sprenkle (Ed.), *Divorce therapy*. New York: Haworth.

Sayer, L., & Bianchi, S. M. (2000). Women's economic independence and the probability of divorce. *Journal of Family Issues, 21*, 906–942.

Sayer, L. C. (2006). Economic aspects of divorce and relationship dissolution. In M. Fine & J. Harvey (Eds.), *Handbook of divorce and relationship dissolution* (pp. 385–406). New Jersey: Lawrence Erlbaum.

Sayer, L. C., England, P., & Allison, P. (2005). *Gains to marriage, relative resources, and divorce initiation*. Unpublished manuscript.

Schoen, R., Astone, N., Rothert, K., Standish, N., & Kim, Y. (2002). Women's employment, marital happiness and divorce. *Social Forces, 81*, 643–662.

Sorensen, E. (1997). A national profile of nonresidential fathers and their ability to pay child support. *Journal of Marriage and Family, 59*, 785–797.

South, S. J. (2001). Time dependent effects of wives' employment on marital dissolution. *American Sociological Review, 66*, 226–43.

Spanier, G., & Thompson, L. (1984). *Parting: The aftermath of separation and divorce*. Thousand Oaks, CA: Sage.

Spanier, G. B., & Lewis, R. A. (1980). Marital quality: A review of the seventies. *Journal of Marriage and the Family, 42*, 825–839.

Sprenkle, D. (1985). *Divorce therapy*. New York: Haworth Press.

Sprenkle, D. (1989). The clinical practice of divorce therapy. In M. Textor (Ed.), *The divorce and divorce therapy handbook* (pp. 171–195). New Jersey: Jason Aronson.

Sprenkle, D. (1996). Divorce therapy. In F. Piercy, D. Sprenkle, J. Wetchler, & Associates (Eds.), *Family therapy sourcebook* (2nd ed.). New York: Guilford.

Stanley, S. M., Bradbury, T. N., & Markman, H. J. (2000). Structural flaws in the bridge from basic research on marriage to interventions for couples. *Journal of Marriage and the Family, 62*, 256–264.

Stewart, A. J., Copeland, A. P., Chester, N. L., Malley, J. E., & Barenbaum, N. B. (1997). *Separating together: How divorce transforms families*. New York: Guilford.

Tashiro, T., Frazier, P., & Berman, M. (2006). Stress related growth following divorce and relationship dissolution. In M. Fine & J. Harvey (Eds.), *Handbook of divorce and relationship dissolution* (pp. 361–384). Mahwah, NJ: Lawrence Erlbaum.

Teachman, J. D. (2003). Premarital sex, premarital cohabitation, and the risk of subsequent marital dissolution among women. *Journal of Marriage and the Family, 65,* 444–456.

Thibaut, J. M., & Kelley, H. H. (1959). *The social psychology of groups.* New York: Wiley.

Thompson, R., & Amato, P. (1999). *The post divorce family.* Thousand Oaks, CA: Sage.

U.S. Bureau of the Census. (2000). *Census 2000.* Washington, DC. Retrieved February 22, 2007 from http://www.census.gov

Van Laningham, J., Johnson, D., & Amato, P. (2001). Marital happiness, marital duration, and the U-shaped curve: Evidence from a five-wave panel study. *Social Forces, 79,* 1313–1341.

Vaughan, D. (1986). *Uncoupling: Turning points in intimate relationships.* New York: Oxford University Press.

Waite, L. J., & Gallagher, M. (2000). *The case for marriage: Why married people are happier, healthier, and better off financially.* New York: Doubleday.

Wallerstein, J. S., & Blakeslee, S. (2003). *What about the kids? Raising your children before, during, and after divorce.* New York: Hyperion.

Wallerstein, J. S., & Lewis, J. M. (2004). The unexpected legacy of divorce: Report of a 25-year study. *Psychoanalytic Psychology, 21*(3), 353–360.

Wang, H., & Amato, P. R. (2000). Predictors of divorce adjustment: Stressors, resources, and definitions. *Journal of Marriage and the Family, 62,* 655–668.

Warren, E., & Tyagi, A. W. (2003). *The two income trap.* New York: Basic Books.

Whitehead, B. (1997). *The divorce culture.* New York: Knopf.

Williams, K. (2003). Has the future of marriage arrived? A contemporary examination of gender, marriage and psychological well-being. *Journal of Health and Social Behavior, 44,* 81–98.

11
Remarital Issues in Couple Therapy

MARCIA L. MICHAELS

Contents

Remarriage and Stepfamily Literature	191
Remarriages Follow Multiple Losses	191
Dreams Are Built on Unrealistic Expectations	191
Remarried Couple Relationship	192
Family Relationships That Impact the Couple	193
Family Boundary Issues	194
Lesbian, Gay, Ethnic Minority Stepfamilies	195
Recommendations for Clinicians	196
Assessment of the Family System	196
Education Is Key to Creating a Context for Change	197
Strengthen the Couple Bond and Develop Co-Parenting Team	298
Nurture All Family Relationships to Create a New Family Identity	200
Conclusion	201
References	201

Remarriage is quickly becoming a societal norm. Statistics reveal that approximately 40%–50% of legal marriages are remarriages for one or both partners and about 65% of those remarriages include children from a former relationship (U.S. National Center for Health Statistics, 1991). Furthermore, remarriages are ending in divorce more rapidly than in the past (Castro Martin & Bumpass, 1989; U.S. Bureau of the Census, 1992a), occurring in less than 4 years after a divorce (Wilson & Clarke, 1992). In addition, cohabitation has significantly increased in the last half of the twentieth century, is more common prior to a second marriage (Bumpass & Sweet, 1989; Smock & Gupta, 2002), and is more unstable than legal marriages (Axinn & Thornton, 1992; L. Bumpass & Lu, 2000). More than half of cohabiting couples contain one partner who has been married previously (L. Bumpass & Lu; U.S. Bureau of the Census, 1998), and it is important to note that a majority of children enter stepfamilies through the less traditional paths of nonmarital birth and cohabitation (L. L. Bumpass, Raley, & Sweet, 1995). These statistics reveal that a significant number of couples and their families are experiencing serial marriages or marriage-like relationships during their lifetime. Moreover, there is substantial evidence that these multiple family disruptions have a negative

190 • Handbook of Clinical Issues in Couple Therapy

impact on the mental health of all family members (e.g., Amato & Keith, 1991a, 1991b; O'Leary, Christian, & Mendell, 1994). Some of these couples and families will seek therapy; however, they may not identify themselves as remarried or as members of stepfamilies due to the stigma associated with divorce, remarriage, and cohabitation.

These statistics on remarriage make it evident that marriage and family therapists and other mental health professionals will encounter remarried couples in their clinical practice. When that happens, clinicians need to think of the couple in the context of a stepfamily; as part of a larger and more complex family system that may be struggling through family reorganization issues and other unique challenges faced by stepfamilies. Clinicians must have knowledge of the remarriage and stepfamily literature and be able to distinguish between typical issues encountered in first marriages and those encountered in remarriages. Why is this important? Because there is evidence that therapy may not be successful if clinicians are unaware of the unique challenges facing remarried couples or if they believe that rules and roles found in first marriages can be applied to remarriages (McGoldrick & Carter, 2005; Pasley, Rhoden, Visher, & Visher, 1996; Visher, Visher, & Pasley, 1997). Consider these comments from stepfamily members who were asked about their therapy experiences (Visher et al.).

> We saw three therapists in a period of five years before we got to one who knew anything AT ALL about stepfamilies. Our situation continued to deteriorate, and we couldn't understand what's wrong that we couldn't be helped. (p. 207)

> She [the therapist] seemed judgmental and she generalized too much or acted as if our problems were insignificant and we exaggerated their importance. (p. 206)

> The therapist did not have stepfamily experience. She treated us like we were a family with children. She had no concept of the bonding problem, alienation, or loyalty problems. (p. 207)

In a related study, Pasley et al. (1996) found that 48.6% (N = 267) of respondents identified "the therapist's lack of training, skill, and knowledge about stepfamily issues as the most unhelpful aspect of the process and structure of therapy" (p. 353). These findings emphasize the need for clinicians to know the current research and clinical literature on stepfamilies, and to be aware of their biases so they do not negatively impact therapy.

This chapter outlines research and clinical findings on remarriage and stepfamilies to provide clinicians with a general understanding of the issues and challenges associated with this family form. This literature allows mental health professionals to place the remarried couple within a larger systemic and developmental context; to understand how history, family structure, societal values, and relationship dynamics impact the couple relationship.

Furthermore, knowledge of this literature allows clinicians to educate and normalize the experiences of remarried couples seen in therapy. For simplicity, the terms "marital," "remarriage," and "remarried couple" will be used throughout the chapter, however, the terms are meant to include couples in long-term committed relationships who are not legally married. Due to the dearth of research on lesbian, gay, and ethnic minority remarried couples, limited findings are presented here.

Remarriage and Stepfamily Literature

Remarriages Follow Multiple Losses

Many remarriages and cohabiting relationships form shortly after the dissolution of the prior relationship. In fact, about 30% of divorced adults remarry within 1 year of their divorce (Wilson & Clarke, 1992). These transitions represent significant changes and losses that affect every family member leading to changes in relationships, roles, and family identity. The family may not have enough time to adjust before another transition occurs. Furthermore, these changes involve profound losses that must be mourned. Adults have lost an intimate partner and the dreams they shared for their future together. Lifestyles may have radically changed due to a move from the family home and loss of income. Noncustodial parents lose opportunities to maintain the close parent–child relationship they had prior to the divorce, and may face competition with a stepparent when the former partner remarries. Children have lost their "family," that sense of safety and security that comes with knowing their parents will always be there to protect them. With a remarriage, children lose the full attention of the custodial parent to a new partner and perhaps to stepsiblings. If these losses are not resolved, they can interfere with the health of the couple relationship and the stepfamily formation process (Burt & Burt, 1996; Ganong, Coleman, & Weaver, 2002; Sager et al., 1983; Visher & Visher, 1996). Therefore, clinicians should consider that unresolved loss may be a contributing factor to the problems being presented in therapy.

Dreams Are Built on Unrealistic Expectations

Although there is evidence that healthy, successful remarried couples have realistic expectations about the new marriage and family (e.g., Kelley, 1995), many couples enter a remarriage with unrealistic expectations (Kaufman, 1993; Papernow, 1993; Visher & Visher, 1996). This occurs, in part, because couples are using a nuclear family model as their guide. Remarried couples believe the new family will be no different than a nuclear family, so they fail to discuss role and relationship expectations or issues associated with joining two families. There is a sense that the families will effortlessly join together and all family members will instantly love one another. Stepparents and stepchildren are expected to immediately feel love for each other. Further, it is believed that stepchildren will readily accept discipline from their stepparent.

192 • Handbook of Clinical Issues in Couple Therapy

These unrealistic expectations place too much pressure on fragile relationships. Stepparents experience guilt when they do not feel love for their stepchildren that is equal to the love for their biological children. Children have no emotional bond with the stepparent so they become resistant toward the stepparent who tries to discipline. In addition, biological and stepparents may find they do not agree on the appropriate disciplinary approach to take with the children. Consequently, expectations fail to materialize and everyone feels hurt, confused, frustrated, angry, and disillusioned. If these feelings are not expressed in a constructive manner, family relationships will suffer and may eventually deteriorate beyond repair. In addition, if unrealistic expectations are not replaced with more realistic expectations, more pain, frustration, and anger will occur. Clinicians who are familiar with the remarriage and stepfamily literature are a valuable resource for remarried couples because they help couples identify realistic expectations for their family, and they know the harm caused by using the nuclear family as a model.

Remarried Couple Relationship

Remarried couples do experience a brief honeymoon period in which their marital satisfaction is higher than couples in their first marriage (Deal, Stanley Hagan, & Anderson, 1992). However, the honeymoon does not last long. Longitudinal research reveals that remarried couples experience sharper declines in marital quality than couples in their first marriage (Booth & Edwards, 1992; J. H. Bray & Berger, 1993). In part, the decline may be due to the presence of children and/or unrealized expectations. When children are present, couples do not have time alone to form a strong marital bond, and they may find that their expectations of a loving and supportive partner and co-parent do not materialize. Whatever the reason for the decline, divorce is a viable option for these couples (Booth & Edwards, 1992). Some have speculated that the willingness to divorce may be linked to findings that remarriages are based on pragmatic considerations to a greater degree than first marriages (e.g., Ganong & Coleman, 1994). For example, divorced women may be looking for someone to relieve their loneliness, to lessen the financial burden of single parenthood, and to help raise the children.

Even though some remarriages may fail because they were formed for pragmatic reasons, other research evidence implicates unhealthy family interactions. For instance, remarried couples rate their families as less cohesive, more distant, and more conflicted than intact families (Brand & Clingempeel, 1987; Hetherington, 1993; Pill, 1990). Remarried couples display more coercion and negativity and less positive interactions than do couples in their first marriage (Anderson & Greene, 1999; J. Bray, 1988). There is also evidence that remarried couples display less competence at problem solving, conflict resolution, and communication (J. Bray; Larson, & Allgood, 1987). Longitudinal research reveals that interactions between spouses become more negative and less positive over time, especially when children move into adolescence (Hetherington, 1993). In fact, many of the couple's conflicts focus on children and discipline (Hobart, 1991). Therefore, a clinician would be wise to consider contributing factors outside of the couple relationship (e.g., stepparent's disciplining practices with the stepchildren) when addressing unhealthy couple communication patterns.

Power and equity in the remarital relationship reflects the nontraditional quality of the stepfamily form. For instance, remarried couples view their relationship as more egalitarian regarding shared childcare and household tasks than do first married couples (Hetherington, 1993). In addition, research reveals that women have more power than men in remarriages and are more active in decision making (Hobart, 1991). Reasons for this distribution of power may be related to increased responsibility as a single parent and the greater resources women bring to the remarriage.

In general, findings on the remarried couple relationship emphasize the need for healthy communication, problem resolution, and conflict management skills. Further, establishing a strong couple relationship will allow the family to accommodate disagreements on issues related to the family formation process (e.g., defining roles, rules, and responsibilities).

Family Relationships That Impact the Couple

Research on stepfamilies has revealed that the stepparent–stepchild relationship can affect marital and family satisfaction (J. H. Bray & Berger, 1993; Clingempeel, Brand, & Ievoli, 1984; Crosbie-Burnett, 1984). Since stepfather families make up 82% of remarried families (U.S. Bureau of the Census, 1992a, 1992b), research has focused on the stepfather–stepchild relationship. That research reveals the lack of a socially prescribed role as a major source of stress for stepparents (Peck, Bell, Waldren, & Sorrell, 1988). Role ambiguity leads families to adopt a traditional parent role. In fact, remarried mothers often want their new husbands to step into the disciplinary role immediately (e.g., Santrock, Sitterle, & Warshak, 1988). However, remarried families who adopt the traditional nuclear family model find that problems arise. That is, when stepfathers try to assume a disciplinarian role too soon after family formation, it can negatively impact the marital relationship and impede family integration (Hetherington, Cox, & Cox, 1982; Visher & Visher, 1982).

Given the lack of clear role expectations, shared family history and paternal bond with their stepchildren, it is not surprising that many stepfathers initially have distant relationships with their stepchildren. When compared to nondivorced fathers, stepfathers make few attempts to monitor or control behavior, and they lack closeness and rapport with their stepchildren (Hetherington, 1993; Stanley Hagan, Hollier, O'Connor, & Eisenberg, 1992). Unfortunately, stepfathers tend to become more disengaged as parents over time (Anderson & Greene, 1999; Hetherington) and there is evidence that child behavior may be driving that disengagement. That is, when stepfathers' efforts to form a positive stepparent–stepchild bond are rebuked by their stepchildren, they begin to withdraw from that relationship (Hetherington & Clingempeel, 1992). As a result, the stepfather–stepchild relationship becomes more negative over time (J. Bray, 1992). Negativity in the stepparent–stepchild relationship also adversely affects the marital relationship (Clingempeel et al., 1984). Therefore, efforts to improve the stepfather–stepchild relationship may benefit the marital relationship.

Approximately 86% of custodial parents are biological mothers (U.S. Bureau of the Census, 1992a, 1992b), so the majority of studies on noncustodial parents focus on biological fathers. There is evidence that noncustodial biological fathers have a positive effect on child adjustment (Hetherington, 1989). However, few children may benefit from that relationship because noncustodial parental contact begins a rapid decline in the first year after divorce (Furstenberg, Morgan, & Allison, 1987; Seltzer, 1991). The level of noncustodial parent involvement cannot be predicted from the predivorce relationship with the child (Hetherington, 1993). Instead, the quality of the custodial–noncustodial parent relationship, satisfaction with one's parenting performance, and legal custody status have been identified as factors that influence noncustodial parental involvement (Hetherington, 1993; Madden-Derdich & Leonard, 2000; Minton & Pasley, 1996). The best predictor of continued noncustodial father involvement is the relationship with the custodial parent and perceived involvement in decision making (Braver et al., 1993). Hetherington (1989) found that the positive effect that noncustodial involvement had on children was contingent upon the health of the co-parental relationship. That is, noncustodial father involvement has a positive influence on children only when the relationship between the custodial and noncustodial parent is low in conflict. It is important to note that a cooperative parental relationship benefits both parents and children, and therefore, the health of the entire family.

Family Boundary Issues

Stepfamilies are a complex family form because children are members of two households. When two households are involved, they share legal, financial, and child-rearing rights and responsibilities. There is evidence that children in families with joint physical or legal custody (versus sole-custody) are better adjusted, family relationships are more positive and biological co-parental relationships are less conflicted (Bauserman, 2002). However, movement between two households gives rise to logistical and emotional complications. For instance, children may live in two homes with conflicting household rules. Adjusting to two sets of rules and expectations may be difficult for children and it may increase conflict between the former partners (Visher & Visher, 1988). In an effort to gain more control, families may adopt a more traditional family model and tighten the boundaries around the immediate family so that the other household is excluded. This will only lead to further conflict between former partners and loyalty conflicts for children because they feel forced to choose between parents (Ganong & Coleman, 2004). When the relationship between biological parents is cooperative, stepfamilies report greater cohesion, less conflict, and more open communication (Giles-Sims, 1987). In addition, remarried couples and stepfamilies are more successful when they display greater flexibility in their definition of family and family roles and when coordinating activities that involve child movement between households (Kelley, 1995).

Lesbian, Gay, Ethnic Minority Stepfamilies

Although there is very little research on lesbian-headed and gay stepfamilies, there are indications that these couples and their families share similar challenges to those found in heterosexual remarried couples and stepfamilies (Fredriksen-Goldsen & Erera, 2003; Lynch, 2000; Lynch & McMahon-Klosterman, 2006; van Dam, 2004). For instance, they enter new relationships with unrealistic expectations, they experience boundary ambiguity and divided loyalties, and they have no clearly defined roles or a family model to use as a guide (Fredriksen-Goldsen & Erera, 2003; Lynch, 2000). Furthermore, there is evidence that lesbian-headed stepfamilies need to be flexible and adaptive just like heterosexual stepfamilies (Fredriksen-Goldsen & Erera, 2003; Lynch & McMahon-Klosterman, 2006).

Even with these similarities, lesbian-headed and gay stepfamilies are considered a distinct family form. That is, they share a similar structure to heterosexual stepfamilies but they also share gender composition with lesbian and gay families (Lynch, 2000). The most prevalent type of lesbian-headed stepfamily is formed after the divorce of a heterosexual relationship (i.e., children are born into a heterosexual relationship but the biological mother later forms a lesbian relationship). Inherent in this type of stepfamily is the issue of sexual identity of the birth mother (Fredriksen-Goldsen & Erera, 2003). Integrating a new sexual identity, while creating a new stepfamily, further complicates the already challenging process of family formation. Thus, clinicians should be aware of the identity transformation process individuals go through (Lynch, 2004a, 2004b).

Another difference between lesbian-headed/gay stepfamilies and heterosexual stepfamilies is the extent of discrimination experienced by lesbian and gay stepfamilies (Fredriksen-Goldsen & Erera, 2003; Lynch, 2000; van Dam, 2004). Fear of discrimination and/or a desire to protect the children may lead lesbian and gay parents to alter their behavior (Lynch & McMahon-Klosterman, 2006). For instance, they may not show affection toward each other in front of the children or introduce their partner to others. The biological parent may be the only parent attending parent–teacher conferences to shelter the children from discrimination or to protect the family from a custody battle should a former partner become aware of the parent's new sexual identity. Further complicating the process of family formation in lesbian and gay stepfamilies is the fact that they are unable to legitimize their couple relationship in most states and countries (Berger, 1998).

Most of the research on racial/ethnic minority remarried couples is limited to information on the prevalence and stability of marriages and remarriages. First, there is evidence that African Americans spend more years in a nontraditional female-headed household than Latinos or Anglos (L. Bumpass, Sweet, & Castro Martin, 1990). Second, research suggests that marriages and remarriages are much less stable for African Americans than for Anglos or Latinos (Bramlett & Mosher, 2001). Finally, remarriage rates for African Americans are about one quarter of those for Anglos, and Latino rates of remarriage are about half those of Anglos (L. Bumpass et al., 1990). The limited research available on stepfamily dynamics provides some evidence that African American stepfamilies show similarities to Anglo stepfamilies (Berger, 1998; Fine, McKenry, Donnelly, & Voydanoff, 1992), however, African American families also display important culturally based strengths. That is, African American families are receptive to divergent family configurations that include members with no biological connections and tend to display permeable family boundaries that allow children to move between extended kin networks (Berger, 1998). This cultural characteristic seems to provide an environment in which the stepfamily configuration is viewed as normal and legitimate. Therefore, some of the typical challenges faced by Anglo stepfamilies may be less of an issue for African American stepfamilies.

Clinicians who choose to work with lesbian, gay, and ethnic minority remarried couples should be knowledgeable of the remarriage and stepfamily literature, however, they must also be aware of lesbian and gay issues, and be sensitive to ethnic/cultural differences in their clients. More importantly, clinicians must come to terms with their values regarding cohabitation, divorce, and remarriage, and their biases toward lesbians, gays, and people of color to ensure that their values and biases do not negatively influence therapy.

Recommendations for Clinicians

Assessment of the Family System

All clinicians conduct assessments of the client system when therapy begins. In the case of remarried couples, the assessment phase of treatment has unique qualities in that both assessment and intervention occur simultaneously. Throughout the assessment, the clinician is normalizing the experiences of remarried couples and educating them about the processes of family reorganization and formation. This may be the first time remarried couples have expressed their feelings and discussed their experiences with an outsider due to the stigma associated with remarriage. Combining assessment and intervention in this manner encourages hope for the success of their new marital relationship as well as trust in the therapist's ability to help the couple.

Assessment with a remarried couple should include a thorough assessment of the family system even if the couple is presenting only with marital relationship issues. Include an assessment of the immediate family subsystems (i.e., marital, stepparent–stepchild, biological parent–child) and extended family relationships (e.g., biological parents, relationship of new partner to former partner). Since the marital relationship is affected by other family relationships, this information is necessary to formulate a treatment plan. The genogram and timelines can be helpful tools for assessment. The genogram can provide clinicians with important information on family relationships (e.g., communication patterns, coalitions, boundaries) and family composition (e.g., custody and visitation arrangement) while allowing clients to see the complexity of their family system. It also offers an opportunity for clinicians to normalize feelings the couple express about their relationship. Assessing the developmental stage of each family is also helpful. For instance, the wife may have young children (e.g., 3 and 5 years old) while the new husband may have older adolescents (e.g., 16 and 17 years old). Each of these families are at different stages of the family life cycle and those differences may be a contributing factor to the problems being presented to the clinician. For example, the 16 and 17 year old adolescents may be more reticent to accept a stepmother into their family, and would be much less interested in doing "family activities" than would 3 and 5 year old children. In addition, the stepfather who is nearing the launching phase of parenthood may become discouraged to find himself with two young children, especially if he was looking forward to decreased parental responsibilities. Finally, a timeline of significant events assists in the identification of issues that may be contributing factors to the marital problems presented in therapy (e.g., multiple affairs, a quick succession of family transitions that do not allow for successful family reorganization).

The assessment provides the clinician with important information on family history, developmental issues, and current family functioning. Clinicians must quickly assess the health of all family subsystems to identify the focus of treatment that will assist the couple in their efforts to strengthen their bond and form a new family. This rapid assessment of such a large quantity of information may seem overwhelming even to mental health professionals trained as family therapists. However, the intensity and complexity of issues presented by remarried couples and stepfamilies demand quick synthesis of the important information. Key to the clinician's ability to formulate a successful course of treatment is a thorough knowledge of remarriage and stepfamily issues and respect for the challenges faced by remarried couples (Pasley et al., 1996).

Education Is Key to Creating a Context for Change

Education about remarriage and stepfamily issues and challenges is a major part of early treatment. It is typical for remarried couples and stepfamilies to use the traditional nuclear family as their model and to enter the remarriage with unrealistic expectations. Consequently, they come to therapy dissatisfied with their progress in creating a strong marital relationship, co-parenting team, and wonder if their children will ever accept the new family. When remarried couples are unaware of the normal challenges stepfamilies face such as role ambiguity, loyalty conflicts, and unrealistic expectations, they are unable to understand why they are experiencing so many problems. Clinicians are able to use their knowledge on remarriage to normalize the feelings their clients are experiencing. Both education and normalization assist remarried couples in developing more realistic expectations and promote a context to make healthy changes in the couple and family relationships.

Stepfamilies have their own unique family formation process that can take as few as 4 years and as many as 12 years to complete (Papernow, 1993). Several models of stepfamily development have been proposed that have utility for clinicians (e.g., J. H. Bray & Berger, 1993; Mills, 1984; Papernow, 1993). These models describe individual and family developmental stages that stepfamilies go through and include developmental tasks that should be accomplished at each stage. For instance, Papernow's model includes three stages of family development. In the early stage of development, the family is divided along biological lines with strong parent–child coalitions governing the rules and routines followed in the stepfamily. During this stage, family members need to constructively express their feelings and expectations for family members. Unrealistic expectations must be identified and discarded for more reasonable ones. During the middle stage of development, parent–child coalitions weaken and restructuring of the stepfamily begins to occur. At this point, new boundaries and subsystems emerge which strengthen the family as a unit. During this stage, family members need to openly discuss differences between family cultures, and hear the experiences of both insiders and outsiders (e.g., men experience being an outsider when their wives bring biological children to the remarriage). Steps to constructively influence the reorganization of the family will strengthen the family as a unit. In the final stage, a new family is formed, complete with its own rules, traditions, and identity. By the time the family reaches this stage of development, the stepparent role has been clearly defined and accepted, as have other new roles within the family. The marital relationship is typically strong and healthy at this point.

Understanding the process of stepfamily formation, with all of its complexities, provides a context for clinicians working with remarried couples. When clinicians provide information on the developmental process to remarried couples, it highlights the accomplishments already achieved by the couple and family and it provides a roadmap to guide them through the remainder of the process.

Strengthen the Couple Bond and Develop Co-Parenting Team

A healthy marital relationship is the bond that holds the family together, and it should be the focus of early therapy sessions even if other issues are presented.

Since conflict in other family relationships, such as the stepparent–stepchild relationship and custodial–noncustodial parent relationship, put strain on the marital relationship, couples will need help in managing the stress until it can be resolved. Education can relieve some of the pressure because it helps couples put their problems into context, and it normalizes the thoughts and emotions they have been experiencing. Once initial work with the couple is complete, the clinician may want to work with multiple family configurations simultaneously (e.g., the couple, stepparent–stepchild, and biological parent–child subsystems, and the family unit).

Depending upon the needs of the couple, therapy may include a focus on communication or negotiation skills, but there will also be an emphasis on forming a boundary around the marital subsystem. Remarried couples are in a unique situation because they bring children into the home which makes it very difficult to focus their efforts on nurturing the marital bond. Depending upon the age of the children, the length of the time between divorce and remarriage, and the biological parent–child relationship prior to the remarriage (e.g., child may have taken on a confidant role with parent after the divorce), creating a boundary around the marital system may be met with great resistance. In that case, the therapist can help the couple find creative ways to strengthen their relationship and still nurture the biological parent–child relationship. It is important to note that these couples also may be experiencing typical presenting problems usually brought into couple therapy. The problems may be unrelated to the family reorganization process, but they may be exacerbated by that process.

When working with a remarried couple, it is equally important to establish a co-parenting team, especially since many fights revolve around children and discipline (Hobart, 1991). There is no established role definition for a stepparent, so the couple will have to define the stepparent's role. The role may be different with each child due to the age of the child, the child's personality, and living situation (i.e., living in the home full time versus occasional visits). Setting aside time for stepparents to spend with their stepchildren will be essential for establishing a bond. Once a bond begins to form, it becomes easier for stepparents to enforce rules in the home. Usually, rules that were previously established by the biological parent will be used in the new family until the new co-parenting team slowly establishes a new set of rules. Children are typically less resistant to the old rules so allowing those rules to stand decreases the incidence of resistance. Since it is typically inadvisable for stepparents to immediately begin disciplining their stepchildren, the couple will need to discuss how the stepparent can be supportive of the biological parent when disciplining the children. Once the co-parent team is established, it is recommended they act as a "united front" to their children especially when enforcing rules and discipline. This display of a strong co-parenting team may also decrease the resistance children have to the marital relationship.

200 • Handbook of Clinical Issues in Couple Therapy

When working with the couple, homework assignments focusing on building a healthy stepparent–stepchild relationship can be utilized to decrease conflict in the marital relationship and to speed the process of successful family formation.

A third couple relationship in this family, and another relationship that impacts the remarried couple, is the co-parent team of biological parents. It is difficult, yet essential, to keep the co-parenting relationship with the former partner from intruding on the remarried couple relationship when both share parenting responsibilities (Crosbie-Burnett, 1989). The fact that there are so many couple subsystems in the family emphasizes the challenges faced by remarried couples. That is, the remarried couple assumes marital and parental roles yet parenting is also shared with the former partner (and maybe the partner's new spouse). Distinctions between marital subsystems and parental subsystems may be fuzzy in these families so efforts to distinguish the tasks and responsibilities associated with each role can be very helpful. To compound the issue associated with multiple parents, stepparents have no legal relationship with their stepchildren and therefore have no rights (Fine & Fine, 1992). This is another reason why parenting decisions are typically made by the biological parents. If a healthy biological co-parent relationship has been established and conflict kept to a minimum, intrusion on the remarried couple relationship should be minimal. If the relationship is not healthy, the clinician may want to assist the biological parents in their efforts to evaluate the effects of their parenting on the children. Any therapy with this couple subsystem would focus solely on their co-parenting responsibilities and should not be done if it would negatively impact the health of the remarried couple relationship. Since it is possible to change the biological co-parenting team relationship without directly working with the noncustodial biological parent, therapy with only the custodial parent is sufficient. Homework assignments that encourage custodial parents to find ways to include the noncustodial parent in their children's lives can improve their co-parenting relationship (e.g., offer to send pictures of the children to the noncustodial parent when the noncustodial parent cannot attend a special event).

Nurture All Family Relationships to Create a New Family Identity

Many times, it is conflict in other family relationships that bring remarried couples in for treatment. The bond between the biological parent and child may need repair if this relationship was neglected after the remarriage or if the child lost an important role when the new partner arrived (e.g., confidant to biological parent). Biological parents may continue to feel anger and resentment toward their former partner. Therefore, they may need encouragement to show respect for each other and learn to cooperate even when they disagree with some of the former partner's parenting practices. Improvement in this relationship positively impacts the children because they experience fewer loyalty conflicts. Stepparents need time with their stepchildren so they can form a closer relationship, and biological parents need to allow this to happen. Clinicians may find that biological parents will state that they want their new partner to form a close relationship with their biological children, but then block every attempt to do so. Clinicians who can simultaneously focus on each of these relationships while strengthening the marital relationship will see change occur more readily.

Creating an environment that is inclusive of all family members encourages cooperation, open communication, and reduces loyalty conflicts. Encouraging families to establish new family traditions, and take time for family activities, creates a shared history and a sense of family identity. Homework assignments focusing on the creation of new family traditions, rituals, and identity, along with activities to build and nurture family relationships, reinforce the therapeutic work occurring in session. All of these efforts will improve the couple relationship, strengthen the family unit, and speed up the family formation process.

Conclusion

Given the increasing number of remarriages and cohabiting relationships, mental health professionals will encounter remarried couples in their clinical practice. These couples present unique issues and challenges for clinicians; issues that may be overlooked, if the professional is unfamiliar with the literature. To be effective with these couples, clinicians must be aware of the unique factors that negatively and positively impact the marital relationship. Stepfamilies are a complex family form so clinicians will need to quickly assess complex family interaction patterns, and manage multiple and competing relationships as the family members create a new family. These families can be a challenge to clinicians, but they are a very rewarding challenge.

References

Amato, P. R., & Keith, B. (1991a). Parental divorce and the well-being of children: A meta-analysis. *Psychological Bulletin, 100,* 26–46.

Amato, P. R., & Keith, B. (1991b). Parental divorce and adult well-being: A meta-analysis. *Journal of Marriage and the Family, 53,* 43–58.

Anderson, E. R., & Greene, S. M. (1999). Children of stepparents and blended families. In W. K. Silverman & T. H. Ollendick (Eds.), *Developmental issues in the clinical treatment of children* (pp. 342–357). Boston: Allyn and Bacon.

Axinn, W. G., & Thornton, A. (1992). The relationship between cohabitation and divorce: Selectivity or causal influence? *Demography, 29,* 357–374.

Bauserman, R. (2002). Child adjustment in joint-custody versus sole-custody arrangements: A meta-analytic review. *Journal of Family Psychology, 16,* 91–102.

Berger, R. (1998). *Stepfamilies: A multi-dimensional perspective.* Binghamton, NY: Haworth Press.

Booth, A., & Edwards, J. N. (1992). Starting over: Why remarriages are more unstable. *Journal of Family Issues, 13,* 179–194.

202 • Handbook of Clinical Issues in Couple Therapy

Bramlett, M. D., & Mosher, W. D. (2001). *First marriage dissolution, divorce, and remarriage: United States*. Advance data from vita and health statistics; no. 323. Hyattsville, MD: National Center for Health Statistics.

Brand, E., & Clingempeel, G. (1987). The interdependence of marital and stepparent-stepchild relationships and children's psychological adjustment: Research findings and clinical implications. *Family Relations, 36*, 140–145.

Braver, S. L., Wolchik, S. A., Sandler, I. N., Sheets, V. L., Fogas, B., & Bay, R. C. (1993). A longitudinal study of noncustodial parents: Parents without children. *Journal of Family Psychology, 7*, 1–16.

Bray, J. (1988). Children's development during early remarriage. In M. Hetherington & J. Arastech (Eds.), *Impact of divorce, single parenting, and stepparenting on children* (pp. 279–298). Hillsdale, NJ: Erlbaum.

Bray, J. (1992). Family relationships and children adjustment in clinical and nonclinical stepfather families. *Journal of Family Psychology, 6*, 60–68.

Bray, J. H., & Berger, S. H. (1993). Developmental issues in StepFamilies Research Project: Family relationships and parent-child interactions. *Journal of Family Psychology, 7*, 76–90.

Bumpass, L., & Lu, H. H. (2000). Trends in cohabitation and implications for children's family contexts in the United States. *Population Studies, 54*, 29–41.

Bumpass, L., Sweet, J., & Castro Martin, T. (1990). Changing patterns of remarriage. *Journal of Marriage and the Family, 52*, 747–756.

Bumpass, L. L., Raley, R. K., & Sweet, J. A. (1995). The changing character of stepfamilies: Implications of cohabitation and nonmarital childbearing. *Demography, 32*, 425–436.

Bumpass, L. L., & Sweet, J. A. (1989). National estimates of cohabitation. *Demography, 26*, 615–625.

Burt, M. S., & Burt, R. B. (1996). *Stepfamilies: The step by step model of brief therapy*. New York: Brunner/Mazel.

Clingempeel, W. G., Brand, E., & Ievoli, R. (1984). Stepparent-stepchild relationships in stepmother and stepfather families: A multimethod study. *Family Relations, 33*, 465–473.

Crosbie-Burnett, M. (1984). The centrality of the step relationship: A challenge to family theory and practice. *Family Relations, 33*, 459–464.

Crosbie-Burnett, M. (1989). Impact of custody arrangement and family structure on remarriage. *Journal of Divorce, 13*, 1–16.

Deal, J. E., Stanley Hagan, M., & Anderson, E. R. (1992). The marital relationship in remarried families. *Monographs of the Society for Research in Child Development, 57*(2–3, Serial No. 227), 73–93.

Fine, M. A., & Fine, D. R. (1992). Recent changes in laws affecting stepfamilies: Suggestions for legal reform. *Family Relations, 41*, 334–340.

Fine, M. A., McKenry, P. C., Donnelly, B. W., & Voydanoff, P. (1992). Perceived adjustment of parents and children: Variations by family structure, race, and gender. *Journal of Marriage and the Family, 54*, 118–127.

Fredriksen-Goldsen, K. I., & Erera, P. I. (2003). Lesbian-headed stepfamilies. *Journal of Human Behavior in the Social Environment, 8*, 171–187.

Furstenberg, F. F., Morgan, P. S., & Allison, P. D. (1987). Paternal participation and children's well-being after marital dissolution. *American Sociological Review, 52*, 695–701.

Ganong, L. H., & Coleman, M. (1994). *Remarried family relationships*. Thousand Oaks, CA: Sage.

Ganong, L. H., & Coleman, M. (2004). *Stepfamily relationships: Development, dynamics, and interventions*. New York: Plenum.

Ganong, L. H., Coleman, M., & Weaver, S. (2002). Relationship maintenance and enrichment in stepfamilies: Clinical applications. In J. H. Harvey & A. Wenzel (Eds.), *A clinician's guide to maintaining and enhancing close relationships* (pp. 105–129). Mahwah, NJ: Lawrence Erlbaum.

Giles-Sims, J. (1987). The stepparent role: Expectations, behavior, sanctions. *Journal of Family Issues, 5*, 116–150.

Hetherington, E. M. (1989). Coping with family transitions: Winners, losers, and survivors. *Child Development, 60*, 1–14.

Hetherington, E. M. (1993). An overview of the Virginia longitudinal study of divorce and remarriage with a focus on early adolescence. *Journal of Family Psychology, 7*, 39–56.

Hetherington, E. M., & Clingempeel, W. G. (1992). Coping with marital transitions: A family systems perspective. *Monographs of the Society for Research in Child Development, 57*(2–3, Serial No. 227), 1–14.

Hetherington, E. M., Cox, M., & Cox, R. (1982). Effects of divorce on parents and children. In M. E. Lamb (Ed.), *Nontraditional families* (pp. 233–288). Hillsdale, NJ: Lawrence Erlbaum.

Hobart, C. (1991). Conflict in remarriages. *Journal of Divorce and Remarriage, 15*, 69–86.

Kaufman, T. S. (1993). *The combined family: A guide to creating successful step-relationships.* New York: Plenum Press.

Kelley, P. (1995). *Developing healthy stepfamilies: Twenty families tell their stories.* New York: Harrington Park Press.

Larson, J. H., & Allgood, S. M. (1987). A comparison of intimacy in first-married and remarried couples. *Journal of Family Issues, 8*, 319–331.

Lynch, J. M. (2000). Considerations of family structure and gender composition: The lesbian and gay stepfamily. *Journal of Homosexuality, 40*, 81–95.

Lynch, J. M. (2004a). Becoming a stepparent in gay/lesbian stepfamilies: Integrating identities. *Journal of Homosexuality, 48*, 45–60.

Lynch, J. M. (2004b). The identity transformation of biological parents in lesbian/gay stepfamilies. *Journal of Homosexuality, 47*, 91–107.

Lynch, J. M., & McMahon-Klosterman, K. (2006). Guiding the acquisition of therapist ally identity: Research on the GLBT stepfamily as resource. In J. J. Bigner & A. R. Gottlieb (Eds.), *Interventions with families of gay, lesbian, bisexual, and transgender people: From the inside out* (pp. 123–150). New York: Haworth Press.

Madden-Derdich, D. A., & Leonard, S. A. (2000). Parental role identity and fathers' involvement in coparental interaction after divorce: Fathers' perspectives. *Family Relations, 49*, 311–318.

Martin, T. C., & Bumpass, L. L. (1989). Recent trends in marital disruption. *Demography, 26*, 37–51.

McGoldrick, M., & Carter, B. (2005). Remarried families. In B. Carter & M. McGoldrick (Eds.), *The expanded family life cycle: Individual, family, and social perspectives* (3rd ed., pp. 417–435). New York: Pearson.

Mills, D. (1984). A model for stepfamily development. *Family Relations, 33*, 365–372.

Minton, C., & Pasley, K. (1996). Fathers' parenting role identity and father involvement: A comparison of nondivorced, divorced, nonresident fathers. *Journal of Family Issues, 17*, 26–45.

O'Leary, K. D., Christian, J. L., & Mendell, N. R. (1994). A closer look at the link between marital discord and depressive symptomatology. *Journal of Social and Clinical Psychology, 13*, 33–41.

Papernow, P. L. (1993). *Becoming a stepfamily: Patterns of development in remarried families.* San Francisco: Jossey-Bass.

204 • Handbook of Clinical Issues in Couple Therapy

Pasley, K., Rhoden, L., Visher, E. B., & Visher, J. S. (1996). Successful stepfamily therapy: Clients' perspectives. *Journal of Marital and Family Therapy, 22,* 343–357.

Peck, C., Bell, N., Waldren, T., & Sorrell, G. (1988). Patterns of functioning in families in remarried and first-married couples. *Journal of Marriage and the Family, 50,* 699–708.

Pill, C. J. (1990). Stepfamilies: Redefining the family. *Family Relations, 39,* 186–193.

Sager, C. J., Brown, H. S., Crohn, H., Engel, T., Rodstein, E., & Walker, E. (1983). *Treating the remarried family.* New York: Brunner/Mazel.

Santrock, J. W., Sitterle, K. A., & Warshak, R. A. (1988). Parent-child relationships in stepfather families. In P. Bronstein & C. P. Cowen (Eds.), *Fatherhood today: Men's changing roles in the family* (pp. 144–165). New York: Wiley.

Seltzer, J. A. (1991). Relationships between fathers and children who live apart: The father's role after separation. *Journal of Marriage and the Family, 53,* 79–101.

Smock, P. J., & Gupta, S. (2002). Cohabitation in contemporary North America. In A. Booth & A. C. Crouter (Eds.), *Just living together: Implications of cohabitation on families, children, and social policy* (pp. 53–84). Mahwah, NJ: Lawrence Erlbaum.

Stanley Hagan, M., Hollier, E. A., O'Connor, T. G., & Eisenberg, M. (1992). Parent-child relationships in nondivorced, divorced single-mother, and remarried families. *Monographs of the Society for Research in Child Development, 57*(2–3, Serial No. 227), 94–148.

U.S. Bureau of the Census. (1992a). *Marriage, divorce, and remarriage in the 1990's* (Current Population Reports P23–180). Washington, DC: U.S. Government Printing Office.

U.S. Bureau of the Census. (1992b). *Studies in marriage and the family: Married couple families with children* (Current Population Reports Series P-23, No. 162). Washington, DC: U.S. Government Printing Office.

U.S. Bureau of the Census. (1998). *Unpublished tables B marital status and living arrangements: March 1998(update)* (Current Population Reports P20–514). Washington, DC: U.S. Government Printing Office.

U.S. National Center for Health Statistics. (1991). *Advance report of final marriage statistics, 1988* (Monthly Vital Statistics Report, Vol. 40, No. 4, Supplement, DHHS Pub. No. PHS 91–1120). Hyattsville, MD: Public Health Service.

van Dam, M. A. (2004). Mothers in two types of lesbian families: Stigma experiences, supports, and burdens. *Journal of Family Nursing, 10,* 450–484.

Visher, E. B., & Visher, J. S. (1982). Children in stepfamilies. *Psychiatric Annals, 12,* 832–841.

Visher, E. B., & Visher, J. S. (1988). *Old loyalties, new ties.* New York: Brunner/Mazel.

Visher, E. B., & Visher, J. S. (1996). *Therapy with stepfamilies.* New York: Brunner/Mazel.

Visher, E. B., Visher, J. S., & Pasley, K. (1997). Stepfamily therapy from the client's perspective. *Marriage and Family Review, 26,* 191–213.

Wilson, B. F., & Clarke, S. C. (1992). Remarriages: A demographic profile. *Journal of Family Issues, 13,* 123–141.

IV
Sociological Issues

12

Awareness of Culture
Clinical Implications for Couple Therapy

SHRUTI S. POULSEN and VOLKER THOMAS

Contents

Introduction	207
Shifting Paradigms	208
Ethics and Cross-Cultural Couple Therapy	208
Impact of Culture in Couple Therapy	209
Defining Culture	209
Conclusion	221
References	222

Introduction

I (SP) am sitting with my partner in our couple therapist's office engaged in a discussion of the issues that have brought us in for therapy when I focus my attention on the fact that my husband is Caucasian as is our therapist and that both are male while I am an Asian Indian female. I am distracted from the therapy process as I ponder whether our therapist has any clue of what my experience as an Asian Indian woman in an interracial relationship with a Caucasian male is really like. The issue never surfaces and I am left wondering if anyone else even noticed or thought it relevant to the process of therapy.

A few days later, I find myself again in a therapy office but this time I'm in the therapist's chair and am discussing issues with my own clients who are a young Caucasian couple in their early twenties from a working-class background. Again, I find myself distracted by this awareness of cultural differences and wonder whether I am qualified to help this couple given our seemingly different socioeconomic, educational, and cultural backgrounds. What is the magic trick, I wonder, to that balance between attention to and respect for cultural difference and still effectively helping couples deal with issues that seem to cross cultural boundaries and are common to couple relationships? We may not discover the "magic trick" and that optimal balance. However, we do hope this chapter will address the ethical issues related to culture and therapy, the impact of culture in couple therapy, the implications for clinicians and their work with couples, an overview of the current couple intervention research, and provide a forum for further exploration and discourse on the issue of culture and couple therapy.

Shifting Paradigms

According to Pare (1995), family therapy in general has undergone a transformation of sorts with an "evolving epistemology" (p. 2) that now includes literary deconstruction, feminism, and cross-cultural studies. This transformation in how therapists know what they know has an impact as well on couple therapy, and in particular on how therapists become aware of and approach culture in couple therapy. Pare suggests that social constructionism with its focus on meaning and interpretation within a person's context has deep implications for a more complex understanding of our clients' cultural experiences from their own perspectives and allows it to be expressed in language that is meaningful to them. Thus, it would seem that a postmodern approach with an emphasis on meaning, interpretation, language, and subjective experience would provide a valuable paradigm for understanding cultural differences and similarities and the cultural experiences of clients.

Ethics and Cross-Cultural Couple Therapy

Although not explicitly stated, the American Association of Marriage and Family Therapy professional code of ethics (2001) highlights the profession's commitment to cultural competence and the role of family and couple therapists as ambassadors of social justice and ethical treatment. The ethical principle of professional competence and integrity highlights the importance of therapists staying abreast of new developments and knowledge in the field, obtaining training, education and supervision, and practicing within the boundaries of their competencies. This particular principle implicitly emphasizes the importance of cultural competence and therapists' obligation to obtain the necessary knowledge and training required to treat ethically a diverse client population.

Principle 6 of the AAMFT code of ethics (2001) encompasses issues related to marriage and family therapists' responsibilities to the profession of marriage and family therapy. This principle emphasizes the ethical obligation of therapists to work toward the betterment of community and society and challenging and changing systems that serve to undermine fairness and justice for all families. Again, though not explicit in its charge to therapists, this principle implies the need for couple and family therapists to work actively toward a community and society that supports and nurtures a diversity of perspectives and an active attention to cultural context. Beyond formal codes of ethics, therapists need to consider their own personal values and ethics in the face of increasing cultural and ethnic diversity in the overall population of our society and certainly in the increasing cultural diversity of our clients.

From an ethical standpoint, a "diversity of perspectives" would allow for a more just and balanced approach to couples' work where there is room for exploration, learning, and understanding both for the experiences that we as therapists may have in common with our clients and for those experiences that are particularly influenced by the cultural frameworks of race, gender, socioeconomic class, and sexual orientation. In an article on sexual and marital therapy, the authors discuss the ethical ramifications of a one-dimensional perspective (generally one that reflects Western middle-class individualistic beliefs) on the values inherent in couple therapy and state that providing ethical therapeutic services "should reflect the cultural variations that exist" (Wylie & Perrett, 1999, p. 220). In other words, the authors believe that therapists and clients bring their own culture, values, and beliefs to the therapy setting and therapists have an ethical obligation to understand and be aware of their own and their clients' cultural values so that there is space for a multiplicity of perspectives in the voices that are privileged.

One of the ethical issues that Wylie and Perrett (1999) point out is that congruence between therapist and client values is associated with positive therapeutic outcome and culture has an impact on a person's values. Therefore, it is imperative that therapists be cognizant of the potential for differing values and beliefs when working with couples from different cultural backgrounds, and be prepared to deal with these issues in the therapeutic setting. The authors (Wylie & Perrett) suggest that therapists using particular therapeutic models with culturally different couples should question the assumptions and values upon which the models are based and not assume that all models can be appropriately adjusted to equally serve all clients across all cultures. The authors also suggest that seeking supervision and working with a co-therapist are effective methods that provide therapists with opportunities to question their assumptions, seek differing perspectives, and challenge their belief systems when confronted with differing cultural value systems.

Professional guidelines of ethical conduct such as AAMFT's code of ethics (2001) provide an institutional framework for therapists to engage in clinical practice that is ethical, appropriate, and demonstrates competence. However, beyond formal professional codes of ethics, couple therapists should consider their own cultural context, the cultural contexts of their clients, their own and their clients' values and worldviews, and the importance of imbuing their practice with openness to and expression of a diversity of cultural perspectives and experiences.

Impact of Culture in Couple Therapy

Defining Culture

The term "culture" encompasses a myriad of implicit and explicit variables including race, socioeconomic class, gender, and sexual orientation. In its broadest sense, culture is defined as a set of shared symbols, beliefs, and customs that shape individual and group behavior (Goodenough, 1999). Culture also provides us with a set of guidelines for speaking, doing, interpreting, and assessing actions and reactions in life (Dilworth-Anderson, Burton, & Klein, 2005). Broadly speaking, culture and cultural experiences provide definition to almost every aspect of our lives from our worldviews, values and beliefs to how we dress, speak, work, play, and engage with the world around us. Therapists frequently face overt experiences of cultural differences in couples and need to find ways of dealing with those differences respectfully. According to Bhugra and De Silva (2000) cultural differences are particularly challenging in the couple therapy setting because of the variety of ways they might manifest themselves—for example, the therapist is from the majority culture while both partners of the couple are from a minority culture or vice versa, or where both therapist and couple come from the same or different minority cultures, or where each partner in the couple comes from different cultural backgrounds.

Bhugra and De Silva (2000) state that therapists should attend to cultural differences in couple therapy because power differences are inherent to the therapeutic relationship and reflect the broader sociopolitical context. The therapist not only represents professional authority but may also represent power if she or he is from the majority culture while the client is from a minority culture. Couples who are from a minority culture may experience that imbalance more acutely and bringing culture to awareness is important to the process of being more open about the potential for power imbalances in the therapeutic relationship. Even in the age of postmodern and feminist thought, Mirkin and Geib (1999) believe that the majority culture continues to imbue therapists with the message that it is not necessary or even okay to be aware of culture or cultural differences and that context really does not matter because each individual has the power within her or himself to fix their own problems if they just work at it hard enough. Mirkin and Geib suggest that therapists should employ therapeutic techniques that help bring to consciousness an awareness of context in all its varied forms, through the expansion of narrow stories, through naming and making that which is implicit more explicit, and through reframing and working collaboratively with clients. The authors encourage the use of inquiring questions that explore meaning rather than impose meaning and help therapists and couples work collaboratively (Mirkin & Geib).

In attending to culture and bringing it to consciousness, several issues need to be considered. According to Bhugra and De Silva (2000), culture may have an impact on issues such as sense of self, help-seeking patterns, openness to therapeutic interventions, definitions of family, and the varied and complex functioning in the couple and family relationships. Therefore, therapists need to be aware of these issues, have knowledge about such cultural implications, and be sensitive to the variations couples might present with in therapy. Bhugra and De Silva also suggest that assessing cultural norms for roles and responsibilities within the relationship is important as is assessing the strength and weaknesses of the relationship so that appropriate interventions can be applied in couple therapy.

An additional consideration when exploring the issue of culture and couple therapy is an understanding of the overall culture of therapy itself.

Awareness of Culture • **211**

In comparison to many other cultural contexts such as particular ethnic groups, the culture of therapy may be a relatively low-context culture. In Hall and Hall's (1990) discourse about cultural variation and communication, the author addresses the issue of high-context and low-context cultures. High-context cultures tend to be those cultures that rely less on verbal communication with information being transmitted through the context of the situation, the relationships between people and physical cues in one's environment. Understanding between members of a high-context culture is generated through shared experiences, shared history, and implicit messages (1990). In comparison, low-context cultures rely on precise, direct, and logical verbal communication. Low-context cultures tend to be less attuned to environmental cues and unarticulated moods. Although the goal of most relational therapists is to pay attention to and honor contextual issues and to the importance of history, environment, implicit and explicit interactions and relationships, it is possible that the broader "culture" of the therapy process is itself low context in that it relies heavily on and encourages direct, precise, and logical communication in the relational context. Given this seeming disparity in cultural perspectives, it seems important to consider that a critical and discerning approach to therapy is necessary when working with couples from either low- or high-context cultures.

It is beyond the scope of this chapter to address in detail all of the relevant literature and issues related to culture and couple therapy. However, the following section will briefly summarize cultural issues such as race and ethnicity, gender, socioeconomic status, and sexual orientation and their implications for couple therapy.

Race and Ethnicity   Several scholars have explored the implications of race and ethnicity on family therapy interventions and practice (Asai & Olson, 2004; Berg & Jaya, 1993; Burton, Winn, Stevenson, & Clark, 2004; Daniels, 1997). From this literature it is possible to extrapolate the implications of such issues as race and ethnicity in the couple therapy setting.

Daniels (1997) addresses the issue of race and therapy by exploring the implications on the therapeutic process of an African American therapist providing family and couple therapy to clients from the majority White culture. The author suggests that openly and directly addressing the racial and cultural differences with clients at the beginning of therapy helps to put both client and therapist at ease and aids in the joining process. One conclusion that can be drawn from Daniel's work is that for couple therapy it would seem important to address early on in the therapy process any cultural and racial differences between therapist and couple thereby sending the clear message that the therapy setting is safe and open enough to tolerate challenging and sensitive issues.

In working with African American couples, therapists who are not from the same racial background can help facilitate discussion regarding racial and

212 • Handbook of Clinical Issues in Couple Therapy

ethnic differences by first having a better understanding of their clients' context. One important contextual issue for African American couples and families is the concept of "homeplace" (Burton et al., 2004). The authors describe the concept of "homeplace" as an emotional, mental, and physical "sanctuary for healing and renewal from frequent discriminatory assaults" (Burton et al., p. 400). The authors view the "homeplace" as a source of strength and support for African American families and couples and important as an anchor and resource in their lives. Integrating and utilizing the concept of "homeplace" in the therapeutic process includes such tasks as the therapist increasing her or his own racial identity consciousness and awareness through a process of self-reflection and self-critique, approaching African American clients from a "both/and" framework that allows for dialogue about the complexities of their experiences, using a communal framework that helps clients explore, understand, and access their social and familial networks, and helping clients understand their own critical consciousness which involves exploring not only the physical aspects of "homeplace" but also the emotional and less tangible aspects of "homeplace" (Burton et al.). For therapists working with African American couples, integrating the concept of "homeplace" in the therapy setting, in the couple relationship, and in the clients' understanding of their own resources and strengths, could provide a powerful means of support for couples.

The concept of "homeplace" appears to be implicitly understood in the African American family context. Given this implicit understanding and awareness of this resource, this may be an area where African American culture could be viewed as a high-context culture where norms and relationships are understood through a variety of situational contexts and cues. By making the concept of "homeplace" an explicit and key component in working with African American couples, therapists can honor both the culture of therapy and its overall goals of directness and explicitness and an important cultural aspect for African American couples.

When considering couple therapy with Asian American couples, it is important to understand that the term "Asian American" encompasses several different ethnic and cultural groups such as Koreans, Chinese, Japanese, Indian, Pakistani, etc. While there is much overlap between the types of experiences and needs of these different ethnic groups, there is also a great deal of variation and diversity between and within the groups. The literature tends to clump all these groups under the umbrella term of Asian American or may consider only Far East Asian groups such as Chinese, Japanese, and Korean as part of the larger Asian American category (Berg & Jaya, 1993; Ramisetty-Mikler, 1993).

When working with Asian American couples, some generalities can be ascertained that may be useful in working with couples from a variety of Asian American backgrounds. Berg and Jaya (1993) offer some general strategies for working with Asian American couples and families that can be adapted to the particularities of the clients' culture and ethnicity. These strategies include acknowledging the value of cultural differences and not assuming that these are always a problem to the couple. It also includes understanding that for many Asian American couples *how* things are done is sometimes more important than *what* is done. For example, it may be important to the couple to know information about the therapist such as the therapist's age, marital status, and whether the therapist has children. This information is helpful to the client in understanding his or her own role and the therapist's role in the therapy process and the hierarchy in the therapeutic relationship. Other strategies include combining a focus on finding pragmatic solutions as well as exploration of feelings, and focusing on the good of the family rather than on the individual. Therapy with Asian American couples may be more efficacious if a positive outcome in the couple relationship can be demonstrated to result in positive outcomes for the familial relations as a whole. Berg and Jaya (1993) also recommend particular attention to the issue of "saving face," which entails not embarrassing family members in front of each other and providing positive reframes along with compliments thereby preserving the couple's sense of dignity while also helping to solve problems.

Berg and Jaya (1993) emphasize the importance of working with clients from their particular starting point. For most Asian Americans, the use of mental health services of any kind is not the first option or resource. Therefore, clinical contact with Asian American couples may focus on crisis intervention, be relatively brief, and focused on finding immediate solutions (1993). Clinicians should consider this when working with Asian American couples to ensure that the couple's goals, needs, and immediate concerns are honored and addressed.

Several of Berg and Jaya's (1993) recommendations for working with Asian American families are echoed in literature focusing on therapy with Asian Indians (Durvasula & Mylvaganam, 1994; Ramisetty-Mikler, 1993). These authors also bring to light other issues that may be relevant to couple therapy with Asian Indians. For example, issues such as religion and philosophy of life, family structure and kinship, ethics and value systems, family roles and expectations, parenting, language, and immigration experiences may need to be explored and understood by the therapist seeking to provide effective therapy to Asian Indian couples. Ramisetty-Mikler recommends a systems approach based within an ecological framework that takes into account social networks and family roles to effectively work with couples of Asian Indian background. Additionally, a psychoeducational approach that explores current skills and teaches new skills for interpersonal interactions may be more effective than solely focusing on exploration of feelings, changing philosophical orientations, or focusing on the past (Ramisetty-Mikler).

Racial and ethnic diversity may also entail an awareness and acknowledgement of religious diversity in the couple therapy setting. Many traditions and rituals couples and families celebrate and engage in are influenced by their religious values and beliefs. In a review of Muslim families and family therapy, Daneshpour (1998) highlights the importance of a thorough understanding of the underpinnings and belief system of religious systems and their impact on family and couple life and dynamics. Issues related to connectedness, independence, interdependence, boundary flexibility, communication inside and outside of the immediate family system, are all significantly influenced by the religious culture of the family (1998).

Strategies for working with Latino couples may also be applied to therapy with couples of other racial and ethnic backgrounds. For example, in a case study by Barry and Bullock (2001) the use of rituals and creativity is recommended to increase cultural understanding between client and therapist. The rituals used in treatment involved the use of the couple's extensive multiethnic doll collection to frame discussions around culture, race, immigration, and family traditions. Experiential activities such as watching culturally relevant movies and discussing family traditions were used to explore the couple's difficulties of being part of and estranged from their various contexts. In using such rituals and experiential activities, the therapist was able to help the couple feel less estranged from each other, let go of their past histories, and develop a stronger support network that met their needs while at the same time helped the therapist to gain an in-depth understanding of the couple's cultural context and experience (Barry & Bullock).

Assessment is an important part of any therapy process and therapists may often use standardized assessment tools to gain a better understanding of their clients' experience and realities. An important issue in the use of existing assessment tools is the applicability and appropriateness of using these tools with culturally diverse clients (Asai & Olson, 2004). Thorough assessments are a cornerstone of couple and family therapy and therapists use a variety of formal and informal tools to engage in this process. The use of the genogram is one such example of an assessment tool that can be valuable in couple therapy particularly when exploring and assessing for sociopolitical and cultural factors (Daneshpour, 1998; McGoldrick, Gerson, & Shellenberger, 1999). The genogram is a tool that is highly sensitive and applicable to the understanding of cultural contexts and requires little or no adaptation. Other tools however, such as the PREmarital Personal and Relationship Evaluation (PREPARE) Inventory, may require adaptation to be used in a culturally sensitive manner with diverse client populations. Asai and Olson (2004) adapted the PREPARE inventory to use with Japanese premarital couples. The authors found that adapting the instrument to attend to cultural issues such as past and future extended family relationships and dynamics, provided useful information on the process of cultural adaptation of assessment tools and highlighted the overall importance of sensitive cultural adaptation of clinical tools and interventions (2004).

Gender Culture encompasses the experience of gender and gender is a cultural component that frequently underlies the overall process of couple therapy regardless of the clients' and the therapist's racial and ethnic background. Knudson-Martin (1997) states that gender and family are inseparable and that clients and therapists engage in a social construction of gender whether they are aware of it or not. The author provides suggestions for the clinical practice of couple therapy that incorporate a process-oriented view of gender that helps men and women develop more consciousness of their own patterned ways of relating. These include asking questions about how gender is part of what is happening in the relationship and in the couples' context, not assuming equality or no gender bias, actively encouraging male as well as female accommodation toward relationship stability, asking "gendercentric" questions that highlight gender as an important part of relationship processes, address gender as a part of day-to-day, ongoing relationship interactions, identify and overtly express the gender issues that are present, and frame gender issues in the context of the larger culture so couples can begin to see it as part of a collective struggle rather than just their own personal struggle (Knudson-Martin).

A common dilemma for therapists dealing with gender in couple therapy is to take a "men are from Mars and women are from Venus" approach to gender differences (Parker, 1999, p. 2) thus highlighting primarily the differences between men and women in heterosexual relationships. Parker recommends an approach to couple therapy that takes into consideration not only the differences between men and women in language, behavior, and roles but also the larger societal context of gender issues that give way to inequality between the genders where women frequently are disadvantaged. Parker emphasizes the need to name or acknowledge openly gender differences in an effort to understand and deal with what these differences mean for the couple relationship. Parker also recommends open discussion and exploration of gender stereotypes and polarizations that each partner holds, and their socialization experiences that have had an impact on the beliefs and assumptions each partner holds regarding gender.

Clinical skills that help couples move away from a polarized experience of gender in their relationship include empowering couples, creating empathy for each partner as a way to improve understanding of each partner's reality, bringing social analysis to the therapy process, and openly addressing issues related to conflict (Rampage, 1995). According to Rampage, empowerment allows both partners to explore opportunities and resources and provides a view of couplehood that includes self-agency and access to the benefits of being a couple for both partners. Clients are frequently unaware of their partner's experience and may base what understanding they do have on societal expectations and stereotypes of gender. Helping clients to develop empathy and a genuine understanding for their partner's lived experiences can make space

216 • Handbook of Clinical Issues in Couple Therapy

for openness of expression and the ability to define and express needs more clearly. One way to create empathy is to encourage social analysis in therapy and explore the ways in which cultural expectations and social contexts affect the experience of couple relationship. This allows the couple to examine societal constraints that keep their relationship from becoming what they truly desire it to be (1995). Issues to explore with couples as they engage in social analysis can include issues such as housework, money, intimacy, and sex.

Another important topic and focus of social analysis in couple therapy is the issue of partner communication. According to Donohue and Crouch (1996), communication training (CT) is a valuable aspect of marital therapy many couple therapists incorporate in their work. However, the authors suggest that an in-depth understanding and awareness of the impact of gender, gender stereotypes, and biases in mixed-couple relationships is critical to the utilization of approaches such as CT. In their review of communication behaviors and gender, the authors highlight the importance of assessing couples' communication patterns for quantitative and qualitative features that include length of speech, duration of talk, and choice of words. Also important for assessment are issues such as interactional styles and nonverbal behaviors. Effective CT can be further facilitated by a thorough exploration of each partner's own perspectives, biases, stereotypes, and beliefs about gender and communication (1997). The authors suggest "gender-sensitive practices" in CT that include making gender visible and addressing it directly in the therapy context (p. 97, 1997). Similar to Rampage's (1995) recommendation to facilitate gender understanding and knowledge, Donohue and Crouch suggest encouraging "gender empathy" (1996, p. 98) in couple relationships. Increasing gender empathy helps to create an atmosphere of understanding and support rather than an atmosphere of criticism and judgment and allows for a more open and honest assessment of gender biases and stereotyping that each partner brings to the relationship. Finally, the authors also recommend that the therapist's own "gender-related communication expectations and patterns" (1997, p. 98) be adequately explored and their impact on the couple therapy process be acknowledged.

In addition to heightening clients' awareness of the impact of gender biases, gender stereotyping and misunderstanding, therapists' own recognition and awareness of these issues is an important component to an overall sensitivity toward gender in the couple therapy setting. In a study exploring therapist gender-related attributions in couple therapy, the authors found that therapists might bring their own assumptions, perceptions, and expectations to the couple therapy process (Stabb, Cox, & Harber, 1997). Although the results of the study were not conclusive, the authors indicated that gender-based attributions do exist and could potentially bias clinical judgments in couple therapy. Based on their findings, the authors recommended that couple therapy training include a focus on understanding gender issues from a feminist perspective and including self-monitoring methods that trainees could utilize to monitor their own self-awareness of gender-based attribution patterns (1997).

Social Class Although not always tangibly and overtly evident in couple therapy, the social class of clients and therapists is an aspect of cultural differences that may manifest itself in a variety of ways. Educational differences between client and therapist may be one way that social class issues may present themselves in therapy. Therapy and counseling tend to be perceived as "white-collar" professions therefore clients coming from more "blue-collar," working class types of backgrounds may experience a difference in social class status and power in the therapy setting. Therapists tend to exhibit a limited understanding and awareness of social class as a cultural construct for a variety of reasons (Liu, Soleck, Hopps, Dunston, & Pickett Jr., 2004). According to Liu et al., social class may be generally perceived by researchers and therapists as a demographic variable rather than a cultural concept therefore they are less apt to pay attention to it as part of the therapeutic process.

In working with clients from different social class backgrounds, it is important for therapists to consider their own attitudes of classism that may include such beliefs as "White trashism" or "trailer-parkism" (Liu et al., 2004). The authors also recommend that therapists examine issues of money, socioeconomic status, and employment status in their own family-of-origin and with their clients in an attempt to understand their clients' struggles. Liu et al. suggest that addressing issues of social class in therapy is not only an ethical obligation but also an issue of social justice as therapists are in a unique and privileged position to take action when confronted with poverty and economic disparities and the classist attitudes their clients may frequently face in the their larger cultural contexts.

Family and couple therapists have largely neglected the issues of economic marginalization in their work with couples and families (Ziemba, 2001). To address this gap in the clinical and research literature, Ziemba has proposed applying the principles of feminist family therapy for developing a model of "class-conscious" therapy. These principles include: (a) attention to the family's social and larger ecological context; (b) gender as a topic of therapy including the discussion of larger cultural contexts of power, hierarchy, social pressure, and stereotypes; (c) encouraging egalitarian couple relationships which may enhance couple's coping with financial difficulties; (d) empowerment as personal strength and finding alternative solutions; (e) nonhierarchical therapeutic relationship which can be helpful in finding solutions that work for the client; (f) therapist non-neutrality and understanding one's own values and beliefs that implicitly or explicitly enter the therapeutic context; and (g) attention to individual and family well-being and strengths to encourage self-care behavior as a way of coping with the stress of dealing with poverty. Increased awareness of one's own values and beliefs on social class and applying

218 • Handbook of Clinical Issues in Couple Therapy

principles of feminist family therapy are some ways in which couples' therapists address issues of social class in therapy while continued dialogue and clinical research is needed to further therapists' understanding of working with couples from different socioeconomic backgrounds.

Sexual Orientation   Straight therapists working with homosexual, bisexual, lesbian, or transgendered individuals and couples bring a wide range of understanding, comfort levels, and awareness of homophobia and heterosexist perspectives to the therapy setting (Bernstein, 2000). According to Bernstein few mainstream heterosexual therapists are properly prepared or trained to cross the cultural divide that presents itself when working with couples of different sexual orientations. The author recommends a "cultural competency" model of therapy that includes the need for self-education and case consultation, examining ones own attitudes, biases, heterosexist beliefs and assumptions, and examining heterosexual assumptions of therapy models. Applying a cultural competency model for working with gay and lesbian couples should also include taking an "anthropological" approach that allows for therapist and client to make meaning collaboratively rather than the therapist imposing her or his perspectives on the client (Bernstein).

Supporting Bernstein's (2000) recommendation of a cultural competency model of therapy and an anthropological approach to understanding gay and lesbian relationships, Bepko and Johnson (2000) add that an ethnographic stance is important for therapists who seek to understand the larger cultural context of their clients. Understanding these cultural contexts includes recognizing the stereotypes and attitudes toward gender norms in lesbian and gay relationships, the process of coming out to self and others and its impact on the client and her or his social network, exploring the client's social support, understanding family of origin tensions and alternatives such as family of choice, and understanding how gay couples and lesbian couples may be different and the same.

Working with lesbian couples from an ethnographic stance includes understanding the normative development and challenges of healthy and functioning lesbian couples (Brown, 1995). Understanding the critical issues related to the family life cycle development of lesbian couples includes knowledge about the decision-making process related to having and raising children, the coming out process, the decision-making process of setting up a household and pursuing employment. As with lesbian couples, working with gay male couples includes taking a data-gathering approach that provides the clinician with a rich and in-depth understanding of the dynamics of the couple relationship. The social analysis approach recommended by Rampage (1995) can work equally well with gay and lesbian couples to help them to explore and understand their experience of gender, the impact of cultural and societal expectations and constraints on their relationship, and to develop empathy for their partner's reality.

Clinicians working with LGBT clients may also need to develop their practical skills and knowledge to be effective sources of support. Such practical skills and knowledge includes understanding and awareness of legal ramifications and needs of non-married domestic partnerships, legal agreements for living together, separation, and division of property and custody and visitation issues for any children involved. Additionally, same-sex couples should be encouraged to become aware of the laws and restrictions related to health issues and their rights in regards to their role as "next of kin" (Brown, 1995). Finally, Brown encourages clinicians to embrace the perspective that gay and lesbian couples should be treated with the same regard and sense of hopefulness that heterosexual relationships in treatment are considered. According to Brown, same-sex couples in therapy "deserve the same chances at healing and competent therapeutic interventions as do heterosexual ones" (p. 289).

Couple and family therapists in general come poorly prepared to work sensitively and effectively with LGBT clients (Long & Serovich, 2003). Long and Serovich state that most marriage and family therapy training programs do not provide adequate exposure to and training for working clinically with LGBT clients, and may inadvertently ignore heterosexist bias in existing curricula and training methods. Although MFT training programs need to continue to take steps toward providing more inclusive clinical training, didactic, and professional opportunities for marriage and family trainees (Long & Serovich), the overall field of multicultural counseling has with its long history been able to provide a great deal to LGBT counseling and therapy (Israel & Selvide, 2003).

Multicultural counseling models take into account issues such as clinician knowledge, attitudes, and skills which are necessary for competent work with diverse populations (Israel & Selvide, 2003). While this literature does not focus specifically on couple therapy, it does provide insight on how multicultural counseling models are relevant to therapy with LGBT couples. According to Israel and Selvidge, the knowledge component of a multicultural counseling model is intended to expose trainees to unfamiliar cultures while the attitudes component focuses on helping trainees explore their own stereotypes, values, and biases in relation to diverse cultures. The skills component in multicultural counseling focuses on trainees developing accurate assessment skills, treatment planning and implementation skills, and advocacy skills that are appropriate and accurate given the particular cultural context that the couple's experience is embedded in (Israel & Selvidge). Although multicultural counseling models are useful in working effectively with LGBT couples, the authors are quick to caution clinicians that some specific issues need to be kept in mind regarding working with this population of clients. These include therapists actively developing a knowledge base regarding resources and support services specific to LGBT couples' needs, developing knowledge of human sexuality and a comfort level for addressing these issues openly, being able to help couples address their own sense of internalized homophobia and spirituality

220 • Handbook of Clinical Issues in Couple Therapy

and religious issues (Israel & Selvidge). The authors also reiterate that because LGBT couples are often not from environments that are supportive of LGBTs and that LGBT couples are not readily or overtly identifiable as an ethnic or cultural minority, it is even more imperative that therapists create a therapeutic environment that is supportive of all couples in order to be effective with those couples who are lesbian, gay, bisexual, or transgendered (Israel & Selvidge).

Overlap of Cultural Variables   The previous sections provide an overview of several cultural categories and the implications for couple therapy but describe these categories in a manner that implies they are discrete and separate. Guanipa and Wooley (2000) illustrate the tendency for categorization and compartmentalization in relation to such issues as culture and gender in their study that explores marriage and family therapy trainees' conceptualization of gender in the clinical setting. The authors found that trainees tended to focus on one particular cultural variable, gender, while ignoring other cultural variables such as historical contexts, ethnicity, and religion (2000). The study highlighted the importance of supervisors helping their trainees to think more analytically and with greater complexity and attention to all the various intersections of a variable such as gender with other multicultural issues.

Clearly, it is important to understand that therapists working with diverse couples may in reality, encounter a variety of configurations and overlap of these cultural categories. Therefore, in becoming more aware and attuned to the presence of culture in couple therapy, it is imperative to recognize the complex ways in which race and ethnicity, gender, social class, and sexual orientation interact and intersect. The task of the couple therapist becomes a complex and multilayered process of attention and sensitivity to all the possible explicit and implicit manifestations of culture in the therapy setting.

Culture and Making Meaning   In addition to the more obvious manifestations of culture, relationship researcher John Gottman (1999) highlights the importance of therapists understanding how all couples engage in the process of creating a unique culture of their own within their relationship. According to Gottman, making meaning in a relationship is a cultural issue and each partner brings to the relationship her or his own set of values, beliefs, experiences, and background. Therefore, while acknowledging and becoming aware of the overt manifestations of culture in the couple therapy setting, clinicians must attend to cultural meanings couples bring to the everyday events experienced in couple and family life. As couples engage and interact in their relationship, they are "constantly creating a culture" and shared meaning (Gottman, 1999, p. 108).

Gottman suggests several ways in which clinicians can explore shared meanings and the implicit and explicit cultures couples create and experience within their relationship. Exploring such issues such as rituals, roles, goals, and symbols are all ways in which a clinician can work with couples to elaborate and express their sense and experience of culture within their relationship. Rituals encompass daily activities such as routines and functions as simple as sharing meals or dealing with chores, and they include understanding couples' meanings around larger events such as holidays, spending time with extended family, and vacations. Exploring and understanding the different roles (e.g., spouse, father, mother, worker, son, daughter) each partner plays in the relationship and the meanings each person attaches to these roles is important in understanding the couple's cultural experience. The long-term and short-term goals partners incorporate into their family and couple life should be explored. Finally, couples should be encouraged to explore the symbolic aspects of concepts such as home, love, family, interdependence, and so on and what these mean to them in their lives and relationships (1999, p. 108).

Another research-based approach to couple therapy is Johnson's Emotionally Focused Couple Therapy, EFT (2004). Similar to Gottman's approach to understanding couples' experiences of culture and making cultural meaning in couple relationships, EFT promotes a therapeutic stance that is open, respectful, and focused on understanding meaning from the client's perspective (Johnson & Denton, 2002). According to Johnson and Denton, every couple represents in a sense, a unique culture that the therapist must learn about and understand. In particular, EFT focuses on understanding and exploring a couple's emotional experiences and the ways in which people manage and regulate emotions (Johnson, 2004). Therefore, while the experience of emotions and the need for connection may be universal to all cultures, couples from different cultural backgrounds bring different understanding to the regulation of emotions and different rules for the expression of emotions in relationships (Johnson). Critical to working with couples from different cultural backgrounds is getting a clear understanding of these rules and expectations as they relate to the experience and expression of emotions and the meanings couples create.

Conclusion

In a decade review of couple therapy, Johnson and Lebow (2000) outline several important themes in the continuing evolution of couple therapy. Attention to factors such as gender, postmodern perspectives, and awareness of couple and family diversity in all its various forms, were highlighted as challenges for the future of couple therapy. Integrating couple treatment and assessment models in ways that are respectful and attentive to culture in all its manifestations is a challenge for couple therapy. Applying a postmodern perspective to understanding the implications of gender, ethnicity, race, socioeconomic status, sexual orientation, and couples' own unique creations of culture, allows clinicians to regard clients as experts on their own experience and reality. Adhering rigidly to models of couple intervention without

222 • Handbook of Clinical Issues in Couple Therapy

regard to our clients' experience of culture weaken the field of couple therapy and ignore the continuing dramatic changes in the cultural landscape of current society (2000).

Multiculturalism and cross-cultural issues in couple therapy are complex and dynamic issues involving a diversity of variables. A strength of the systemic perspective in which couple therapy is based, is that it implicitly acknowledges the importance of context and larger systems such as culture and sociopolitical factors. On the other hand, couple therapists may automatically assume that this implicit acknowledgment is enough in our work with clients from a diversity of backgrounds. An ongoing challenge for couple therapists is to be able to take a "both/and" approach to the issue of culture and couple therapy. This approach acknowledges not only the explicit manifestations of culture such as gender and race that couples bring to the therapy setting, but also the implicit aspects that acknowledge the very individual meaning, expression, and experience of culture of every person. While this chapter highlights some of the ethical issues related to culture, the impact of culture in couple therapy, and the implications for clinicians in working with couples, current couple intervention research, it also provides a forum for further discourse and exploration of these issues and of the challenges couple therapists face in creating a balanced therapeutic environment for all couples.

References

American Association for Marriage and Family Therapy. (2001). *AAMFT Code of Ethics.* Retrieved September 25, 2007, from http://www.aamft.org/resources/lrmplan/ethics/ethicscode2001

Asai, S. G., & Olson, D. H. (2004). Culturally sensitive adaptation of prepare with Japanese premarital couples. *Journal of Marital and Family Therapy, 30,* 411–426.

Barry, D. T., & Bullock, W. A. (2001). Culturally creative psychotherapy with a Latino couple by an Anglo therapist. *Journal of Family Psychotherapy, 12,* 15–30.

Bepko, C., & Johnson, T. (2000). Gay and lesbian couples in therapy: Perspectives for the contemporary family therapist. *Journal of Marital and Family Therapy, 26,* 409–419.

Berg, I. K., & Jaya, A. (1993). Different and same: Family therapy with Asian-American families. *Journal of Marital and Family Therapy, 19,* 31–38.

Bernstein, A. C. (2000). Straight therapists working lesbians and gays in family therapy. *Journal of Marital and Family Therapy, 26,* 443–454.

Bhugra, D., & De Silva, P. (2000). Couple therapy across cultures. *Sexual and Relationship Therapy, 15,* 183–192.

Brown, L. (1995). Therapy with same-sex couples. In N. S. Jacobsen & A. S. Gurman (Eds.), *Clinical handbook of couple therapy* (2nd ed., pp. 274–291). New York: The Guilford Press.

Burton, L. M., Winn, D. M., Stevenson, H., & Clark, S. L. (2004). Working with African American clients: Considering the "Homeplace" in marriage and family therapy practices. *Journal of Marital and Family Therapy, 30,* 397–410.

Daneshpour, M. (1998). Muslim families and family therapy. *Journal of Marital and Family Therapy, 24*(3), 355–390.

Daniels, D. D. (1997). Race in family therapy: "Unnoticeable" or relevant? *Journal of Family Psychotherapy, 8*, 55–60.

Dilworth-Anderson, P., Burton, L. M., & Klein, D. M. (2005). Contemporary and emerging theories in studying families. In V. L. Bengtson, A. C. Acock, K. R. Allen, P. Dilworth-Anderson, & D. M. Klein (Eds.), *Sourcebook of family theory and research* (pp. 35–58). Thousand Oaks, CA: Sage Publications, Inc.

Donohue, W. O., & Crouch, J. L. (1996). Marital therapy and gender-linked factors in communication. *Journal of Marital and Family Therapy, 22*(1), 87–101.

Durvasula, R. S., & Mylvaganam, G. A. (1994). Mental health of Asian Indians: Relevant issues and community implications. *Journal of Community Psychology, 22*, 97–108.

Goodenough, W. H. (1999). Outline of a framework for a theory of cultural evolution. *Cross-Cultural Research: The Journal of Comparative Social Science, 33*(1), 84–107.

Gottman, J. M. (1999). *The marriage clinic: A scientifically based marital therapy* (pp. 108–109). New York: W. W. Norton & Company, Inc.

Guanipa, C., & Wooley, S. R. (2000). Gender biases and therapists' conceptualizations of couple difficulties. *The American Journal of Family Therapy, 28*, 181–192.

Hall, E. T., & Hall, M. R. (1990). *Understanding cultural differences: Germans, French, and Americans* (pp. 7–10). Boston: Intercultural Press.

Israel, T., & Selvide, M. M. D. (2003). Contributions of multicultural counseling to counselor competence with lesbian, gay, and bisexual clients. *Journal of Multicultural Counseling and Development, 31*, 84–99.

Johnson, S. M. (2004). *The practice of emotionally focused couple therapy: Creating connection.* New York: Brunner-Routledge.

Johnson, S. M., & Denton, W. (2002). Emotionally focused couple therapy: Creating secure connections. In A. S. Gurman & N. S. Jacobsen (Eds.), *Clinical handbook of couple therapy* (3rd ed., pp. 221–250). New York: Guilford Press.

Johnson, S. M., & Lebow, J. (2000). The "coming of age" of couple therapy: A decade review. *Journal of Marital and Family Therapy, 26*, 23–28.

Knudson-Martin, C. (1997). The politics of gender in family therapy. *Journal of Marital and Family Therapy, 23*, 421–437.

Liu, W. M., Soleck, G., Hopps, J., Dunston, K., & Pickett Jr., T. (2004). A new framework to understand social class in counseling: The social class worldview model and modern classism theory. *Journal of Multicultural Counseling and Development, 32*, 95–122.

Long, J. K., & Serovich, J. M. (2003). Incorporating sexual orientation into MFT training programs: Infusion and inclusion. *Journal of Marital and Family Therapy, 29*, 59–67.

McGoldrick, M., Gerson, R., & Shellenberger, S. (1999). Genograms: Assessment and interventions (2nd ed.). New York: W. W. Norton & Company.

Mirkin, M. P. & Geib, P. (1999). Consciousness of context in relational couples therapy. *Journal of Feminist Family Therapy, 11*, 31–51.

Pare, D. A. (1995). Of families and other cultures: The shifting paradigm of family therapy. *Family Process, 34*, 1–34.

Parker, L. (1999). Bridging gender issues in couples work: Bringing "Mars and Venus" back to Earth. *Journal of Family Psychotherapy, 10*, 1–15.

Ramisetty-Mikler, S. (1993). Asian Indian immigrants in American and sociocultural issues in counseling. *Journal of Multicultural Counseling and Development, 21*, 36–49.

Rampage, C. (1995). Gendered aspects of marital therapy. In N. S. Jacobsen & A. S. Gurman (Eds.), *Clinical handbook of couple therapy* (2nd ed., pp. 261–273). New York: The Guilford Press.

224 • Handbook of Clinical Issues in Couple Therapy

Stabb, S. D., Cox, D. L., & Harber, J. L. (1997). Gender-related therapist attributions in couples therapy: A preliminary multiple case study investigation. *Journal of Marital and Family Therapy, 23*(3), 335–346.

Wylie, K., & Perrett, A. (1999). Ethical issues in work with couples. *Sexual and Marital Therapy, 14,* 219–237.

Ziemba, S. J. (2001). Therapy with families in poverty: Application of feminist family therapy principles. *Journal of Feminist Family Therapy, 12,* 205–237.

13
Fostering Strength and Resiliency in Same-Sex Couples

JANIE K. LONG and BARBARA V. ANDREWS

Contents

Introduction	225
Family Strength and Family Resiliency	226
Family Functions	226
Application With Same-Sex Couples	227
A Caveat: Same-Sex Couples and Potential Gender Role Bias	228
Family Formation and Membership	230
Diversity	230
Marriage/Civil Unions	233
Families of Origin	234
Children: To Have or Not to Have?	235
Nurturance, Education, and Socialization	236
Exploration and Development of Gender Roles	236
Spirituality and Religiosity	238
Sexual Fulfillment	239
Support Networks	240
Protection of Vulnerable Members	240
Self-Disclosure and Power	241
Legal Protection	241
Conclusion	242
References	243

Introduction

A family system is defined as two or more individuals and the patterns or relationships that exist between them (Bateson, 1972). In this chapter, the couple, one form of family structure, will be examined through the unique lens of same-sex couples. We will attempt to place these couples within cultural contexts and discuss how those contexts might influence the strength and resilience of their relationships. We are particularly interested in the ability of the same-sex couple relationship to fulfill family functions that serve the social, psychological, and physical needs of each of the partners and society

(J.M. Patterson, 2002a). Walsh (2002) notes that same-sex couples are expanding the view of committed relationships in society yet recognizes that these couples face the ongoing challenges of stigma and discrimination that can work to undermine them. She concludes, "Application of a family resilience lens can normalize and contextualize their struggles, affirm their desires for loving relationships, and applaud their courage and perseverance in forging new models of human connectedness despite the barriers they face" (p. 133). Modcrin and Wyers (1990) found that 54% of lesbian couples and 32% of gay male couples had previously sought the services of a mental health professional to address problems in their relationship, moreover, "86% of lesbians and 60% of gay males in their sample stated that they would seek professional help in the future if problems arose in their relationships" (Means-Christensen, Snyder, & Negy, 2003). We believe training couple therapists to work from a strength and resiliency base is crucial in working with same-sex couples.

Family Strength and Family Resiliency

There is a discourse in the field of family science that focuses on the definition of the construct of family resilience (J. M. Patterson, 2002a; Walsh, 1998). J. M. Patterson (2002b) postulates that practitioners and researchers have used the concept of resilience differently. She suggests practitioners have used the term *resilience*, to focus on family strengths as opposed to deficits and that family researchers have used the term to examine "unexpected competent functioning among families (and individuals) who have been exposed to significant risk(s)" (p. 349). For the purposes of this paper, we include the concepts of both family strengths and family resilience because we believe both have relevance for practitioners working with same-sex couples. Family strengths are also sometimes described as family capabilities, for example, resources and coping behaviors that enable couples to fulfill normative family functions. We also believe, as Walsh (2002) suggests, that same-sex couples often exemplify family resilience against the chronic high risk of homophobic prejudice and discrimination, especially when the couples do not have ample social support. Social isolation usually contributes to significant risk (J. M. Patterson, 2002b). Thus, family strength is evidenced by the couple's ability to fulfill family functions, and family resiliency is conceptualized as the couple's ability to provide family functions in the face of significant risk. Our intent is not to determine nor define family strength and resiliency in same-sex couples, but rather to highlight the cultural contexts that may influence the couple's capabilities in both arenas.

Family Functions

Ooms (1996) identifies several important functions that families fulfill for their members. Three of those functions, family formation and membership, nurturance and socialization, and protection of vulnerable members, are particularly germane to same-sex couples. The family function Ooms identifies as *family*

Fostering Strength and Resiliency in Same-Sex Couples • **227**

formation and membership provides couples and their families with a sense of belonging, personal and social identity, and meaning and direction for life. The second family function, *nurturance and socialization,* provides the partners and any children with physical, psychological, social, and spiritual development and instills social values and norms. The third salient family function, *protection of vulnerable family members*, provides protective care and support for vulnerable members of the family (J. M. Patterson, 2002a). The degree to which a couple is able to fulfill these functions is indicative of its level of functioning.

Application With Same-Sex Couples

We have identified several categories related to the relationship experiences of same-sex couples that we believe are examples of areas that may need to be addressed in therapy in order to assist same-sex couples in fulfilling these basic family functions and thus keep them strong and resilient (see Table 13.1). We do not propose that we have captured every experience of all same-sex

Table 13.1 Core Family Functions for Same-Sex Couples

Family Function	Individual/Couple Benefits	Potential Relationship Experiences
Membership and couple formation	Provides a sense of belonging	Recognition of diverse family forms
	Provides personal and social identity	Recognition of marriage and civil unions
	Provides meaning and direction for life	Establishes independence but not cut-off from families-of-origin
		Addition of children is planned and desired
Nurturance, education, and socialization	Provides for physical, social, psychological, and spiritual development	Exploration and development of gender roles
	Provides opportunities for security and attachment to grow	Establishing relationships with other same-sex couples
	Provides opportunities to become a part of a larger community	Roles of spirituality and religiosity
		Sexual fulfillment
		Development of support networks including families of choice
Protection of vulnerable members	Provides protective care and support for vulnerable members	Power related to self-disclosure legal protection

228 • Handbook of Clinical Issues in Couple Therapy

couples, but we have included those factors that the literature suggests are important. We also acknowledge that the experiences we have related to each function are not unrelated to other functions, for example, the role of spirituality and/or religiosity. For some couples a similar religious identity or upbringing, in addition to providing a sense of nurturance, may be part of what initially draws the couple together. Feeling a sense of spiritual or religious connection and participating in a particular faith community may also provide couples with some feelings of protection against stigma and prejudice. Thus, we realize that these functions and experiences within functions are somewhat fluid rather than concretized. Before outlining each of the family functions and noting important areas to be addressed to keep lesbian and gay male couples resilient and strong, we caution therapists to address potential bias within themselves before beginning work with these couples.

A Caveat: Same-Sex Couples and Potential Gender Role Bias

While working with same-sex couples clinicians need to attend to multiple levels of potential bias. Two case examples will be helpful in assisting us to examine our initial thoughts about possible gender bias on the part of the therapist related to differences and similarities in gay male and lesbian couples, as well as, similarities and differences between same-sex and opposite-sex couples.

Example 13.1

Ben and Roger have been together as a couple for 8 years. Both men are in their forties with Ben being 8 years older than Roger. When they met, Roger was still living at home with his parents and was not out to them, nor in his professional life, even though he had identified as gay in his teens. Ben has been openly gay for many years in both his personal and professional lives. Ben is more established professionally than Roger and makes more money. Roger does not have any siblings while Ben is a favored uncle by several nieces and nephews. Ben has known for several years that he wanted to form a living together, committed partnership with Roger. They have lived a few hours from one another throughout their relationship, which has meant mostly weekend contact. Roger did move into his own apartment 4 years ago but says that even though he loves Ben he cannot move in with or even live in the same town as Ben until both his parents, who are in their seventies, die. Ben also loves Roger and is trying to figure out if he can be at peace with the relationship as is.

Example 13.2

Angelina and Carmen have had an on and off relationship for about 8 months. Angelina is Caucasian and in her early forties and Carmen is Hispanic and is in her mid-thirties. Angelina is out in every aspect of her life and has two adolescent sons. This is the first woman-to-woman relationship for Carmen who was previously married to a man. She is still uncertain whether she considers herself a lesbian and would not be comfortable being out either with her family or in her work environment. She is attracted to Angelina on multiple levels but also feels torn about the relationship. She has withdrawn from the relationship several times in the past 8 months but eventually returns. Angelina is going to be moving in a few months to live closer to her children's father. She would like for Carmen to move with her. Carmen does not know how to make this commitment given that she would have to explain the changes in her life to her parents and friends.

Both of these couples are facing numerous challenges to their relationships. Several questions arise related to potential bias in how we present and scrutinize them including: Does their level of functioning differ because they are same-sex couples versus opposite-sex couples? What advantages might they have as a same-sex couple? Are they representative of the issues most same-sex couples encounter?

Several authors have written about the importance of the need for balance in looking at differences between opposite-sex couples and same-sex couples neither viewing them as having no differences nor viewing them as being completely different (Basham, 1999; Bernstein, 2000; Green & Mitchell, 2002; Long & Serovich, 2003). Hare-Mustin (1987, p. 15) warns against "alpha bias" (the exaggeration of differences between groups of people) and "beta bias" (ignoring differences that do exist). This type of binary thinking minimalizes the complexity of relationships. In the context of same versus opposite-sex partners, alpha bias would mean, for example, focusing only on sexual or gender identity differences between partners as an explanation for relationship difficulties. Beta bias would then totally ignore the influence of sexual or gender identity differences on the couple's relationship. It is important for the clinician to pay close attention to the individual constructions of the partners rather than operating out of cultural stereotypes. However, a balance between putting too much emphasis on the differences and not attending enough to differences is important.

In assessing similarities between opposite-sex and same-sex couples, clinicians can also examine areas of typical stressors between all couples including family-of-origin issues, gender issues, and difficulties related to money, children, and sex. An example of beta bias in this situation would be to treat sexual difficulties in a lesbian relationship from a hetero-normative posture. The couple's sexual relationship would then be considered abnormal if they were not focused on penetration and orgasm. An example of alpha bias would be to only focus on the differences in each partner's gendered norms regarding sexuality (Long, 2003). So while acknowledging that all gay male couples and lesbians couples are not the same either within groups or between groups, we also believe it is important to present some of the challenges the literature suggests they face in meeting basic family functions.

230 • Handbook of Clinical Issues in Couple Therapy

Family Formation and Membership

Stereotypically, gay males and lesbians are believed neither to desire nor be capable of permanence in relationships. Yet research indicates that between 45% and 80% of lesbians and 40% and 60% of gays are involved in steady relationships at any given time (Peplau & Cochran, 1990), and many lesbians and gays establish lifelong partnerships (McWhirter & Mattison, 1987). The U.S. Census of the year 2000 (U.S. Census Bureau, 2001a) showed that same-sex couples comprised approximately 2% of all households, which translates into approximately 1 million same-sex couples in the United States (Means-Christensen et al., 2003). In addition, state laws against prohibiting same-sex couples from marrying makes it likely that there is a high percentage of this population that are in committed relationships that are not currently identified as such (Means-Christensen et al.). Recent prolonged and arduous efforts by many lesbians, gay males, and heterosexuals to pass laws upholding the rights of same-sex couples to marry in the face of huge opposition to such rights would seem to render this notion of lack of desire for permanence obsolete.

Also, stereotypically, gay male and lesbian relationships are believed to be less satisfactory than heterosexual relationships. Yet when the relationship satisfaction of lesbians and gay male couples is compared to heterosexual couples, few if any differences emerge (Kurdek & Schmitt, 1986; Peplau & Cochran, 1990). Following are some of the areas most often reviewed in the literature that we believe hold salience for same-sex couple formation and membership in providing a sense of belonging, personal and social identity, and meaning and direction for life.

Diversity

Family diversity is common throughout history and across different cultures (Coontz, 1997). Walsh (2002) points out that there is a growing body of research that supports the fact that well-functioning couples and families and well-adjusted children are found in a plethora of formal and informal kinship arrangements. Lesbian and gay male couples also display diversity in several forms including couples comprised of members who identify as bisexual, transsexual, intersexed, and transgendered. These persons may also identify as being a part of a same-sex couple. For example, a post-op male to female transsexual who is in a committed relationship with another woman may identify that relationship as lesbian. A bisexual man who is in a committed relationship with another male may identify his relationship as a gay male relationship. These variations add unique aspects to the relationship that are different from the experiences of two partners who both identify as lesbian or gay.

It is not within the scope of this paper to identify all of the possible combinations of sexual orientation relationships and the resulting challenges.

Fostering Strength and Resiliency in Same-Sex Couples • **231**

However, clinicians who work with same-sex couples should be aware that these variations in sexual identity and gender expression do exist and need to be considered when working with same-sex couples. For example, within some same-sex couple relationships, one or both of the partners identifies as bisexual. Issues for these couples often include sexual health, monogamy/non-monogamy, feelings of competition, and judgments of others. These couples often lack support from the lesbian and gay community as well. Ossana (2000) states that therapists should "help mixed-orientation couples negotiate the specifics of a relationship style … that works for both partners," (p. 293) and validate the couples' choices.

Lesbians and gays are meeting and entering into relationships with partners from increasingly varied backgrounds including race,* culture, and class. Census data offer us one view of the numbers of interracial couples in this country. The 2000 U.S. census revealed that most partners (married and unmarried) are of the same race but that unmarried partners are about twice as likely to be of different races than married partners (Fields & Casper, 2001). In the 2000 census 4% of unmarried partners were of different races as compared to 2% of married couples (U.S. Census Bureau, 2001a, p. 14). It is impossible to obtain accurate readings of the numbers of same-sex couples including lesbian couples with the current format of the census (Fields & Casper). However, one could make the case that because the numbers of interracial couples are increasing that the number of interracial lesbian and gay male couples is also increasing. Census data also suggest that persons of color have become the numerical majority in the United States (U.S. Census Bureau Web site, 2001b). This rise has brought about increased complexity in the multiple layers of multiculturalism. How might racial or cultural differences matter to same-sex couples?

Managing multiple differences can be a challenge facing interracial or intercultural same-sex couples (Long, 2003; Nazario, 2003). Differences may include race, ethnicity, class, current socioeconomic status, and religion. These differences are often experienced in conjunction with one another further complicating the issues. The differences may conjure up one's own prejudices, but they also heavily influence one's value and belief systems. Some of the cultural differences include: obligations to immediate and extended families, money, time management, styles of parenting, and child rearing (Pearlman, 1996).

---

* Ruth Frankenberg (1993) highlighted the notion of race as a social construction, rather than, an inherently meaningful category. Frankenberg suggests that there is more variability within one traditionally biologically defined racial category than there is between two categories. Frankenberg and others present the view that the salience of racial difference still holds true in our society because of the social and political contexts in which racial difference is constructed. Austin (2001) points out that as a socially constructed category; race is then linked to relations of power. This worldview does not minimize the social and political reality of race.

232 • Handbook of Clinical Issues in Couple Therapy

Interracial same-sex couples each holding minority status, share experiences of oppression as persons of color and as sexual minorities. For these reasons, they may assume more similarity between them than is the case (Greene & Boyd-Franklin, 1996). They are both still members of different cultures and of different families with potentially different values. Both partners in an interracial relationship experience interracial relationship prejudice. Prejudice and racism may come from family members, friends, co-workers, and the society at large. A partner from the dominant culture may experience racial prejudice for the first time. The couple may no longer be welcome in certain neighborhoods and they may not be safe in others. If both partners are from different minority cultures, the prejudice may be compounded by the fact that neither one has dominant cultural privilege (Long, 2003).

Some same-sex partners in interracial relationships believe that they are more easily identifiable as a couple due to their racial differences (Greene & Boyd-Franklin, 1996; Pearlman, 1996). When this is the case, they may become easier targets of discrimination and hate. Interracial and intercultural same-sex couples must deal with the effects of this discrimination upon their relationships. For example, Greene and Boyd-Franklin address the devalued position of African American lesbians within the social hierarchy as "triple jeopardy" (p. 49). They often face racial, gender, and heterosexist institutional oppression all of which have influence on their optimal development and the development of their relationships (Greene, 1994a, 1994b). Greene and Boyd-Franklin note that some dominant culture partners may then under-react (feel that a partner's anger over racism is inappropriate or exaggerated) or over-react (become critical of a partner for not more actively resisting oppression, or attempt to become the rescuer). The African American partner may then "find the assumption of this protective role presumptuous, unwanted, unneeded, and even patronizing" (Greene & Boyd-Franklin, p. 56).

After being in a relationship for some time, white partners in an interracial relationship may fall into the mistaken notion that they somehow know what the experience of racism is like for their partners, ignoring the fact that their minority partners have lived their entire lives in a position of oppression. As white partners become more aware of privilege and gain in their knowledge and understanding of their experiences, minority partners may feel somewhat displaced or even threatened about whom in the relationship has more authority regarding race, prejudice, and discrimination (Long, 2003). Out of feelings of guilt, white partners may also try to right the injustices of years of oppression, which may leave their partner feeling frustrated and angry due to the lack of psychological armor and defensive coping strategies that their minority partners have developed.

Due to their attraction to a member of the dominant culture, partners from minority cultures may struggle with questions of internalized racism. Partners from the minority may also struggle with anger toward the majority

Fostering Strength and Resiliency in Same-Sex Couples • **233**

partner as an artifact of the prejudice and discrimination they experience on a daily basis from members of the majority culture. Jealousy and resentment over the lover's privileged status in the dominant culture and within the gay community may arise (Greene & Boyd-Franklin, 1996).

Immigrants in same-sex couples may still be making adjustments to a new culture. How much does one want to hold onto one's own traditions and how much does one adopt the traditions of the dominant culture? Sometimes these adjustments are not chosen but are imposed by the dominant culture. Due to bias, persons coming from other cultures who were raised in higher classes may find themselves struggling with maintaining a sense of privilege within American culture (Long, 2003). For example, some partners from India may be treated in the United States as though they are from a lower class, when in fact they were from a very high caste in India. This drop in social standing may be very difficult for the Indian partner to accept thus placing an added strain on the relationship. If the white partner is from a high social class, the Indian partner may resent the perceived differences that society places upon them or may struggle with a diminished sense of self-esteem.

Lesbians of color do not necessarily share the same priorities as white, Anglo lesbians who often dominate lesbian communities (Laird, 2000). For example, lesbians of color have challenged white lesbian feminists regarding gender assumptions. These differences have created tensions within many lesbian communities and left some lesbians of color feeling unwelcome. Greene and Boyd-Franklin (1996) acknowledge that African American lesbians are marginalized within the lesbian community and Nazario suggests the same marginalization of gay Latinos within the Latino community (2003). Even though there is sparse literature to support the assumption that other racial minority groups also experience marginalization within the gay and lesbian communities, it seems likely, not only due to philosophical differences, but also because of the existence of prejudice and racism. These communities do not exist in a vacuum but are reflective of the society. Just because lesbians and gay males are objects of prejudice and discrimination based on their sexual orientation, does not mean that they are immune to racism. Interracial and intercultural couples may distance themselves from lesbian and gay communities in order to protect themselves from further negation and discrimination.

Marriage/Civil Unions

Currently there are no recognized rituals of marriage for same-sex couples that are universally sanctioned in this country or within this culture. Civil unions, currently legalized in Connecticut, New Hampshire, New Jersey, and Vermont, and same-sex marriages, currently recognized in the state of Massachusetts and California, are not recognized or validated in any other states or by the Federal government (Connors, 2003). These sanctions offer some of the advantages of marriage to same-sex couples, yet are far

234 • Handbook of Clinical Issues in Couple Therapy

from equal in provision of rights to those available through heterosexual marriage. Civil unions do provide a format for same-sex couples to have a socially recognized commitment, some state-based tax benefits, health care/insurance options for partners, hospital visitation rights, and the ability for partners to make life/health decisions for each other. Yet the Federal government does not recognize these marriages and civil unions. In addition to a lack of governmental and legal support, many religions will not recognize unions or blessings of same-sex couples. Therapists can offer much support by acknowledging the importance and commitment of the couple to each other and can help the couple create their own rituals and celebrations of their union.

Families of Origin

The family is our primary socializing agent. It is where we first learn what our culture deems appropriate and acceptable (Andrews, 2004). Family of origin is the family we are born into or the family who raised us. Our families of origin often foster a sense of duty to hold similar values, beliefs, and interests. Kerr and Bowen (1988) postulated that when individuals leave their parental home they must establish intergenerational emotional boundaries that allow for connection as well as protection of the integrity of their new relationships. Therapists working with same-sex couples can help them identify patterns, roles, and expectations that each person brings to the relationship from their families of origin and their community. They can help the couple negotiate the roles, values, and beliefs they wish to continue to hold onto within their present relationship. Family of origin dynamics becomes even more complicated when one or both of the same-sex partners are from other marginalized groups. How might multiple minority status affect relationships with the family of origin especially in interracial same-sex couples?

Interracial same-sex couples like many interracial opposite-sex couples may face antagonism from their families of origin (Nazario, 2003). Greene and Boyd-Franklin report, however, that while opposite-sex interracial couples often lack family support; lesbian interracial relationships face an even greater challenge. One partner's race may become the focus of the other partner's family's anger. When racial differences exist, a partner's position as an outsider to the family and to the ethnic group makes him or her a target of blame or the scapegoat for "turning" the family member into a "gay" person (Greene & Boyd-Franklin, 1996, p. 54). Both partners may be perceived as lacking loyalty to their own families and/or ethnic or racial groups and may begin to feel ashamed of their involvement in the relationship (Falco, 1991). Partners may feel pulled between their loyalty to their partner versus loyalty to their family and their community. These feelings further complicate the resolution of issues within the relationship.

Children: To Have or Not to Have?

Historically, same-sex parented families were created when one or both of the parents brought children to the family from a previous heterosexual union (Johnson & O'Connor, 2002; C. J. Patterson, 1992). Advances in science and technology have increased the potential for couples of all sexual orientations to become parents. For the purpose of this chapter, we will focus on same-sex partners. Some researchers have referred to this movement as the *gay baby boom* (Johnson & O'Connor). More gay male and lesbian couples are choosing to have children by a variety of means. Regardless of how children come into this world, parents of various sexual orientations face common issues such as: discipline, rule and boundary setting, financial planning, health care needs, and childcare responsibilities.

Same-sex parents face some unique concerns as well as those shared by all parents. The choice of whether or not to have children is the first of many significant parenting choices same-sex couples face. Other considerations include: how to conceive, who will bear the child (same issue but slightly different for lesbian and gay male couples), how to choose a donor, whether the donor will be known or unknown, and whether this donor will be part of the child's life or not. Many issues go into these decisions, and the therapist needs to be able to address these issues, without judgment, and with knowledge of the resources available to the couple. Additional important issues for the couple to consider include: desirability of roles, how to navigate reactions of significant others in the couples' lives, employment, insurance coverage, and even what the children will call their two mothers or fathers.

Same-sex parented families also face challenges such as (a) lack of availability of family health care benefits; (b) lack of survivor and insurance coverage benefits; (c) lack of spousal and family insurance benefits; (d) lack of recognition of same-sex families in the arenas of health care (e.g., within physicians' offices, hospitals, and schools); (e) school systems' lack of recognition of all functional parents involved in a child's life; (f) lack of legal rights and benefits; (g) complicated and unvalidated relationship issues around separation, divorce, child custody, and child support; (h) scarce or nonexistent community recognition and support; and (i) the process of coming out. All of these challenges affect and impact their families' acceptance within a community (Andrews, 2004; C. J. Patterson, 1992; Tasker & Golombok, 1997). Therapists' knowledge and awareness of the unique challenges same-sex couples face can offer much support and assistance as the families navigate through some of these unique challenges. In the event of the dissolution of a same-sex parented family, the therapist will need to be prepared to help the family negotiate through issues of separation, child custody, child support, and the determination of each partner's rights and responsibilities.

236 • Handbook of Clinical Issues in Couple Therapy

One of the unique challenges for same-sex couples is the coming out process. This is a difficult one for all involved and creates the need for substantial emotional support for both parents and children. The family needs guidance and support around the consequences of children telling their friends about their parents, attitudes of their peers, and the family's acceptance at school and in the community (Casper & Schultz, 1999). Therapists can assist the parents through this process, with the hurdles and transitions involved around decision making regarding timing of coming out, to whom, preparing for possible consequences, and helping the family identify and create support networks.

Some same-sex parents may feel forced to conceal their sexual identity, may be denied parental or spousal benefits, and may experience lack of recognition and support from the community, their child's school, their work environment, and their own extended families. Sometimes same-sex parents may not be recognized as both being parents outside of their own nuclear family. This inconsistency presents their children with a striking dichotomy between their public and private lives (Andrews, 2004; Casper & Schultz, 1999). Helping same-sex couples identify and connect with support and resources will be crucial to their successful navigation through some of these challenges.

Nurturance, Education, and Socialization

The second major family function for same-sex couples is the provision of experiences that provide the couple with nurturance, education, and socialization. These functions foster physical, social, psychological, and spiritual development. Feelings of security and attachment are nurtured and allowed to grow within the couple relationship. And when these needs are finally met, same-sex couples grow in their feelings of being a part of a larger community. Following are some of the key areas we believe provide same-sex couples with nurturance, education, and socialization.

Exploration and Development of Gender Roles

Gender roles are stereotypical sets of acceptable behavior adopted by a culture for males and females. They have been described as "how one acts in relation to the current social construction of expected behaviors based on outwardly determined gender. In our culture, for instance, girls are 'expected' to be made of 'sugar and spice and everything nice,' namely to play with dolls, act feminine, and be squeamish." Boys, on the other hand, are "socially 'expected' to play in a rough –and-tumble manner with trucks and cars and act masculine," (Sanders & Kroll, 2000, p. 433). Any deviation from these expectations and the children are considered gender-atypical (Sanders & Kroll). Stereotypically, expectations of men in society have involved providing for the family, while those for women have involved roles of nurturing. Same-sex couples have the same needs of providing and nurturing as heterosexual couples, yet typically have little outward support for these roles as they differ from what is stereotypical for their gender. There are no clear guidelines and role models for how gender roles may differ when a couple is comprised of two members of the same sex. Same-sex couples are often very resilient and creative in meeting the needs of their family. Therapists can help the couple identify their areas of strength and areas for growth within the relationship, and perhaps help the couple find or build a support network within their community. There are many commonalities shared among couples regardless of their sexual orientation, such as the desire for intimacy, companionship, and love. Other similarities involve more practical considerations such as money, sex, communication, conflict resolution, balancing work and personal commitments, and children—just to name a few. Historically, women have been socialized to value and express intimacy, emotional sensitivity, nurturing, and commitment to relationships while men have been socialized to value emotional stoicism, independence, leadership, and providing for the family (Ossana, 2000). These are important roles that many same-sex couples struggle with, regardless of gender, within their relationships. In the absence of role models and rituals for same-sex couples, gays and lesbians are left to be more flexible and creative about their roles within their relationships as couples (Peplau, 1991), often needing to take on roles culturally associated with the opposite gender.

Some issues lesbian couples historically brought into therapy were seen as connected to an overly deep level of emotional enmeshment or "fusion." Fusion was described as a relationship in which the boundaries between the individual partners were blurred (Ossana, 2000), and was seen as more pathological. However, currently this deep emotional connection is viewed as more of a survival or coping mechanism created as the couple has been faced with navigating the many challenges and incredible odds presented them by a lack of support and recognition of their union within the greater society (Long, 1996; Slater & Mencher, 1991). Therapists can help facilitate growth within the relationship by helping each partner find themselves within the merger, and help the couple work to create a better balance of merger and separation (Long).

It has been noted that for male couples, their presenting concerns have historically involved difficulties with intimacy and emotional distancing often used as a coping mechanism (Martin, 1990). Both of these extremes could be related to gender role socialization creating challenges for two members of the same gender forming a couple. As noted earlier, therapists can support the couple in what has worked well for them as a coping mechanism against a hostile environment and can help the couple continue to maintain independence, while also identifying ways of creating greater intimacy within their union.

Some of the outward supports that help validate and encourage couples are often missing for same-sex couples such as rituals, outward recognitions, and celebrations that undergird the couple. Heterosexual couples have the constructs of engagement, marriage, and anniversaries that are both recognized

238 • Handbook of Clinical Issues in Couple Therapy

and celebrated by society. However, same-sex couples typically do not have these outward forms of support for their coupling. Gays and lesbians continue to fight for same-sex marriage or civil unions between same-sex couples in an effort to seek recognition and support from local, state, and Federal governments, as well as from society as a whole. Therapists can show much support for gay and lesbian couples by expressing respect for each partner's commitment to the other, and further validating the couple by recognizing significant events and milestones in the relationship while helping the couple plan and create their own celebrations.

Spirituality and Religiosity

Spirituality is based in one's belief in the sacredness of life and generally evidenced by one's efforts to find meaning, harmony, value, and purpose in life (Aponte, 2002). One's religiosity is the degree to which one embraces the beliefs and practices of an organized religious institution. Because spirituality and religiosity play an important role in the lives of so many people it is important for the clinician to explore spiritual and/or religious thoughts, feelings, and beliefs with same-sex couples. As in other areas of life, same-sex couples may either be in sync on their spiritual journeys or they may hold widely different views and be in different stages of faith development. They may also choose to be very active in organized religion or not, and they may vary drastically in their levels of participation.

Theological debates surrounding issues related to sexual orientation are among the most controversial topics in organized religion today. The Southern Baptist Convention, the Assemblies of God, the United Methodist Church, the Presbyterian Church USA, and the Evangelical Lutheran Church in America are among the faith communities in the United States in heated debate over issues of the ordination of lesbians and gays, the conduct of same-sex unions, and even the inclusion of sexual minorities in the membership of the church. The Metropolitan Community Church, the Unitarian Universalist Fellowship, and the United Church of Christ provide faith communities where sexual minorities are accepted. Even among mainline Protestant denominations one can find certain groups that are supportive and known as reconciling or affirming congregations. Therefore, same-sex couples who want to be involved in organized religion may have to switch their primary faith affiliation or look for particular congregations within their denomination to be accepted. They may also struggle with some of the negative messages put forth by their previous faith communities including their beliefs in the sinful nature of same-sex orientation and the message of some faith communities that people who are lesbian and gay can and should "change their orientation" (Long, 1998). These negative messages may serve to undercut the important role that spirituality and religiosity can play in nurturing the same-sex couple relationship. Therefore, it is important that the clinician be informed about faith communities and clergy, priest, and rabbis in their area who are accepting and supporting of same-sex orientation and unions.

Sexual Fulfillment

Ritter and Trendrup (2002) have recently noted the virtual silence in the professional literature about the sexual expression of same-sex couples. As in other aspects of same-sex relationships, gay and lesbian couples share some sexual problems that are common with heterosexual couples, but they also face unique challenges. The sexual complaints that often bring lesbians and gay men to sex therapy, including oral sex aversions and anal sex difficulties, are largely ignored in the literature (Rosser, Short, Thurmes, & Coleman, 1998).

The literature that does exist suggests that female couples may face the stigma attached to sexual and erotic behaviors in women, or alternatively, that woman-to-woman sex can only be a magical experience that is a cure-all for any type of sexual difficulty (Brown & Zimmer, 1986). Women may also be concerned about gender conceptualizations that tend to dichotomize sexual norms, such as the belief that initiating sex is only a masculine role (Slater & Mencher, 1991). It is not surprising then that the most frequently reported sexual difficulty between lesbians is discrepancy in sexual desire (Schwartz, 1998).

Gay men are also influenced by gender role socialization and heterosexist beliefs. They may struggle with the need to split their sexuality from their emotional needs (Canarelli, Cole, & Rizzuto, 1999), or become overly focused on performance, constantly monitoring how their partner is responding and how they are performing (George & Behrendt, 1987). How do two gay males, socialized to believe that men should focus on sex in relationships and that a real man has many sexual conquests, handle the idea of monogamy?

Sexual orientation includes not only sexual behavior, but also erotic fantasies and interpersonal affection. Good therapy involves helping couples explore what they want, which may require that we explore possibilities and issues of both commitment and sexual non-monogamy (Bernstein, 2000; Shernoff, 1999). "Clinicians need to understand what issues such as sexual fidelity, sexual dysfunction, and compulsive sexuality mean to each couple, rather than seeing these behaviors through the lens of psychopathology or the values of a heterosexist society" (Ritter & Trendrup, 2002, p. 348). For example, Hall (1987) indicates that women who are each other's best friend, political ally, social support, and perhaps business partner may decrease sexual contact in order to create some distance. Is this sexual dysfunction or establishing healthy boundaries?

Therapists need to consider the range and meanings of sexual expression among same-sex couples in all of their diversity, challenge their homophobia and heterosexism, examining how such biases may be infiltrating the choices they make and the possibilities they recognize; re-examine their beliefs about

240 • Handbook of Clinical Issues in Couple Therapy

and opinions of issues such as monogamy, boundaries, and gender roles; and, finally, work through any discomfort and/or fascination with practices and couple arrangements that are different from those of opposite-sex couples (Long & Pietsch, 2004).

Support Networks

There is a paucity of research related to the family context in which same-sex couples negotiate their relationships and lives (Rostosky et al., 2004). Perceived family support has been shown to be a significant factor in the development and stability of heterosexual relationships (Parks & Eggert, 1991). Lesbian and gay male couples are reported to receive less emotional support from families of origin than opposite-sex couples and also often experience those relationships as difficult and stressful (Kurdick & Schmitt, 1987; Laird, 1996; Laird & Green, 1996). Recent research suggests that same-sex couples who are challenged to build and maintain strong and resilient relationships in the context of a stigmatized social identity also feel the negative effects of lack of family support on the quality of their relationship (Rostosky et al.), thus, making supportive families of choice even more important in the lives of same-sex couples.

Resiliency and strength in same-sex couples may then partially depend on creating "a reciprocal flow of social support" across both families of origin, as well as, families of choice (Oswald, 2002, p. 381). One's family of choice is created by joining together with others who are not blood related who share common values, experiences, ideals, and/or beliefs in committed relationships of care and responsibility for one another. Same-sex couples often choose to surround themselves with close friends and others who share similar lifestyles, values, interests, and beliefs to create their own nurturing family environment. These families create their own celebrations of important events within their lives, when society at large does not otherwise do so.

Protection of Vulnerable Members

The third family function particularly salient for same-sex couples is the protection and support of vulnerable members. The ubiquitous existence of homophobia and hate crimes against sexual minorities is the most obvious area where same-sex couples are vulnerable; however, heterosexual bias also exists and is harmful. Spaulding (1999) defines heterosexism as, "a form of social control in which values, expectations, roles, and institutions normalize heterosexuality, which, in turn, is promoted and enforced formally and informally by [social] structures" (p. 13). As Hartman (1999) points out, the United States is experiencing a social revolution of acceptance in attitudes and policies toward lesbians and gay men; nevertheless, widespread tolerance, protection, and equality are yet to be attained. Heterosexist bias still pervades our

Fostering Strength and Resiliency in Same-Sex Couples • **241**

culture and our belief systems. Helping same-sex couples battle the negative effects of homophobia and heterosexism is one of the most cited therapeutic intervention areas clinicians are called to address (Green & Mitchell, 2002). We discuss the provision of protection related to issues of self-disclosure and power within the relationship, as well as, how to facilitate couples putting into place legal protection for themselves as a couple.

Self-Disclosure and Power

Internalized homophobia, a common and problematic condition in which sexual minorities internalize the heterosexism and homophobia of the dominant culture, is highlighted by a number of authors (Crawford, 1987; Green & Mitchell, 2002). Some partners in same-sex couples are not able to openly identify because they are struggling with these internal constructs. Others are largely self-accepting but remain closeted to family and friends fearing rejection. Societal homophobia and heterosexism also play a part in comfort with self-disclosure as they have historically determined outcomes in cases of custody disputes between a straight parent and a gay/lesbian parent with the latter being denied custody. In addition, gay and lesbian couples hoping to adopt may hide their sexual identities from adoption agencies (Munzio, 1999). Some partners are not able to self-disclose their relationship in their work environments for fear of losing their jobs. These types of discrimination increase feelings of vulnerability within same-sex couple relationships and can unbalance the power dynamics within the relationship particularly when one partner lives in fear of disclosure and the other does not. Partners from the dominant culture including race, ethnicity, class, physical ability, etc. are less likely to feel the effects of the fear of disclosure. Therapists need to be aware of the potential differences in levels of comfort with open identification and the many issues of power that surround those decisions.

We must attend to power issues both inside and outside the therapy room. We can increase our clients' awareness of dominant stories created by powerful people and groups in society and collaboratively examine how these dominant stories—such as those that reinforce homophobia and heterosexism—inform the problems same-sex couples bring to our attention (Long & Pietsch, 2004).

Legal Protection

Sexual minorities are not legally protected to the same degree as other U.S. residents and are therefore vulnerable in several areas of their lives that can affect couple relationships including: unfair employment practices, unequal access to housing, denial of marriage and family privileges and benefits, refusal of parental and custodial rights, lack of assurances of physical safety, and immigration status (Ritter & Trendrup, 2002). Even though clinicians

242 • Handbook of Clinical Issues in Couple Therapy

do not themselves offer legal advice, they do need to be aware of the potential legal consequences of issues clients bring to therapy.

> Because sexual minority couples and their families lack legal recognition and protection (e.g., legal and medical powers of attorney; tax equity; and rights of guardianship, survivorship, and inheritance), the concept of domestic partnership was developed as a basis for legitimizing same-sex relationships

(Ritter & Trendrup, 2002, p. 72)

As noted earlier, some same-sex couples have the option of marriage or civil unions but to date those options are very restricted within the United States.

Hertz (1998) points out that partners in same-sex relationships often feel fragile because of beliefs like (a) society is convinced our relationship will not last, and the law reinforces that sentiment; (b) we were raised to believe we could never get married or even have long-term relationships; (c) we were raised to believe we could never have children; (d) the legal and economic rules for our lives establish a reign of separateness, and if we want to merge our property we have to go to great lengths to try to protect ourselves and our future. Therapists working with same-sex couples need to understand both the potential effects of these belief systems and also that those same-sex couples, who are mostly forced to live outside the traditional marriage system, have more choices related to things like gender roles and traditional family structures. Therapists have an opportunity to help these couples identify their needs and wants, leading to customized legal agreements that incorporate their identities and allow them both the levels of emotional freedom and sense of commitment that they desire (Hertz).

Conclusion

In conclusion, we believe that mental health professionals who work with same-sex couples must do so from a culturally responsive base that fosters the family functions of *formation and membership, nurturance and socialization,* and *protection of vulnerable members,* if these couples are to thrive. Becoming informed about the realities of institutionalized discrimination toward same-sex couples is crucial to culturally competent therapy. Assisting couples in undertaking advance legal planning helps them to decrease the vulnerability that they will lose their rights to care for their couple and family units in the event one or both of them become impaired. We must help them foster multiple nurturing networks including, when appropriate, families of origin; families of choice; ethnic groups; and spiritual communities, while also addressing with them unjust social and institutional policies that may compromise the health and well-being of their relationships.

References

Andrews, B. (2004). An examination of the factors affecting school counselors' competency to address the needs of same-sex parented families (Doctoral dissertation, University of Northern Colorado, 2004). *Dissertation Abstracts International,* *65*(12), 4471A.

Aponte, H. J. (2002). Spirituality: The heart of therapy. *Journal of Family Psychotherapy,* *13*, 13–27.

Austin, S. (2001). Race matters. *Radical Psychology, 2.* Retrieved January 12, 2002, from http://www.radpsy.yorku.ca/vol2-1/austin.htm

Basham, K. K. (1999). Therapy with a lesbian couple: The art of balancing lenses. In J. Laird (Ed.), *Lesbians and lesbian families* (pp. 143–177). New York: Columbia University Press.

Bateson, G. (1972). *Steps to an ecology of mind.* New York: Ballantine.

Bernstein, A. C. (2000). Straight therapists working with lesbians and gays in family therapy. *Journal of Marital and Family Therapy, 26,* 443–454.

Brown, L. S., & Zimmer, D. (1986). An introduction to therapy issues of lesbian and gay male couples (pp. 451–468). In N. S. Jacobson & A. S. Gurman (Eds.), *Clinical handbook of marital therapy.* New York: The Guilford Press.

Canarelli, J., Cole, G., & Rizzuto, C. (1999). Attention vs. acceptance: Some dynamic issues in gay male development. *Gender and Psychoanalysis, 4,* 47–70.

Casper, V., & Schultz, S. B. (1999). *Gay parents/straight schools: Building communication and trust.* New York: Teachers College Press.

Connors, P. G. (2003). *Same-sex marriages and civil unions. Michigan Legislative Service Bureau Legislative Research Division Research Report, 23*(1), January 2003.

Coontz, S. (1997). *The way we really are: Coming to terms with America's changing families.* New York: Basic Books.

Crawford, S. (1987). Lesbian families: Psychosocial stress and the family-building process. In Boston Lesbian Psychologies Collective (Ed.), *Lesbian psychologies: Explorations and challenges* (pp. 195–214). Chicago: University of Illinois.

Falco, K. L. (1991). *Psychotherapy with lesbian clients.* New York: Brunner-Mazel.

Fields, J., & Casper, L. M. (2001). *America's families and living arrangements: March 2000. Current Population Reports,* 20-537. Washington, DC: U.S. Census Bureau.

Frankenberg, R. (1993). *White women race matters: The social construction of whiteness.* Minneapolis, MN: University of Minnesota Press.

George, K. D., & Behrendt, A. E. (1987). Therapy for male couples experiencing relationship problems and sexual problems. *Journal of Homosexuality, 14,* 77–85.

Green, R. J., & Mitchell, V. (2002). Gay male and lesbian couples in therapy: Homophobia, relational ambiguity, and social support. In A. S. Gurman & N. J. Jacobson (Eds.), *Clinical handbook of couple therapy* (3rd ed., pp. 546–568). New York: Guilford.

Greene, B. (1994a). Ethnic-minority lesbians and gay men: Mental health and treatment issues. *Journal of Consulting and Clinical Psychology, 62,* 243–251.

Greene, B. (1994b). Lesbian women of color: Triple jeopardy. In L. Comas-Diaz & B. Greene (Eds.), *Women of color: Integrating ethnic and gender identities in psychotherapy* (pp. 389–427). New York: Guilford Press.

Greene, B., & Boyd-Franklin, N. (1996). African American lesbian couples: Ethnocultural considerations in psychotherapy. In M. Hill & E. D. Rothblum (Eds.), *Women and therapy* (pp. 49–60). New York: The Haworth Press.

Hall, M. (1987). Sex therapy with lesbian couples: A four stage approach. *Journal of Homosexuality, 14,* 137–156.

244 • Handbook of Clinical Issues in Couple Therapy

Hare-Mustin, R. T. (1987). The problem of gender in family therapy theory. *Family Process, 26,* 15–27.

Hartman, A. (1999). The long road to equality. In J. Laird (Ed.), *Lesbians and lesbian families: Reflections on theory and practice* (pp. 91–120). New York: Columbia University Press.

Hertz, F. (1998). *Legal affairs: Essential advice for same-sex couples.* New York: Henry Holt and Co.

Johnson, S. M., & O'Connor, E. (2002). *The gay baby boom: The psychology of gay parenthood.* New York: New York University Press.

Kerr, M. E., & Bowen, M. (1988) Family evaluation: An approach based on Bowen theory. New York: W.W. Norton and Co.

Kurdek, L. A., & Schmitt, J. P. (1986). Relationship quality of partners in heterosexual married, heterosexual cohabiting, and gay and lesbian relationships. *Journal of Personality and Social Psychology, 14,* 57–68.

Laird, J. (1996). Invisible ties: Lesbians and their families of origin. In J. Laird & R. J. Green (Eds.), *Lesbians and gays in couples and families: A handbook for therapists* (pp. 8–122). San Francisco: Jossey-Bass.

Laird, J. (2000). Gender in lesbian relationships: Cultural, feminist, and constructionist reflections. *Journal of Marital and Family Therapy, 26,* 455–467.

Laird, J., & Green, R.-J. (Eds.). (1996). *Lesbians and gays in couples and families: A handbook for therapists.* San Francisco: Jossey-Bass.

Long, J. K. (1996). Working with lesbians, gays, and bisexuals: Addressing heterosexism in supervision. *Family Process, 35,* 377–388.

Long, J. K. (1998). Love the sinner but hate the sin?: Gays and lesbians in the church family. *Family Therapy News, 29,* 4–5.

Long, J. K. (2003). Interracial and intercultural lesbian couples: The incredibly true adventures of two women in love. In V. Thomas, T. Karis, & J. Wetchler (Eds.), *Clinical issues with multiracial couples: Theory and research* (pp. 85–101). Binghamton, NY: The Haworth Press.

Long, J. K., & Pietsch, U. (2004). How do therapists of same-sex couples "do it"? In S. Greene & D. Flemons (Eds.), *Quickies: Brief approaches to sex therapy* (pp. 171–188). New York: Norton.

Long, J. K., & Serovich, J. M. (2003). Incorporating sexual orientation into MFT training programs: Infusion and inclusion. *Journal of Marital and Family Therapy, 29*(1), 59–68.

Martin, C. L. (1990). Attitudes and expectations about children with nontraditional and traditional gender roles. *Sex Roles, 22,* 151–165.

McWhirter, D. P., & Mattison, A. M. (1987).Male couples: The beginning years. *Journal of Social Work and Human Sexuality, 5*(2), 67–78.

Means-Christensen, A. J., Snyder, D. K., & Negy, C. (2003). Assessing nontraditional couples: Validity of The Marital Satisfaction Inventory-Revised with gay, lesbians, and cohabiting heterosexual couples. *Journal of Marital and Family Therapy, 29*(1), 69–83.

Modcrin, M. J., & Wyers, N. L. (1990). Lesbian and gay couples: Where they turn when help is needed. *Journal of Gay and Lesbian Psychotherapy, 1*(3), 89–104.

Munzio, C. (1999). Lesbian co-parenting: On being/being with the invisible (m)other. In J. Laird (Ed.), *Lesbians and lesbian families* (pp. 180–196). New York: Columbia University Press.

Nazario, A. (2003). Latino cross-cultural same-sexsame-sex male relationships: Issues of ethnicity, race, and other domains of influence. In V. Thomas, T. Karis, & J. Wetchler (Eds.), *Clinical issues with multiracial couples: Theory and research* (pp. 103–113). Binghamton, NY: The Haworth Press.

Ooms, T. (1996, July). *Where is the family in comprehensive community initiatives for children and families*. Paper presented at the Aspen Roundtable on Comprehensive Community Initiatives for Children and Families, Aspen, CO.

Ossana, S. M. (2000). Relationship and couples counseling. In R. M. Perez, K. A. DeBord, & K. J. Bieschke (Eds.), *Handbook of counseling and psychotherapy with lesbian, gay, and bisexual clients* (pp. 275–302). Washington, DC: American Psychological Association.

Oswald, R. (2002). Resilience within the family networks of lesbians and gay men: Intentionality and redefinition. *Journal of Marriage and the Family, 64*, 3374–3383.

Parks, M. R., & Eggert, L. L. (1991). The role of social context in the dynamics of personal relationships. In W. H. Jones & D. Perlamn (Eds.), *Advances in personal relationships* (Vol. 2, pp. 1–34). London: Jessica Kingsley.

Patterson, C. J. (1992). Children of lesbian and gay parents. *Child Development, 63*(5), 1025–1042.

Patterson, J. M. (2002a). Understanding family resilience. *Journal of Clinical Psychology, 58*(3), 233–246.

Patterson, J. M. (2002b). Integrating family resilience and family stress theory. *Journal of Marriage and Family, 64*(May), 349–360.

Pearlman, S. F. (1996). Loving across race and class divides: Relational challenges and the interracial lesbian couple. In M. Hill & E. D. Rothblum (Eds.), *Couples therapy: Feminist perspectives* (pp. 25–35). New York: The Haworth Press.

Peplau, L. A. (1991). Lesbian and gay relationships. In J. C. Gonsiorek & J. D. Wienrich (Eds.), *Homosexuality: Research implications for public policy* (pp. 177–196). Newbury Park, CA: Sage.

Peplau, L. A., & Cochran, S. D. (1990). A relationship perspective on homosexuality. In D. McWhirter, S. Sanders, & J. Reinisch (Eds.), *The Kinsey Institute Series; Homosexuality/heterosexuality: Concepts of sexual orientation* (pp. 321–349). New York: Oxford University Press.

Ritter, K. Y., & Trendrup, A. I. (2002). *Handbook of affirmative psychotherapy with lesbians and gay men*. New York: Guilford.

Rosser, B. R. S., Short, B. J., Thurmes, P. J., & Coleman, E. (1998). Anodyspareunia, The unacknowledged sexual dysfunction: A validation study of painful receptive anal intercourse and its psychosexual concomitants in homosexual men. *Journal of Sex and Marital Therapy, 24*, 281–292.

Rostosky, S. S., Korfhage, B. A., Duhigg, J. M., Stern, A. J., Bennett, L., & Riggle, E. D. B. (2004). Same-sex couple perceptions of family support: A consensual qualitative study. *Family Process, 43*(1), 43–57.

Sanders, G. L., & Kroll, I. T. (2000). Generating stories of resilience: Helping gay and lesbian youth and their families. *Journal of Marital and Family Therapy, 26*(4), 433–442.

Schwartz, A. E. (1998). *Sexual subjects: Lesbians, gender, and psychoanalysis*. New York: Routledge.

Shernoff, M. (1999). Monogamy and gay men: When are open relationships a therapeutic option? *Networker, March/April*, 63–71.

Slater, S., & Mencher, J. (1991). The lesbian family life cycle: A contextual approach. *American Journal of Orthopsychiatry, 61*, 372–382.

Spaulding, E. (1999). Unconsciousness-raising: Hidden dimensions of heterosexism in theory and practice with lesbians. In J. Laird (Ed.), *Lesbians and lesbian families: Reflections on theory and practice* (pp. 11–26). New York: Columbia University Press.

Tasker, F. L., & Golombok, S. (1997). *Growing up in a lesbian family: Effects on child development*. New York: Guilford Press.

246 • Handbook of Clinical Issues in Couple Therapy

U.S. Census Bureau. (2001a). *Census 200 profiles of general geographic characteristics: United States.* Washington, DC: Author.

U.S. Census Bureau. (2001b). Publications. Retrieved March 19, 2006, from http://www.census.gov/prod/2001pubs/p20-537.pdf

Walsh, F. (1998). *Strengthening family resilience.* New York: Guilford Press.

Walsh, F. (2002). A family resiliency framework: Innovative practice applications. *Family Relations, 51*(2), 130–137.

14

Couple Therapy and the Integration of Spirituality and Religion

KAREN B. HELMEKE and GARY H. BISCHOF

Contents

Definitions of Spirituality and Religion	248
First Wave 1990–1994: Why Integrate Spirituality/Religion?	249
Incorporation of Spirituality Into Therapy and Training: First Wave 1990–1994	249
Research: First Wave 1990–1994	251
Second Wave 1995–1999: How Does Spirituality/Religion Help and Hinder Therapy?	253
Incorporation of Spirituality/Religion Into Therapy and Training: Second Wave 1995–1999	253
Spirituality Research: Second Wave 1995–1999	257
Third Wave 2000–Present: How Should Spirituality Be Integrated?	258
Incorporation of Spirituality Into Therapy: Third Wave 2000–Present	259
Incorporation of Spirituality Into Training: Third Wave 2000–Present	260
Research on Couple Therapy and Spirituality/Religion: Third Wave 2000–Present	261
Recommendations: Where to Go From Here	264
Systematic Application to Couple Therapy Models	264
Increasing Specificity About Various Religious Groups	264
Expanding Research	264
Utilization of Research From Other Related Fields	265
Increased Attention in Training and Supervision	265
References	266

Couple therapy and its openness to issues of spirituality may seem like a new invention, but no doubt spirituality and religion were integrated in the marriage counseling movement, one of the historical roots of the field of marriage and family therapy (MFT) that began in the early 1930s. Many members of the marriage counseling movement were clergy, who focused on couples and marital distress decades before the development of the discipline of systemic family therapy (Gurman & Fraenkel, 2002). Some have argued that the field of MFT has been the most amenable of the mental health disciplines to the integration of religious and spiritual issues into psychotherapeutic processes

248 • Handbook of Clinical Issues in Couple Therapy

(Watson, 1997). In their survey of therapists in four different mental health professions (i.e., psychiatrists, psychologists, social workers, and marriage and family therapists), Bergin and Jensen (1990) found family therapists to be the most religious of the four, and the ones most consistent with the religious involvement of the general population. These findings were supported by two later surveys of marriage and family therapists. In Prest, Russel, and D'Souza (1999), 72.6% of MFT graduate students not only considered themselves to be spiritual people, but felt strongly about their spirituality. In the second study (T. Carlson, Kirkpatrick, Hecker, & Killmer, 2002), in response to questions designed to find out the importance of spirituality and religion in the lives of MFTs, 95% of 153 MFTs surveyed said that they considered themselves to be a spiritual person and 62% considered themselves to be a religious person.

This early influence of the marriage counseling movement waned, however, as professional and academic influences increased. As the American Association for Marriage and Family Therapy grew in stature, the field stressed being taken seriously as a bona fide mental health discipline. By the 1970s and 1980s, little mention was made of the role of spirituality and religion in clients' lives and in clinical practice.

Another shift occurred in the late 1980s and into the 1990s, as the explicit integration of spirituality and religion in couple therapy once again became more evident. This integration seems to have blossomed in the past 15+ years in three primary waves, with the early wave occurring from roughly 1990–1994, the second wave from 1995 to 1999, and the third wave from 2000 to the present. Key developments of each wave will be described below, and the chapter concludes with recommendations on the further integration of religion and spirituality and couple therapy. Prior to a description of these three waves, we offer a brief discussion on the definitions of religion and spirituality.

Definitions of Spirituality and Religion

For readers familiar with the literature on spirituality and religion and couple therapy, one commonality among almost all of the articles and book chapters is the inclusion of definitions of the terms *religion* and *spirituality*, and recognition that these two terms comprise distinct, yet related areas. Religion has generally been viewed as involvement in a more formal, institutionalized organization with structured belief systems. Spirituality on the other hand has more to do with personal values, meanings, beliefs, and a sense of purpose, which usually, but not necessarily, includes the concept of a God or a transcendent being with whom human beings are in relationship.

According to Stander, Piercy, Mackinnon, and Helmeke (1994):

Religion includes shared and generally institutionalized values and beliefs about God. It implies involvement in a religious community. Spirituality, on the other hand, is a more personal belief in and

Couple Therapy and the Integration of Spirituality and Religion • **249**

experience of a supreme being or the ultimate human condition. It includes an internal set of values and active investment in those values. Spirituality is also a sense of connection, a sense of meaning, and a sense of inner wholeness. (p. 39)

These distinctions are important to make for a number of reasons. Wendel (2003) noted that one of the reasons that research on religion, spirituality, and psychotherapy has been so limited has been the difficulty in reaching a consensus on the definitions of spirituality and religion. The distinction between religion and spirituality has been significant to therapists as well, who express far more comfort in using spiritual interventions in therapy than religious ones (T. Carlson et al., 2002; Prest et al., 1999). This may be because therapists are reluctant to impose their own religious values and beliefs on clients, are uncertain as to what to do when there is a conflict between therapist and client religious belief systems, and have an awareness of the potential of abuse due to holding greater power in the therapeutic system.

First Wave 1990–1994: Why Integrate Spirituality/Religion?

During this first wave of integrating spirituality and couple therapy, significant advancement was made in the field to raise spirituality and religion as topics to be included in MFT, in the training of marriage and family therapists, and in marital research. Very little, however, was written specifically regarding couple therapy and spirituality.

Incorporation of Spirituality Into Therapy and Training: First Wave 1990–1994

Abbott, Berry, and Meredith (1990, p. 446) reported that only a few "maverick" social scientists had considered and discussed the ways a family's religious beliefs and practices might be accessed and used in therapy. The Spring, 1990 volume (27) of *Psychotherapy* had a special issue on psychotherapy and religion. Although none of the articles focused on couple therapy, this special issue included Bergin and Jensen's (1990) classic survey of the religiosity of psychotherapists, and Shafranske and Malony's (1990) survey of over 400 clinical psychologists regarding their religious and spiritual beliefs, their use of therapeutic interventions of a religious nature, and the amount of training received on religious and spiritual issues.

During the first part of this time period, very few articles were published in MFT journals that discussed the incorporation of spirituality into therapy. Stander et al. (1994) did a content analysis of 6 primary MFT journals between 1986 and 1992 and found only 13 articles specifically about religion or spirituality in therapy. None of these focused specifically on couple therapy. Seven of the 13 articles came from the *Family Therapy Networker* alone, meaning that during that 6-year span, the following MFT journals had a total of *only* 6 articles with a focus on spirituality/religion in therapy: *American Journal*

250 • Handbook of Clinical Issues in Couple Therapy

of Family Therapy, Family Process, Contemporary Family Therapy, Family Therapy, and *Journal of Marital and Family Therapy.*

Toward the end of the first wave, more direct attention to the inclusion of religion and spirituality began to appear, and several articles were published that explored how family therapy models, concepts, and interventions could be used to address religious issues in clinical practice. One of the first of these articles to appear in the MFT literature was by Prest and Keller (1993), who, writing from a constructivist perspective, placed an emphasis on clients' language and metaphors. They suggested five therapeutic strategies to use within more traditional belief systems (Protestant, Jewish, Catholic): (1) identifying solutions that have become part of the problem, (2) eliciting fundamental beliefs, (3) using dialogues to discern incongruent spiritual maps, (4) using quotations from religious texts, and (5) sharing the spiritual process: therapist's use of self. Similarly, they identified five strategies of using myths and metaphors with spiritual clients holding nontraditional spiritual beliefs systems: (1) human beings are manifestations of God, (2) God as a stream, and all humans are in the stream, (3) God is "of the dark" as well as "of the light," (4) making friends with one's perceived psychological enemies, and (5) the human as "eco-self," in which the individual is part of the larger world, universe, and God.

In one of the first articles to address training issues regarding spirituality for marriage and family therapists, Stander et al. (1994) suggested ways for the therapist to become more spiritually sensitive, drawing on constructivism and postmodern strategies. Some of these strategies include exploring with clients the role that religion and spirituality plays in their relationship, developing collaborative referral relationships with religious leaders in the community, working in supervision on the therapist's responses to clients' religious and spiritual issues, and dialoguing with those from different cultural and religious backgrounds about religious practices and values, including marital, family, and developmental issues.

Also emerging in the last part of this first wave are the initial articles that integrate spirituality specifically with couple therapy. Rotz, Russell, and Wright (1993, p. 369) discussed the potential problem of a therapist who is perceived by couples as being religious getting triangled as "spiritually correct" by the "spiritually one-up" spouse. Butler and Harper (1994) incorporated both Bowenian and structural approaches to work with the religious belief systems of couples by considering the triadic relationships that develop as a result of each partners' relationship with God, including both healthy and dysfunctional triangles.

Also appearing in this wave was an edited book by Barbara Jo Brothers (1993) called *Spirituality and Couples: Heart and Soul in the Therapy Process.* Writing from a social work perspective, the editor included an interview and analysis of Virginia Satir's treatment approach in terms of spirituality and

Couple therapy, as well as Buddhist and Jewish perspectives. To this day, there exist no other books devoted specifically to the topic of couple therapy and spirituality.

The Fall, 1994 special issue of the *Journal of Systemic Therapies* also focused on spirituality. This special issue included two articles that addressed two different aspects of couple therapy. Stewart and Gale (1994) discussed the importance of understanding spiritual experiences of clients as cultural "ethos" (p. 16), and used marital therapy with couples on the religious right as an example. Stewart and Gale argued that clients from various religious backgrounds should be approached from an "ethno-sensitive" (p. 16) perspective, and proceeded to describe defining features and ethos of the Evangelical Protestantism or the "new religious right" (p. 17), and then gave suggestions on how therapists can enhance marital interventions with evangelical couples. In this article, Stewart and Gale cited a 1992 Gallup Poll in which 66% of surveyed clients preferred a therapist with spiritual values, and 81% desired a therapist who would enable them to integrate their values and beliefs in therapy. A final article by Anderson (1994) asserted that there are times when spiritual phenomena and couple therapy processes comes together. Using a case study to demonstrate how spiritual phenomena can induce change, Anderson described how partners reported a sense of change that was initiated beyond themselves (i.e., transcendent), that resulted in one or both partners relinquishing efforts to control, change, or shape their partner.

Research: First Wave 1990–1994

Almost no research on spirituality or religion and its application in couple therapy appears in this first wave. Worthington, Kurusu, McCullough, and Sandage (1996) reviewed 148 empirical studies of three related areas published between 1984 and 1994: religion and clients, religion and counselors, and religious counseling. It is unfortunate that out of the 36 journals included in their review, only 1 was a major MFT journal, *The American Journal of Family Therapy*. Despite their own lack of focus on MFT literature in their review, the authors adroitly pointed out the that although the most frequent problem seen by religious counselors is marital distress, there is relatively little research on either marriage or marital therapy with explicitly religious couples: "In light of the prevalence of the problem and the surfeit of supposed solutions, one might think that empirical research on the efficacy of religious marital counseling would be a garden of delight. Instead, it is a wasteland" (p. 477).

Although there was almost no research on spirituality or religion and its application in therapy in this first wave, there continued to be research in related fields on the impact of some type of spiritual or religious variable on individuals, marriages, and families. This type of research had been going on for some time, and has come a long way since Ellis's (1981) now ludicrous hypothesis that religiously devout and orthodox people were more

252 • Handbook of Clinical Issues in Couple Therapy

emotionally disturbed than less religious persons. Rather than finding that greater religiosity was associated with pathology, many studies found various aspects of healthy marital and family functioning that were related to the spirituality and religion of clients. Although these studies examined processes occurring outside of therapy, it can be argued that, indirectly, a couple's spirituality and religious background can influence what takes place in therapy, whether or not it is openly acknowledged in therapy itself. Thus it is important for clinicians to be aware of this research, and find clinical applications for it (Williams, Patterson, & Miller, 2006).

Some of the influence of spirituality or religion on couples comes indirectly by benefiting the individuals. Haug (1998) asserts that there is research that supports the view that "spiritual beliefs and practices have a beneficial, stress-buffering effect on people's mental, emotional, and physical well-being" (p. 185). In a survey of MFT graduate students, 86.3% saw a relationship between spiritual health and both physical and mental health (Prest et al., 1999). In a later survey (T. Carlson et al., 2002), a robust 96% of 153 clinical members of the American Association for Marriage and Family Therapy believed there is a relationship between spiritual and mental health.

Although most of this research has found positive associations between spirituality or religion and mental health, many authors have taken pains to include cautionary comments about scenarios in which some aspect of spirituality, or more commonly religion, could harm the individual, couple, or family and to list possible negative effects of religion or spirituality. (e.g., see B. A. Griffith & Rotter, 1999; Sperry & Giblin, 1996.) This effort probably reflects the general attitude of unease and uncertainly that was pervasive during this early wave about whether and how spirituality should be included within the sanctity of a therapy session, as well as a recognition of the dysfunctional elements of religion and the potential for therapists to abuse their positions of power when dealing with clients' religiosity.

Other research also found that religion or spirituality impacted the family, as well as the individual. In researching strong and successful families, family process research found that "transcendent spiritual beliefs and practices are key ingredients in healthy family functioning" (Walsh, 1999a, p. 9). Abbott et al. (1990) found that two important factors in family satisfaction were family members' perceptions that religion was valuable in enhancing social support and that having a personal relationship to a deity in which they could experience divine intervention provided comfort. Although 77% of their respondents agreed that their religious beliefs and practices positively affected their family satisfaction, only 2% reported that their religious beliefs and practices negatively affected family satisfaction.

Finally, there were a number of studies before and during this first wave of research that established that spirituality enhances the marital relationship. Overcoming claims that the findings were due simply to marriage

Couple Therapy and the Integration of Spirituality and Religion • **253**

conventionality (Wilson & Filsinger, 1986), these studies primarily examined the effect of some religious or spiritual variable on marital satisfaction, stability, or adjustment. Many studies found that religious involvement is an important predictor of long-term marriage, marital satisfaction, commitment, happiness, and adjustment. For a review of these studies, see Giblin (1996) and Weaver et al. (2002). In one example from a phenomenological study of 15 couples (Robinson & Blanton, 1993) who had been married for 30 years, religious faith was cited as one of five key characteristics of enduring marriages. Couples indicated that they gained social, emotional, and spiritual support from their faith, all of which in turn supported their marriages. Increased intimacy resulted from sharing the intimacy of one's personal faith. Also helping to strengthen marriages was having shared common elements of their faith. Many experienced increased marital commitment through the religious value placed on marriage. Many others experienced spiritual support and comfort during difficult times, which though an individual experience, also influenced the strength of the marital bond.

In this first wave of research, then, a case was made for the positive association between religiosity and marital satisfaction and adjustment, and attempts had begun to identify more specific components of this association. As for including spirituality in couple therapy, an argument commonly presented in this first wave is that because religion and spirituality are so important for clients, these topics should not be ignored in therapy. This first wave ends, then, with growing calls for spirituality to be incorporated in MFT and training, albeit cautiously and respectfully. Prest and Keller (1993), for instance, argued for the relevancy of spirituality for therapy and invited therapists to "consider the spiritual belief systems of their clients which have served both to strengthen and support their family system and which may also have contributed to the development or maintenance of the presenting problem" (p. 137).

Second Wave 1995–1999: How Does Spirituality/Religion Help and Hinder Therapy?

Incorporation of Spirituality/Religion Into Therapy and Training: Second Wave 1995–1999

Consistent features in the articles and book chapters in the second wave include a continued rationale for why this integration is important, a recognition of how little integration has occurred in the field of psychotherapy, explanations for how the inclusion of spirituality in therapy can enhance the therapeutic process, and cautions about how this integration can be done in the best interests of the client, to assure that therapists do not impose their values and beliefs.

Although spirituality as a topic for inclusion in therapy became more established in this second wave, reflected by the growing number of articles on spirituality and therapy, only a few publications directly addressed the integration of spirituality and religion into couple therapy. One exception is the excellent review of spirituality research by Giblin (1996) that examined marital satisfaction, healthy marital and family functioning, assessment, and clinical practices. Another exception is a book that took existing models of couple therapy and adapted them by including spirituality and religion, *Christian Marital Counseling: Eight Approaches to Helping Couples* (Worthington, 1996). Anderson and Worthen (1997), in another article specifically aimed at couple therapy, viewed spirituality as "subjective engagement with a fourth, transcendent dimension of human experience" (p. 3). The primary focus of their article was the couple therapist, and how the therapist can use one's spirituality as a resource in couple therapy.

Although not specifically addressing couple therapy, an important development regarding spirituality and the field of MFT was the integration of spirituality with specific models of family therapy. For instance, Joanides (1996) applied collaborative family therapy when working with religious families. Sperry and Giblin (1996) looked at including spirituality in marital and family therapy from the vantage of three main metaconstructs derived from most marital and family therapy models and approaches: boundaries or inclusion, power or control, and intimacy. Harris (1998) analyzed three family therapy theories, structural family therapy, object relations theory, and Bowen's family systems theory, to show possible spiritual dimensions in each. T. D. Carlson and Erickson (2000) demonstrated how narrative therapy can be used to re-author clients' personal identity stories and their relationship with God, and they also utilized narrative therapy to describe a four-step process that can be used in supervision to assist therapists in exploring their own spirituality (Carlson & Erickson, 2002b).

During this second wave, the recognition that integrating spirituality into therapy has the potential for harming as well as helping clients became more explicit, as several scholars articulated some of the potential for harm. Sperry and Giblin (1996) offered a sophisticated discussion of some of the potential harm, not only that therapists can do, but that can come from some religious dogmas and practices. Citing previous studies, they identified the following as examples of religious beliefs and practices that have the potential to be harmful to families:

> rigid doctrine that is insensitive to human need; negativity regarding such issues as family planning, sexuality, divorce, and remarriage; and an overemphasis on such concepts as sin-a judgment leading to guilt feelings and low self-esteem ... the promotion of traditional, patriarchal gender roles as bias toward the indissolubility of marriage on any grounds and an emphasis on the individual to the exclusion of emphasis on the family (p. 515).

Couple Therapy and the Integration of Spirituality and Religion • **255**

Other potential problems stemming from religious beliefs and practices include the withholding of emotions, particularly anger, distorted thoughts (e.g., difficulties in life are punishments from God), or dysfunctional behavior, such as a married person who gives up spouse and family in order to "follow the Lord." B. A. Griffith and Rotter (1999) also suggested that overly rigid rules and family structures associated with some religious families can be dysfunctional for individual family members, as can religion that is used to manipulate and control other family members and to produce "irrational guilt or confusion" (p. 162). Some of the same family rules can be found in dysfunctional religious families as in alcoholic families: "'Don't talk,' 'Don't trust,' 'Don't feel,' and 'Don't want'" (p. 162).

Sperry and Giblin (1996) also asserted that harm can come from therapists' interventions, such as trying to solve each presenting problem with a handy scriptural reference, the use of untimely prayer, or by oversimplifying the mysteries and paradoxes of life, and pushing clients to forgive too quickly. They suggested that self-of-the therapist work include an assessment of the type of spirituality that therapists bring to therapy, and presented several themes of inquiry. M. E. Griffith (1995) challenged four "certainties" (p. 123) that therapists hold that can hinder therapeutic work with religious and spiritual clients: (1) I know what God is like for you because I know your religious denomination, (2) I know what God is like for you because I know what your language about God means, (3) I know what God is like for you because your image of God is a reflection of your early attachment figures, and (4) I know what God is like and you need to know God as I do.

As calls for increasing integration of spirituality and religion in therapy increased, and the discomfort with this potential of harm to clients simultaneously increased, we see the beginning of the appearance of articles outlining ethical guidelines, beginning in the second wave and continuing into the third wave. In response to this potential for harm, many have called for an examination of the ethical issues involved in incorporating spirituality or religion into therapy. Aponte (1996) urged that these issues be included in training programs, and addressed the need for psychotherapists to examine self-of-the-therapist issues regarding their own spirituality, religion, and moral values. Haug (1998) recommended that the principles of medical ethics be adopted as guidelines for including a spiritual dimension in therapy: respect for clients' autonomy, safeguarding clients' welfare, protecting them from harm, and treating them justly and honestly. Frame (2000) discussed several ethical issues that arise in integrating spiritual and religious issues in counseling, and cited several standards from America Counseling Association's *Code of Ethics and Standards of Practice* and the *Ethical Code for the International Association of Marriage and Family Counselors*. These include the need to respect diversity in terms of religion, the therapist's competence to treat such issues, and the prohibition from imposing counselor

256 • Handbook of Clinical Issues in Couple Therapy

values on clients or forcing families into prescribed attitudes, roles, or behaviors. Helmeke and Bischof (2002) suggested the need for distinguishing between religious and spiritual issues, with greater caution urged for religious issues, and for distinguishing between who initiated the spiritual or religious topic: the client or the therapist. M. E. Griffith and Griffith (2002b), while acknowledging the healing aspects of including spirituality in therapy, also warned of the need for therapists to understand how spirituality can be expressed destructively.

How well were these ethical issues, as well as other issues pertaining to the integration of spirituality and religion into therapy, being addressed in MFT training programs? In this second wave, several articles related to training emerged. Hines (1996), in a survey of 205 graduates from 28 Commission on Accreditation for Marriage and Family Therapy Education accredited programs, both master's- and doctoral-level graduates said that they had received some training in religious/spiritual issues in their academic program. Of the 162 master's-level therapists, the average amount of training received was 6.48 hr, while for the 43 doctoral level therapists, the average was 1.18 hr. Therapists surveyed felt that they had received insufficient training, and recommended an increase in training in how to address religious and spiritual issues in clinical practice.

Prest et al. (1999) in their survey of 52 MFT graduate students found similar sentiments, as they examined spiritual and religious attitudes and practices in the personal and professional lives of these graduate students. Although 86.3% reported that they thought it was necessary to work with clients' spirituality if they really expected to be able to help them, 92.2% reported that they had not received any training in this area. A key text for novice marriage and family therapists, *Essential Skills in Family Therapy* (Patterson, Williams, Grauf-Grounds, & Chamow, 1998), published during this wave included attention to assessment of clients' religion or spirituality as potential resources for clients and the therapeutic process.

By the end of the second wave, the need for and the benefits of addressing spirituality or religion in therapy was recognized in all of the mental health disciplines, and the discussion began to shift to *how* this integration should occur. This is reflected in the number of books, many of them edited compilations from numerous authors, offering practical guidance for integrating spirituality with psychotherapeutic approaches in clinical practice. Many of these were in related mental health disciplines. The first such book to appear in the field of MFT was Walsh's (1999b) groundbreaking book, *Spiritual Resources in Family Therapy*, which proposed that spirituality can be viewed by therapists as a strength and resource in clinical work. The trend for more explicit guidance and practical clinical suggestions for how to integrate spirituality continues in the third wave. Next we consider research in the second wave.

Couple Therapy and the Integration of Spirituality and Religion • 257

Spirituality Research: Second Wave 1995–1999

Although there was an explosion of literature on integrating spirituality or religion with therapy and training during this period, albeit with only a little of that focused on couple therapy, research examining psychotherapeutic processes and outcomes when religious or spiritual interventions were applied to couple therapy remained nonexistent. However, research studies in related fields began to become more sophisticated as a consensus was reached on the need to understand the complexities of the relationships between some aspect of religion or spirituality and marital satisfaction and stability. The research during this time period began the task, which continues today, of trying to discern specific mechanisms, qualities and aspects of, and ways that spirituality and religion benefit couples and marriages. Research was no longer trying to establish that spirituality or religion in some way is associated with marital satisfaction or adjustment, using simple, unidimensional measures. Instead, more complex constructs of spirituality and religion were used, mediating factors were considered, methodologies using both cross-sectional and longitudinal methods were used, and interaction effects were studied.

Weaver et al. (2002) reviewed quantitative research studies reported in six primary marriage and family journals from 1995 to 1999 and found that 13.2% (114 of 864) of the articles included at least one measure of religion, a higher percentage than was found when doing similar reviews of quantitative research in psychological and psychiatric journals. Of the six journals reviewed, the *Journal of Marital and Family Therapy* had the highest number of research articles that included a religious variable during this time period (24.1%).

Of the 114 studies identified by Weaver et al. (2002), two topics that were represented in at least five different studies were related to couples: (1) marriage preparation, and (2) marital adjustment and satisfaction. Some of the studies involving marriage preparation showed their effectiveness. For example, Hahlweg, Markman, Thurmaier, Engl, and Eckert (1998) showed that after 3 years, the group that went through the 15-hr marriage preparation program had better marital adjustment, lower rates of divorce (9.4% compared to 21.9%), and improved communication. Although there were some mixed findings among the various studies, in general, the studies on marital adjustment and satisfaction found that religious participation and beliefs and joint religious activities were positively associated with marital satisfaction and adjustment.

Weaver et al. (2002) recommended the use of multiple measures of religion, as only a single variable was deemed insufficient. Many of the research studies in this second wave followed this recommendation. Weaver et al. also recommended the inclusion of religious variables in more outcome studies of marriage and family clinical interventions, so that we can better understand

258 • Handbook of Clinical Issues in Couple Therapy

the role that religion plays in the "prevention, onset, status, and resolution of marriage and family mental health problems, as well as with its clinical consequences" (p. 305), and so that we can better understand "how, when, and why religious issues may benefit or damage marriage and family clinical care." These recommendations are as relevant to researching spirituality and religion and couple therapy today as they were in 2002.

In a key study in this second wave, Mahoney et al. (1999) attempted to understand more clearly what it is about religion that relates positively to marriage. Their primary criticism of research in this period is that individually focused measures of spirituality are not adequate to fully assess the ways that religion is a part of a couple's life together and the degree to which their religion impacts their perceptions of their relationship. They called these individually focused measures, such as individual religiousness and religious homogamy, "distal" (p. 321) religious constructs. As a result, Mahoney et al. added two "proximal" (p. 321) measures, constructs that are closely related to couples' experiences and views of their marriage: (1) participation in joint religious activities, such as praying together, attending religious services together, celebrating religious holidays, etc.; and (2) spouses' perceptions of their marriage as having sacred qualities or using spiritual terms to characterize their marriage. They found that better marital functioning (e.g., more perceived benefits of the marriage, less marital conflict, better problem-solving) was associated with both of these more dyadic, proximal measures.

In sum, the second wave was characterized by an acceptance that it is important to address issues of spirituality or religion in MFT, and attention became directed to how do so in a sensitive and ethical manner. Research became more sophisticated in this wave, with increased attention to dyadic variables and teasing out how spirituality and religion impact couple satisfaction. These themes continue in the third wave along with more specifics about how to integrate spirituality and religion into clinical work, and to a limited extent, how this integration can occur in couple therapy specifically.

Third Wave 2000–Present: How Should Spirituality Be Integrated?

With the advent of the new millennium, no longer is it necessary to justify the need for including spirituality and religion in therapy. Instead, recognizing the importance of being sensitive to and incorporating clients' religion and spirituality have become established themes. Although there is agreement *that* spirituality needs to be included, there is still no general consensus on *how* it is to be addressed in therapy. The proliferation of books and articles generated during this third wave have the following tasks as their objectives: synthesizing spirituality with existing models, describing new models and approaches for integrating spirituality in therapy, and offering practical suggestions, techniques, and interventions for how spirituality and religion can be addressed in therapy. This third wave of the integration of spirituality and

Couple Therapy and the Integration of Spirituality and Religion • **259**

therapy has also seen an increase in special issues of journals dedicated to the topic of spirituality in therapy, as well as complete books dedicated to the integration of spirituality. However, despite the rapid growth in the number of articles on spirituality and therapy, there are still relatively few that focus on integrating spirituality specifically into couple therapy, by now a familiar theme. Reflecting the growing literature, we provide separate sections on integration in therapy, training, and research for this third wave.

Incorporation of Spirituality Into Therapy: Third Wave 2000–Present

Special Journal Issues In this third wave, several MFT-related journals have published special issues focused upon the integration of spirituality and family therapy. For instance, the April, 2000 issue of the *Journal of Marital and Family Therapy* has a special section on spirituality and family therapy, although none of the articles are on integrating spirituality specifically with couple therapy. The *Family Therapy Networker*'s cover for the January/February 2000 issue is on "Christian counseling: A journey beyond the self." The *Journal of Family Psychotherapy* dedicates its entire volume in 2002 to spirituality and family therapy, which is copublished simultaneously as the edited book *Spirituality and Family Therapy* (T. D. Carlson & Erickson, 2002a). This book contains sections on spirituality and theory, spirituality research, spirituality and ethics, spirituality and MFT training, and spiritual approaches with specific issues. Only one chapter in this special issue, however, deals specifically with couple therapy (Blanton, 2002). In this chapter, Blanton described clinical guidelines for incorporating Christian meditation into a collaborative language systems approach.

Edited and Authored Books Several additional books have been published in the third wave, similar in form and function to the ones published in the second wave. These collections of theoretical approaches and practical suggestions come from various mental health disciplines. See Sperry (2001), J. L. Griffith and Griffith (2002a), G. Miller (2002), and Sperry and Shafranske (2005) for excellent examples. Sperry's (2001) book also includes approaches for incorporating spirituality into couples' treatment. Richards and Bergin's (2005) second edition of *A Spiritual Strategy for Counseling and Psychotherapy* is another fine example, and their companion (2004) casebook also contains a case description on forgiveness by Krejci (2004), in which a couple in marriage therapy resolves issues of anger. Bill O'Hanlon's (2006) *Pathways to Spirituality* addresses the integration of spirituality with solution-oriented therapy. Berg-Cross (2001), in her book on couple therapy, included a chapter on spirituality and the couple relationship. Serlin (2005) wrote a chapter on religious and spiritual issues in couple therapy in Harway's (2005) *Handbook of Couples Therapy*.

260 • Handbook of Clinical Issues in Couple Therapy

The first similar type of edited book to appear in the field of MFT is a two-book set of *The Therapist's Notebook for Integrating Spirituality in Counseling: Homework, Handouts, and Activities for Use in Psychotherapy* (Helmeke & Sori, 2006a, 2006b), which contains six chapters on spirituality and couple therapy. Baca, Schafer, and Helmeke (2006) discussed three empathy-generating skills designed to increase a couple's empathic attunement with each other in therapy, using adaptations from Imago Relationship Therapy (Hendrix, 1988). Michael (2006) wrote about developing a couple mission statement. Mamalakis (2006) redirected a couple to their wedding vows and their faith to look for ways for the couple to rekindle their love, and Shaw (2006) examined the role of shame in a couple's relationship. Also, Meyerstein (2006) discussed spiritual ramifications of couples' struggles with infertility, and Distelberg and Helmeke (2006) reflected on miscarriage from a father's perspective.

Spirituality and Sex Therapy   Sex therapy is one of the areas of couple therapy that has particularly begun to explore the role of spirituality. Prominent couple and sex therapist David Schnarch (1998) described how fulfilling one's sexual potential leads to spirituality and transcendence, and an ineffable connection and sense of oneness for the couple. Other recent articles have addressed the integration of spirituality and religion with sex therapy, suggesting these two dimensions of experience share a common ground (Ullery, 2004), and that the inherent transcendence of spirituality has implications for greater sexual understanding and fulfillment (Turner, Center, & Kiser, 2004). Boaz and Wiseman (2001) use four case studies to show how the concept of sin contributes to the problem of inhibited sexual desire among Christian couples.

Incorporation of Spirituality Into Training: Third Wave 2000–Present

Also emerging in this third wave of spirituality in MFT is an additional survey related to the training of marriage and family therapists and their opinions on how much training they had received on integrating spirituality and therapy. T. Carlson et al. (2002) found that only 14% of marriage and family therapists surveyed report that spirituality had been emphasized in their training. The authors hypothesize that this lack of education may be related to therapists' discomfort in addressing and integrating spirituality in therapy.

The third wave ushers in several new developments in response to the concern that marriage and family therapists were receiving inadequate training and supervision regarding the integration of religion and spirituality into therapy. Patterson, Hayworth, Turner, and Raskin (2000) describe a graduate-level course on spiritual issues in family therapy, which includes suggested weekly topics and readings, including information on comparative religions. Kimball and Knudson-Martin (2002) proposed a framework for addressing how gender intersects with spirituality, religions, and relationship problems.

Couple Therapy and the Integration of Spirituality and Religion • **261**

These are both tools that will help to equip therapists-in-training to feel more confident in integrating issues of spirituality in training.

Another development, and an additional sign of spirituality and family therapy "having arrived" in this third wave, is that the Commission on Accreditation for Marriage and Family Therapy Education's (version 10.3) requirements for accredited programs included religion and spirituality among other multicultural and diversity issues to be addressed in MFT education.

Rivett and Street (2001) proposed a framework to conceptualize the connection between therapy and spirituality that included two dimensions: an instrumental connection, in which therapists orient themselves to their clients' beliefs, using various clinical strategies, and a metaphysical connection, in which therapists address the way spirituality is linked to therapy by orienting themselves to their own beliefs.

In yet another development, M. M. Miller, Korinek, and Ivey (2004) have created a tool to measure therapists' perceptions of the frequency with which spirituality is addressed in supervision, called the Spiritual Issues in Supervision Scale. The authors assert that this tool is an initial step in the field of MFT to be able to examine spirituality through research and to assess the depth and breadth that spirituality is discussed in supervision. Hodge (2005), in recognition of the lack of training many marriage and family therapists had received regarding integrating spirituality into therapy, provided an overview of six qualitative assessment tools and a decision tree to determine the applicability of their use. These include the use of spiritual histories, life maps, spiritual genograms, and eco-maps. In a discussion of couple therapy supervision, Stratton and Smith (2006) highlight the importance of the supervisor raising issues about how the couple therapist's religious and cultural views can impact their view of couple issues such as cohabitation, infidelity, unplanned pregnancy, and same-sex couples.

As with the rest of the literature, there have been no specific articles relating to training on how to incorporate spirituality in couple therapy, yet it seems clear that therapists welcome and desire this type of training. Haug (1998) agrees that training in spirituality is an important part of therapists' self-awareness: "every practicing therapist holds beliefs about human nature including human suffering, people's capacity to change, and the process of healing" (p. 184), and because therapists' beliefs have an effect on therapy process and outcome, they need to be examined in training, so that therapists can "non-judgmentally and respectfully open space for the discussion of religious or spiritual content that is important to clients" (p. 185).

Research on Couple Therapy and Spirituality/Religion:
Third Wave 2000–Present

The type of research related to couples has continued along the same vein in this third wave as in the first and second waves, although in general, the factors studied and the methodologies used become increasingly more nuanced, as various aspects of couples are studied in relation to spirituality and religion. Further, more studies have begun to make clear the clinical implications of their findings. For example, instead of just looking at the effect of religious intermarriage or heterogamy on the level of couple intimacy or satisfaction, Heller and Wood (2000) reported that intramarried and intermarried couples arrive at similar levels of intimacy, but by different pathways. Although this study was not directly related to couple therapy, the authors do include clinical implications of their findings. Heller and Wood concluded that clinicians and religious leaders should not just assume that because partners come from different religious backgrounds that they are therefore doomed to lower levels of intimacy, but rather they should understand that these couples can have greater intimacy through the very process of negotiating their differences. Similarly, Senter and Caldwell (2002), in studying the ways that spiritual beliefs intersect with women's ability to leave abusive relationships, suggested that clinicians help women explore the spiritual dimension of their decision-making process, recognize that the process of leaving a relationship itself can change clients' relationships with God, and to understand how a client's religious beliefs and resources can assist them.

In a grounded theory qualitative study, 10 Roman Catholic couples were interviewed to understand the effects of their religious beliefs on the ways in which they managed anger and conflict in their marital relationships (Marsh & Dallos, 2001). The authors suggest that clinicians discuss with couples how the discipline of prayer and meditation can contribute to creating calmer conditions under which more constructive problem solving can occur.

Butler, Stout, and Gardner (2002) also reflected on the clinical implications of using prayer as a conflict resolution tactic in marital therapy for religious couples. Butler et al. assessed participants' phenomenological experience of prayer during marital conflict and found that couples associated relationship softening, healing, and perception or experience of responsibility of change with their prayer experience.

As Butler et al. (2002) stated that "much of the existing marriage, family, and therapy research consists of opinion, attitude, and practice surveys only" (p. 20). It must be admitted that some of the surveys have become more focused on couple therapy. For example, Ripley, Worthington, and Berry (2001) surveyed religious couples about their preferences and expectations for four different marital therapy situations and found that although highly religious Christian clients do not necessary seek highly religious Christian therapists, they do reject a marital therapist who is religiously different *and* does not appear interested in the clients' religion.

However, it still remains unfortunately true, with a few exceptions, that there is very little research looking at the effects of spiritual variables on processes and outcomes in couple therapy. As noted above, Worthington et al. (1996) reported that few studies have investigated the role of religion in actual clients' lives during therapy. However, some small advances are being made that push closer to developing studies that examine how various aspects of spirituality affect psychotherapeutic processes and outcomes in couple therapy.

One example of this advance is an ethnographic study of three couples and six practitioners regarding their experiences of spirituality in therapy (Coffey, 2002). Results show that spirituality relates to couple therapy in three ways: (1) practitioners' perceptions, (2) couples' experiences of spirituality, and (3) open exchanges among the participants. Two of the couples reported that spirituality was central to their experiences in therapy, and all of the participants considered spirituality to be additive to the process and outcome of couple therapy. In another advance, Carson, Carson, Gil, and Baucom (2004) have studied the effects of a particular spiritual intervention, a program called Mindfulness-Based Relationship Enhancement that was designed to enhance the relationships of relatively healthy couples. Although this is not couple therapy per se, this relationship enhancement intervention does show improvement in individual relaxation, acceptance of partner, confidence in ability to cope, and overall relationship satisfaction.

In addition, there have been several articles detailing some type of spiritual intervention in couple therapy that also include a case study. For example, Blanton (2002) using a collaborative language systems perspective to incorporate Christian meditation with religious couples, shared transcripts of a therapy session. Sperry (2007) described how a relatively new cognitive behavioral approach, called Cognitive Behavioral Analysis System of Psychotherapy, can be used to address patterns of spiritual issues that emerge in couple therapy when one partner has a chronic illness. Included in the case study is a transcript of a couple therapy session that illustrates how the nine steps of CBASP are applied. Although he does not include a case study, Laaser (2006), described working with couples when one partner is a sex addict from a faith based or spiritual perspective, and gives examples of reflection questions to pose in couple therapy. Worthington, Mazzeo, and Canter (2005) describe a psychoeducational intervention to promote forgiveness among couples, and include a case study. Weld and Eriksen (2006) applied nine strategies discussed in previous literature in a case study of a couple presenting with religious differences. Finally, Blanton (2004) used three case studies to illustrate the use of postmodern interventions that make couple therapy a meaningful and respectful experience for evangelical Christian couples. These case studies and others like these will likely pave the way for the next wave of research in the field that moves beyond case study reports to more sophisticated research investigating the influence of integrating spirituality or religion on the outcome and process of couple therapy.

264 • Handbook of Clinical Issues in Couple Therapy

Recommendations: Where to Go From Here

Although tremendous strides have been made in suggesting how spirituality can be included in couple therapy, much yet remains to be done. Several areas are especially promising, which we discuss below.

Systematic Application to Couple Therapy Models

The review above reveals the lack of application of spirituality to couple therapy models, with minor exceptions. What is principally missing is any systematic application to prominent couple therapy models. This would be a logical next step in the development of this integration. Religion and spirituality could be applied to prominent models of couple therapy such as Emotionally Focused Therapy, Integrative Behavioral Couple Therapy, Gottman's Sound Relationship House Theory, and Imago Relationship Therapy (Hendrix, 1988), showing how outcomes from these models might be enhanced by such an application.

Increasing Specificity About Various Religious Groups

Thus far, again with few exceptions, only a general discussion about integrating religion and spirituality with couple therapy exists. As this integration further develops, a growing sophistication regarding specific religions or religious denominations is called for. As has been increasingly true for other facets of multiculturalism, such as ethnicity and race, greater understanding about specific denominations and spiritual practices seems appropriate. It would be helpful for clinicians to know critical differences among various religions, understand basic doctrine, to become familiar with the "ethos" (e.g., language, nonverbal symbols, rituals, norms, patterns of relationships, Stewart & Gale, 1994) of specific religious subcultures, and to understand how such sensitivity can enhance clinical practice. Stewart and Gale can serve as a guideline for this type of work, as they spell out the ethos of protestant evangelicals, and derive clinical interventions appropriate for working with a couple from this background.

Expanding Research

Even now, research on psychotherapeutic processes and outcome in couple therapy and the integration of spirituality or religion is almost nonexistent. As Butler et al. (2002) note, existing research about the application of spirituality to MFT, and by association couple therapy, has been limited to opinion, attitude, and practice surveys only. Though helpful to justify integration, it is time to move beyond such surveys. Research is needed that studies how various aspects of spirituality affect psychotherapeutic processes and outcomes in couple therapy in order to discern specific mechanisms, qualities, and ways that spirituality and religion benefit couples and aid the therapeutic process. For instance, one might explore the impact on therapy if the therapist uses

Couple Therapy and the Integration of Spirituality and Religion • **265**

religious or spiritual techniques, shows respect for religious or spiritual heritage and practices, or uses religious language and metaphors, and how these factors might affect the clients' perception of the therapist, perceptions of therapeutic alliance, and various therapeutic processes. One example of such clinically relevant research is Butler et al., who, in studying the technique of using prayer as a conflict resolution tactic in marital therapy for religious couples, found that couples associated relationship softening, healing, and perception or experience of responsibility of change with their prayer experience. Notice that the concepts of softening and partners taking responsibility for their part in interactions are two common elements of most effective couple therapy models. Qualitative and quantitative studies are both appropriate for better understanding therapeutic processes impacted by the inclusion of spirituality. Consistent with a trend in MFT research, accessing clients' perspectives is also recommended. One earlier study emphasizes the value of gaining clients' perspectives. Lindgren and Coursey (1995) conducted a study in which 34% of the clients wanted to discuss spirituality with their therapist "very much" or "occasionally" but had never done so. Only half of the clients surveyed who wanted to discuss their spirituality in therapy felt free to do so.

Utilization of Research From Other Related Fields

Couple therapists would be wise to draw from findings in other related disciplines, such as family studies and family sociology, which have addressed the role of religion or spirituality for couple and family relationships. A thorough review of the literature for this chapter revealed that a substantial amount of useful information exists, though not necessarily in primary MFT journals and publications. Such information on the science of the role of religion or spirituality and the study of healthy, well-functioning couples has much to offer clinicians in their work with couples experiencing problems in their relationships. For instance, it is well established that spirituality enhances the marital relationship, and that religious involvement is an important predictor of long-term marriage, marital satisfaction, commitment, and happiness. For one review of these studies, see Weaver et al. (2002).

Increased Attention in Training and Supervision

Finally, it is apparent that attention to matters of religion and spirituality is woefully inadequate in MFT training programs. As noted above, although trainees and clinicians value spirituality in their own lives and believe that these resources could be useful to tap in clinical work, they are hesitant to address these matters directly, and generally fail to do so, especially for religion (T. Carlson et al., 2002; Prest et al., 1999). We concur with these authors who conclude that a lack of education is likely related to therapists' discomfort and reluctance in addressing and integrating religion and spirituality in therapy.

266 • Handbook of Clinical Issues in Couple Therapy

Training programs and supervisors are encouraged to include discussion of these topics as part of a general consideration of multicultural and diversity issues for clients and therapists. These topics could also be infused into existing courses where appropriate, and when feasible, a specialized course could also be offered. Educators and supervisors can provide permission to explore and integrate religion and spirituality in clinical work, as well as offer guidance about how to do so in a sensitive, respectful manner that assists therapeutic goals and enhances the therapeutic process. American Association for Marriage and Family Therapy Approved Supervisor training and refresher trainings could also include attention to the integration of spirituality and religion in couple and family therapy.

In summary, we see in these three waves an increase in the acceptance of integrating spirituality and religion in MFT as well as a greater refinement in how these important dimensions of people's experience may be applied to clinical work, training, and research. It is interesting to note that the time frame in which couple therapy has developed as a distinct discipline within the field of MFT has paralleled the time frame in which the growth of the application of spirituality and religion in our field has occurred. We foresee that one of the future developments in the next wave for both couple therapy and the integration of spirituality in therapy will be the dovetailing of these two areas: couple therapy will integrate what we have learned about spirituality and religion with greater sophistication and spirituality and religion will be more fully utilized in the realm of couple therapy. In doing, the promise of appreciating the role of spirituality and religion that our early marriage counselor predecessors held will be not only reclaimed, but expanded.

References

Abbott, D., Berry, M., & Meredith, W. H. (1990). Religious belief and practice: A potential asset in helping families. *Family Relations, 39*, 443–448.

Anderson, D. A. (1994). Transcendence and relinquishment in couple therapy. *Journal of Systemic Therapies, 13*, 36–41.

Anderson, D. A., & Worthen, D. (1997). Exploring a fourth dimension: Spirituality as a resource for the couple therapist. *Journal of Marital and Family Therapy, 23*, 3–12.

Aponte, H. J. (1996). Political bias, moral values, and spirituality in the training of psychotherapists. *Bulletin of the Menninger Clinic, 60*(4), 488–502.

Baca, B. J., Schafer, S. L., & Helmeke, K. B. (2006). Empathic attunement in marital therapy as a spiritual state: Some thoughts and strategies for its development. In K. B. Helmeke & C. F. Sori (Eds.), *The therapist's notebook for integrating spirituality in counseling: Homework, handouts, and activities for use in psychotherapy* (pp. 129–137). New York: Haworth Press.

Berg-Cross, L. (2001). *Couples therapy* (2nd ed.). New York: Haworth Clinical Practice Press.

Bergin, A. E., & Jensen, J. P. (1990). Religiosity of psychotherapists: A national survey. *Psychotherapy, 27*, 3–7.

Blanton, P. G. (2002). The use of Christian meditation with religious couples: A collaborative language systems perspective. *Journal of Family Psychotherapy, 13*, 291–307.

Couple Therapy and the Integration of Spirituality and Religion • **267**

Blanton, P. G. (2004). Opening space for dialogue between postmodern therapists and evangelical couples. *The Family Journal, 12*, 375–382.

Boaz, B. J., & Wiseman, C. (2001). Problems of the heart: Overcoming spiritual issues associated with inhibited sexual desire in Christian marriage. *Marriage & Family: A Christian Journal, 4*, 229–238.

Brothers, B. J. (Ed.). (1993). *Spirituality and couples: Heart and soul in the therapy process.* Binghamton, NY: Haworth Press.

Butler, M. H., & Harper, J. M. (1994). The divine triangle: God in the marital system of religious couples. *Family Process, 33*, 277–286.

Butler, M. H., Stout, J. A., & Gardner, B. C. (2002). Prayer as a conflict resolution ritual: Clinical implications of religious couples' report of relationship softening, healing perspective, and change responsibility. *American Journal of Family Therapy, 30*, 19–37.

Carlson, T., Kirkpatrick, D., Hecker, L., & Killmer, M. (2002). Religion, spirituality, and marriage and family therapy: A study of family therapists' beliefs about the appropriateness of addressing religious and spiritual issues in therapy. *American Journal of Family Therapy, 30*, 157–171.

Carlson, T. D., & Erickson, M. J. (2000). Re-authoring spiritual narratives: God in persons' relational identity stories. *Journal of Systemic Therapies, 19*, 65–83.

Carlson, T. D., & Erickson, M. J. (2002a). *Spirituality and family therapy.* New York: Haworth Press.

Carlson, T. D., & Erickson, M. J. (2002b). The spiritualities of therapists' lives: Using therapists' spiritual beliefs as a resource for relational ethics. *Journal of Family Psychotherapy, 13*(3–4), 215–236.

Carson, J. W., Carson, K. M., Gil, K. M., & Baucom, D. H. (2004). Mindfulness-based relationship enhancement. *Behavior Therapy, 35*, 471–494.

Coffey, A. D. (2002). *Spirituality and couples therapy: Ethnographic perspectives from therapy experiences.* Unpublished doctoral dissertation, Texas Women's University.

Distelberg, B., & Helmeke, K. B. (2006). Am I a father? A husband's miscarriage. In K. B. Helmeke & C. F. Sori (Eds.), *The therapist's notebook for integrating spirituality in counseling II: More homework, handouts, and activities for use in psychotherapy* (pp. 231–241). New York: Haworth Press.

Ellis, A. (1981). Science, religiosity, and rational emotive psychology. *Psychotherapy: Theory, research and practice, 18*, 155–158.

Frame, M. W. (2000). Spiritual and religious issues in counseling: Ethical considerations. *The Family Journal, 8*, 72–74.

Giblin, P. (1996). Spirituality, marriage, and family. *The Family Journal, 4*, 46–52.

Griffith, B. A., & Rotter, J. C. (1999). Families and spirituality: Therapists as facilitators. *The Family Journal, 7*, 161–164.

Griffith, J. L., & Griffith, M. E. (2002a). *Encountering the sacred in psychotherapy: How to talk with people about their spiritual lives.* New York: Guilford.

Griffith, M. E. (1995). Opening therapy to conversations with a personal God. *Journal of Feminist Family Therapy, 7*, 123–139.

Griffith, M. E., & Griffith, J. L. (2002b). Addressing spirituality in its clinical complexities: Its potential for healing, its potential for harm. *Journal of Family Psychotherapy, 13*, 167–194.

Gurman, A. S., & Fraenkel, P. (2002). The history of couple therapy: A millennial review. *Family Process, 41*, 199–260.

Hahlweg, K., Markman, H. J., Thurmaier, F., Engl, J., & Eckert, V. (1998). Prevention of marital distress: Results of a German prospective longitudinal study. *Journal of Family Psychology, 12*, 543–556.

268 • Handbook of Clinical Issues in Couple Therapy

Harris, S. M. (1998). Finding a forest among trees: Spirituality hiding in family therapy theories. *Journal of Family Studies, 4,* 77–86.

Harway, M. (Ed.). (2005). *Handbook of couples therapy.* New York: John Wiley & Sons.

Haug, I. E. (1998). Including a spiritual dimension in family therapy: Ethical considerations. *Contemporary Family Therapy, 20,* 181–194.

Heller, P. E., & Wood, B. (2000). The influence of religious and ethnic differences on marital intimacy: Intermarriage versus intermarriage. *Journal of Marital and Family Therapy, 26,* 241–252.

Helmeke, K. B., & Bischof, G. H. (2002). Recognizing and raising spiritual and religious issues in therapy: Guidelines for the timid. *Journal of Family Psychotherapy, 13,* 195–214.

Helmeke, K. B., & Sori, C. F. (2006a). *The therapist's notebook for integrating spirituality in counseling: Homework, handouts, and activities for use in psychotherapy.* New York: Haworth Press.

Helmeke, K. B., & Sori, C. F. (2006b). *The therapist's notebook for integrating spirituality in counseling II: More homework, handouts, and activities for use in psychotherapy.* New York: Haworth Press.

Hendrix, H. (1988). *Getting the love you want: A guide for couples.* New York: Harper Perennial.

Hines, M. (1996). Follow-up survey of graduates from accredited degree-granting marriage and family therapy training programs. *Journal of Marital and Family Therapy, 22,* 181–194.

Hodge, D. (2005). Spiritual assessment in marital and family therapy: A methodological framework for selecting among six qualitative assessment tools. *Journal for Marital and Family Therapy, 31,* 341–356.

Joanides, C. J. (1996). Collaborative family therapy with religious family systems. *Journal of Family Psychotherapy, 7,* 19–35.

Kimball, L. S., & Knudson-Martin, C. (2002). A cultural trinity: Spirituality, religion and gender in clinical practice. *Journal of Family Psychotherapy, 13,* 145–166.

Krejci, M. J. (2004). Forgiveness in marital therapy. In P. S. Richards & A. E. Bergin (Eds.), *Casebook for a spiritual strategy in counseling and psychotherapy* (pp. 87–102). Washington, DC: American Psychological Association.

Laaser, M. R. (2006). Working with couples from a spiritual perspective [Special issue: Sexual addiction and the family]. *Sexual Addiction & Compulsivity, 13,* 209–217.

Lindgren, K. N., & Coursey, R. D. (1995). Spirituality and serious mental illness: A two-part study. *Psychosocial Rehabilitation Journal, 18,* 93–111.

Mahoney, A., Pargament, K. I., Jewell, T., Swank, A. B., Scott, E., Emery, E., & Rye, M. (1999). Marriage and the spiritual realm: The role of proximal and distal religious constructs in marital functioning. *Journal of Family Psychology, 13,* 321–338.

Mamalakis, P. (2006). WWJD: Using a couple's faith to fall back in love. In K. B. Helmeke & C. F. Sori (Eds.), *The therapist's notebook for integrating spirituality in counseling: Homework, handouts, and activities for use in psychotherapy* (pp. 149–155). New York: Haworth Press.

Marsh, R., & Dallos, R. (2001). Roman Catholic couples: Wrath and religion. *Family Process, 40,* 343–360.

Meyerstein, I. (2006). Spiritual steps for couples recovering from fetal loss. In K. B. Helmeke & C. F. Sori (Eds.), *The therapist's notebook for integrating spirituality in counseling II: More homework, handouts, and activities for use in psychotherapy* (pp. 223–229). New York: Haworth Press.

Couple Therapy and the Integration of Spirituality and Religion • **269**

Michael, R. (2006). Developing a couples mission statement: A resource for couples facing career decisions/transitions. In K. B. Helmeke & C. F. Sori (Eds.), *The therapist's notebook for integrating spirituality in counseling: Homework, handouts, and activities for use in psychotherapy* (pp. 139–147). New York: Haworth Press.

Miller, G. (2002). *Incorporating spirituality in counseling and psychotherapy: Theory and technique*. Hoboken, NJ: Wiley.

Miller, M. M., Korinek, A., & Ivey, D. C. (2004). Spirituality in MFT training: Development of the Spiritual Issues in Supervision Scale. *Contemporary Family Therapy, 26,* 71–81.

O'Hanlon, W. (2006). *Pathways to spirituality: Connection, wholeness and possibility for therapist and client*. New York: Norton.

Patterson, J., Hayworth, M., Turner, C., & Raskin, M. (2000). Spiritual issues in family therapy: A graduate course. *Journal of Marital and Family Therapy, 26,* 199–210.

Patterson, J., Williams, L., Grauf-Grounds, C., & Chamow, L. (1998). *Essential skills in family therapy: From the first interview to termination*. New York: Guilford.

Prest, L. A., & Keller, J. F. (1993). Spirituality and family therapy: Spiritual beliefs, myths, and metaphors. *Journal of Marital and Family Therapy, 19,* 137–148.

Prest, L. A., Russel, R., & D'Souza, H. (1999). Spirituality and religion in training, practice, and personal development. *Journal of Family Therapy, 21,* 60–78.

Richards, P. S., & Bergin, A. E. (Eds.). (2004). *Casebook for a spiritual strategy in counseling and psychotherapy*. Washington, DC: American Psychological Association.

Richards, P. S., & Bergin, A. E. (2005). *A spiritual strategy for counseling and psychotherapy* (2nd ed.). Washington, DC: American Psychological Association.

Ripley, J. S., Worthington, E. L., Jr., & Berry, J. W. (2001). The effects of religiosity on preferences and expectations for marital therapy among married Christians. *American Journal of Family Therapy, 29,* 39–58.

Rivett, M., & Street, E. (2001). Connections and themes of spirituality in family therapy. *Family Process, 40,* 459–467.

Robinson, L. C., & Blanton, P. W. (1993). Marital strengths in enduring marriages. *Family Relations, 42,* 38–45.

Rotz, E., Russell, C. S., & Wright, D. W. (1993). The therapist who is perceived as "spiritually correct": Strategies for avoiding collusion with the "spiritually one-up" spouse. *Journal of Marital and Family Therapy, 19,* 369–375.

Schnarch, D. (1998). *Passionate marriage*. New York: Owl Books/Henry Holt.

Senter, K. E., & Caldwell, K. (2002). Spirituality and the maintenance of change: A phenomenological study of women who leave abusive relationships. *Contemporary Family Therapy, 24,* 543–564.

Serlin, I. (2005). Religious and spiritual issues in couples therapy. In M. Harway (Ed.), *Handbook of couples therapy* (pp. 352–369). New York: John Wiley & Sons.

Shafranske, E. P., & Malony, H. N. (1990). Clinical psychologists' religious and spiritual orientations and their practice of psychotherapy. *Psychotherapy, 27,* 720–728.

Shaw, R. S. (2006). I reject that shame. In K. B. Helmeke & C. F. Sori (Eds.), *The therapist's notebook for integrating spirituality in counseling: Homework, handouts, and activities for use in psychotherapy* (pp. 157–164). New York: Haworth Press.

Sperry, L. (2001). *Spirituality in clinical practice: Incorporating the spiritual dimension in psychotherapy and counseling*. New York: Brunner-Routledge.

Sperry, L. (2007). Dealing with the spiritual issues of chronically ill clients in the context of couples counseling: A unique application of cognitive behavioral analysis system of psychotherapy (CBASP). *The Family Journal, 15,* 183–187.

270 • Handbook of Clinical Issues in Couple Therapy

Sperry, L., & Giblin, P. (1996). Marital and family therapy with religious persons. In E. P. Shafranske (Ed.), *Religion and the clinical practice of psychology*. Washington, DC: APA.

Sperry, L., & Shafranske, E. P. (Eds.). (2005). *Spiritually oriented psychotherapy*. Washington, DC: American Psychological Association.

Stander, V., Piercy, F., Mackinnon, D., & Helmeke, K. (1994). Spirituality, religion and family therapy: Competing or complementary worlds? *American Journal of Family Therapy, 22,* 27–41.

Stewart, S. P., & Gale, J. E. (1994). On hallowed ground: Marital therapy with couples on the religious right. *Journal of Systemic Therapies, 13,* 16–25.

Stratton, J. S., & Smith, R. D. (2006). Supervision of couples cases. *Psychotherapy: Theory, Research, Practice, Training, 43,* 337–348.

Turner, T. E., Center, H., & Kiser, J. D. (2004). Uniting spirituality and sexual counseling. *The Family Journal, 12,* 419–422.

Ullery, E. K. (2004). Consideration of a spiritual role in sex and sex therapy. *The Family Journal, 12,* 78–81.

Walsh, F. (1999a). Religion and spirituality: Wellsprings for healing and resilience. In F. Walsh (Ed.), *Spiritual resources in family therapy* (pp. 3–27). New York: Guilford Press.

Walsh, F. (Ed.). (1999b). *Spiritual resources in family therapy*. New York: Guilford Press.

Watson, W. H. (1997). Soul and system: The integrative possibilities of family therapy. *Journal of Psychology and Theology, 25,* 123–135.

Weaver, A. J., Samford, J. A., Morgan, V. J., Larson, D. B., Koenig, H. G., & Flannelly, K. J. (2002). A systematic review of research on religion in six primary marriage and family journals: 1995–1999. *The American Journal of Family Therapy, 30,* 293–309.

Weld, C., & Eriksen, K. (2006). The challenge of religious conflicts in couples counseling. *The Family Journal, 14,* 383–391.

Wendel, R. (2003). Lived religion and family therapy: What does spirituality have to do with it? *Family Process, 42,* 165–179.

Williams, L. M., Patterson, J. E., & Miller, R. B. (2006). Panning for gold: A clinician's guide to using research. *Journal of Marital and Family Therapy, 32,* 17–32.

Wilson, M. R., & Filsinger, E. E. (1986). Religiosity and marital adjustment: Multidimensional interrelationships. *Journal of Marriage and the Family, 48,* 147–151.

Worthington, E. L., Jr. (Ed.). (1996). *Christian marital counseling: Eight approaches to helping couples*. Grand Rapids, MI: Baker Books.

Worthington, E. L., Jr., Kurusu, T. A., McCullough, M. E., & Sandage, S. J. (1996). Empirical research on religion and psychotherapeutic processes and outcomes: A 10-year review and research prospectus. *Psychological Bulletin, 119,* 448–487.

Worthington, E. L., Jr., Mazzeo, S. E., & Canter, D. E. (2005). Forgiveness-promoting approach: Helping clients REACH forgiveness through using a longer model that teaches reconciliation. In L. Sperry (Ed.), *Spiritually oriented psychotherapy* (pp. 235–257). Washington, DC: American Psychological Association.

15
Feminist Couple Therapy

ANNE M. PROUTY and KEVIN P. LYNESS

Contents

The Continued Deconstruction of Gender	271
Gender Deconstruction to Reconstruction	272
Gender Roles in Feminist Couple Therapy	272
Cultural Diversity, Racism, and Couples	273
Self-of-the-Therapist: Know and Educate Oneself	273
Honoring Aspects of Heritage That Are Congruent With Feminist Goals	274
Honoring Uniqueness, Transitions, and Innovations: Working With Intercultural Couples	275
Understanding the Pressures of Racism on Couples' Relationships	275
The Importance of Community Support for Changes	276
Connection as a Focus and as a Process	276
Redefining Sex Therapy	277
The Pervasiveness of Power	279
Deconstruction and Reconstruction of Relationship Power	279
Negotiating Family and Work Responsibilities	280
Power and Gendered Communication	281
Feminist Therapy for Couple Violence	281
Conclusion	283
References	284

Feminist couple therapy now spans four decades of critiquing, expanding, and strengthening our work with individuals, couples, families, and larger systems. Feminists have been at the forefront of bringing aspects of human diversity to couple therapy in order to make oppression overt and to not perpetuate it within treatment. In this chapter, we focus on the literature of recent years.

The Continued Deconstruction of Gender

Most of the early feminist family therapy scholarship focused on the effects of gender as a major organizing principle of intimate relationships, families, and society. Upon this work, feminists have continued to build a sophisticated examination of gender in therapy.

Gender Deconstruction to Reconstruction

Feminists have continued to focus on the importance of identifying societal scripts about "natural" differences between men and women and to help same-sex and heterosexual couples to deconstruct these scripts so as to enable more flexible options (Bepko & Johnson, 2000; Halstead, 2003; Knudson-Martin, 1995; Knudson-Martin & Mahoney, 1999; Rampage, 2003; Sims, 1996). Rampage worked toward meaningful gender reconstruction at the behavioral, emotional, and cognitive levels. Freedman and Combs (2002) helped partners to discover gender stories in which they have more choices about how to be women and men. This idea was extended by Prouty and Protinsky (2002) in the use of internal family systems therapy with couples working with balancing parts of their personalities as related to gendered interactions and other aspects of the couple relationship.

The importance of deconstructing and reconstructing gender applied to heterosexual, lesbian, and gay couples, but feminists were aware that stereotypes about gender added an extra layer of gender bias with lesbian and gay couples because gender and sexual orientation have been confused—one of many layers of gendered heterosexism (Bepko & Johnson, 2000). Bepko and Johnson challenged therapists' ideas about the necessity or naturalness of a socially constructed masculine or feminine role complementarity. They suggested that couple therapists be aware of the potential for both the heterosexist and the shaming effects on clients of stereotyped ideas. Along those lines, Knudson-Martin and Laughlin (2005) called for a postgendered approach as they discussed gender and sexual orientation as socially constructed, politically laden, and culturally influenced stereotypes that could never reflect human diversity or couple's diverse needs.

Feminists have also continued to talk about gender roles within the couple dynamics when a mental illness is diagnosed. Knudson-Martin (2001) discussed the role of the social construction of gender on women's mental health and provided a model of couple therapy based on a feminist interpretation of emotional differentiation. Papp (2000, 2003) and her colleagues at the Ackerman Institute's Depression Project focused feminists' attentions to the gendered constructions of depression and depression's part in couple dynamics. And, Jackson (2005) delivered a thought-provoking discussion of the interaction effects of poverty, oppression, chronic stress, and depression in women's lives and relationships.

Gender Roles in Feminist Couple Therapy

During recent years, feminists have continued to focus on the social construction of gender roles and how these affect couples. A good deal of the recent work in this area has focused on how gender role constructions influenced couple's feelings of closeness and distance (Conway, 2000; Guilbert, Vace, & Pasley, 2000; Philpot, Brooks, Lusterman, & Nutt, 1997; Schneider, 1996).

Levant and Philpot (2002) summarized work on the gender role strain paradigm and how it affected couples. Other foci within this area included gender myths, particularly in the treatment of infidelity (S. Johnson, 2005); how gender role constructions influenced communication (O'Donohue & Crouch, 1996); and female and male perceptions within relationships (Gilbin & Chan, 1995; Guilbert et al., 2000), and the effects of racism in stereotyping gender roles. "Slavery has had a long-term impact on the gender roles of African American men and women" (p. 86). The "invisibility syndrome" (p. 87) continues to not just affect people, but to affect their gender roles in intimate relationships, *and* to influence the intimate relationships themselves.

Feminists recommended psychoeducation about the socially constructed nature of gender roles, including information on cultural differences of gender roles (Conway, 2000; Gilbin & Chan, 1995; Guilbert et al., 2000; Levant & Philpot, 2002; Philpot et al., 1997; Rabin, 1996). Whether through psychoeducation or more active therapeutic interventions, feminist were helping couples to develop greater understandings of the role gender played in relationship functioning and greater understanding and acceptance of their partner (and of their differences) in order to build empathy and mutuality (Philpot et al.; Rabin; Schneider, 1996). Vatcher and Bogo (2001) and S. M. Johnson (2004) suggested a feminist integration with emotionally focused therapy for couples, specifically in addressing "gender roles and individual emotional experience using a systemic framework for understanding couple interaction" (Vatcher & Bogo, p. 69).

Cultural Diversity, Racism, and Couples

Feminists "seek to establish a non-Eurocentric worldview, both in content and methodology, that relies heavily on the phenomenological experiences of ethnically and culturally diverse men and women living in our contemporary global world" (Parks, Cutts, Woodson, & Flarity-White, 2001, p. 18).

Self-of-the-Therapist: Know and Educate Oneself

Feminist therapists believed it essential to acknowledge inequities of class, gender, power, and safety among participants in therapy, including the therapist (Mac Kune-Karrer & Weigel Foy, 2003; Turner & Avis, 2003). To do this opened discussions about diversity and minimized covert collusion with racism, classism, heterosexism, and other forms of oppression. This collusion includes the minimization or avoidance of talking about ethnic history, experience, and differences in couple therapy. Feminists emphasized perpetual self-assessment of personal biases, privilege, and inexperience of human cultural diversity and of the monitoring of countertransference (Hays, 1996; Long, 2003; Pearlman, 1996; Pinderhughes, 2002). Tubbs and Rosenblatt (2003) suggested family of origin message analysis. Hays introduced the ADDRESSING acronym: age, developmental and acquired disabilities, religion, ethnicity,

274 • Handbook of Clinical Issues in Couple Therapy

social status, sexual orientation, indigenous heritage, national origin; and gender. Pearlman challenged therapists to monitor their heterosexism, no matter one's own sexual orientation, and to be sensitive to issues around coming and being out. Being sensitive to people from different cultures required that the therapist be knowledgeable and trustworthy, and may have more to do with what one has experienced in life and with one's own family than with any academic training (Perel, 2000).

Tamasese (2003) asserted that one cannot privilege gender over culture because they are woven together in the experience of life. She analyzed how White feminist's cultural privilege allowed a rendering of White culture invisible to the dominant discourse, but that it has never been invisible to those whose cultures have been colonized, oppressed, and ignored. Another one of Tamasese's many contributions to the feminist literature was to raise the discussion to the process of human diversity via the ability to be with people's pain and to help them and ourselves, if we allow the process of therapy to really work, as we discover people's stories of strength and resiliency. Thereby, therapy is revealed as a recursive process by which couples and families change therapists, and therapy can be an experience of family and community renewal and resilience, instead of yet another form of White colonization.

Honoring Aspects of Heritage That Are Congruent With Feminist Goals

Rather than trying to colonize couple's with White feminist constructions of gender equity, Tamasese and her colleagues in New Zealand (Tamasese, 2003; Tamasese & Laban, 2003; Tamasese & Waldegrave, 2003) also encouraged couple therapists to help uncover the traditions of gender arrangements that were traditional in people's cultures and that facilitated equity, respect, reciprocity, accountability, and empathy. Tien and Olson (2003) did just that when they drew from the Confucion Code to inform their work with Asian American couples. Paying attention to their generation in the United States and their unique familial integration of these codes of behaviors, Tien and Olsen helped clients to reimmerse themselves in their family values and to find facets that could be honored and focused in ways that provided greater freedom for both men and women. Similarly, Hays (1996) warned therapists not to view differences as deficiencies, and to be sure to notice creativity, commitment, and prior efforts at resolution. She emphasized the importance of culturally congruent framing of the problem and the solutions. Along these lines, Falicov (1998) talked about the concepts of fairness and justice being culturally congruent, as well as the positive aspects of both machismo and hembrismo, like loyalty to family, courage, strength, and putting family first, and urged feminists to draw upon these aspects when trying to help couples become more flexible around gender and power issues. Boyd-Franklin (2003), Black (2000), Falicov (1998), and R. L. Hall and Greene (2003) also focused on culturally informed stances of equity and resiliency. These included: self-care;

resiliency as protection; cautious boundaries with people until one knows they will honor and respect you; the importance of extended family and fictive kin to the couple's relationship; the concept of women being "softly strong" (R. L. Hall & Greene, p. 117); the value of acquiring direct experience; and the importance of the couple's relationship as parents.

Honoring Uniqueness, Transitions, and Innovations: Working With Intercultural Couples

When working with interracial and intercultural couples, feminists wrote about helping clients to discern when their differences were based in common personal preference, when their perspectives were informed by gender or ethnicity, and how to identify their strengths (Hays, 1996; K. Killian, 2003; Laird, 1994, 2000; Long, 2003; Pinderhughes, 2002) and when differences provided challenges that could create a richer couple experience (Root & Suyemoto, 2005). Falicov (1995) suggested the frame of the "cultural transition" (p. 236) to prevent stereotyping of differences and to create a more balanced approach to couples' explorations. Perel (2000) suggested introducing the metaphor of being a tourist in each other's culture in order to construct positions of interest, curiosity, respect, and to create a process of lifelong learning. Several feminist clinicians and clinical researchers suggested helping couples to focus on constructing empowering stories and identities (Hill & Thomas, 2002; K. D. Killian, 2001a; Tamasese, 2003; Wieling, 2003). Feminists were helping couples to express emotion, connection, physical affection, roles, power distribution, parenting, meanings of love, and methods of communication by eliciting rich life and cultural stories; resisting stereotypes, and validating experiences, feelings, goals, and values (Daneshpour, 2003). And, Wieling encouraged interracial couples to look at life cycle transitions and larger family dynamics that increased the possibility of stress. Feminist couple therapists warned against both presumptions of differences and ignoring differences between lesbian women of different ethnic backgrounds. Feminists facilitated lesbian couples' examinations of values, styles, and loyalties with extended family, money, time, styles of mothering and child-rearing, sources of identity and self-esteem, options and access to power (and privilege), and access to familial and cultural rituals while avoiding heteronormative assumptions regarding anything, including sexual constructions (Daneshpour; Halstead, 2003; Laird & Green, 1996; Long, 2003).

Understanding the Pressures of Racism on Couples' Relationships

Greene and Boyd-Franklin (1996) asserted that traditional approaches to couple therapy reinforced the triple discrimination (racism, sexism, and heterosexism) that African American women and lesbian couples faced in their daily lives. Pinderhughes (2002) discussed societal projection process (see Bowen, 1978) as a way to understand the effects of external and internal racism, classism,

276 • Handbook of Clinical Issues in Couple Therapy

and sexism on African American heterosexual couples. Black (2000) and R. L. Hall and Greene (2003) emphasized helping couples to understand the importance of working as a team against racism, while the couple is renegotiating empathy and relatedness, as shielding each other from either partner's pain can create isolation and disconnection; and helping partners to provide each other with emotional support and validation to facilitate emotional intimacy.

K. Killian (2003) also discussed respecting interracial couple's strategies for survival in a racist society: including within their own families, their work environments, and their communities. He suggested helping couples to talk about the benefits and limitations their survival strategies offer them in order to help couples to develop strategies that promoted strength, connection, positive identity, and continuity.

The Importance of Community Support for Changes

Several feminists working with couples wrote about it being essential to understand how couples can be intimately tied to family and community; sometimes to permit or sustain positive change and sometimes as essential to sustain the couple itself. For example, Falicov (1995) cautioned not request changes in Latino couples' gendered communication, power, or the sharing of emotions without first creating a supportive context within the larger family system. She emphasized encouraging emotional breadth, mutual responsibility, care and empathy, decreased stress and conflict, and promoting the greatest number of options that could be supported by the larger family and community system.

Black (2000) discussed the role of education in African American families' fight against racism, and the growth of the Black middle and professional classes. She urged therapists to recognize when couples were experiencing isolation from African American peers and to help couples find ways to reconnect through secular, political, and spiritual organizations. The latter could be especially important as a deep spirituality has been a common source of identity and resiliency to people of African heritage for many centuries (Black). Feminist couple therapists talked about the importance of being sensitive to Black lesbian women's complex loyalties to self, family, community, and culture and similarly complex methods for preserving and challenging them. Looking at communities of support, Black noted that African American gay and lesbian couples have often experienced heterosexism within religious communities. Black urged the importance of helping gay and lesbian African American couples to locate supportive spiritual communities if this previously had been a source of strength and well-being.

Connection as a Focus and as a Process

One of the primary themes in the clinical work of feminist couple therapists was on building connection within the couple (which, as noted above, is often negatively influenced by gender role constructions). What follows is a summary of some of the most influential and clear examples of this theme within the feminist couple therapy literature.

Rabin (1996) described a couple therapy model for building equal partnerships based on the primary notion of friendship; from an explicitly feminist perspective. Rabin's book was full of examples and data from studies of couples in both the United States and in Israel. A theme in Rabin's book that is common to several other books was attention to the gendered nature of the pursuer–distancer dynamic (see also Jacobson & Christensen, 1996; S. M. Johnson, 2004), the effects of power imbalances on relationships, and the effects of the larger cultural system. She discussed egalitarian relationships as involving a great deal of effort and a pay off (this is mirrored in Schwartz's 1994 self-help book for couples called *Love Between Equals: How Peer Marriage Really Works*). The two primary treatment goals of Rabin's therapy were (1) overcoming the gender gap in communications, which also included reducing men's avoidance of conflict and celebrating gender differences; and (2) fostering a shared ideology, which included relationship quality as a shared value and community involvement. Other treatment themes in Rabin's work included "helping couples become friends" (p. 117) and "shared power as mutual empowerment" (p. 84). Rabin combined individual interventions that focus on education regarding gender and couple interventions that focus on empathy building and changing power dynamics.

Many other feminist therapists had an explicit focus on building connection, particularly through empathy (Bergman & Surrey, 1999; S. M. Johnson, 2004; Laennec & Syrotinski, 2003; Schneider, 1996; Snyder, 1996; Vatcher & Bogo, 2001). Creating empathy between partners can be a critical role in understanding each other's experience and being willing to give up roles and entitlements (Knudson-Martin & Mahoney, 2005). Information, familiarity, and empathy can become antidotes to intolerance, misattributions, and projections.

Redefining Sex Therapy

Feminist couple therapists have continued to critique traditional methods of and conceptualizations of human sexuality and sex therapy—even questioning whether the medical community and mental health practitioners may have created problems in order to fix them. Recently, feminists have expanded their critique and developed client-focused methods of working with couples that take into account gender, culture, and power dynamics.

Redefining Sex   Most gendered and cultural stereotypes about sex and sexuality separate the people from their relationships and overly focus on the genitals, ignoring the rest of the body and the mind (Brooks, 2001). Feminists reported redirecting couples' attentions from a focus on genitals to uncovering the origins of their ideas about sex and sex roles, the influence of social

278 • Handbook of Clinical Issues in Couple Therapy

and gendered power inequities on their relationship, to revaluing their personal experiences and communicating them to each other (Stock & Moser, 2001). Several feminists asserted that we need a new way of naming, even of conceptualizing sexuality, sexual behaviors, and sexual problems (Tiefer, 2001) so as to incorporate women's experiences of their bodies, their relationships, and their cultures. M. Hall (1996) suggested that therapists who worked with lesbian couples should consider and expand their own ideas about sexual desire and what is defined as sexual behavior so as not to falsely construct problems in need of solving. Tiefer (2001) suggested new interpersonal constructions of sexual issues such as desire discrepancy or Schnarch's (1997) use of natural systems concepts to understand the role of sex in people's relationships. Similarly, Kleinplatz (2001) criticized traditional sex therapy as being too much of a "one size fits all goals" (p. 115), thereby ignoring diversity rather than including it. She wrote about working with couples whose sexuality was invisible within the sex therapy literature, such as disabled and older people. She suggested that therapists write more about working with diverse couples with diverse constructions of their sexualities—for the benefit of all couples. Feminist couple therapists stressed supporting people, and especially women, to construct their own repertoires of connection and physical pleasure, and for these to be built upon affirming self-images and interrelational patterns. Feminist couple therapists also stressed the importance of both partners taking responsibility for establishing rituals of connection that might include sex.

Sex Therapy as Relational Work   M. Hall (1996, 2001) emphasized validating diverse forms of intimacy, and helping clients to construct meaningful and mutually satisfying repertoires. Connor (2003) and Rampage (2003) both focused on helping partners to identify and remove constraints through constructing empathy, acceptance, vulnerability, intensity, and collaboration. Daniels, Zimmerman, and Bowling (2002) focused on helping couples to break down barriers and build bridges to facilitate connecting sexually. Stock and Moser (2001) cautioned against using sexual arousal enhancement drugs as a chemical bypass to the relational work, especially in an attempt to bypass creating power equity. What this literature revealed was that feminist sex therapists have emphasized on helping couples to build sensuality and emotional intimacy, to know each other's experiences and value systems, and to redefine sexual interludes as erotic encounters so as to enhance their relationship and to enhance their relationship in order to facilitate sexual pleasure. The focus for couples was often on redefining success into a continuum of erotic connecting, being present in the relationship, and mutual enjoyment of the process, and to seeing their sexual arousal as part of a larger ebb and flow within their relationship and their lives (Brooks, 2001; Ellison, 2001).

Inclusion and Special Issues of Same-Sex Couples   Iasenza (2004) wrote about helping lesbian couples to build "an appreciation of the familial, community, and societal influences that contribute to the presenting problems" (p. 15), including heterosexist and sexist ideas in mental health and the broader culture. Iasenza based her sex therapy on Carter's (1993) model of multicontextual therapy within the life-cycle framework of Carter and McGoldrick (1999). Long and Pietsch (2004) wrote about how traditional sex therapy and its constructions of sexuality were inherently heterosexist and limiting for everyone. They advocated for clinicians to educate themselves about same-sex couple intimate behavior and ways of connecting intimately so as to be able to help couples to explore what they want within the context of the multiple layers of legal and cultural power within same-sex couples' sexual relationships.

The Pervasiveness of Power

Feminist couple therapists have expanded their analysis of power in couple therapy to more sophisticated discussions of changing power dynamics, work and family, and violence.

Deconstruction and Reconstruction of Relationship Power

Several feminists compared couples' stated therapy goals with their patterns of decision to uncover habits based in gendered power (Knudson-Martin & Mahoney, 1999; Prouty & Protinsky, 2002; Rampage, 2002). Knudson-Martin and Mahoney (1999) paid attention to couples' struggles to become more congruent with their values by attending to language in therapy. Similarly, Parker (1997, 2003) cautioned therapists about falling into traps that collude with privilege like when a partner claims to care less about something in order to avoid responsibility or skill development or when one claims to care more in order to maintain control. She proposes that raising the issues of power in therapy *is* the challenge to the inequitable process.

Intentionality and deconstruction of the patterns and assumptions places presenting problem within its larger context and facilitates partners' conscious reconstruction of their relationship within its context. Feminists used deconstructing questions to help people connect their positions in dyadic power dynamics to the larger cultures in which their relationships were embedded (Blanton & Vandergriff-Avery, 2001; Parker, 2003; Parks et al., 2001; Rabin, 1998; Rampage, 2002, 2003; Temesese, 2003). Thereby, feminists helped the couple to discover how culture, gender, sexual orientation, age, socioeconomics, religion, and all of their experiences and socializations contributed to their stuckness (Rabin, 1998). Knudson-Martin and Mahoney (2005) found that when couples, who have a goal of equality, are made aware of unequal processes in their relationship based on covert, gendered entitlements, most made changes by sharing responsibilities and developing new competencies. As a part of the unraveling of power in couple therapy, Imber-Black (2003)

280 • Handbook of Clinical Issues in Couple Therapy

talked about the importance of couples noticing the power in secrets and in the privilege of naming decisions and behaviors as *private*. Both dynamics are a means by which a partner can exert and protect his or her power. Naming things as secrets often covers a person's vulnerabilities, insecurities, or lack of skill. Rebalancing power in an intimate relationship requires that each person acknowledge their limitations. Rebalancing also requires that the person with more power understands and wants the benefits of giving up some of his or her power. It also might require encouraging one's partner to access more power (relationships, education, money, knowledge, etc.) outside of the relationship. Rice (2003) suggested looking at divorce as women's adaptive resistance in instances in which power could not be equilibrated within a marital relationship. Power was discussed as both the distribution and access to resources and options: both perceived and real. Qualls (1995) wrote about how this remained true across the lifespan and could surface anew with the role shifts, changes in finances, and changes in physical health of later life couples. Helping couples to maintain their connection to emotional support and develop mutually nurturing roles can help them to renegotiate power within their relationship and with their larger family system.

Negotiating Family and Work Responsibilities

Feminist couple therapists (S. Haddock & Bowling, 2001; S. Haddock & Rattenborg, 2003; S. Haddock, Zimmerman, Current, & Harvey, 2001; S. A. Haddock, Zimmerman, Lyness, & Ziemba, 2006; S. Haddock, Zimmerman, Ziemba, & Current, 2001; Levner, 2000; Viers & Prouty, 2001; Zimmerman, Haddock, Ziemba, & Rust, 2001) asserted the importance of knowing the research supporting the methods by which couples could succeed, as well as being informed of the continued contextual restraints in the workplace and in the larger culture that often hampered families from feeling successful. Some of these restraints included gender role stereotyping by employers, friends, family, and the couple about who should parent; a lack of balance of power and decision making within the couple; heterosexism, racism, and classism; too few critical supports like close, safe, and culturally respectful daycare; flexible work schedules; a poverty of social support; and lack of safe neighborhoods and schools. Feminist therapists established a context of care (Bacigalupe, 2001; Parker & Almeida, 2001) in which they helped couples to examine both internal and external restraints, and provided hope that people could successfully integrate work and family life (MacDermid, Leslie, & Bissonnette, 2001). S. Haddock and Bowling (2001) offered a list of resources for both therapists and dual-earner couples about successfully navigating family and work based on research of families who did this well. And, Levner helped couples to rework the way they approached work and family with her conception of the three career family: each partner's career plus sharing the career of home and family.

Several feminist clinical scholars have emphasized the importance that families needed consistent social support, whether it be from an extended kinship network, a family of choice, religious or secular organizations, or neighborhoods who band together to help families accommodate to the daily and developmental requirements of family and work (Bacigalupe, 2001; Boyd-Franklin, 2003; Brockwood, Hammer, Neal, & Colton, 2001; Falicov, 1998; Parker & Almeida, 2001). This is especially necessary from a feminist perspective as it is often women who carry the responsibility to organize interior family life and interactions with the exterior community (Parker & Almeida). Parker and Almeida reminded us that those with more social power and privilege were often aided in balancing their lives with the labor of those with less social power and privilege. They asserted that

> Feminist work needs to occur on both the public social level as well as on the personal private level…We must work to establish protective measures and legislation regarding discrimination and harassment due to race, gender, social class, sexual orientation, age, or physical ability. (p. 158)

Power and Gendered Communication

One of the primary areas of feminist research has been on the study of the gendered nature of communication in couple therapy (Deinhart, 2001; S. Haddock & Lyness, 2002; Harris, Moret, Gale, & Kampmeyer, 2001; Stabb, Cox, & Harber, 1997; Stratford, 1998; Werner-Wilson, Price, Zimmerman, & Murphy, 1997; Werner-Wilson, Zimmerman, Daniels, & Bowling, 1999). Knudson-Martin and Mahoney (1999) examined the language that White, middle-class couples used to negotiate equality and the language they used to diffuse and avoid an incongruence between the equality they said they wanted and couple dynamics that indicated otherwise. Quite a few feminist couple therapists are applying feminist principles to interracial couples (K. D. Killian, 2001a, 2001b, 2001c, 2003; Wieling, 2003). The specific focus in these articles is on the role of power and how couples negotiate racial, gender, and class differences.

Feminist Therapy for Couple Violence

The primary focus in the couple violence literature is on men's violence against women, but with recent additional focus on gay and lesbian violence. The feminist critique has long argued for gendered constructions of violence, in particular males violence in couples.

Screening Gauthier and Levendosky (1996) made several initial suggestions for therapists working with couples in assessing violence. However, in the couple therapy field, Bograd and Mederos (1999) wrote a more often-cited article on

282 • Handbook of Clinical Issues in Couple Therapy

universal screening and selection of treatment modality in battering and couples therapy, and they particularly cited the ongoing controversy over treatment modality (conjoint versus other). The basis of this article was that conjoint therapy may be ethical and effective for certain groups but not others, and they laid out specific guidelines for selecting treatment modality that have been lacking in the field. They offered specific and detailed suggestions for assessment and screening and stringent criteria for the use of conjoint therapy in violent couples.

Building on this work and on his own work, Brian Jory has developed the Intimate Justice Scale (2004). Jory has been building the Intimate Justice model for some time (Jory & Anderson, 1999, 2000; Jory, Anderson, & Greer, 1997). The Intimate Justice model is one which focuses on ethics and is built on feminist conceptions of family violence and the contextual theory of Boszormenyi-Nagy. There are three key concepts, each with subconcepts: equality, which includes freedom, respect, and accountability; fairness, which includes reciprocity, mutuality, and accommodation; and care, which includes empathy, attachment, and nurturance.

Expansion of the Focus Much of what is "cutting edge" in the treatment of intimate violence in the feminist literature has been an increasing focus on issues of culture, including race, class, and sexual orientation, and the difficulties in determining power roles since they are not ascribed by gender (Almeida & Durkin, 1999; Almeida, Woods, Messineo, Font, & Heer, 1994; Bograd, 1999; Istar, 1996; Rasche, 1995) using the concept of *intersectionality*. Specific focus has been placed on how racism affects gendered couple violence as well (Boyd-Franklin & Franklin, 1998). Parks et al. (2001) explore several layers of socialization with African American lesbian couples with a member with a history of sexual abuse. Parks and his colleagues stressed the importance of emotional supports for both the couple and the therapist during therapy, and of the ethical mandate for therapists to get training and supervision about African American families, gender role socialization, coming-out issues, couple issues, sexuality, and sexual abuse dynamics when intertwined with racism, sexism, and heterosexism. This focus in the couple violence literature mirrored this larger trend in the feminist couple therapy literature.

Increasing Sophistication of Clinical Methods Goldner (1999), in summarizing 10 years of the Ackerman Institute's Gender and Violence Project, talked about the need to not just focus on power and inequity in examining couple violence, but to also look at complex emotional connections in those relationships. She highlighted the need to look beyond gender inequity to issues of race and class (themes mirrored in much of this literature). She posited that the family violence field is moving toward a position of increasing sophistication of theory and research as well. She argued for taking a position of "multiplicity" (p. 328)—of holding multiple, often competing, perspectives.

Feminist Couple Therapy • **283**

A theme in Goldner's work was "taking responsibility" (p. 329), which was seen elsewhere as well (see Jenkins, 1990). Goldner also addressed gendered patterns of moral reasoning and the issue of morality in the therapeutic situation: "It has been our experience that working at the moral edge with clients seems to inspire them to go beyond the notion of change as a way to feel better, to change as a way to be better" (p. 334).

Training   S. A. Haddock (2002) published a training curriculum for assessment and intervention in couple therapy for partner abuse, which provides a summary of the feminist critique through her recommendations for sections of the curriculum. There are sections on the phenomenon of partner abuse, a review and critique of explanatory theories of partner abuse, feminist-informed and culturally sensitive theories and practices, assessment and modality selection protocols, therapy for survivors of abuse and for perpetrators of abuse, and a final section on addressing these issues in couple therapy. Like others (Almeida & Durkin, 1999), Haddock recommends the use of movie segments in teaching about dynamics of partner abuse.

Conclusion

Feminist thought is influencing every area of couple therapy—one could say that the state of the art in couple therapy is *feminist* couple therapy. While continuing to focus on how gender influences couple relationships and how power dynamics related to gender influence couples, feminist therapists have expanded their focus to look at the multiple ways society affects power in couples through intersections of race, culture, class, ability and disability, sexual orientation, and gender identity. This focus on people's experiences of the intersections can be found in a great deal of the feminist literature on couple therapy today.

Feminist couple therapy has moved to a position of embracing complexity and diversity—not just diversity of clients or therapists, but diversity of ideas and interventions. This diversity can be found in areas of feminist couple therapy as disparate as therapy for violent couples and sex therapy. This diversity means that feminist thought is influenced by writers from diverse cultural backgrounds and even by many males embracing feminist philosophy. Mainstream couple and family therapy models and theories are being influenced by feminist thinking as well—not just in the feminist critique of family systems theory but in the expansions of emotionally focused therapy for couples, narrative therapy, solution-focused therapy, and so forth. Feminist writers are expanding every couple therapy model that does not explicitly address gender and power issues already. Feminist writers are influencing other areas as well. In fact, there are so many areas where feminists are influencing couple therapy that our first draft of this chapter was nearly 60 pages long! We explored how feminists are influencing research on couples and couple therapy, how feminist thinking is influencing training and supervision in couple

284 • Handbook of Clinical Issues in Couple Therapy

therapy, and many interventions and additions to the field that we could not include here. Another area we had to cut short was an acknowledgement of the history behind today's current trends. We feel that it is unfair to look at the state of the art today without looking at the foundation that art is built upon. However, there is only so much room and we will have to leave our tribute to that history to this short acknowledgement.

References

Almeida, R. V., & Durkin, T. (1999). The cultural context model: Therapy for couples with domestic violence. *Journal of Marital and Family Therapy, 25*, 313–324.

Almeida, R. V., Woods, R., Messineo, T., Font, R. J., & Heer, C. (1994). Violence in the lives of the racially and sexually different: A public and private dilemma. *Journal of Feminist Family Therapy, 5*(3/4), 99–126.

Bacigalupe, G. (2001). Is balancing family and work a sustainable metaphor? *Journal of Feminist Family Therapy, 14*(2/3), 5–20.

Bepko, C., & Johnson, T. (2000). Gay and lesbian couples in therapy: Perspectives for the contemporary family therapist. *Journal of Marital and Family Therapy, 26*, 409–419.

Bergman, S. J., & Surrey, J. L. (1999). Couple therapy: A relational approach. *Journal of Feminist Family Therapy, 11*(2), 21–48. (Also published in *The complexity of connection: Writings from the Stone Center's Jean Baker Miller Training Institute*, pp. 167–193, by J. V. Jordan, M. Walker, & L. M. Hartling, Eds., 2004, New York: Guilford).

Black, L. W. (2000). Therapy with African American couples. In P. Papp (Ed.), *Couples on the fault line* (pp. 205–221). New York: Guilford.

Blanton, P. W., & Vandergriff-Avery, M. (2001). Marital therapy and marital power: Constructing narratives of sharing relational and positional power. *Contemporary Family Therapy, 23*(3), 295–308.

Bograd, M. (1999). Strengthening domestic violence theories: Interactions of race, class, sexual orientation, and gender. *Journal of Marital and Family Therapy, 25*, 275–289.

Bograd, M., & Mederos, F. (1999). Battering and couples therapy: Universal screening and selection of treatment modality. *Journal of Marital and Family Therapy, 25*, 291–312.

Boyd-Franklin, N. (2003). *Black families in therapy* (2nd ed.). New York: Guilford.

Boyd-Franklin, N., & Franklin, A. J. (1998). African American couples in therapy. In M. McGoldrick (Ed.), *Re-visioning family therapy: Race, culture, and gender in clinical practice* (pp. 268–281). New York: Guilford.

Bowen, M. (1978). *Family therapy in clinical practice*. New York: Jason Aronson.

Brockwood, K. J., Hammer, L. B., Neal, M. B., & Colton, C. L. (2001). Effects of accommodations made at home and at work on wives' and husbands' family and job satisfaction. *Journal of Feminist Family Therapy, 14*(2/3), 41–64.

Brooks, G. R. (2001). Challenging dominant discourses of male (hetero) sexuality: The clinical implications of new voices about male sexuality. In P. J. Kleinplatz (Ed.), *New directions in sex therapy: Innovations and alternatives* (pp. 50–68). Philadelphia: Brunner-Routledge.

Carter, B. (1993). A multicontextual framework for assessing families. On *Clinical dilemmas in marriage: The search for equal partnership* [Videotape]. New York: Guilford.

Carter, B., & McGoldrick, M. (1999). *The expanded family lifecycle: Individual, family and social perspectives* (3rd ed.). Boston: Allyn and Bacon.

Conner, J. (2003). Vulvar vestibulitis syndrome: Therapeutic implications for couples. In A. M. Prouty Lyness (Ed.), *Feminist perspectives in medical family therapy* (pp. 89–98). New York: Haworth.

Conway, C. E. (2000). Using the crucial Cs to explore gender roles with couples. *The Journal of Individual Psychology, 56*, 495–501.

Daneshpour, M. (2003). Lives together, worlds apart? The lives of multicultural Muslim couples. *Journal of Couple & Relationship Therapy, 2*(2/3), 57–71.

Daniels, K. C., Zimmerman, T. S., & Bowling, S. W. (2002). Barriers in the bedroom: A feminist application for working with couples. *Journal of Feminist Family Therapy, 14*(2), 21–50.

Deinhart, A. (2001). Engaging men in family therapy: Does the gender of the therapist make a difference? *Journal of Family Therapy, 23*, 21–45.

Ellison, C. R. (2001). Intimacy-based sex therapy: Sexual choreography. In P. J. Kleinplatz (Ed.), *New directions in sex therapy: Innovations and alternatives* (pp. 163–184). Philadelphia: Brunner-Routledge.

Falicov, C. J. (1995). Cross cultural marriages. In N. S. Jacobson & A. S. Gurman (Eds.), *Clinical handbook of couple therapy* (pp. 231–246). New York: Guilford.

Falicov, C. J. (1998). *Latino families in therapy*. New York: Guilford.

Freedman, J., & Combs, G. (2002). *Narrative therapy with couples...and a whole lot more*. Adelaide, South Australia: Dulwiche Centre.

Gauthier, L. M., & Levendosky, A. A. (1996). Assessment and treatment of couples with abuse male partners: Guidelines for therapists. *Psychotherapy, 33*, 403–417.

Gilbin, P., & Chan, J. (1995). A feminist perspective. *The Family Journal: Counseling and Therapy for Couples and Families, 3*, 234–238.

Goldner, V. (1999). Morality and multiplicity: Perspectives on the treatment of violence in intimate life. *Journal of Marital and Family Therapy, 25*, 325–336.

Greene, B., & Boyd-Franklin, N. (1996). African American lesbian couples: Ethnocultural considerations in psychotherapy. *Women & Therapy, 19*(3), 49–60.

Guilbert, D. E., Vace, N. E., & Pasley, K. (2000). The relationship of gender role beliefs, negativity, distancing, and marital instability. *The Family Journal: Counseling and Therapy for Couples and Families, 8*, 124–132.

Haddock, S., & Bowling, S. W. (2001). Therapists' approaches to the normative challenges of dual-earner couples: Negotiating outdated societal ideologies. *Journal of Feminist Family Therapy, 14*(2/3), 91–120.

Haddock, S., & Lyness, K. P. (2002). Three aspects of the therapeutic conversation in couples therapy: Does gender make a difference? *Journal of Couple and Relationship Therapy, 1*(1), 5–24.

Haddock, S., & Rattenborg, K. (2003). Benefits and challenges of dual-earning: Perspectives of successful couples. *The American Journal of Family Therapy, 31*, 325–344.

Haddock, S., Zimmerman, T. S., Current, L. R., & Harvey, A. (2001). *Journal of Feminist Family Therapy, 14*(2/3), 37–55.

Haddock, S., Zimmerman, T. S., Ziemba, S. J., & Current, L. R. (2001). Ten adaptive strategies for family and work balance: Advice from successful families. *Journal of Marital and Family Therapy, 27*, 445–458.

Haddock, S. A. (2002). Training family therapists to assess for and intervene in partner abuse: A curriculum for graduate courses, professional workshops, and self-study. *Journal of Marital and Family Therapy, 28*, 193–202.

Haddock, S. A., Zimmerman, T. S., Lyness, K. P., & Ziemba, S. J. (2006). Practices of dual earner couples balancing work and family. *Journal of Family and Economic Issues, 27*, 207–234.

Hall, M. (1996). Unsexing the couple. *Women and Therapy, 19*(3), 1–11.

286 • Handbook of Clinical Issues in Couple Therapy

Hall, M. (2001). Beyond forever after: Narrative therapy with lesbian couples. In P. J. Kleinplatz (Ed.), *New directions in sex therapy: Innovations and alternatives* (pp. 279–301). Philadelphia: Brunner-Routledge.

Hall, R. L., & Greene, B. (2003). Contemporary African American families. In L. B. Silverstein & T. J. Goodrich (Eds.), *Feminist family therapy: Empowerment in social context* (pp. 107–120). Washington, DC: American Psychological Association.

Halstead, K. (2003). Over the rainbow: The lesbian family. In L. B. Silverstein & T. J. Goodrich (Eds.), *Feminist family therapy: Empowerment in social context* (pp. 39–50). Washington, DC: American Psychological Association.

Harris, T., Moret, L. B., Gale, J., & Kampmeyer, K. L. (2001). Therapists' gender assumptions and how these assumptions influence therapy. *Journal of Feminist Family Therapy, 12*(2/3), 33–60.

Hays, P. A. (1996). Cultural considerations in couples therapy. *Women & Therapy, 19*(3), 13–23.

Hill, M., & Thomas, V. (2002). Racial and gender identity development for Black and White women in interracial partner relationships. *Journal of Couple & Relationship Therapy, 1*(4), 1–35.

Iasenza, S. (2004). In S. Green & D. Flemons (Eds.), *Quickies: The handbook of brief sex therapy* (pp. 15–25). New York: Norton.

Imber-Black, E. (2003). Women's secrets in therapy. In L. B. Silverstein & T. J. Goodrich (Eds.), *Feminist family therapy: Empowerment in social context* (pp. 189–198). Washington, DC: American Psychological Association.

Istar, A. (1996). Couple assessment: Identifying and intervening in domestic violence in lesbian relationships. *Journal of Gay & Lesbian Social Services, 4*(1), 93–106.

Jackson, V. (2005). Robbing Peter to pay Paul: Reflections on feminist therapy with low-wage earning women. In M. P. Mirkin, K. L. Suyemoto, & B. F. Okun (Eds.), *Psychotherapy with women: Exploring diverse contexts and identities*. New York: Guilford.

Jacobson, N. S., & Christensen, A. (1996). *Acceptance and change in couple therapy: A therapist's guide to transforming relationships*. New York: Norton.

Jenkins, A. (1990). *Invitations to responsibility: The therapeutic engagement of men who are violent and abusive*. Adelaide, South Australia: Dulwich Centre Publications.

Johnson, S. (2005). Your cheatin' heart: Myths and absurdities about extradyadic relationships. *Journal of Couple and Relationship Therapy, 4*(2/3), 161–172.

Johnson, S. M. (2004). *The practice of emotionally focused couple therapy: Creating connection* (2nd ed.). New York: Brunner-Routledge.

Jory, B. (2004). The Intimate Justice Scale: An instrument to screen for psychological abuse and physical violence in clinical practice. *Journal of Marital and Family Therapy, 30*, 29–44.

Jory, B., & Anderson, D. (1999). Intimate Justice II: Fostering mutuality, reciprocity, and accommodation in therapy for psychological abuse. *Journal of Marital and Family Therapy, 25*, 349–364.

Jory, B., & Anderson, D. (2000). Intimate Justice III: Healing the anguish of abuse and embracing the anguish of accountability. *Journal of Marital and Family Therapy, 26*, 329–340.

Jory, B., Anderson, D., & Greer, C. (1997). Intimate Justice: Confronting issues of accountability, respect, and freedom in treatment for abuse and violence. *Journal of Marital and Family Therapy, 23*, 399–419.

Killian, K. (2003). Homogamy outlaws: Interracial couples' strategic responses to racism and to partner differences. *Journal of Couple and Relationship Therapy, 2*(2/3), 3–21.

Killian, K. D. (2001a). Crossing borders: Race, gender, and their intersections in interracial couples. *Journal of Feminist Family Therapy, 13*(1), 1–31.

Killian, K. D. (2001b). Differences making a difference: Cross-cultural interactions in supervisory relationships. *Journal of Feminist Family Therapy, 12*(2/3), 61–103.

Killian, K. D. (2001c). Reconstituting racial histories and identities: The narratives of interracial couples. *Journal of Marital and Family Therapy, 27*, 27–42.

Kleinplatz, P. J. (2001). A critique of the goals of sex therapy, or the hazards of safer sex. In P. J. Kleinplatz (Ed.), *New directions in sex therapy: Innovations and alternatives* (pp. 109–131). Philadelphia: Brunner-Routledge.

Knudson-Martin, C. (1995). Constructing gender in marriage: Implications for counseling. *The Family Journal: Counseling and Therapy for Couples and Families, 3*(3), 188–199.

Knudson-Martin, C. (2001). Women and mental health: A feminist family systems approach. In M. M. McFarlane (Ed.), *Family therapy and mental health: Innovations in theory and practice* (pp. 331–360). Binghamton, NY: Haworth.

Knudson-Martin, C., & Laughlin, M. J. (2005). Gender and sexual orientation in family therapy: Toward a postgender approach. *Family Relations, 54*, 101–115.

Knudson-Martin, C., & Mahoney, A. R. (1999). Beyond different worlds: A "postgender" approach to relational development. *Family Process, 38*, 325–340.

Knudson-Martin, C., & Mahoney, A. R. (2005). Moving beyond gender: Processes that create relationship equality. *Journal of Marital and Family Therapy, 31*, 235–246.

Laennec, C., & Syrotinski, M. (2003). Insiders' perspectives on a feminist marriage. *Feminism and Psychology, 13*, 454–458.

Laird, J. (1994). Lesbian and gay families. In M. P. Mirkin (Ed.), *Women in context: Toward a feminist reconstruction of psychotherapy* (pp. 118–148). New York: Guilford.

Laird, J. (2000). Gender in lesbian relationships: Cultural, feminist, and constructionist reflections. *Journal of Marital and Family Therapy, 26*, 455–467.

Laird, J., & Green, R. (1996). *Lesbians and gays in couples and families: A handbook for therapists.* San Francisco: Jossey-Bass.

Levant, R. F., & Philpot, C. L. (2002). Conceptualizing gender in marital and family therapy research: The gender role strain paradigm. In H. A. Liddle & D. A. Santisteban (Eds.), *Family psychology: Science-based interventions* (pp. 301–329). Washington, DC: American Psychological Association.

Levner, L. (2000). The three-career family. In P. Papp (Ed.), *Couples on the fault line* (pp. 29–47). New York: Guilford.

Long, J. (2003). Interracial and intercultural lesbian couples: The incredibly true adventures of two women in love. *Journal of Couple & Relationship Therapy, 2*(2/3), 85–101.

Long, J., & Pietsch, U. (2004). How do therapists of same-sex couples "do it"? In S. Green & D. Flemons (Eds.), *Quickies: The handbook of brief sex therapy* (pp. 171–188). New York: W. W. Norton

Mac Kune-Karrer, B., & Weigel Foy, C. (2003). The gender metaframework. In L. B. Silverstein & T. J. Goodrich (Eds.), *Feminist family therapy: Empowerment in social context* (pp. 351–363). Washington, DC: American Psychological Association.

MacDermid, S., Leslie, L. A., & Bissonnette, L. (2001). Walking the walk: Insights from research on helping clients navigate work and family. *Journal of Feminist Family Therapy, 14*(2/3), 21–40.

O'Donohue, W., & Crouch, J. L. (1996). Marital therapy and gender-linked factors in communication. *Journal of Marital and Family Therapy, 22*, 87–101.

Papp, P. (2000). *Couples on the fault line.* New York: Guilford.

Papp, P. (2003). Gender, marriage, and depression. In L. B. Silverstein & T. J. Goodrich (Eds.), *Feminist family therapy: Empowerment in social context* (pp. 211–224). Washington, DC: American Psychological Association.

288 • Handbook of Clinical Issues in Couple Therapy

Parker, L. (1997). Unraveling power issues in couples therapy. *Journal of Feminist Family Therapy, 9*(2), 3–20.

Parker, L. (2003). Brining power from the margins to the center. In L. B. Silverstein & T. J. Goodrich (Eds.), *Feminist family therapy: Empowerment in social context* (pp. 225–238). Washington, DC: American Psychological Association.

Parker, L., & Almeida, R. (2001). Balance and fairness for whom? *Journal of Feminist Family Therapy, 14*(2/3), 153–168.

Parks, C. W., Cutts, R. N., Woodson, K. M., & Flarity-White, L. (2001). Issues inherent in the multicultural feminist couple treatment of African-American, same gender loving female adult survivors of child sexual abuse. *Journal of Child Sexual Abuse, 10*(3), 17–34.

Pearlman, S. F. (1996). Loving across race and class divides: Relational challenges and the interracial lesbian couple. *Women & Therapy, 19*(3), 25–35.

Perel, E. (2000). A tourist's view of marriage: Cross-cultural couples—Challenges, choices, and implications for therapy. In P. Papp (Ed.), *Couples on the fault line* (pp. 178–204). New York: Guilford.

Philpot, C. L., Brooks, G. R., Lusterman, D., & Nutt, R. L. (1997). *Bridging separate gender worlds: Why men and women clash and how therapists can bring them together.* Washington, DC: American Psychological Association.

Pinderhughes, E. B. (2002). African American marriage in the 20th century. *Family Process, 41*, 269–282.

Prouty, A. M., & Protinsky, H. O. (2002). Feminist-informed internal family systems therapy with couples. *Journal of Couple and Relationship Therapy, 1*(3), 21–36.

Qualls, S. H. (1995). Marital therapy with later life couples. *Journal of Geriatric Psychiatry, 28*(2), 139–163.

Rabin, C. (1996). *Equal partners, good friends: Empowering couples through therapy.* New York: Routledge.

Rabin, C. (1998). Gender and intimacy in the treatment of couples in the 1990s. *Sexual and Marital Therapy, 13*(2), 179–190.

Rampage, C. (2002). Marriage in the 20th century: A feminist perspective. *Family Process, 41*, 261–268.

Rampage, C. (2003). Gendered constraints to intimacy in heterosexual couples. In L. B. Silverstein & T. J. Goodrich (Eds.), *Feminist family therapy: Empowerment in social context* (pp. 199–210). Washington, DC: American Psychological Association.

Rasche, C. (1995). Minority women and domestic violence: The unique dilemmas of battered women of color. In B. Raffel Price & N. Solokoff (Eds.), *The criminal justice system and women: Offenders, victims, and workers* (2nd ed., pp. 246–261). New York: McGraw Hill.

Rice, J. K. (2003). "I can't go back": Divorce as adaptive resistance. In L. B. Silverstein & T. J. Goodrich (Eds.), *Feminist family therapy: Empowerment in social context* (pp. 51–64). Washington, DC: American Psychological Association.

Root, M. P. P., & Suyemoto, K. L. (2005). Race, gender, class, and culture through the looking glass of interracial and intercultural intimate relationships. In M. P. Mirkin, K. L. Suyemoto, & B. F. Okun (Eds.), *Psychotherapy with women: Exploring diverse contexts and identities.* New York: Guilford.

Schnarch, D. (1997). *Passionate marriage.* New York: Norton.

Schneider, P. (1996). Mutuality in couples therapy. In *The Hatherleigh guide to marriage and family therapy* (pp. 267–284). New York: Hatherleigh Press.

Schwartz, P. (1994). *Love between equals: How peer marriage really works.* New York: Free Press.

Sims, J. M. (1996). The use of voice for assessment and intervention in couples therapy. *Women & Therapy, 19*(3), 61–77.

Snyder, M. (1996). Intimate partners: A context for the intensification and healing of emotional pain. *Women & Therapy, 19*(3), 79–92.

Stabb, S. D., Cox, D. L., & Harber, J. L. (1997). Gender-related therapist attributions in couples therapy: A preliminary multiple case study investigation. *Journal of Marital and Family Therapy, 23*, 335–346.

Stock, W., & Moser, C. (2001). Feminist sex therapy in the age of Viagra. In P. J. Kleinplatz (Ed.), *New directions in sex therapy: Innovations and alternatives* (pp. 139–162). Philadelphia: Brunner-Routledge.

Stratford, J. (1998). Women and men in conversation: A consideration of therapists' interruptions in therapeutic discourse. *Journal of Family Therapy, 20*, 383–394.

Tamasese, K. (2003). Gender and culture—Together. In C. Waldegrave, K. Tamasese, F. Tuhaka, & W. Campbell (Eds.), *Just therapy: A journey* (pp. 203–206). Adelaide: Dulwich Centre Publications.

Tamasese, K., & Laban, L. W. (2003). Gender—The impact of western definitions of womanhood on other cultures. In C. Waldegrave, K. Tamasese, F. Tuhaka, & W. Campbell (Eds.), *Just therapy: A journey* (pp. 207–213). Adelaide: Dulwich Centre Publications.

Tamasese, K., & Waldegrave, C. (2003). Cultural and gender accountability in the 'just therapy' approach. In C. Waldegrave, K. Tamasese, F. Tuhaka, & W. Campbell (Eds.), *Just therapy: A journey* (pp. 81–96). Adelaide: Dulwich Centre Publications.

Tiefer, L. (2001). Feminist critique of sex therapy: Foregrounding the politics of sex. In P. J. Kleinplatz (Ed.), *New directions in sex therapy: Innovations and alternatives* (pp. 29–49). Philadelphia: Brunner-Routledge.

Tien, L., & Olson, K. (2003). Confucian past, conflicted present: Working with Asian American families. In L. B. Silverstein & T. J. Goodrich (Eds.), *Feminist family therapy: Empowerment in social context* (pp. 135–146). Washington, DC: American Psychological Association.

Tubbs, C. Y., & Rosenblatt, P. C. (2003). Assessment and intervention with Black-White multiracial couples. *Journal of Couple and Relationship Therapy, 2*(2/3), 115–129.

Turner, J., & Avis, J. M. (2003). Naming injustice, engendering hope: Tensions in feminist family therapy training. In L. B. Silverstein & T. J. Goodrich (Eds.), *Feminist family therapy: Empowerment in social context* (pp. 365–378). Washington, DC: American Psychological Association.

Vatcher, C., & Bogo, M. (2001). The feminist/emotionally focused therapy practice model: An integrated approach for couple therapy. *Journal of Marital and Family Therapy, 27*, 69–83.

Viers, D., & Prouty, A. (2001). We've come a long way? An overview of the research of dual-career couples' stressors and strengths. *Journal of Feminist Family Therapy, 14*(2/3), 169–190.

Werner-Wilson, R. J., Price, S. J., Zimmerman, T. S., & Murphy, M. J. (1997). Client gender as a process variable in marriage and family therapy: Are women clients interrupted more than men clients? *Journal of Family Psychology, 11*, 373–377.

Werner-Wilson, R. J., Zimmerman, T. S., Daniels, K., & Bowling, S. M. (1999). Is therapeutic alliance influenced by a feminist approach to therapy? *Contemporary Family Therapy, 21*, 545–550.

Wieling, E. (2003). Latino/a and White marriages: A pilot study investigating the experiences of interethnic couples in the United States. *Journal of Couple and Relationship Therapy, 2*(2/3), 41–55.

Zimmerman, T. S., Haddock, S. A., Ziemba, S., & Rust, A. (2001). Family organizational labor: Who's calling the plays? *Journal of Feminist Family Therapy, 14*(2/3), 65–90.

V
Primary Prevention Issues

16

One Size Does Not Fit All

Customizing Couple Relationship Education for Unique Couple Needs

JEFFRY LARSON and W. KIM HALFORD

Contents

The Rationale for Marriage and Couple Relationship Education	294
Current Status of Marriage and Couple Relationship Education	295
Targeting and Customizing Couple Relationship Education	297
Targeting Relationship Education	297
Customizing Relationship Education	398
The Stepped Approach to Couple Relationship Education	300
Research on CRE Stepped Approaches	302
An Example of Customized-Stepped CRE:	
RELATE With Couple CARE	302
Conclusion	305
References	306

Marriage and couple relationship education (CRE) is offered to couples to enhance their relationship knowledge, attitudes, and skills (Halford, Markman, Stanley, & Kline, 2003). The goals are to assist as a many couples as possible to sustain long-term relationship satisfaction and to reduce the prevalence of relationship distress, violence, and separation. In this chapter, we argue that, in order for CRE to achieve its stated goals, three innovations are required. First, the reach of evidence-based programs needs to be extended. Second, couples need to be offered education in which the content is customized to their assessed needs. Third, education needs to be provided that is stepped in intensity, so that couples at the highest risk of future relationship problems receive the most education and assistance. In developing the rationale for a customized-stepped approach to CRE, we begin by reviewing the evidence of CRE's efficacy. We analyze the tendency of most programs to offer a standardized, universal content without attending to the diversity of couples' entry background, knowledge, or relationship skills. We also document the limited reach of current relationship education. Finally, we describe a new customized-stepped model of flexible relationship education utilizing empirically supported methodologies.

294 • Handbook of Clinical Issues in Couple Therapy

The Rationale for Marriage and Couple Relationship Education

The vast majority of people in the world marry by age 50, across almost all countries, cultures, and religions (United Nations Economic and Social Affairs Population Division, 2003). Even among those who choose not to marry, in Western countries the vast majority of people enter "marriage-like" cohabiting couple relationships (Australian Bureau of Statistics [ABS], 2003; Statistics Canada, 2003; United States Census Bureau, 2003).

The expectations of marriage vary considerably across cultures and history (Coontz, 2005). In Western countries, there has been a historical shift from marriage being viewed as an economic partnership embedded in family and community obligations to being viewed as predominantly a love-based, companionate, private arrangement founded on the partners having a mutually satisfying relationship (Coontz). Social and economic changes have freed many more people—especially women—to leave marriages that do not meet their expectations (United Nations Economic and Social Affairs Population Division, 2003). Divorce rates have increased markedly in most countries compared to historically low rates, particularly in the developed nations where the median divorce rate increased between 1970 and 2000 from 13 to 25 per 1000 population (United Nations Economic and Social Affairs Population Division).

Some of the world's increased divorce rate reflects more people now being legally and economically able to leave relationships with long-standing, severe problems such as recurrent intense conflict, violence, or infidelity (de Graaf & Kalmjin, 2006). However, the majority of current divorces, at least in Western countries, are not people leaving relationships with such severe problems. Rather most people leaving relationships do so because they evaluate the relationship to be insufficiently satisfying (Amato & Rogers, 1997; Kalmijn & Poortman, 2006).

Evidence has accumulated that a strong, mutually satisfying relationship is a source of great psychological support for both partners (Cutrona, 1996), and a very powerful predictor of positive health and well-being for both adults and their children (Amato, 2000; Waite & Gallagher, 2000). Indeed, evidence accumulates that children raised by their own parents in the same home are advantaged on many dimensions (McLanahan & Sandefur, 1996). Yet the high divorce rates, combined with an increased prevalence of unstable cohabiting parent relationships, has led to ever increasing numbers of children being raised without both parents in the home (Raley & Bumpass, 2003). Concern about the high rates of relationship dissolution of married and cohabiting couples, and the impact on adults and children, has led policy makers across many nations to implement policies intended to help couples achieve their aspirations for a mutually satisfying, stable relationship (van Acker, 2003). The provision of CRE has been central to these efforts (Halford et al., 2003; van Acker, 2003).

Current Status of Marriage and Couple Relationship Education

CRE is becoming increasingly available in most Western countries but most programs offered have not been rigorously evaluated within randomized controlled trials (Halford, 2004; Halford et al., 2003). Many CRE providers develop their own programs, often in response to perceived local needs, and most of these programs are not documented in a way that permits evaluation (Halford & Simons, 2005).

Existing evidence-based CRE is of two forms. The first is the use of structured inventory-based assessments with one or more hours of feedback session used to provide couples with information about their level of risk for future relationship problems (Larson, Newell, Topham, & Nichols, 2002). This approach is based on the assumption that such feedback can guide couples to take appropriate remedial action. The most widely used inventories provide scores on dimensions like shared realistic relationship expectations, effective communication and conflict resolution skills, emotional health, and effective personal stress management. Scores on these questionnaires predict newlywed couple's future relationship satisfaction and stability (Larson et al.), showing they do assess relevant aspects of couple relationships.

There have been three recent studies evaluating the effects of assessment and feedback on couple relationships. The first was a quasi-experimental study by Knutson and Olson (2003) who found that assessment and feedback using the PREPARE inventory program significantly improved premarital couples' relationship satisfaction. Two randomized controlled trials evaluated assessment with feedback with the Internet-based, self-interpretive RELATE inventory. Both studies showed increases in relationship satisfaction and commitment in couples in early-stage committed relationships (Busby, Ivey, Harris, & Ates, 2007; Larson, Vatter, Galbraith, Holman, & Stahmann, 2007). The Busby et al. (2007) study was the only one to evaluate maintenance of effects, and they found relationship satisfaction and commitment were sustained at a high level for at least 6 months after completing RELATE. Each of the samples of couples in these three studies were well educated and in early-stage committed relationships (long-term dating or engaged), and the generalizability to less-educated or longer established relationships is untested. Whether the effects of assessment and feedback persist for years also is unknown. It is known that some couples lack key relationship skills like effective communication and conflict management (Halford et al., 2003). Assessment with feedback might be insufficient to allow such couples to sustain high relationship satisfaction, thus they might benefit from relationship skill training.

The second evidence-based approach to CRE seeks to teach couples crucial relationship skills, typically in a face-to-face course of 12–15 contact hours with use of procedures like modeling, rehearsal, and feedback on skills. It is well established that skill-focused relationship education can teach couples

296 • Handbook of Clinical Issues in Couple Therapy

key relationship skills such as positive communication and conflict management, and these skills are maintained for at least a year or two after training (Halford et al., 2003). Moreover, couples that initially have somewhat low relationship satisfaction show immediate increases in relationship satisfaction (Giblin, Sprenkle, & Sheehan, 1985).

There are benefits from skill-based CRE in helping couples sustain long-term relationship satisfaction, but these benefits seem to be primarily for couples at high risk for future relationship difficulties. Several quasi-experimental studies have shown long-term (3–4 year) universal benefit for couples from skill-based education (e.g., Bodenmann, Pihet, Shantinath, Cina, & Widmer, 2006; Markman, Renick, Floyd, Stanley, & Clements, 1993). However, as Halford et al. (2003) noted these effects might be due to couples self-selecting into receiving CRE. Only randomized controlled trials with adequate follow-up can clearly establish an effect of CRE on maintaining relationship satisfaction and stability.

To determine the current state of CRE research using randomized controlled trials with at least 6-month follow-up evaluations, we conducted a search of the psychinfo data base using the terms *marriage education, couple education*, and "relationship education" for articles published in refereed journals between January 1980 and December 2006. We selected articles that met the following criteria: The study included a randomized controlled trial of CRE; the relationship education sought to enhance couple interaction, relationship satisfaction or prevent relationship separation; and the study included at least a 6-month follow-up assessment of the effects of the education on relationship satisfaction or stability. We added to the identified articles by searching for similar articles, and articles that had cited the identified articles, which met the selection criteria. Eleven such studies were found, five that targeted early-stage couple relationships, two that focused on long-established couple relationships, and four that worked with couples having their first child (see Halford, in press for detailed information).

Of the five studies evaluating CRE's effects on relationship satisfaction or stability in early-stage relationships, three were universal programs (Bagarozzi, Bagarozzi, Anderson, & Pollane, 1984; Laurenceau, Stanley, Olmos-Gallo, Baucom, & Markman, 2004; Wampler & Sprenkle, 1980), one examined effects with couples at high risk of future relationship problems (Bouma, Halford, & Young, 2004), and one examined risk as a moderator of the effect of education (Halford, Sanders, & Behrens, 2001). Only one of the three universal programs found there was a positive effect of education on future relationship satisfaction (6 months post-test) (Wampler & Sprenkle, 1980), whereas two found no sustained effect (Bagarozzi et al., 1984; Laurenceau et al., 2004). The Bouma et al. (2004) study found education enhanced relationship stability in a high-risk sample of couples. Halford et al. (2001) found high- but not low-risk couples had enhanced maintenance of relationship satisfaction after receiving CRE.

One of the two trials of education with long-established (average 11 years) couple relationships seeking relationship enrichment found enhanced maintenance of relationship satisfaction (Kaiser, Hahlweg, Fehm-Wolfsdorf, & Groth, 1998), but the other did not (van Widenfelt, Hosman, Schaap, & van der Staak, 1996). The Kaiser et al. (1998) sample had a substantial proportion of couples with mild to moderate relationship distress, and the findings are consistent with many other studies showing couples with distress can benefit from CRE. However, it is questionable if this is really prevention or indicated early intervention.

All four of the trials of relationship education with couples making the transition to parenthood found enhanced maintenance of relationship satisfaction resulting from education (Midmer, Wilson, & Cummings, 1995; Petch, Halford, & Creedy, 2007; Schulz, Cowan, & Cowan, 2006; Shapiro & Gottman, 2005), though one study found this effect only for women but not men (Petch et al., 2007). All of these programs were universal. That is, there was no selection for couples at high risk of future relationship problems. However, the transition to parenthood is a time associated with rapid decline in relationship satisfaction with a substantial proportion of couples (e.g., Twenge, Campbell, & Foster, 2003). Thus, all these couples could be regarded as at high risk of future relationship deterioration.

In summary, couples who consistently show sustained benefits from skill-based CRE seem to be: Couples in early-stage relationships at high risk of future relationship problems; couples making the transition to parenthood (who also are at risk for future problems); and couples who already have some relationship distress. There is little evidence for a universal benefit that lasts 6 months or longer from skill-based CRE.

Targeting and Customizing Couple Relationship Education

Most existing CRE programs are offered universally to couples in a one-size-fits-all (universal) manner (Halford, 2004). This approach has two major limitations: (1) It fails to target relationship education on those who might benefit the most, and (2) it fails to address the unique needs, risks, and protective factors of couples by having a relatively fixed curriculum.

Targeting Relationship Education

In Australia and the United States more than 50% of couples who marry remain together for the rest of their lives, the vast majority of these couples report being satisfied in their relationship at least most of the time (ABS, 2007; United States Census Bureau, 2003), and most of these couples have not attended any form of relationship education (Halford, O'Donnell, Lizzio, & Wilson, 2006). Thus, it is clear many couples can have successful relationships without formal relationship education. A universal offering of relationship education likely makes little difference to the many couples at low-risk of future problems.

298 • Handbook of Clinical Issues in Couple Therapy

It is possible to identify, albeit with limited accuracy, the couples who are at high risk for future relationship problems. For example, couples who have divergent or unrealistic expectations of their relationship; who have deficits in their expression of affection, sharing of positive activities, or supporting of each other; who have negative communication styles or ineffective conflict management; who are forming stepfamilies; or who experienced parental separation or violence in their family of origin, are at high risk of deteriorating relationship satisfaction and separation (Bradbury & Karney, 2004; Larson & Holman, 1994). If these high-risk couples self-selected to attend relationship education, then the current system of universal offerings might be effective. However, data suggests that high-risk couples are somewhat less likely to attend current offerings than low-risk couples (Halford et al., 2006; Sullivan & Bradbury, 1997). Therefore, providing an easily accessible assessment to help couples evaluate their need for relationship education would seem useful.

Helping couples produce sustained changes in their relationships that enhance the chance of sustained relationship satisfaction and stability is a major challenge. No existing psychological interventions produce life-long protection against occurrence of psychological problems (Kendall, 1989), and it is probably unrealistic to expect that one course of CRE could permanently inoculate couples against relationship problems. In the longest term evaluation of skill-based relationship education, effects do attenuate over a 3–4 year period (Markman et al., 1993). In recent work with couples married 5–10 years, a follow-up session 1 year after initial skill-based relationship education helped couples sustain relationship satisfaction (Braukhaus, Hahlweg, Kroeger, Groth, & Fehm-Wolfsdorf, 2003). Booster sessions might assist long-term maintenance of CRE effects in newlywed couples. Assessments that are easy to access could allow couples to evaluate at various points in their life together whether they needed relationship education booster sessions.

Customizing Relationship Education

Almost all current skill-based CRE provides a universal curriculum. This approach fails to address the unique relationship challenges particular couples have in their relationship. For example, the popular and empirically supported Prevention and Relationship Enhancement Program (PREP) (Markman, Stanley, & Blumberg, 1994) has more extensive efficacy data than any other CRE program (Halford et al., 2003; Jakubowski, Milne, Brunner, & Miller, 2004; Schilling et al., 2003). PREP has multiple components in its 12–15 h standard curriculum, but it is clear it cannot cover all of the potential risk factors relevant to couples. For example, remarried couples bring a range of unique challenges to their relationship, such as developing shared and realistic expectations of the step parent role (Halford, Nicholson, & Sanders, in press). These issues are not covered in the standard PREP curriculum.

One approach to address more of couples' needs has been to expand the curriculum of CRE. Probably the lengthiest and most comprehensive CRE program is the *Practical Application of Intimate Relationship Skills (PAIRS)* program (Gordon, 1994). The Relationship Mastery Program of PAIRS (PAIRS, 2006) is a semester-long program—16 weeks of classes (3 h per week) with four intensive weekend workshops (18 h per workshop), which together total 120 h of training. A total of 60 relationship skills are taught (PAIRS) ranging across communication, self-awareness, existential meaning, sensuality, sexuality, commitment, jealousy, decision making, and creating a committed and passionate partnership. Although impressive in its scope and intensity, there is doubt that all couples need or can use all of the PAIRS content. Moreover, such a comprehensive program is very expensive to deliver, and couples must devote a large amount of time to complete such a program.

The briefer duration of the PREP program makes it more affordable than PAIRS, and probably more acceptable to couples in terms of the level of effort and costs involved. The content of PREP is focused upon skills that research has identified as the most common challenges couples encounter in sustaining relationship satisfaction. However, even the most central of PREP content is not relevant to all couples. Enhancing couple communication and preventing destructive conflict is a key ingredient in PREP and central to its claimed benefits (Markman et al., 1994). This focus on enhancing communication is based on research showing that negative communication in newlyweds predicts poor couple outcomes (Heyman, 2001). However, this prediction results from the heterogeneity of couples on initial couple communication skills. In other words, differences between newlywed couples' communication predict differences in future relationship satisfaction and stability. It follows that many marrying couples have low levels of negative communication that predict them being able to sustain high relationship satisfaction. Such couples seem unlikely to benefit from education that teaches communication emphasizing reduction of negative communication, as PREP does. Consistent with this interpretation, Halford et al. (2001) found only couples with initially high levels of negative communication showed long-term (after 4 years) gains in relationship satisfaction from skill training focused on communication. Thus, for many couples it appears that communication skills training may not be necessary.

Because not all couples need all components of a program, participating in a fixed curriculum program means many couples may waste valuable time and money participating. Couples report it is unhelpful to work through materials that are not directly applicable to their unique relationship needs (Busby et al., 2007), and learning concepts and skills irrelevant to their unique needs may de-motivate the learner to participate in other curriculum components more relevant to their needs (Duncan & Goddard, 2005). For example, individuals who have excellent communication skills but poor

300 • Handbook of Clinical Issues in Couple Therapy

financial management skills may show low engagement with, or even drop out, of programs practicing communication skills.

A challenge in offering customized CRE is that many current providers of relationship education do not have the professional skills to carry out relationship assessments that might guide customizing (Doherty & Anderson, 2004). This has lead some leaders in the field to suggest that only highly trained mental health professionals should offer CRE (Gottman, 1999). However, such an approach is likely to severely limit the accessibility of CRE. There are not enough highly trained professionals to provide such services, and even if there were the acceptability of such intensive interventions to couples is doubtful. Furthermore, the cost of universal application of such interventions would likely be prohibitive. One possible means to customize relationship education is with the use of easily accessed, web-based assessments like RELATE, which is self-scoring and provides clear interpretative guidelines to educators and couples.

In summary, CRE needs to better account for the different risk and protective factors couples bring to their relationships (Halford, 2004). Trying to cover all risk factors makes CRE unnecessarily costly and time consuming as many risks are relevant to only a few couples. For example, reducing hazardous drinking to safe levels enhances couple relationship stability, but is only relevant for a minority of marrying couples (Bouma et al., 2004). Rather, what is required is assessment and customizing of the content of CRE for each couple's unique relationship risks and strengths profile. The problem with nearly all existing CRE programs is a lack of such comprehensive preprogram assessment even though this preliminary step is acknowledged to be important in effective CRE (Arcus, Schvaneveldt, & Moss, 1993; Duncan & Goddard, 2005).

The Stepped Approach to Couple Relationship Education

The stepped approach to offering psychological interventions has been gradually gaining acceptance in the clinical literature (Davison, 2000) but has not been applied much in the context of CRE. The core concept of a stepped approach is to offer a range of interventions varying in intensity from brief, inexpensive, often self-directed programs, to more extended, expensive, and often professionally delivered programs. A key rationale for a stepped approach is to offer the least intensive program needed to achieve the desired goal. The wide offering of less intensive programs can often address many people's needs and enable limited resources to be concentrated in such a way that those in most need of them get the most intensive programs (Davison).

Applying the concept of a stepped approach to CRE, a brief intervention might take the form of offering books that describe evidence-based approaches to relationship enhancement like Markman et al.'s (1994) *Fighting for Your Marriage*. If such brief interventions meet many couples' needs, then more

One Size Does Not Fit All • **301**

intensive interventions like PREP, or even an individually tailored CRE program, can be offered selectively to those couples likely to benefit the most from the program.

There are a number of assumptions implicit in a stepped approach to CRE. First, that many couples do not need intensive relationship education. We have already argued that the evidence supports this assumption. Second, that low intensity interventions can have wide appeal and can be effective for at least some people. We know that low intensity education can have an extensive reach. For example, couples are more likely to read self-help books on relationships than seek couple education or therapy (Doss, Rhoades, Stanley, & Markman, 2009; Norcross, 2006). Low intensity CRE interventions like books, DVDs, CDs, and Internet sites are extremely popular. For example, *Why Marriages Succeed or Fail* by John Gottman (1994) has been read by millions of couples. Moreover, we know that substantial numbers of couples report that they have experienced and overcome relationship distress without direct contact with professional assistance (Norcross, 2006; Waite & Gallagher, 2000).

To date, there has not been an evaluation of whether very brief couple interventions like reading a book or watching a DVD can contribute to the self-correction of couples' relationships, but this does seem plausible. As noted earlier, completing the web-based RELATE assessment and reviewing the report does have a positive effect on couple relationships. Furthermore, evidence-based advice is finding its way into widely distributed sources such as self-help books (see Norcross et al., 2003 for comprehensive guidelines on selecting these sources). As the information and advice offered in books come to better reflect the available research, that might well enhance the effects of brief couple interventions.

One unresolved issue is the effect of participating in low intensity CRE on later use of more intense CRE. A positive experience of using low-intensity CRE might build motivation for change, and increase the chance of couples later engaging in a more intensive program. For example, there is evidence that people seeking education or therapy often do so after reading a book on relationships (Doss et al., 2009). Some relationship educators have expressed the view that positive experiences of CRE might enhance later presentation for further education or even couple therapy, when they are required (Stanley, 2001). On the other hand, Wilson, Vitousek, and Loeb (2000) cautioned clinicians that "Failure to respond to an initial low-intensity level of care [could] discourage patients from seeking subsequent treatment or undermine their response to such treatment" (p. 564). An analogous problem might occur with stepped CRE; ineffective low intensity programs might have a negative impact on partners' self-efficacy, reduce their motivation for change, and discourage them from seeking future relationship education. Research is needed to evaluate the effects of using low-intensity CRE on the later accessing of CRE.

302 • Handbook of Clinical Issues in Couple Therapy

Research on CRE Stepped Approaches

Two studies suggest that stepped approaches may be effective in CRE. Ford, Bashford, and DeWitt (1984) tested the effects of three steps (levels of intensity) of communication skills training with 64 couples relative to a wait-list control. The three steps in order of increasing intensity were (1) bibliotherapy, consisting of reading, written exercises, and weekly telephone contacts by a relationship educator; (2) observation, consisting of watching audiovisual demonstrations of communication skills training between a couple and educator, combined with structured exercises; and (3) face-to-face training, consisting of individualized modeling, rehearsal, and feedback on communication skills with structured homework exercises. All three program steps were beneficial, and the initial characteristics of the couples moderated response to the education. For example, couples with initially low relationship satisfaction and emotional expressiveness benefited most from the intense face-to-face program, whereas couples with initially high relationship satisfaction benefited equally well from that condition or the observational learning condition. Thus, providing couples with the intensity of education they needed seemed to enhance outcomes. More recently, Busby et al. (2007) demonstrated in a randomized controlled study with 79 couples that face-to-face interaction is not universally necessary in CRE. They found the web-based RELATE assessment and the computer-generated and self-interpretive report produced more positive changes in couple relationship satisfaction and commitment than a 6-h face-to-face skill training program (Busby et al.). The couples who received the assessment-based (RELATE) program reported it provided high levels of individualized information, whereas the couples who received the standardized training sessions reported that much of the content was not relevant to them.

The Ford et al. (1984) and Busby et al. (2007) studies lacked long-term follow-up, but do show at least short-term benefits from low-intensity CRE. In a comprehensive review of types of CRE Hawkins, Carroll, Doherty, and Willoughby (2004) noted that low-intensity, largely self-guided CRE is one of the most common, accessible, and promising approaches to improving relationships.

An Example of Customized-Stepped CRE: RELATE With Couple CARE

Based on the above review of evidence, we concluded that it is desirable to integrate a standardized, self-scoring assessment with relationship skills building into CRE. Such a system would allow an easy way to customize content, and to evaluate with the couple the intensity of CRE most likely to meet their needs. An example of such an integrated program is our RELATE-Couple CARE program, which we have developed and evaluated. RELATE is the assessment tool whereas Couple CARE provides skill training in a flexible, individually customized way. An advantage of this combined program is it can be completed in a variety of formats, either being done entirely by couples at home, or in a mix of at-home and face-to-face sessions with an educator.

RELATE is a 271-item online comprehensive assessment of a couple's relationship. RELATE is completed by both partners, and takes about 55 min to complete (Busby, Holman, & Taniguchi, 2001). RELATE provides self- and partner reports of personal characteristics and values, self-reports of family-of-origin background and interaction processes, and self- and partner reports of current relationship satisfaction, communication, conflict management, and aggression. These factors predict marital satisfaction and stability in newlywed couples (Holman & Associates, 2001). Relationship risk is operationalized as the number of relationship challenges a couple has, as assessed by RELATE, which has been shown to predict newlywed's future relationship satisfaction and separation status (Holman & Associates).

Couple CARE is a 6-unit at-home program in which couples are asked to complete each unit in about a week. Completing each unit consists of three steps. First, the couple watches a 12- to 15-min segment of videotape that introduces key concepts and models relevant relationship skills. Second, they complete individual and conjoint tasks described in a guidebook given to each partner, which take approximately 50 min to complete. The tasks assist the couple to relate the concepts and skills shown in the videotape to their own relationship, to prompt relationship goal setting, to self-direct change in their relationship behaviors. Third, the couple shares a telephone call of about 45 min with a marriage educator who reviews the concepts covered in the unit and helps the couple implement individual self-change plans.

The content of each of the six units of Couple CARE is presented in Table 16.1. A distinguishing feature of Couple CARE is a focus on relationship self-regulation, which is the extent to which the partners each actively work on their relationship. Partners are assisted to self-evaluate their behavior across a range of domains of relationship interaction, to select goals for personal change, and to implement and evaluate their change efforts. For example, across Units 2 and 3 of Couple CARE, participants watch videotape segments illustrating positive couple communication. The guidebook describes communication tasks the partners do together, after which each partner self-evaluates his or her current communication skills using a form provided in the guidebook. Each identifies specific behavioral goals to improve one's own communication, again using a form provided in the guidebook. The self-evaluation and goals are discussed with the relationship educator during the telephone call, and the partners are assisted to implement their self-change goals for communication enhancement. As a second example, in the final unit on adapting to change, each partner is asked to identify the likelihood that a range of life changes (e.g., have a child, change job), might occur to him or her in the next 12 months, and the positive and negative relationships consequences of such a change.

304 • Handbook of Clinical Issues in Couple Therapy

Table 16.1 Content of Couple CARE Relationship Education Program

Unit	Content
1. Self-change	Introduction to program and structure; relationship goal setting; commitment to relationship enhancement; producing self-change in relationships
2. Communication	Model of effective couple communication; self-evaluation of communication; self-change for communication enhancement
3. Intimacy and caring	Importance and review of expression of affection, social support, and positive shared activities; self-change plan
4. Managing differences	Review of the positive effects of differences; model of effective conflict management; self-evaluation of current conflict management; self-change plan
5. Sexuality	Common myths about sexual expression; assessment of current sexual behavior within the relationship; self-change plan
6. Adapting to change	The impact of life events on relationships; assessment of likely life changes for couple and possible relationship effects; review of how to maintain a relationship focus in a busy life; self-change plan

The couple then discuss their goals in managing such a change and identify individual actions that would help them manage such changes as a couple.

In the combined RELATE with Couple CARE program couples first complete RELATE on the web, or if they do not have Internet access RELATE is provided in written form. The couple receives a 10-page computer-generated RELATE report that is self-interpretive, which documents their relationship strengths and challenges. A 1-h feedback session with an educator (usually by telephone but may be face-to-face) is used to discuss this report of relationship strengths and challenges, and to assist couples to formulate specific relationship enhancement goals. Couples with many relationship strengths and few challenges (low-risk couples) are given brief advice to assist them achieve their goals by self-directed fine tuning of any areas of concern. Moderate- to high-risk couples go on to complete the Couple CARE program (or selected units from Couple CARE) to develop the knowledge and skills necessary to achieve their stated relationship goals. Some couples with sufficient relationship distress may need to be referred to couple therapy. Thus, the integrated RELATE with Couple CARE system provides a customized-stepped approach to CRE based on assessed risk, as depicted in Table 16.2.

The RELATE with Couple CARE approach to CRE differs from previous approaches by using a flexible-delivery format, so that couples can complete the program in their own time and pace and in the privacy of their own home.

Table 16.2 RELATE With Couple CARE: A Customized-Stepped Approach to Couple Relationship Education

| Risk | Prevention | | | Indicated |
	Low	Medium	High	
Intervention	RELATE			
		RELATE plus some Couple CARE		
			RELATE plus all of Couple CARE	
				Couple therapy

Research suggests, although most couples' express willingness to utilize education to enrich their relationship (Johnson et al., 2002) only one third actually do so (Halford et al., 2006; Sullivan & Bradbury, 1997). Traditional CRE programs adopt a face-to-face format with small groups of couples (Halford & Moore, 2002). However, many couples indicate that they do not attend CRE due to its time intensity and lack of privacy (Christensen & Jacobson, 1994; Simons, Harris, & Willis, 1994). RELATE with Couple CARE is brief and convenient for couples, and is conducted in their home using the Internet and telephone. This mode of delivery aims to facilitate couple recruitment and retention and to assist those who are more geographically isolated to access CRE.

The RELATE with Couple CARE relationship education program also differs from previous programs by using a customized-stepped approach, which provides couples with only as much education as they need. When necessary couples can emphasize an area of their relationship that especially needs enrichment by spending more time on a particular unit (see Table 16.2). In addition, they can retake RELATE to monitor relationship changes. This has the potential to create an ongoing commitment to relationship checkups to monitor their relationship as it evolves (see Larson, 2000, 2003). RELATE alone is likely to assist many couples, whereas high-risk couples that lack key relationship skills are likely to benefit from the additional skills training provided in Couple CARE.

Conclusion

The limitations of universal CRE programs, and the advantages and limitations of customized-stepped CRE programming have been discussed. Research on the effectiveness of customized-stepped CRE is in its infancy but preliminary studies suggest it is a promising future form of CRE. Psychometrically sound comprehensive assessment questionnaires are already available to the field including RELATE, PREPARE/ENRICH, and FOCCUS (see Larson et al., 2002). Empirically supported relationship skills programs are also readily available. It is now time to combine assessment

306 • Handbook of Clinical Issues in Couple Therapy

with programming that recognizes unique couple strengths and challenges and enriches only where needed in an efficient, customized-stepped method. The wide-scale availability of computers, DVD players, and high-tech telephones make a wide variety of CRE more accessible than before. These technologies can be more creatively used to conduct customized-stepped CRE as we are doing with RELATE with Couple CARE. We believe this type of programming can reach more couples, take less time to complete, cost less, and increase convenience for couples to access CRE and enrich their relationships.

References

Amato, P. R. (2000). Consequences of divorce for adults and children. *Journal of Marriage and the Family, 58*, 356–365.

Amato, P. R., & Rogers, S. H. (1997). A longitudinal study of marital problems and subsequent divorce. *Journal of Marriage and the Family, 59*, 612–624.

Arcus, M. E., Schvaneveldt, J. D., & Moss, J. J. (1993). The nature of family life education. In M. E. Arcus, J. D. Schvaneveldt, & J. J. Moss (Eds.), *Handbook of family life education* (Vol. 1, pp. 1–25). Newbury Park, CA: Sage.

Australian Bureau of Statistics. (2003). *Marriage in Australia.* Canberra: Australian Bureau of Statistics.

Australian Bureau of Statistics. (2007). *Social trends.* Canberra, Australia: Australian Bureau of Statistics.

Bagarozzi, D. A., Bagarozzi, J. I., Anderson, S. A., & Pollane, L. (1984). Premarital Education and Training Sequence (PETS): A 3-year follow-up of an experimental study. *Journal of Counseling & Development, 63*, 91–100.

Bodenmann, G., Pihet, S., Shantinath, S. D., Cina, A., & Widmer, K. (2006). Improving dyadic coping in couples with a stress-oriented approach: A 2-year longitudinal study. *Behavior Modification, 30*, 571–597.

Bouma, R. O., Halford, W. K., & Young, R. M. (2004). Evaluation of the Controlling Alcohol and Relationship Enhancement (CARE) program with hazardous drinkers. *Behavior Change, 21*, 1–22.

Bradbury, T. N., & Karney, B. R. (2004). Understanding and altering the longitudinal course of intimate partnerships. *Journal of Marriage and the Family, 61*, 451–463.

Braukhaus, C., Hahlweg, K., Kroeger, C., Groth, T., & Fehm-Wolfsdorf, G. (2003). The effects of adding booster sessions to a prevention training program for committed couples. *Behavioural and Cognitive Psychotherapy, 31*, 325–336.

Busby, D. M., Holman, T. B., & Taniguchi, N. (2001). RELATE: Relationship evaluation of the individual, family, cultural and couple contexts. *Family Relations, 50*, 308–317.

Busby, D. M., Ivey, D. C., Harris, S. M., & Ates, C. (2007). Self-directed, therapist-directed, and assessment-based interventions for premarital couples. *Family Relations, 56*, 279–290.

Christensen, A., & Jacobson, N. S. (1994). Who (or what) can do psychotherapy: The status and challenge of nonprofessional therapies. *Psychological Science, 5*, 8–14.

Coontz, S. (2005). *Marriage, a history.* New York: Penguin.

Cutrona, C. (1996). *Social support in couples: Marriage as a resource in times of stress.* Thousand Oaks, CA: Sage.

Davison, G. C. (2000). Stepped care: doing more with less? *Journal of Consulting and Clinical Psychology, 68*, 580–585.

One Size Does Not Fit All • **307**

de Graaf, P. M., & Kalmjin, M. (2006). Divorce motives in a period of rising divorce: evidence from a Dutch life-history survey. *Journal of Family Issues, 27*, 483–505.

Doherty, W. J., & Anderson, J. R. (2004). Community marriage initiatives. *Family Relations, 53*, 425–432.

Doss, B. D., Rhoades, G., Stanley, S., & Markman, H. J. (2009). Marital therapy, retreats, and books: the who, what, when and why of relationship help-seeking. *Journal of Marital and Family Therapy, 35*, 18–29.

Duncan, S. F., & Goddard, H. W. (2005). *Family life education: Principles and practices for effective outreach.* Thousand Oaks, CA: Sage.

Ford, J. D., Bashford, M. B., & DeWitt, K. N. (1984). Three approaches to marital enrichment: Toward optimal matching of participants and interventions. *Journal of Sex and Marital Therapy, 10*, 41–48.

Giblin, P., Sprenkle, D. H., & Sheehan, R. (1985). Enrichment outcome research: A meta-analysis of premarital, marital, and family interventions. *Journal of Marital and Family Therapy, 11*, 257–271.

Gordon, L. H. (1994). *PAIRS curriculum guide and training manual.* Falls Church, VA: PAIRS Foundation. Retrieved July 1, 2007, from http://www.pairs.com/downloads/resource.pdf

Gottman, J. (1994). *Why marriages succeed or fail.* New York: Simon and Schuster.

Gottman, J. M. (1999). *The marriage clinic: A scientifically-based marital therapy.* New York: W. W. Norton & Company.

Halford, W. K. (2004). The future of couple relationship education: Suggestions on how it can make a difference. *Family Relations, 53*, 559–571.

Halford, W. K. (in press). *Marriage and relationship education: What works and how to provide it.* New York: Guilford.

Halford, W. K., Markman, H. J., Stanley S. M., & Kline, G. (2003). Best practice in couple relationship education. *Journal of Marital and Family Therapy, 29*, 385–406.

Halford, W. K., & Moore, E. (2002). Relationship education and the prevention of couple relationship problems. In A. S. Gurman (Ed.), *Clinical handbook of couple therapy* (3rd ed., pp. 400–419). New York: Guilford.

Halford, W. K., Nicholson, J. M., & Sanders, M. R. (in press). Couple communication in step families. *Family Process.*

Halford, W. K., O'Donnell, C., Lizzio, A., & Wilson, K. L. (2006). Do Couples at high-risk of relationship problems attend pre-marital education? *Journal of Family Psychology, 20*, 160–163.

Halford, W. K., Sanders, M. R., & Behrens, B. C. (2001). Can skills training prevent relationship problems in at-risk couples? Four year effects of a behavioral relationship education program. *Journal of Family Psychology, 15*, 750–768.

Halford, W. K., & Simons, M. (2005). Couple relationship education in Australia. *Family Processes, 44*, 147–259.

Hawkins, A. J., Carroll, J. S., Doherty, W. J., & Willoughby, B. (2004). A comprehensive framework for marriage education. *Family Relations, 53*, 547–558.

Heyman, R. E. (2001). Observation of couple conflicts: Clinical assessment applications, stubborn truths, and shaky foundations. *Psychological Assessment, 13*, 5–35.

Holman, T. B., & Associates. (2001). *Premarital prediction of marital quality or break up: Research, theory and practice.* New York: Kluwer.

Jakubowski, S. F., Milne, E. P., Brunner, H., & Miller, R. B. (2004). A review of empirically supported marital enrichment programs. *Family Relations, 53*, 528–536.

Johnson, C. A., Stanley, S. M., Glenn, N. D., Amato, P. R., Nock, S. L., Markman, H. J., & Dion, M. R. (2002). *Marriage in Oklahoma: 2001 baseline statewide survey on marriage and divorce.* Oklahoma: Oklahoma Department of Human Services.

308 • Handbook of Clinical Issues in Couple Therapy

Kaiser, A., Hahlweg, K., Fehm-Wolfsdorf, G., & Groth, T. (1998). The efficacy of a compact psychoeducational group training program for married couples. *Journal of Consulting and Clinical Psychology, 66,* 753–760.

Kalmijn, M., & Poortman, A. (2006). His or her divorce? The gendered nature of divorce and its determinants. *European Sociological Review, 22,* 201–214.

Kendall, P. C. (1989). The generalization and maintenance of behaviour change: Comments, considerations, and the "no-cure" criticism. *Behavior Therapy, 20,* 357–364.

Knutson, L., & Olson, D. H. (2003). Effectiveness of PREPARE program with premarital couples in community settings. *Marriage and Family, 6,* 529–546.

Larson, J. H. (2000). *Should we stay together? A scientifically proven method for evaluating your relationship and improving its chances for long-term success.* San Francisco: Jossey-Bass.

Larson, J. H. (2003). *The great marriage tune-up book.* San Francisco: Jossey-Bass.

Larson, J. H., & Holman, T. B. (1994). Premarital predictions of marital quality and stability. *Family Relations, 43,* 228–237.

Larson, J. H., Newell, K., Topham, G., & Nichols, S. (2002). A review of three comprehensive premarital assessment questionnaires. *Journal of Marital and Family Therapy, 28,* 233–239.

Larson, J. H., Vatter, R. S., Galbraith, R. C., Holman, T. B., & Stahmann, R. F. (2007). The RELATionship Evaluation (RELATE) with therapist-assisted interpretation: Short-term effects on premarital relationships. *Journal of Marital and Family Therapy, 33,* 364–374.

Laurenceau, J. P., Stanley, S. M., Olmos-Gallo, A., Baucom, B., & Markman, H. J. (2004). Community-based prevention of marital dysfunction: Multi-level modeling of a randomized effectiveness study. *Journal of Consulting and Clinical Psychology, 72,* 933–943.

Markman, H. J., Renick, M. J., Floyd, F. J., Stanley, S. M., & Clements, M. (1993). Preventing marital distress through communication and conflict management training: A 4- and 5-year follow-up. Special Section: Couples and couple therapy. *Journal of Consulting and Clinical Psychology, 61,* 70–77.

Markman, H. J., Stanley, S. M., & Blumberg, S. L. (1994). *Fighting for your marriage: Positive steps for preventing divorce and preserving a lasting love.* San Francisco: Jossey-Bass.

McLanahan, S., & Sandefur, G. (1996). *Growing up with a single parent: What hurts, what helps.* Cambridge, MA: Harvard University Press.

Midmer, D., Wilson, L., & Cummings, S. (1995). A randomized, controlled trial of the influence of prenatal parenting education on postpartum anxiety and marital adjustment. *Family Medicine, 27,* 200–205.

Norcross, J. C. (2006). Integrating self-help into psychotherapy: 16 practical suggestions. *Professional Psychology: Research & Practice, 37,* 683–693.

Norcross, J. C., Santrock, J. W., Campbell, L. F., Smith, T. P., Sommer, R., & Zuckerman, E. L. (2003). *Authoritative guide to self-help resources in mental health.* New York: Guilford.

PAIRS. (2006). *For individuals and couples.* Retrieved June 15, 2007, from http://www.pairs.com/public/index.php

Petch, J., Halford, W. K., & Creedy, J. (2007). Promoting a positive transition to parenthood: A randomized controlled trial of the Couple Care for Parents Program. Manuscript submitted for publication.

Raley, R. K., & Bumpass, L. (2003). The topography of the divorce plateau: Levels and trends in union stability in the United States after 1980. *Demographic Research, 8*, 245–260.

Schilling, E. A., Baucom, D. H., Burnett, C. K., Sandin-Allen, E., & Ragland, L. (2003). Altering the course of marriage: The effect of PREP communication skills acquisition on couple's risk of becoming marital distressed. *Journal of Family Psychology, 17*, 41–53.

Schulz, M. S., Cowan, C. P., & Cowan, P. A. (2006). Promoting healthy beginnings: A randomized controlled trial of a preventive intervention to preserve marital quality during the transition to parenthood. *Journal of Consulting and Clinical Psychology, 74*, 20–31.

Shapiro, A. F., & Gottman, J. M. (2005). Effects on marriage of a psycho-communicative-educational intervention with couples undergoing the transition to parenthood, evaluation at 1-year post intervention. *The Journal of Family Communication, 5*, 1–24.

Simons, M., Harris, R., & Willis, P. (1994). *Pathways to marriage: Learning for married life in Australia*. Adelaide, Australia: Centre for Research in Education and Work, University of South Australia.

Stanley, S. M. (2001). Making the case for premarital training. *Family Relations, 50*, 272–280.

Statistics Canada. (2003). Update on families. *Canadian Social Trends, Summer 2003*. Ottawa, Canada: Statistics Canada.

Sullivan, K. T., & Bradbury, T. N. (1997). Are premarital prevention programs reaching couples at risk for marital dysfunction? *Journal of Consulting and Clinical Psychology, 65*, 24–30.

Twenge, J. M., Campbell, W. K., & Foster, C. A. (2003). Parenthood and marital satisfaction: A meta-analytic review. *Journal of Marriage and the Family, 65*, 574–583.

United Nations Economic and Social Affairs Population Division. (2003). *World fertility report*. New York: United Nations.

United States Census Bureau. (2003). *Census 2000 special report: Married couples and unmarried partner households 2000*. Washington, DC: Author.

van Acker, L. (2003). Administering romance: Government policies concerning pre-marriage education programs. *Australian Journal of Public Administration, 62*(1), 15–23.

van Widenfelt, B., Hosman, C., Schaap, C., & van der Staak, C. (1996). The prevention of relationship distress for couples at risk: A controlled evaluation with nine-month and two-year follow-ups. *Family Relations, 45*, 156–165.

Waite, L. J., & Gallagher, M. (2000). *The case for marriage: Why married people are happier, healthier, and better off financially*. New York: Doubleday.

Wampler, K. S., & Sprenkle, D. (1980). The Minnesota Couple Communication Program: A follow-up study. *Journal of Marriage and the Family, 42*, 577–585.

Wilson, G. T., Vitousek, K. M., & Loeb, K. L. (2000). Stepped care treatment for eating disorders. *Journal of Consulting and Clinical Psychology, 68*, 564–572.

17
Premarital Counseling
Promises and Challenges

LEE WILLIAMS

Contents

Skills-Based Programs	312
Relationship Enhancement	312
COUPLE COMMUNICATION	312
Prevention and Relationship Enhancement Program	313
Practical Application of Intimate Relationship Skills	314
Premarital Inventories	314
Premarital Counseling Within Church Settings	315
Premarital Counseling With Clergy	315
Engaged Encounter	316
Mentor Couples	316
Daylong Workshops	316
Other Approaches to Premarital Counseling	316
Relevant Research	318
Effectiveness of Premarital Counseling	318
Empirical Support for Specific Programs	319
Research on Designing Premarital Counseling Programs	320
Challenges Within Premarital Counseling	321
Conclusion	322
References	323

Beginning in the 1960s, the divorce rate dramatically climbed to unprecedented levels. Although the divorce rate is no longer increasing, a recent study found that 43% of first marriages end in divorce or separation within 15 years (Bramlett & Mosher, 2001). The high divorce rate has focused attention on the need to better prepare couples for building and sustaining a healthy marriage (Stanley, 2001). In response to this need, a variety of approaches have been developed in the premarital counseling field. The goal of this chapter is to briefly describe the approaches that are commonly used in premarital counseling. In addition, the research on premarital counseling will be briefly summarized, as well as three important challenges facing the premarital counseling field.

311

312 • Handbook of Clinical Issues in Couple Therapy

Skills-Based Programs

Several programs have been developed that teach couples skills for communicating and handling conflict. Some programs also address other topics, such as nurturing positive aspects of the relationship. These programs are traditionally offered in a group format, but the concepts can be used with couples in therapy. Brief descriptions of four of the most well-known and empirically supported programs are included in this section.

Relationship Enhancement

Relationship enhancement (RE) is a skills-based program to help couples effectively communicate and problem-solve issues (Cavedo & Guerney, 1999). Individuals learn, for example, how to identify needs, desires, and feelings, and to express them in a way that will minimize the listener's defensiveness. Individuals also learn how to empathically respond to the speaker's message by asking how they would think and feel in similar circumstances. Couples learn other skills to help them maintain a positive atmosphere when discussing issues, uncover the deep feelings and root issues, exit negative communication cycles, promote change within themselves and their partner, and find creative solutions through problem-solving skills. RE participants practice the skills through role-playing and discussing issues in the relationship. Coaches provide participants with feedback on how effectively they are using the skills.

COUPLE COMMUNICATION

COUPLE COMMUNICATION also teaches couples communication and conflict resolution skills (Miller & Sherrard, 1999). Like RE, a key part of the program is practicing the skills and getting feedback from coaches who observe the couples as they apply the skills. COUPLE COMMUNICATION is typically divided into four 2-hr sessions.

The first session focuses on caring for self, and emphasizes themes of self-esteem and how each individual is unique. Couples are taught how to use the Awareness Wheel, a 30-in. floor map divided into different sections to help individuals explore their experiences. Individuals first step onto the skill mat and state the issue they want to talk about, and then step on other parts of the mat to explore and articulate other aspects of the issue such as their experiences, feelings, thoughts, wants for self or others, and actions.

In the second session, the focus is on caring for your partner by developing effective listening skills, including practicing the Listening Cycle framework (also printed on a skill map). Individuals are taught, for example, how to allow the speaker rather than the listener to direct the conversation. The importance of seeking understanding first before trying to reach an agreement is also emphasized.

In the third session, couples are taught an eight-step process for resolving conflicts called "mapping an issue." After defining the problem, the couple is encouraged to understand the issue completely, including each partner's wants. Part of the process also involves generating options and evaluating which ones to implement.

In the fourth session, couples learn about different negative and positive styles of communication, and practice positive communication styles while discussing an issue.

Prevention and Relationship Enhancement Program

Prevention and Relationship Enhancement Program (PREP) is a 12-hr program that is typically delivered to couples in a group format, although PREP can be easily incorporated into work with individual couples. The four primary goals of PREP are to help couples develop better communication and conflict resolution skills, explore their expectations for the relationship, explore their attitudes and choices around commitment, and enhance their relationship bond through fun, friendship, and sensuality (Stanley, Blumberg, & Markman, 1999). A variety of strategies are used to achieve these goals (Markman, Stanley, & Blumberg, 2001).

To help couples handle conflict in a positive manner, PREP teaches couples the "speaker–listener technique." Using this technique, one individual is the "speaker," while the other individual assumes the "listener" role. The speaker follows certain guidelines, such as speaking only about their own experience, while the listener paraphrases what the speaker says. Couples are also taught ground rules to avoid harmful approaches for handling conflict, such as taking "time outs" when their discussions escalate to the point of being damaging or unproductive.

To aid couples in exploring expectations in a number of different areas (e.g., sexuality, children, spending time together, communication, and decision making), couples are given a set of questions to answer and share with their partners. Another exercise encourages couples to identify and share their core belief system, which includes religious and spiritual values, core relationship values, and moral views.

To foster commitment, couples are instructed to focus their thoughts and energy on improving the current relationship rather than alternatives. Couples are encouraged to take a long-term view of marriage, rather than a short-term view, which tends to be more reactive to current events in the relationship. PREP also invites individuals to explore whether their choices reflect their life priorities.

PREP helps couples strengthen their relationship bond in a variety of areas. Couples are asked to brainstorm fun activities they can do together and set aside time for these activities. To nurture the friendship part of their relationship, couples are encouraged to find time to share and talk with one another. Couples are taught how to separate sexuality from sensuality and are asked to do exercises that promote physical affection (e.g., hugging, massage) outside of sexual intercourse.

Practical Application of Intimate Relationship Skills

Practical Application of Intimate Relationship Skills (PAIRS) is a comprehensive 120-hr program that emphasizes both learning skills and an in-depth exploration of the self (Gordon & Durana, 1999). PAIRS is divided into five sections. In the first section, participants learn communication skills and skills for effectively resolving conflict. Couples, for example, are taught how to use the PAIRS "dialogue guide" to express a range of thoughts, feelings, and assumptions by completing sentences that begin with word stems such as "I notice," "I assume," "I am hurt by," or "I appreciate." Participants also learn to identify caring behaviors and uncover hidden expectations or beliefs about love and relationships.

The second section focuses on exploration of the self. Participants uncover what early messages they learned about love and relationships, and explore how family of origin rules, myths, or loyalties may affect their current relationships. The creation of a genogram, a multigenerational family map, is used to facilitate this exploration. The impact that different roles or personality styles can have on intimacy is also addressed.

The third section focuses on bonding, which the program emphasizes is essential to sustaining an intimate relationship. This section includes building empathy for one's partner, differentiating the need for bonding from the need for sex, and freeing repressed emotions from the childhood and recent past. Couples also identify caring behaviors they would like from their partners, and identify "turn-ons/turn-offs."

In the fourth section, couples explore the pleasures of physical bonding and touch, as well as their sensuality and sexuality. Early sexual decisions, sexual myths, and jealousy are also addressed. The fifth and final section is devoted to clarifying expectations and goals. Using the skills and insights developed throughout the program, couples negotiate a contract or set of expectations for their relationship.

Premarital Inventories

Premarital inventories are commonly used in marriage preparation or premarital counseling. The basic idea behind premarital inventories is to provide engaged couples individualized feedback about their relationship. Premarital inventories explore the couple's relationship in a number of areas including communication, conflict resolution, personality match, marital expectations, financial matters, leisure activities, family, friends, sexuality, spirituality, and children. The inventories indicate to the couple areas that are potential strengths and potential areas for growth for the couple.

Beyond identifying possible strengths and areas for growth, the inventories are intended to facilitate dialogue between the couple about their relationship. The inventories are not to be used as a test to determine whether a couple should get married, although some couples may conclude they are not suitable for one another based on the inventory results. In a review of premarital inventories, Larson, Newell, Topham, and Nichols (2002) identified PREPARE, FOCCUS, and RELATE as psychometrically sound inventories, each with its own strengths and limitations. PREPARE and FOCCUS have been designed so that couples process the feedback from the inventory with a facilitator (e.g., clergy, counselor). In contrast, RELATE is self-administered, with individuals taking the inventory and receiving the results online.

FOCCUS, PREPARE, and RELATE have different versions for addressing couples with special circumstances. PREPARE has customized versions based on the couple's characteristics (e.g., couples with children, cohabitating couples, couples over 50). FOCCUS also has various editions (general, Catholic, nondenominational, Orthodox Christian), with additional sets of questions for remarried, interfaith, and cohabitating couples. FOCCUS is also available in an abridged edition that is designed for couples with lower reading and education levels. In addition to the general RELATE inventory for couples, there is also a special version for single individuals (READY) who want to discover their relationship readiness.

PREPARE has some unique elements compared to the other inventories (Olson & Olson, 1999). PREPARE, for example, includes four relationship dynamic scales that measure assertiveness, self-confidence, avoidance, and partner dominance. Assertiveness and self-confidence mutually reinforce one another in a positive cycle. In contrast, avoidance and partner dominance mutually reinforce each other in a negative or undesirable way. PREPARE also measures the level of cohesion and flexibility in the individual's family of origin, as well as cohesion and flexibility in the couple's current relationship. The results from both partners are plotted on the Couple and Family Map to help the couple explore how experiences from their families of origin may influence their perceptions or expectations about their own relationship. Couples who take PREPARE also receive a *Building a Strong Marriage Workbook*, which contains several couple exercises to develop skills and strengthen the relationship.

Premarital Counseling Within Church Settings

The majority of premarital counseling today is offered through churches (Stahmann & Hiebert, 1997). Some churches require couples to participate in some form of marriage preparation before getting married. The use of premarital inventories is common practice within many churches. Some churches also use skills-based programs, such as Christian PREP, a version of PREP that incorporates Scriptural guidelines (Stanley & Trathen, 1994). Couples also encounter other forms of premarital counseling within church settings, which are described below.

Premarital Counseling With Clergy

A common format for premarital counseling within the church setting is for a couple to meet privately with a clergy person. The number and nature of

316 • Handbook of Clinical Issues in Couple Therapy

these meetings depends upon the clergy person. On one end of the spectrum, clergy may have only one session with the couple and focus primarily on wedding plans. On the opposite end, clergy may devote several sessions to marriage preparation, exploring a variety of areas in the relationship. The most common areas for premarital counseling to address include communication, conflict resolution, egalitarian roles, sexuality, commitment, finances, and personality issues (Silliman & Schumm, 1999).

Engaged Encounter

Engaged Encounter, a variation of Marriage Encounter (Elin, 1999), is another approach used in churches, especially the Catholic Church. Engaged Encounter weekends are led by a team of married couples (and perhaps a clergy person), who give several presentations on marriage. After the presentations, individuals are given time to reflect and write about their feelings. Individuals are also given opportunities to privately share their reflections with their partner.

Mentor Couples

Another approach that some churches use is to have engaged couples meet with a married couple that will provide mentoring. Typically the engaged couple meets in the home of the mentor couple over a period of time (e.g., 4 weeks), and the two couples complete a workbook with exercises that explore important aspects of marriage. The married couple typically completes the exercises in the workbook and shares their responses with the engaged couple so they can benefit from their experiences.

Daylong Workshops

Another common approach, especially within the Catholic Church, is to have couples attend a daylong workshop. These workshops typically have multiple speakers that present on a number of different topics, including building effective communication, developing and nurturing spirituality within the marriage, dealing with financial matters, natural family planning, or other topics. Speakers may include married couples, clergy, or experts (including therapists) within the specific area.

Other Approaches to Premarital Counseling

In addition to those already discussed, other approaches to premarital counseling also exist. Stahmann and Hiebert (1997), for example, have outlined an approach that includes using premarital inventories, conducting a thorough relationship history, and exploring the couple's families of origin. The detailed history of the couple's relationship is intended to uncover relational dynamics, issues, and patterns. For example, the premarital counselor can explore how the couple decided to date one another seriously and how they became engaged, revealing how the couple developed a bond and commitment to one another. A couple's first fights and decisions can also give insight into the couple's conflict resolution skills and the distribution of power within the relationship. Family of origin issues are explored by constructing a three-generation family map or genogram of each partner's family. Questions about individual family members, sibling interactions, parent–child interactions, and husband–wife interactions are included as part of the exploration.

Another premarital counseling program that explores transgenerational themes is *Saving Your Marriage Before it Starts* (SYMBIS) by Parrott and Parrott (1999). The SYMBIS model relies heavily on Bowen theory and encourages couples to explore how their family legacies may create unconscious roles or unspoken rules that impact their relationship.

The SYMBIS model is typically offered in a 10-session model. The first session includes administering PREPARE and constructing a genogram. The second session focuses on challenging common marital myths and developing realistic expectations, with the goal of helping the couple develop a healthy shared vision for their marriage. Couples are also encouraged to develop a realistic understanding of love (session three), as well as life attitudes that will sustain the marriage (e.g., "avoiding the blame game," "adjusting to things beyond your control"). Couples also learn about communication skills (session five), conflict resolution skills (session seven), and common gender differences (session six). The focus of the eighth session is on spiritual issues for the couple. The final sessions provide the couple feedback from PREPARE and match the couple with a mentor couple. Engaged couples meet with the mentor couple at least three times after the wedding (e.g., 3 months, 7 months, 1 year). Others have also suggested that post-wedding sessions can be valuable to couples (e.g., Guldner, 1971; Stahmann & Hiebert, 1997).

Murray and Murray (2004) described a solution-focused approach to conducting premarital counseling. In this approach, the premarital counselor first helps the couple develop a shared vision for their marriage. The counselor uses a strength-based approach to aid couples in identifying resources that they can use to achieve their vision. One such intervention is the Couple's Resource Map, a process through which couples identify resources for their marriage on the personal, relational, and contextual levels. Solution-focused questions (e.g., miracle question, looking for exceptions) are also used within this framework.

Couple CARE, which is based largely on PREP, uses a novel system for delivering instruction (Halford, Moore, Wilson, Farrugia, & Dyer, 2004). Couples receive a videotape that goes over the key concepts in the program. In addition, the couples complete a workbook of structured activities. The couples also have a series of telephone consults with a therapist who reviews the couple's progress and helps them troubleshoot issues they may be encountering. This type of program may be especially suitable for couples that have limited access to services because they live in rural areas.

318 • Handbook of Clinical Issues in Couple Therapy

A new program entitled *The First Dance* has been developed that targets the stresses that engaged couples face in planning a wedding (Doherty & Thomas, 2006). The philosophy behind the program is to meet engaged couples where they are at—preparing (and preoccupied) with planning a wedding. By teaching couples principles for managing couple and family dynamics that can arise when planning a wedding, the program hopes to provide the couple with lessons that can be applied to their marriage and extended family after the wedding.

The Coalition for Marriage, Family and Couples Education (2007) runs a web site (http://www.smartmarriages.com) that provides numerous resources on marriage education. Individuals can find other marriage preparation or marriage education programs on this site, as well as links to other web sites that offer marriage preparation and marriage education resources.

Relevant Research

Effectiveness of Premarital Counseling

Research conducted to date generally supports the effectiveness of premarital counseling. Some evidence for the effectiveness of premarital counseling comes from meta-analyses. Meta-analysis is an approach that allows researchers to combine the results of several experimental studies by standardizing their results through the calculation of a common statistic called an effect size. A recent meta-analysis of premarital prevention programs found an effect size of 0.80 compared to no treatment controls (Carroll & Doherty, 2003). Two earlier meta-analysis studies also showed positive results. Giblin, Sprenkle, and Sheehan (1985) found an average effect size of 0.53 for premarital programs compared to no treatment controls, while Hahlweg and Markman (1988) found an effect size of 0.55 for behavioral premarital intervention programs. Effect sizes of these magnitudes are considered in the medium to large range (Wampler & Serovich, 1996).

Survey research also suggests that premarital counseling is helpful to couples. A survey among married couples that had marriage preparation within the Catholic Church found that individuals perceived their marriage preparation experience to be valuable (Williams, Riley, Risch, & Van Dyke, 1999). Among those married 12 months or less, 87.5% agreed marriage preparation had been a valuable experience. By the seventh and eighth year of marriage, however, 50.0% and 52.7% of individuals, respectively, agreed marriage preparation had been a valuable experience. Thus, benefits may wear off with time, suggesting the possible need for booster sessions. Or, marriage preparation may be most helpful in terms of the initial adjustment to marriage. Programs that prepare couples for later marital transitions, such as being first-time parents, may be of value to couples.

A large survey of individuals (n = 3034) within Oklahoma, Arkansas, Kansas, and Texas (Stanley, Amato, Johnson, & Markman, 2006) also suggests that premarital counseling may be helpful. In this study, individuals who had some form of marriage preparation had a 31% less chance of having been divorced compared to those with no marriage preparation. In addition, having marriage preparation was predictive of higher marital satisfaction, higher commitment, and lower conflict, although the effect sizes for each were very modest (0.15–0.21). The study is correlational, which makes it possible that healthier couples sought out premarital counseling. The authors note, however, that other analyses and results from the study suggest premarital education does indeed have positive effects.

One of the potential benefits of premarital counseling is that couples may be more receptive to seeking out therapy if problems arise later (Stanley, 2001). A survey among 1285 recently married Army soldiers found those who had premarital counseling were more likely to have sought out marital and family therapy during their marriage (Schumm, Silliman, & Bell, 2000). Although not conclusive, the study also found evidence that those who had premarital counseling appeared to have benefited more from marital and family therapy. The authors speculate that this may be because individuals who have had premarital counseling may seek out help at an earlier stage of distress, making it easier to resolve issues.

Empirical Support for Specific Programs

There is good empirical support for the skills-based programs described earlier. Cavedo and Guerney (1999) stated that RE was compared to several couple programs and "was found to be generally superior to the alternative treatment on either outcome or process measures" (p. 99). They also note that in the meta-analysis by Giblin et al. (1985), RE demonstrated the largest effect size (0.96) among marriage enrichment programs.

COUPLE COMMUNICATION has also been extensively studied. Miller and Sherrard (1999) reported that over 40 independent, outcome studies were conducted. These studies support that COUPLE COMMUNICATION leads to better communication, improved relationship quality, and improved self-esteem. A meta-analysis comparing COUPLE COMMUNICATION to no treatment control found an effect size of 0.52 (Wampler & Serovich, 1996).

In a review of PREP outcome studies, Halford, Markman, Kline, and Stanley (2003) noted that in three of the four studies, PREP promoted sustained relationship satisfaction and stability. PREP couples, for example, had a lower incidence of divorce compared to control couples. In addition, one study found that PREP couples reported fewer instances of spouse physical abuse compared to control couples across 3-, 4-, and 5-year follow-ups.

One of the most impressive aspects of the PREP research is the length of time that couples are followed. PREP is the only program to have a published outcome study to have followed couples more than 1 year (Halford et al., 2003). Following couples longitudinally over a significant period of time is important for two reasons (Stanley et al., 1999). First, differences between

320 • Handbook of Clinical Issues in Couple Therapy

treatment and no treatment groups are difficult to break out initially because most engaged couples are highly satisfied with their relationship. Second, one of the outcomes of most interest is whether a couple stays married or divorces. Couples need to be followed over a sufficient length of time to see if the interventions impact the long-term stability of the relationship.

In a review of PAIRS research, Gordon and Durana (1999) discussed several studies that suggested PAIRS could lead to improvements in several areas such as marital satisfaction, cohesion, and emotional well-being. A key limitation of the research, however, is that few controlled studies have been done with PAIRS. Gordon and Durana cited an unpublished study by Turner that compared PAIRS participants to control participants and found that the PAIRS intervention had a positive impact on interaction style, social support, and marital discord.

Research on Designing Premarital Counseling Programs

A study on marriage preparation among Catholics examined several aspects of marriage preparation design (Williams et al., 1999). Although conducted among Catholics who received preparation primarily in a church setting, the results provide important clues on designing marriage preparation programs. In terms of length of preparation, the study clearly showed that one session was not very helpful. Rather, eight to nine sessions appeared to provide optimum results, with more sessions not necessarily being more helpful. Another study (Stanley et al., 2006) supports the fact that there may be a point of diminishing returns in terms of hours of marriage preparation. In this study, increasing hours of premarital counseling up to 9 hr was associated with decreasing levels of marital conflict. However, there was little additional reduction in marital conflict for those who had more than 9 hr of premarital counseling. Similarly, increasing hours of premarital counseling up to 20 hr improved marital satisfaction, but additional hours beyond that did little to improve marital satisfaction.

Marriage preparation was perceived as most helpful if presented by a team of providers, suggesting that both clergy and married couples should be included in marriage preparation if done in a church setting (Williams et al., 1999). The study also found that private meetings with clergy, weekend programs, and meetings with married couples were the three formats rated most helpful. The use of premarital inventories was also found to be a helpful component of marriage preparation.

In addition, the study (Williams et al., 1999) found that marriage preparation was most helpful to couples if it enabled them to spend time with one another and learn more about each other. Learning more about marriage, deepening one's relationship with God, and learning more about one's self were also important elements or benefits of marriage preparation. The topics rated most helpful in marriage preparation were collectively labeled the five C's: communication, commitment, conflict resolution, children, and church (a composite of religion and values with marriage covenant). In another study, Risch, Riley, and Lawler (2003) found that balancing job and family, frequency of sexual relations, and financial issues were the three primary issues that couples faced in the early years of marriage, and suggested that premarital counseling target these issues. Sullivan and Anderson (2002) discovered that communication, finances, problem-solving, and having children were the most important topics that engaged couples reported they wanted addressed through premarital counseling.

Research by Russell and Lyster (1992) suggested that the timing of premarital counseling might be important. They found that couples who participated in premarital counseling within 2 months of the wedding found the experience less helpful compared to couples whose wedding was more than 2 months away. Russell and Lyster recommended that couples receive premarital counseling well in advance of the wedding. Otherwise, they speculate, the couple may not be open to an honest and open exploration of issues with an impeding wedding.

Challenges Within Premarital Counseling

The field of premarital counseling faces a number of challenges. Despite the availability of several types of programs, Silliman and Schumm (1999) cited studies that indicated only 10%–35% of couples received any type of marriage preparation. Thus, one of the challenges facing the field (and perhaps society) is how to get a higher percentage of couples to seek out premarital counseling (Sullivan & Anderson, 2002).

A variety of approaches have been used to encourage couples to seek out premarital counseling. Some faith-based organizations like the Catholic Church mandate that couples receive some form of premarital counseling. Williams (1992) found that whether or not premarital counseling was mandatory was the best predictor of whether a couple attended premarital education. The potential downside to making premarital counseling mandatory, however, is that some couples may resent being forced to attend premarital counseling. Some states now offer incentives for couples to participate in some form of premarital counseling (Gardiner, Fishman, Nikolov, Glosser, & Laud, 2002). In Minnesota, for example, the legislature passed a law that gives couples $50 off their marriage license if they have received at least 12 hr of premarital counseling.

A second challenge facing the premarital counseling field is to develop further evidence as to the effectiveness of its approaches (Carroll & Doherty, 2003; Stanley, 2001). In church settings, where the majority of premarital counseling is performed today, there is limited empirical support for many of the approaches that are commonly used. Although premarital inventories like FOCCUS, PREPARE, and RELATE are commonly used in premarital counseling, limited research has been done to show that taking a premarital inventory leads to better outcomes compared to those who do not take an inventory. A recent study showed that couples who took RELATE had better relationship outcomes compared to couples who did not (Larson, Vatter, Galbraith, Holman, & Stahmann, 2007). Similar research could be done with FOCCUS and PREPARE. In addition, it is important to assess if the benefits of taking a premarital inventory extend beyond the three months tested in the RELATE study. Skills-based programs that teach couples communication and conflict-resolution skills have the strongest empirical support to date. Even among these programs, however, only one program (PREP) has published outcome studies that extend beyond a year (Halford et al., 2003). Thus, there is a strong need for additional research to demonstrate the long-term benefits of premarital counseling.

A third challenge that needs to be addressed is to develop and evaluate programs that target special needs or populations. For example, couples where one or both partners are remarrying often have special needs or considerations that other couples do not have, especially if one or both partners bring children into the relationship. Although some guidelines for working with those preparing for remarriage have been developed (e.g., Lyster, Russell, & Hiebert, 1995; Stahmann & Hiebert, 1997), there has been little research looking at the effectiveness of premarital counseling with remarried couples (Carroll & Doherty, 2003).

Couples from different religious faiths or backgrounds are another special population that premarital counselors frequently encounter. Research suggests that couples from different religious backgrounds are at greater risk for divorce (e.g., Center for Marriage and Family, 1999; Heaton, 2002; Heaton & Pratt, 1990, Lehrer & Chiswick, 1993). *Two Churches, One Marriage* (Williams, 2004) is a free web-based program (http://www.sandiego.edu/interchurch) that addresses a number of challenges that couples from different religious backgrounds can face, including managing religious differences, building a joint religious and spiritual life, considering whether to change religious affiliation, and the religious upbringing of children.

Premarital counseling with diverse racial or ethnic groups is another special population that deserves attention. Most research evaluating the effectiveness of premarital counseling has been based primarily on White, middle-class individuals (Carroll & Doherty, 2003). Research is needed to demonstrate if current programs are equally effective with culturally diverse groups, or if programs need to be tailored to various racial/ethnic groups. This is an important question to address given that different cultural groups may have different values or beliefs regarding marriage that needed to be considered.

Conclusion

The divorce rate in recent decades has highlighted the struggle that many couples face in developing a stable and satisfying marriage. Unfortunately, marital therapy has been an incomplete answer to this problem. Many couples do not seek help for their marriages until they are highly distressed, if they even seek help at all. In contrast, premarital counseling follows the advice given by Benjamin Franklin: "An ounce of prevention is worth a pound of cure." A number of different approaches to premarital counseling have developed over time, each with the goal of preparing couples for marriage. As the field evolves, it will need to find new ways to encourage engaged couples to participate in premarital counseling. It will also need to continue to develop programs that have empirical support for their effectiveness, including programs that address specific needs or populations.

References

Bramlett, M. D., & Mosher, W. D. (2001). *First marriage dissolution, divorce, and remarriage: United States.* (Advanced Data from Vital and Health Statistics; No. 323). Hyattsville, MD: National Center for Health Statistics.

Carroll, J. S., & Doherty, W. J. (2003). Evaluating the effectiveness of premarital prevention programs: A meta-analytic review of outcome research. *Family Relations, 52,* 105–118.

Cavedo, C., & Guerney, B. J. (1999). Relationship Enhancement enrichment and problem-prevention programs: Therapy-derived, powerful, versatile. In R. Berger & M. T. Hannah (Eds.), *Preventive approaches in couples therapy* (pp. 73–105). Philadelphia: Brunner/Mazel.

Center for Marriage and Family. (1999). *Ministry to interchurch marriages: A national study.* Omaha, NE: Creighton University.

Coalition for Marriage, Family and Couples Education. (2007). *Smart marriages.* Retrieved August 2, 2007, from http://www.smartmarriages.com

Doherty, W. J., & Thomas, E. (2006). *The first dance.* Retrieved August 2, 2007, from http://www.thefirstdance.com

Elin, R. J. (1999). Marriage Encounter: A positive preventive enrichment program. In R. Berger & M. T. Hannah (Eds.), *Preventive approaches in couples therapy* (pp. 55–72). Philadelphia: Brunner/Mazel.

Gardiner, K. N., Fishman, M. E., Nikolov, P., Glosser, A., & Laud, S. (2002). *State policies to promote marriage.* United States Department of Health and Human Services. Retrieved July 25, 2007, from http://aspe.hhs.gov/hsp/marriage02f

Giblin, P., Sprenkle, D. H., & Sheehan, R. (1985). Enrichment outcome research: A meta-analysis of premarital, marital and family interventions. *Journal of Marital and Family Therapy, 11,* 257–271.

Gordon, L. H., & Durana, C. (1999). The PAIRS Program. In R. Berger & M. T. Hannah (Eds.), *Preventive approaches in couples therapy* (pp. 217–236). Philadelphia: Brunner/Mazel.

Guldner, C. A. (1971). The post-marital: An alternative to premarital education. *The Family Coordinator, 20,* 115–119.

Hahlweg, K., & Markman, H. J. (1988). Effectiveness of behavioral marital therapy: Empirical status of behavioral techniques in preventing and alleviating marital distress. *Journal of Consulting and Clinical Psychology, 56,* 440–447.

Halford, W. K., Markman, H. J., Kline, G. H., & Stanley, S. (2003). Best practice in couple relationship education. *Journal of Marital and Family Therapy, 29,* 385–406.

Halford, W. K., Moore, E. M., Wilson, K. L., Farrugia, C., & Dyer, C. (2004). Benefits of a flexible delivery relationship education: An evaluation of the Couple CARE program. *Family Relations, 53,* 469–476.

324 • Handbook of Clinical Issues in Couple Therapy

Heaton, T. B. (2002). Factors contributing to increasing marital stability in the United States. *Journal of Family Issues, 23*, 392–409.

Heaton, T. B., & Pratt, E. L. (1990). The effects of religious homogamy on marital satisfaction and stability. *Journal of Family Issues, 11*, 191–207.

Larson, J. H., Newell, K., Topham, G., & Nichols, S. (2002). A review of three comprehensive premarital assessment questionnaires. *Journal of Marital and Family Therapy, 28*, 233–239.

Larson, J. H., Vatter, R. S., Galbraith, R. C., Holman, T. C., & Stahmann, R. F. (2007). The RELATionship Evaluation (RELATE) with therapist-assisted interpretation: Short-term effects on premarital relationships. *Journal of Marital and Family Therapy, 33*, 364–374.

Lehrer, E. L., & Chiswick, C. U. (1993). Religion as a determinant of marital stability. *Demography, 30*, 385–404.

Lyster, R. F., Russell, M. N., & Hiebert, J. (1995). Preparation for remarriage: Consumers' views. *Journal of Divorce and Remarriage, 24*, 143–157.

Markman, H. J., Stanley, S. M., & Blumberg, S. L. (2001). *Fighting for your marriage: Positive steps for preventing divorce and preserving a lasting love* (Rev. ed.). San Francisco: Jossey-Bass.

Miller, S., & Sherrard, P. (1999). COUPLE COMMUNICATION: A system for equipping partners to talk, listen, and resolve conflicts effectively. In R. Berger & M. T. Hannah (Eds.), *Preventive approaches in couples therapy* (pp. 125–148). Philadelphia: Brunner/Mazel.

Murray, C. E., & Murray, T. L. (2004). Solution-focused premarital counseling: Helping couples build a vision for their marriage. *Journal of Marital and Family Therapy, 30*, 349–358.

Olson, D. H., & Olson, A. K. (1999). PREPARE/ENRICH Program: Version 2000. In R. Berger & M. T. Hannah (Eds.), *Preventive approaches in couples therapy* (pp. 196–216). Philadelphia: Brunner/Mazel.

Parrott, L., & Parrott, L. (1999). Preparing couples for marriage: The SYMBIS Model. In R. Berger & M. T. Hannah (Eds.), *Preventive approaches in couples therapy* (pp. 237–254). Philadelphia: Brunner/Mazel.

Risch, G. S., Riley, L. A., & Lawler, M. G. (2003). Problematic issues in the early years of marriage: Content for marriage education. *Journal of Psychology and Theology, 31*, 253–269.

Russell, M. N., & Lyster, R. F. (1992). Marriage preparation: Factors associated with consumer satisfaction. *Family Relations, 41*, 446–451.

Schumm, W. R., Silliman, B., & Bell, D. B. (2000). Perceived premarital outcomes among recently married Army personnel. *Journal of Sex & Marital Therapy, 26*, 177–186.

Silliman, B., & Schumm, W. R. (1999). Improving practice in marriage preparation. *Journal of Sex and Marital Therapy, 25*, 23–43.

Stahmann, R. F., & Hiebert, W. J. (1997). *Premarital and remarital counseling: The professional's handbook.* San Francisco: Jossey-Bass.

Stanley, S. M. (2001). Making a case for premarital education. *Family Relations, 50*, 272–280.

Stanley, S. M., Amato, P. R., Johnson, C. A., & Markman, H. J. (2006). Premarital education, marital quality, and marital stability: Findings from a large, random household survey. *Journal of Family Psychology, 20*, 117–126.

Stanley, S. M., Blumberg, S. L., & Markman, H. J. (1999). Helping couples fight for their marriages: The PREP approach. In R. Berger & M. T. Hannah (Eds.), *Preventive approaches in couples therapy* (pp. 279–303). Philadelphia: Brunner/Mazel.

Stanley, S. M., & Trathen, D. W. (1994). Christian PREP: An empirically based model for marital and premarital intervention. *Journal of Psychology and Christianity*, *13*, 158–165.

Sullivan, K. T., & Anderson, C. (2002). Recruitment of engaged couples for premarital counseling: An empirical examination of the importance of program characteristics and topics to potential participants. *The Family Journal: Counseling and Therapy for Couples and Families*, *10*, 388–397.

Wampler, K. S., & Serovich, J. M. (1996). Meta-analysis in family therapy research. In D. H. Sprenkle & S. M. Moon (Eds.), *Research methods in family therapy*. New York: Guilford Press.

Williams, L. M. (1992). Premarital counseling: A needs assessment among engaged individuals. *Contemporary Family Therapy*, *14*, 505–518.

Williams, L. M. (2004). *Two churches, one marriage*. Retrieved August 2, 2007, from http://www.sandiego.edu/interchurch

Williams, L. M., Riley, L. A., Risch, G. S., & Van Dyke, D. T. (1999). An empirical approach to designing marriage preparation programs. *American Journal of Family Therapy*, *27*, 271–283.

VI
Training Issues

18

What Is Unique About Supervising Couple Therapists?

One Supervisor's Beginning Answer

CHERYL L. STORM

Contents

Emphasizing Clinical Competence in Supervision	331
Values and Beliefs and Their Influence on CT	331
Therapeutic Alliance: Critical and Complex	333
Attention to Emotions in CT	335
Emphasizing Professional Competence in Supervision	336
Ambiguity, Unpredictability of Relationships, Patience, and Hope	337
Comfort in Exploring "Sensitive" Areas in Couple Relationships	339
Evolving to a More Sophisticated Answer	341
References	341

Supervisors are becoming increasingly curious about supervising couple therapists for several understandable reasons. First, in the past decade there has been a resurgence of interest in couples therapy (CT), which has stimulated renewed curiosity by supervisors about the experience of supervising therapists working with couples and in the advancement of this aspect of supervision. Up until now, the supervision of couple therapists for most supervisors has *not* been seen as a unique process but either as encapsulated within the supervision process of relationally oriented therapists or based on training of couple therapists in a specific model of CT. For many supervisors, including myself, the centerpiece of supervision has been focused on processes that assist therapists in practicing from a relationship paradigm whether working with individuals, couples, or families. For those supervisors training couple therapists in a specific CT model, supervision processes have been dictated from the model.

Second, supervisors are recently receiving guidance regarding which specific change procedures and events that if targeted in supervision have the potential to increase their supervisees' CT proficiency. In the last decade, there has been a search for common processes across therapy models (Blow & Sprenkle, 2001) and as CT is "coming of age" (Johnson & Lebow, 2000, p. 23), it is becoming clearer what specific therapeutic processes couple therapists

329

330 • Handbook of Clinical Issues in Couple Therapy

may need to have special proficiency in beyond that of *any* relationally oriented therapist. Johnson (2003) argued that a revolution in CT was occurring because CT research was now becoming significant to practicing clinicians. Research is "beginning to provide direct clinical guidance for the therapist in his or her efforts to initiate specific change procedures and events" (Johnson, p. 378) especially with Caucasian, heterosexual, middle-class couples.

Finally, because these advancements are widely known by clinicians and written about in the CT literature, we are now at a point in time when there is a need for supervision practices that support them. Attention to supervision historically lags behind most therapy advances. When therapy advances lead to developments in supervision, they tend to first emerge in the form of applying the ideas of a therapy approach isomorphically in the supervision context, for example, the articles by Betchen (1995) and Glickauf-Hughes and Cummings (1995) where they describe supervision based on their preferred CT models. I believe that we are now at a point when teasing out what is unique to supervising couple therapists and what is not is relevant and timely for supervisors and the field.

In this chapter, I offer a beginning answer to the following question: What is unique about supervising couple therapists? In a review of the supervision literature, Morgan and Sprenkle (2007) found that supervisors differ greatly in their emphasis in supervision on a continuum ranging from a focus on developing clinical competency to a focus on developing professional competency with many supervisors believing both are important. I initially address ways to develop the clinical competency of couple therapists by focusing on processes that have emerged as important from recent advancements in CT. I then address ways to develop the professional competency of couple therapists by focusing on two personal qualities required of effective couple therapists. After briefly describing each process or personal quality and why it is viewed as important in CT, I suggest ways supervisors can assist interested supervisees in becoming more proficient in them and ways to stimulate growth in the self-of-the-couple therapist. An abbreviated supervision illustration ends each section.

The supervision suggestions throughout the chapter reflect my intersecting multiple social identities as a middle-aged, middle-class, heterosexual, married, female supervisor from Scandinavian descent. The examples reflect my predominant supervision context which has been a small, private, religiously affiliated couple and family therapy (CFT) therapy program where supervisees are just beginning their careers as couple therapists. My supervisory responses are only one of a myriad of possible ways to engage in supervision relationships with couple therapists.

By no means are the processes below the only relevant ones. However, they were chosen because they have been recurrent themes in my supervision with couple therapists and are emerging in the clinical literature as important in

What Is Unique About Supervising Couple Therapists? • **331**

CT with research findings supporting their importance; thus they have reasonable clinical, theoretical, and research credibility. In answering the question by focusing on both ends of the continuum of emphasis in supervision (i.e., clinical and professional development of supervisees), I hope to spark dialogue about what is unique in supervising couple therapists among supervisors across the continuum.

Emphasizing Clinical Competence in Supervision

The guidance supervisors are receiving about supervision that increases the clinical competence of couple therapists is not readily accessible for most practicing supervisors because little direct attention is paid in the literature to the implications for supervision based on recent advancements in CT. As a result, many supervisors may be supervising blindly and unintentionally ignoring the processes that we are learning are especially important to facilitate in effective CT. In addition, some authors are concerned that many couple therapists have never received supervision addressing the unique processes involved in CT (Doherty, 2002; Stahmann, 2002).

Values and Beliefs and Their Influence on CT

The values and beliefs that couples and therapists (and also supervisors) have regarding gender roles and relationship equality, the meaning of commitment/ marriage, sexuality, acceptance of same sex coupling and marriage, and spiritual and cultural ideas of relationship (e.g., individualistic, collectivist) come to the forefront in CT. It is important to attend to couples' values and beliefs about coupling because research findings are beginning to establish strong links between them and couple functioning, especially for White, middle-class heterosexual couples. For example, gender roles and the balance of power in relationships are associated with couple functioning (Johnson, 2003). Johnson and Lebow (2000) concluded in their decade review of CT that there is general broad understanding that CT "cannot be effective if it does not include an understanding of gender and the part it plays in the issues of concern" (p. 30). There is also "considerable evidence that most couples fall into unequal relationship patterns without their conscious intention or awareness" (Knudsen-Martin & Mahoney, 2005, p. 235). As research continues, the link between coupling values and beliefs will likely evolve for more diverse couples and for other relevant areas. (See Chapter 6 on sexuality and CT and all of the chapters in Part IV, Sociological Issues, of this book for an expanded discussion of the influence of values and beliefs on CT.)

It is important to attend to therapists' values and beliefs about coupling because they often subtly affect the process of CT. There is agreement in the field that the multiple intersecting social identities of couple therapists affect definitions of effective relationships, intimacy, commitment, gender roles, sexuality, and power in relationships. Doherty (2002) argued that the widely

332 • Handbook of Clinical Issues in Couple Therapy

held belief that therapists should be neutral regarding decisions regarding marriage and divorce which is endorsed in ethical codes, along with the individualistic cultural underpinnings in the United States, undermine therapists' valuing of commitment in couple relationships. As a result, he believes many couple therapists encourage couples to end relationships prematurely. Long and Serovich (2003) were concerned about the effects on CT of personal and religious beliefs of some therapists whose values result in them being aversive to working with same sex couples or believing that marriage is reserved for heterosexual couples. Zimmerman (2002) called for couple therapists not only to declare their values but also to critically analyze them paying particular attention to the ways that popular culture may be unknowingly shaping them.

Supervisory Response: Uncovering Values and Beliefs About Coupling in Supervision Supervisors can invite supervisees into a conversation where they identify, understand, and clarify their own and their clients' values and beliefs about coupling and how these reflect their intersecting multiple social identities, and assess the intentional and unintentional effects on CT. Supervisees may be more satisfied with supervision if this step is taken when multicultural competency is a stated goal of supervision (Inman, 2006). Ladany, Brittan-Powell, and Pannu (1997) found that supervisors and supervisees who had common cultural values and beliefs were more likely to address them during supervision. When supervision is occurring; the supervisor's values and beliefs are added to the mix. For example, my companionship-based meaning of marriage that stems from a combination of ethnic, generational, racial, and class influences has led me to focus intensely with my supervisees on engaging both partners in CT in an effort to avoid being privy to feelings about the relationship that is unknown to the other partner.

Uncovering values and beliefs require creating a climate for respectful dialogue in supervision by acknowledging supervisory power (Murphy & Wright, 2005), so that it does not silence supervisees from expressing their values and beliefs but is used benevolently to encourage useful reflection. I have found that sharing my understanding of my values about coupling and how it shapes my CT, noting how couples I work with have values and beliefs that are at times different than mine, and wondering about my supervisees' values and beliefs has led to fruitful discussions in supervision about the meaning of coupling and its effect in CT. The Power Equity Guide is a useful resource for stimulating discussion about gender and power differentials in CT during supervision (Haddock, Zimmerman, & MacPhee, 2000). The Sexual Orientation Matrix for Supervision (Long & Lindsey, 2004) is a useful resource for self-examination and for beginning dialogue about supervisors' and supervisees' level of acceptance of same sex relationships. By uncovering values and beliefs, supervisors and supervisees may discover they have differences in their values and beliefs as in the case below.

What Is Unique About Supervising Couple Therapists? • 333

Supervisory Group Wrestles With Beliefs and Values Regarding Same Sex Couples   In group supervision with supervisees with a variety of spiritual/religious affiliations but homogeneous in sexual affiliation, a supervisee presented a case where a female client, who had sought therapy for the effects of being sexually abused as a child, came out to her and requested CT. Although the supervisee felt she could work with the couple even though her religious convictions were opposed to same sex relationships, she wanted to explore the sexual abuse further before beginning CT. She explained that the abuse could be associated with the client's attraction to women. As a nonpracticing Lutheran supervisor supportive of same sex relationships, I struggled with how do I "show respect for differences, and not discriminate on the basis of sexual orientation or religion, especially with *supervisees of* conservative religious groups?" (Long & Serovich, 2003, p. 63, italics added). My overarching goal was to have a respectful dialogue about a wide range of values and beliefs about same sex coupling and CT. After I noted the client's trust in the therapist to have risked sharing her sexual orientation, I asked group members their reactions to the supervisees' belief and timing for CT. There was a wide range of reactions from support for delaying CT to questioning the underlying premise of the supervisee that being gay is "pathological" or "problematic." There were varying degrees of comfort in proceeding with same sex CT. It became apparent our views of how to proceed in therapy were sometimes subtly and sometimes overtly effected by our spiritual/religious beliefs, personal relational affiliations, and political alliances. I followed many of the supervisory recommendations of Long and Serovich, which admittedly were consistent with my values and beliefs. We talked about adding a co-therapist to the case who was more comfortable with same sex CT thus honoring the client's request, our ethical responsibilities to clients, when a referral is appropriate, and ways of proceeding in CT.

Therapeutic Alliance: Critical and Complex

The therapeutic alliance, "the development of a positive working relationship between the therapist and clients" (Odell, Butler, & Dielman, 2005, p. 2) in CT is critically important yet complex. It is critically important because premature termination in CT is higher than individual therapy (Bischoff & Sprenkle, 1993) and evidence is growing that a strong therapeutic alliance is necessary for CT to be successful (Bedi & Horvath, 2004; Garfield, 2004; Knobloch-Fedders, Pinsof, & Mann, 2007). The importance of the therapeutic alliance as a key process is cited in many specific CT approaches (Odell et al.; Palmer & Johnson, 2002; Pinsof & Catherall, 1986; Prouty & Protinsky, 2002). It is complex because it involves establishing multiple alliances; one with each partner and the therapist and one simultaneously with the dyad and the therapist. And this must be accomplished when *it is the dyad relationship that is itself the focus of therapy.* Therapists are "challenged to accommodate the

334 • Handbook of Clinical Issues in Couple Therapy

potentially divergent interests, motivations, goals and values of each partner in the context of the tripartite therapeutic conversation" (Bedi & Horvath, p. 67). A split alliance or a working relationship may occur with one but not both partners.

Supervisory Response: Processing and Strengthening the Therapeutic Alliance Supervisors can reflect with supervisees on their experience of the therapeutic alliance, and ways to attend to the alliance and to strengthen it throughout therapy. Reflecting on supervisees' experiences of the therapeutic alliance involves considering: Are supervisees facilitating a safe, trusting environment where they establish a bond with each partner, validate and understand both partners' perspectives simultaneously while refraining from side-taking and invalidating either partner's experience? Were supervisees drawn to one or the others' viewpoint and if so, what drew them there? Since couples report equal treatment as a helpful aspect of therapy (Bowman & Fine, 2000), was there a balance of speaking time and focus on concerns of each partner? Supervisory questions are especially useful that can promote curiosity in the supervisee about each partner's perspective. What could they explore in the next session that could help them understand this particular person's point of view?

Garfield (2004) presented guidelines for establishing the alliance, avoiding splits and disruptions, balancing relational power differences, and addressing clients' concerns about therapists' gender based on recent research findings. Supervisors may unveil unknown problems with the therapeutic alliance by encouraging supervisees to check with clients frequently to determine if there is agreement in therapy about goals, tasks, and that couples' overall expectations for therapy are being met (Odell et al., 2005). Supervisors and supervisees may find listening to the language (i.e., watching for negativity or subtle agreement with one partner over the other) that is used in therapy helpful in suggesting ways to strengthen the therapeutic alliance. If only one partner shows for therapy, it is especially important to process the therapeutic alliance because it can affect the therapist's ability to form an alliance with the *other partner* as well as the *couple*. Some therapists (especially novices) may unintentionally promote a split alliance by agreeing with the perspective of the participating partner in therapy suggesting the nonattending partner is in the wrong.

The supervision alliance appears to be as crucial for the supervision process as it is for the therapy process (Inman, 2006) with feminist supervisors being especially focused on it and committed to assuming the responsibility for the quality of it (Prouty, 2001). Like the therapeutic alliance, it includes agreement about goals and tasks. Ungar (2006) proposed that the supervisory role is "co-constructed in multiple ways through interaction with supervisees depending on what the supervisee *wants or needs*" (p. 60, italics added). These multiple roles can be served simultaneously or at different points in any one supervision session, and may include supporter, trainer/teacher, supervisor, case consultant, colleague, client advocate, and so on. In the scenario below, I simultaneously filled several roles as we approached the agreed upon task.

Supervisor and Supervisee Respond to a Split Alliance   A recent multiracial supervisee in her early thirties, describing a split alliance, reported having trouble "liking the woman," which was particularly upsetting to her since she had never felt this way about a client before. She was working with a couple with a similar background to her who was in an intense dispute over money. The supervisee found herself privately agreeing with the man that the woman's nonchalant attitude toward finances and spending habits seemed irresponsible. When I inquired about her feeling drawn to the man's perspective, the supervisee became aware that they had a common experience of growing up in financially disadvantaged families while the woman was raised in a more affluent one. As a result of our discussion she became curious about the woman's experience. We agreed her challenge was how she could continue to stay bonded with the man while simultaneously understanding and validating the woman's experience. Once the therapeutic alliance was strengthened she could more easily address issues of power and gender roles around money in the relationship. As a supervisor (with a similar disadvantaged experience), I helped her process the split alliance by: *sharing* her appreciation of the man's experience while *advocating* for an understanding of the woman's, *supervising* her using questions to facilitate her reflection on the therapeutic alliance, *supporting* her search for ways to strengthen the alliance, and *teaching* her about the importance of attending to gender roles and power in relationships in CT.

Attention to Emotions in CT

Couple interaction is often intensely emotional. Johnson and Lebow (2000) noted that "the question for the couple therapist is how to constructively address and use emotion in the process of change" (p. 32). Research suggests effective couple therapists are comfortable with emotional intensity, effective at slowing down couple interaction, skilled at using repetition to process strong emotions, and proactively structure therapy sessions to facilitate interaction between partners (Johnson, 2003). There is evidence that marital distress is associated with the expression of emotion by a spouse that is ignored by his or her partner (Johnson), and the degree of violence in couples seeking CT requires therapists to structure sessions to assess for domestic violence in all CT and to intervene if it is present. All of these findings make a case for addressing emotion in CT and indicate that couples prefer it be done via enactment-based interaction, or couple interaction that is guided by the therapist (Butler & Wampler, 1999; Estrada & Holmes, 1999). Fortunately enactment-based interaction is common across many CT approaches.

Supervisory Response: Supervisors and Supervisees Work With Emotion in CT Supervisors can assist supervisees in becoming comfortable with the expression of emotion and working with it constructively so they refrain from shutting down emotion prematurely or allow it to escalate unproductively in CT sessions. Supervisees may need to debrief the intense emotions expressed in CT as well as develop specific enactment-based interaction skills in supervision. Davis and Butler (2004) offered a conceptual step-by-step framework for facilitating enactments with couples that could be used across models, and Butler and Gardner (2003) provided guidance across the course of CT. Supervisors can assist supervisees to select among methods for working with emotion that fit with their styles and preferred ways of practicing CT (c.f., Bradley & Furrow, 2004 for a way to facilitate softening events in enactments in emotionally focused CT, Dattilio, 2005 for ways of changing schemas associated with emotion in cognitive-behavioral CT, or Sinclair & Monk, 2004 for a discursive process to help couples negotiate conflict).

Mitigating the Effect of a Warring Couple on a Supervisee A Caucasian male supervisee in his forties with considerable social service experience came to supervision quite distraught after his first ever couple session that had not gone well. He had seen an interracial couple, also in their forties, who argued most of the session. The woman of Northern European descent increasingly became angry while her African American partner became more and more quiet, ultimately angrily leaving the session. The therapist was visibly shaken by the emotional intensity, and requested options for addressing conflict in CT. If supervision did not meet his needs, I was concerned about the long-term effects of this experience on the supervisee's interest in CT and in working cross-culturally, and I worried this could create a preference of working with individuals rather than conjointly and an avoidance of working with interracial couples. I explored with him whether a larger repertoire of enactment-based interaction responses on his part would increase his comfort with the expression of emotion in sessions. He hesitantly thought it would. After debriefing his personal reactions to the arguing, we focused on strengthening the therapeutic alliance by finding ways of understanding the experiences of both partners including a consideration of interracial coupling (c.f., Tubbs & Rosenblatt, 2003). Based on this understanding, we explored possible ways to reengage them in CT. We explored how enactments could be used to slow the conflictual interaction down to allow the couple to process it with his help via a micro-analysis of a section of the videotaped session. Although the supervisee left less upset, he needed further encouragement and support to see another overtly conflicted couple.

Emphasizing Professional Competence in Supervision

Supervisors emphasizing professional competence target the personal growth of supervisees or the development of the self-of-the-couple therapist (Morgan & Sprenkle, 2007). CT calls for particular personal qualities from

What Is Unique About Supervising Couple Therapists? • **337**

therapists that are not necessarily unique to CT but are typically more pronounced in the couple context than in therapy in general. The two processes below seem to be key areas of personal growth for many couple therapists.

Ambiguity, Unpredictability of Relationships, Patience, and Hope

As a new couple therapist, I began a silent game of predicting who would remain together and who was likely to part. I saw some couples change their relationship significantly but decide to part, separated couples who seemed to make no progress happily reconcile, other couples who had a relationship that many would envy be dissatisfied, and some couples revitalize their relationship when I secretly felt it was doomed. These couples taught me an important lesson about experiencing compassion, being patient, and remaining hopeful, while living with their ambiguity and the unpredictability of their relationships; a lesson that supervisors frequently are in a position to pass onto supervisees, and one that has guided my supervision with couple therapists over the years.

The importance of the therapist's ability to be compassionate regarding couples' ambiguity, and hopeful and patient regarding change and the benefit of therapy is increasingly receiving support in the literature. In interviews of experienced couple therapists regarding hope in CT, therapists described a continuum of hope of couples seeking therapy. Some couples seek CT with a solid belief that therapy can help, others seek therapy with ambivalence about whether or not the relationship can improve (the largest group), and still others seek therapy with at least one partner wanting out of the relationship (Ward & Wampler, 2007). A frequent refrain in supervision by frustrated couple therapists is that couples can't decide whether to stay together or to part, and therapists aren't sure whether they are doing couple or uncoupling/divorce therapy. Couple therapists are thus frequently called on to be compassionate and hopeful when witnessing heart-wrenching ambiguity as couples wrestle with their relationships.

Therapist patience seems to be another requisite quality of successful CT. Former clients, who participated in successful CT with one of the developers of three different CT models, described a common theme in their therapy of therapists showing "respect for the client's pace of change by being patient with the change process" (Davis & Piercy, 2007, p. 346). The importance of repetition in CT suggested by CT research findings (Davis & Piercy; Johnson, 2003) and by recent advances in neuroscience (Atkinson et al., 2005; Roberts, 2007) also calls for significant patience on the part of couple therapists.

Supervisory Response: Expanding the Capacity for Patience, Compassion, and Hope By focusing on the couple therapist's growth in their capacity for being compassionate, hopeful, and patient, supervisees seem to be able to respect couples' pace of change, accept the starts, stops, and unpredictability of the process when couples are ambiguous about their relationships, and

338 • Handbook of Clinical Issues in Couple Therapy

cover the same ground again and again. The supervisory challenge then is how to facilitate this personal growth in the self-of-the-couple therapist.

In a study of couple and family therapy interns, Paris, Linville, and Rosen (2006) concluded that a positive, reciprocal relationship exists between personal and professional experiences with interns' personal relationships cited as being a source for professional growth and contributing to therapists' hopefulness. Supervisors can help supervisees tap their personal experiences and relationships as a source of growth. Supervisors can encourage them to remember personal relationship difficulties and/or losses, or to talk with couples who are friends and family members about the ups and downs in couple relationships. These experiences can be fertile ground for increasing compassion and understanding of the couple experience and the often illogical, intense, and even seemingly "crazy" behavior (i.e., calling incessantly or with excuses, driving past the loved ones home, and so on) of those in a relationship that is not going well.

Supervisors can help supervisees tap their professional context and relationships as also a source of growth. Supervisors may wish to draw on mindfulness and Buddhist principles to introduce couple therapists to ways of increasing their compassion, engaging suffering, and "mindful presence" where "therapists learn to respond to whatever clients present from a position of nonattached yet fully engaged witnessing of clients and their experience without the desire to change the experience for them" (Gehart & McCollum, 2007, p. 214). Experienced couple therapists cited ongoing supervision as the primary way they maintain and encourage their own hope that couples can change, getting another perspective through consulting about cases with colleagues, turning to professional resources that open up options, and relying on a CT model of change as ways they become more hopeful (Ward, 2006). If these strategies are useful to experienced couple therapists, they are likely to be so for less-experienced couple therapists and to be ways supervisors can contribute to a growth producing context in supervision.

Supervisor and Therapist Prevent Hope From Slipping Away   A recent Caucasian supervisee from Northern European descent in her mid-twenties shared her frustration with a middle-aged Latino couple she was seeing. Neither partner reported being in love and neither partner was making much effort to change, yet the couple expressed a strong desire to continue CT. In the supervisee's somewhat limited relationship history she had easily moved from relationships when she felt there was no future and was having difficulty understanding why this middle-aged couple was staying together. Over several supervision sessions with this couple therapist, we explored a number of differing areas in her personal and professional experiences and relationships with the hopes of expanding her understanding (and hence capacity for compassion for this couple) and to increase her patience with the therapy process and them. In the personal realm, we explored such areas as the many reasons for coupling

What Is Unique About Supervising Couple Therapists? • 339

outside of romantic love and how cultural and family backgrounds influenced choosing a partner and staying committed to a relationship and times in both our lives when we desired a change but it came slowly. In the professional realm, we considered the systemic philosophical underpinnings of her training suggesting couples change in a variety of ways and speeds, and used her postmodern approach to therapy to explore the effects of patience and impatience on relationships in general, this couple's relationship, and therapy. The supervisee found our conversations useful in regaining a sense of hopefulness that she, as well as therapy, could be helpful to the couple. She became more able to be present in therapy and focus on the couples' experience as they all rode the ups, the downs, and the waves of ambiguity about the relationship.

Comfort in Exploring "Sensitive" Areas in Couple Relationships

Couple therapists are in a context where they are expected to enter into what culturally can be considered "sensitive areas" of discussion; those topics that one does not openly talk about with neighbors, friends, or even other family members. What is considered sensitive varies by individuals and is highly influenced by multiculturalism, community dictates, and family background. Common areas noted by couple therapists as sensitive include sexuality, finances, intimate partner violence, and possible affairs. Oftentimes getting to the heart of the matter in CT requires getting into these areas yet couple therapists can be reticence about inquiring, much less addressing head-on, sensitive areas without an overt invitation from couples; even when therapists have received specific training regarding these areas. For example, some couple therapists believe that exploring certain topics is a violation of couple privacy. Some couple therapists are worried that their clients could misinterpret an interest in couples' sexuality as them "coming on" to one of the partners. While some other couple therapists, often women supervisees, express feeling intimidated and backing away from discussing anger and possible intimate partner violence with male clients out of fear of personal safety.

Supervisory Response: Inviting Personal Discovery Increases Comfort Some supervisees seem to just need a little encouragement and support to open-up these areas in therapy with guidance about ways of inquiring that fit the couple, their style of therapy, and are timed well. Some supervisees seem to need help with having a possible direction for therapy once they have opened up a topic. For example, a recent supervisee, who was hesitant to explore intimate partner violence with a couple, needed little encouragement or guidance about how to assess for violence once we discussed the negotiated time-out tool to deescalate violence (Stith et al., 2002) as a next step should she discover it. When this is the situation, supervisors along with supervisees can discover what professional resources are needed whether they are a supervisory suggestion or a full-scale mutually developed therapeutic plan.

340 • Handbook of Clinical Issues in Couple Therapy

Other couple therapists may need more personal understanding about their reticence requiring exploration of the reluctance in supervision. Supervisors can stimulate this understanding and personal growth in the self-of-the-couple therapist by exploring with supervisees whatever is relevant—their personal and family relationships and history, values and beliefs, multicultural influences, dominant ideas in society, their reactions, and so on. A few questions I have found useful are as follows: What do you think will happen if you bring the topic up? What are your hopes and fears? How is a conversation with couples who are clients different from couples who are friends or family members? How did you learn this area was sensitive to talk about, or considered private? How could you discover if the couple feels similarly or different? How could you gain permission from the couple to enter into this arena in therapy? The ultimate goal is the development of the self-of-the-couple therapist in a way that supervisees are personally comfortable in exploring these areas with couples, are compassionate and understanding if couples are also reticent, and are able to talk with couples about these areas in sensitive, caring ways during CT.

Co-Therapists Explore a Hunch and Develop Comfort in Previously Taboo Areas   A heterosexual Caucasian co-therapy team from European Northern descent shared in supervision that they had a hunch that a couple was arguing about their sexual relationship but the problem is masquerading as "communication difficulty." The therapists' hunch was based on the vague and confusing responses to questions about the couple's concerns with their communication. Both therapists were waiting for the couple to bring it up; hoping that their questions about intimacy, closeness, and time together would invite the couple to discuss their sexual life. The male co-therapist felt it was time to be more direct because they would "loose" the male partner if they did not, but was highly uneasy in doing so. The female co-therapist was worried that the male client's ideas about sexuality would supersede the female client's concerns if their hunch played out. We brainstormed ways of opening up the discussion about sexuality that would allow both partners to express their intimacy and sexual desires without either co-opting the therapeutic process, and that reflected both supervisees' perspectives. Most important, we explored each therapist's reticence in raising sexuality with couples—noting that it stemmed from some similar and some differing personal relationship and family experiences, their unique multicultural backgrounds, and their ideas about gender and cross-gender relationships. We identified some issues for each to further think about and explore and a set of questions both felt comfortable in asking and were case appropriate. The co-therapy team returned the next week excited about the therapy session they had with the couple. Their hunch was right on with the couple responding that they weren't sure if it was appropriate to discuss their sex life since the therapists were couple therapists, not sex therapists! My hope was by finding ways of developing

What Is Unique About Supervising Couple Therapists? • 341

questions and taking the risk of following their hunches, the therapists would generalize the process they used to explore sexuality to other potentially sensitive areas in their work.

Evolving to a More Sophisticated Answer

In this chapter, I proposed a beginning answer to what is *unique* to supervising couple therapists by highlighting specific clinical proficiencies and therapist qualities that come to the forefront when working with couples and ways supervisors could facilitate them in supervision. These clinical proficiencies and therapist qualities are likely present in most effective therapists, but seem to be critical for couple therapists. Effective couple therapists are believed to need to be proficient at attending to values and beliefs about the meaning of coupling to couples and themselves, developing the therapeutic alliance which has a unique complexity in CT, and constructively working with emotion prevalent in CT. They are believed to need a certain capacity for compassion, being patient, and remaining hopeful, while living with couples ambiguity and the unpredictability of couples' relationships. Further, they need to be comfortable in exploring areas with couples that are often considered culturally sensitive. Armed with this awareness of clinical proficiencies and qualities that are needed by couple therapists, supervisors can draw on important dimensions of supervision (Morgan & Sprenkle, 2007; Ungar, 2006) to tailor their existing supervision philosophy and practices to supervising couple therapists. As supervisors more intentionally target supervisees' clinical proficiency in CT and the self-of-the-couple therapist, supervision ideas and methods will evolve. Since supervisors are curious and want to tease out the uniqueness of supervising couple therapists, perhaps a more sophisticated answer is just around the corner.

References

Atkinson, B., Atkinson, L., Kutz, P., Lata, J., Wittman Lata, K., Szekely, J., & Weiss, P. (2005). Rewiring neural states in couple therapy: Advances from affective neuroscience. *Journal of Systemic Therapies, 24*(3), 3–17.

Bedi, R., & Horvath, A. (2004). The perceived relative strength of the therapeutic alliance: Perceptions of own and partner's alliance and psychotherapeutic outcome in time-limited couples therapy. *Journal of Couple and Relationship Therapy, 3*(4), 65–80.

Betchen, S. (1995). An integrative, intersystemic approach to supervision of couple therapy. *Journal of Family Therapy, 23*(1), 48–58.

Bischoff, G., & Sprenkle, D. (1993). Dropping out of marital and family therapy: A critical review of the research. *Family Process, 32*, 353–375.

Blow, A., & Sprenkle, D. (2001). Common factors across theories of marriage and family therapy: A modified Delphi study. *Journal of Marital and Family Therapy, 27*, 385–402.

Bowman, L., & Fine, M. (2000). Client perceptions of couples therapy: Helpful and unhelpful aspects. *American Journal of Family Therapy, 28*, 295–310.

342 • Handbook of Clinical Issues in Couple Therapy

Bradley, B., & Furrow, J. (2004). Toward a mini-theory of the blamer softening event: Tracking the moment-by-moment process. *Journal of Marital and Family Therapy, 30*, 233–246.

Butler, M. H., & Gardner, B. C. (2003). Adapting enactments to couple reactivity: Five developmental stages. *Journal of Marital and Family Therapy, 29*, 311–328.

Butler, M. H., & Wampler, K. S. (1999). Couple-responsible therapy process: Positive proximal outcomes. *Family Process, 38*, 27–54.

Dattillio, F. (2005). The restructuring of family schemas: A cognitive-behavioral perspective. *Journal of Marital and Family Therapy, 31*, 15–30.

Davis, S., & Butler, M. (2004). Enacting relationships in marriage and family therapy: A conceptual and operational definition of an enactment. *Journal of Marital and Family Therapy, 30*, 319–334.

Davis, S., & Piercy, F. (2007). What clients of couple therapy model developers and their former students say about change, Part I: Model-dependent common factors across three models. *Journal of Marital and Family Therapy, 33*, 318–343.

Doherty, W. (2002). How therapists harm marriages and what we can do about it. *Journal of Couple Relationships Therapy, 1*(2), 1–18.

Estrada, A., & Holmes, J. (1999). Couples perceptions of effective and ineffective ingredients of marital therapy. *Journal of Sex and Marital Therapy, 25*(2), 151–162.

Garfield, R. (2004). The therapeutic alliance in couples therapy: Clinical considerations. *Family Process, 43*, 457–465.

Gehart, D., & McCollum, E. (2007). Engaging suffering: Towards a mindful re-visioning of family therapy practice. *Journal of Marital and Family Therapy, 33*, 214–226.

Glickauf-Hughes, C., & Cummings, S. (1995). Use of containment in supervising couples therapy, *Family Journal, 3*(2), 149–154.

Haddock, S., Zimmerman, T., & MacPhee, D. (2000). The power equity guide: Attending to gender in family therapy. *Journal of Marital and Family Therapy, 26*(2), 153–170.

Inman, A. (2006). Supervisor multicultural competence and its relation to supervisory process and outcome. *Journal of Marital and Family Therapy, 32*, 73–86.

Johnson, S. (2003). The revolution of couple therapy: A practitioner-scientist perspective. *Journal of Marital and Family Therapy, 29*, 365–384.

Johnson, S., & Lebow, J. (2000). The "coming of age" of couple therapy: A decade review. *Journal of Marital and Family Therapy, 26*, 29–38.

Knobloch-Fedders, L., Pinsof, W., & Mann, B. (2007). Therapeutic alliance and treatment progress in couple therapy. *Journal of Marital and Family Therapy, 33*, 245–257.

Knudsen-Martin, C., & Mahoney, A. (2005). Moving beyond gender: Processes that create relationship equality. *Journal of Marital and Family Therapy, 31*, 235–246.

Ladany, N., Brittan-Powell, C. S., & Pannu, R. K. (1997). The influence of supervisory racial identity interaction and racial matching on the supervisory working alliance and supervisee multicultural competence. *Counselor Education and Supervision, 36*, 284–304.

Long, J., & Lindsey, E. (2004). The sexual orientation matrix for supervision: A tool for training therapists to work with same-sex couples. *Journal of Couple and Relationship Therapy, 23*(2/3), 123–136.

Long, J., & Serovich, J. (2003). Incorporating sexual orientation into MFT training programs: Infusion and inclusion. *Journal of Marital and Family Therapy, 29*, 59–67.

Morgan, M., & Sprenkle, D. (2007). Toward a common-factors approach to supervision. *Journal of Marital and Family Therapy, 33*, 1–17.

Murphy, M., & Wright, D. (2005). Supervisees' perspectives of power use in supervision. *Journal of Marital and Family Therapy, 31*, 283–296.

Odell, M., Butler, T., & Dielman, M. (2005). An exploratory study of clients' experiences of therapeutic alliance and outcome in solution-focused marital therapy. *Journal of Couple and Relationship Therapy, 4*(1), 1–22.

Palmer, G., & Johnson, S. (2002). Becoming an emotionally focused couple therapist. *Journal of Couple and Relationship Therapy, 1*(3), 1–20.

Paris, E., Linville, D., & Rosen, K. (2006). Marriage and family therapist interns' experiences of growth. *Journal of Marital and Family Therapy, 32*, 45–57.

Pinsof, W., & Catherall, D. (1986). The integrative psychotherapy alliance: Family, couple, and individual therapy scales. *Journal of Marital and Family Therapy, 12*, 137–151.

Prouty, A. (2001). Experiencing feminist family therapy. *Journal of Feminist Family Therapy, 12*, 171–203.

Prouty, A., & Protinsky, H. (2002). Feminist-informed internal family systems therapy with couples. *Journal of Couple and Relationship Therapy, 1*(3), 21–36.

Roberts, T. (2007). Brain biology and couple therapy. *Journal of Couple and Relationship Therapy, 6*, 5–16.

Sinclair, S., & Monk, G. (2004). Moving beyond the blame game: Toward a discursive approach to negotiating conflict within couple relationships. *Journal of Marital and Family Therapy, 30*, 335–348.

Stahmann, R. (2002). Marriage doctor or dr. death? A response to Doherty's "how therapists harm marriages and what we can do about it." *Journal of Couple and Relationship Therapy, 4*(1), 25–32.

Stith, S., Rosen, K., & McCollum, E. (2002). Developing a manualized couples treatment for domestic violence: Overcoming obstacles. *Journal of Marital and Family Therapy, 28*, 21–25.

Tubbs, C., & Rosenblatt, P. (2003). Assessment and intervention with black-white multiracial couples. *Journal of Couple and Relationship Therapy, 2*(2/3), 115–129.

Ungar, M. (2006). Practicing as a postmodern supervisor. *Journal of Marital and Family Therapy, 32*, 59–72.

Ward, D. B. (2006). *Moving up the continuum of hope: A qualitative study of hope and its influence in couples therapy.* Unpublished doctoral dissertation, Texas Tech University, Lubbock, Texas.

Ward, D. B., & Wampler, K. (2007). *Moving up the continuum of hope: Developing a theory of hope and understanding its influence in couples therapy.* Unpublished manuscript.

Zimmerman, T. (2002). A feminist perspective on how therapists can harm marriage and what we can do about it. *Journal of Couple and Relationship Therapy, 4*(1), 19–24.

Index

A

AAMFC, *see* American Association of Marriage and Family Counselors

AAMFT, *see* American Association of Marriage and Family Therapists

ABCT, *see* Alcohol behavioral couple therapy

ACTH, *see* Adrenocorticotropic hormone

Acute stress disorder, 131

Addictions
  alcohol abuse
    alcohol behavioral couple therapy, 78–79
    behavioral couples therapy, 78
    community reinforcement and family training program, 77
    community reinforcement approach, 76
    community reinforcement training, 76–77
    couple group therapy, 79–80
    family systems therapy, 80
    interactional therapy, 78
    minimal spouse involvement, 78–79
    pressure to change approach, 77
    traditional inpatient program, 79
    unilateral family therapy, 77
  eating disorders, 84
  gambling, 83
  sexual compulsivity, 82–83
  substance abuse, 81–82
  systemic couples therapy, 85–88

Addiction Severity Index (ASI), 87–88

Adrenocorticotropic hormone (ACTH), 31

AFSI, *see* Alcohol-focused spouse involvement

Agoraphobia, 50

Alcohol abuse
  alcohol behavioral couple therapy, 78–79
  behavioral couples therapy, 78
  community reinforcement and family training program, 77
  community reinforcement approach, 76
  community reinforcement training, 76–77
  couple group therapy, 79–80
  family systems therapy, 80
  interactional therapy, 78
  minimal spouse involvement, 78–79
  pressure to change approach, 77
  traditional inpatient program, 79
  unilateral family therapy, 77

Alcohol behavioral couple therapy (ABCT), 78–79

Alcohol-focused spouse involvement (AFSI), 78–79

Alpha bias, 229

Alzheimer's disease, 64

American Association for Marriage and Family Therapy, 248–250, 266

American Association of Marriage and Family Counselors (AAMFC), 3–4

American Association of Marriage and Family Therapists (AAMFT), 4

American Association of Marriage and Family Therapy (AAMFT) code, 208–209, 248–250, 266

American Association of Marriage Counselors (AAMC), 2–3

American Journal of Family Therapy, 250–251

American Psychological Association (APA), 7

Anxiety disorders
  agoraphobia, 50
  couple intervention, 49–50
  posttraumatic stress disorder, 50–51
  relationship satisfaction, 49

345

346 • Index

APA, *see* American Psychological
    Association
Arousal disorders, 134
ASI, *see* Addiction Severity Index
Asian American couples, 212–213
Attachment theory, 45
Awareness of culture
    ethics and cross-cultural
        therapy, 208–209
    impact of culture
        context, 211
        cultural differences, 210
        culture and making meaning,
          220–221
        definition, 209
        gender, 215–217
        majority culture, 210
        minority culture, 210
        overlap of cultural variables, 220
        race and ethnicity, 211–214
        sexual orientation, 218–220
        socioeconomic class, 217–218
        values and beliefs, 209–210
    shifting paradigms, 208

B

Behavioral couples therapy (BCT)
    alcohol abuse, 78
    substance abuse, 81–82, 119–121
Behavioral marital therapy
    (BMT), 13–14
Bete bias, 229
Binge eating disorders, 84
Bipolar disorders, 47–49
Bisexual, 229
Blue-collar working class, 217
BMT, *see* Behavioral marital therapy
Bowen family systems theory, 149, 157
Brain biology
    attachment bonds, 27–28
    couple therapy
        attachment styles, 33–34
        attunement, 35
        client/therapist relationship, 35
        conscious insight, 34–35
        creative activity, 36
        emotions, rational thinking, 36
        expressive arts, 35–36
        humor, 36–37
        implicit memory, 32–33

        love and romantic feelings, 37
        new experiences, 37
        nonverbal interventions, 35
        pragmatic/experiential therapy
          for couples, 33
        priming, 34
        stress reduction, 37
    learning and memory
        coherent memory, 30–31
        cortisol, 31
        drugs, 31
        glia cells, 28
        hormones, 31
        implicit and explicit memory,
          29–30
        new experiences and
          information, 28
        short-and long-term memory
          formation, 29
        true and false memories, 31
        unconscious, types, 29
        visualization, 29
    neolimbic/neocortex, 25–26
    neuroscience, 24
    paleolimbic/limbic system, 25–26
    rationality and emotionality, 24
    R-complex, 25
Breast cancer
    body image and sexuality, 65–66
    emotional distress, depression, and
        anxiety, 66–67
    life cycle transitions, 67–68
    long-term adjustment, 67
    sexual dysfunction, 66

C

Childhood trauma
    anger, 136
    anxiety, 136
    boundary issues, 134
    cognitive distortions, 135
    communication difficulties, 134
    depression and suicide, 135
    grief sharing, 133
    hypervigilance, 135
    increased relational conflict, 133
    reduced relational intimacy, 132–133
    sexual disorders, 134–135
    spirituality, 136
    tension reducing activities, 136

Christian marital counseling, 254
Church settings, premarital counseling
  clergy, 315–316
  daylong workshops, 316
  engaged encounter, 316
  mentor couples, 316
Class-conscious therapy, 217
Clinical competence in supervision
  effect of warring couple, 336
  emotions in CT, 335–336
  split alliance, 335
  strengthen and processing, alliance,
    334–335
  supervisory group wrestles, 333
  supervisory response, 332
  therapeutic alliance, 333–334
  work with emotion, 336
Code of ethics, 209
Commission on Accreditation for
    Marriage and Family therapy
    Education (COAMFTE), 3
Common couple violence, 118
Community reinforcement and family
    training program (CRAFT)
  alcohol abuse, 77
  substance abuse, 81
Community reinforcement approach
    (CRA), 76
Community reinforcement training
    (CRT)
  alcohol abuse, 76–77
  substance abuse, 81
Confucion code of conduct, 274
Conjoint couple therapy, 13, 282
Cortisol, 31
Couple group therapy, 79–80
Couple relationship education (CRE),
    293–306
  current status of marriage
    assessment and feedback, 295
    couple distress, 297
    effects of assessment and
      feedback, 295
    evaluating CRE effects, 296–297
    evidence-based approach,
      295–296
    inventory based
      assessments, 295
    research, 296
    skill based CRE benefits,
      296–297

customizing relationship education
  challenging CRE, 300
  couples report, 299–300
  negative communication, 299
  PAIRS, 299
  PREP, 298
  risk and protective factors, 300
limitations of CRE programs,
    305–306
rationale for marriage, 294
RELATE-couple CARE program
  assessment, 303
  contents of, 303–305
  evaluate couple intensity, 302
stepped approach
  applying concept, 300–301
  assumptions, 301
  psychological interventions, 300
  research, 302
targeting relationship education,
    297–298
Couples divorce
  divorce theory, 170–171
  emergence of conflict, 169–170
  emotional disaffection, 168–169
  gender roles, 167
  partners' expectations, 167
  premarital sex and
    cohabitation, 168
Couple therapists, supervision
  answer to unique supervision, 343
  clinical competence
    effect of warring couple, 336
    emotions in CT, 335–336
    split alliance, 335
    strengthen and processing,
      alliance, 334–335
    supervisory group wrestles, 333
    supervisory response, 332
    therapeutic alliance, 333–334
    work with emotion, 336
  professional competence
    ambiguity, unpredictability and
      patience, 337
    co-therapists explore, 340–341
    prevent hope, 338–339
    sensitive areas, 339
    supervisory response, 339–340
    work with emotion, 336
  relationship paradigm, 329
  resurgence of interest, CT, 329

348 • Index

specific therapeutic processes,
329–330
supervision suggestions, 330
therapy advances, 330
Couple therapy
behavioral marital therapy, 13–14
briefer interventions, 11
cultural groups, 17
emotionally focused couple therapy,
11–13
family therapy
APA, 7
charismatic proponents, 6
history and origin, 4
mental health treatment, 6
negative consequences, 4
research, 4–5
theories and models, 5–6
history
AAMC, 2–3
AAMFC, 3–4
AAMFT, 4
COAMFTE, 3
helping professions, 1–2
marriage counseling
movement, 2
integrative behavioral couple therapy,
13–15
integrative models, 10–11
maturity, 16
model, 277, 283
practice patterns and consumer
reports study, 7–8
research
couple interactions, 10
divorce and couple relationships,
8–9
effective treatment, 15–16
instruments, 9
marital adjustment test, 8–9
marital conflict, 9
marital dissatisfaction, 8–9
model development, 11
relationship science, 8
specific disorders, 18
training, 17
Couple violence
clinical methods, 282–283
focus on issues, 282
screening, 281–282
training, 283

CRA, *see* Community reinforcement
approach
CRAFT, *see* Community reinforcement
and family training program
CRT, *see* Community reinforcement
training
Cultural competence, 208
Cultural competency model, 218
Cultural contexts, 208–209, 211, 214,
217–218
Cultural experience, 208–209, 221
Cultural transition, 275

D

Depressive disorders
marital discord and depression, 46
treatment, 46–47
Divorcees, 171–173
Divorce rate, 294, 311
Divorce therapy
couples divorce
divorce theory, 170–171
emergence of conflict, 169–170
emotional disaffection, 168–169
gender roles, 167
partners' expectations, 167
premarital sex and
cohabitation, 168
culture of marriage, 166
decision-making phase, 166
definition of, 165
impact of divorce
children, 175–178
partners, 171–175
marital dissolution, 166
marital therapists concept, 180–182
process, 166
pro-marriage, 167
surviving divorce, 178–180
transitional models, 166
Domestic Conflict Containment
Program (DCCP), 120
Domestic violence-focused couples
treatment (DVFCT), 121
Dynamic unconscious, 29

E

Eating disorders, 84
Economic partnership, 294

Emotion-focused therapy (EFT), 11–13, 45–46
Emotions in couple therapists, 335–336
Empirically supported Prevention and Relationship Enhancement Program (PREP), 298
Ethical code, 255
Ethical principle, 208
Ethical ramifications, 209
Ethnic diversity, 208, 213
Explicit memory, 29–30
Expressive arts, 35–36
Eye movement desensitization and reprocessing (EMDR), 140–141

F

False memory, 31
Family diversity
  bisexual, 230
  immigrants, 233
  interracial couples, 231–232
  sexual identify, 230–231
Family functions
  applications, 227–228
  family formation and membership
    children, 235–236
    diversity, 230–233
    marriage/civil unions, 233–234
    origin of, 234
    relationship satisfaction, 230
    U.S. census, 230
  family strength and resiliency, 226
  family structure, 225
  nurturance, education and socialization
    family support, 240
    gender roles, 236–238
    sexual fulfillment, 239–240
    spirituality and religiosity, 238–239
  potential bias, 228–229
  vulnerable members protection
    legal protection, 241–242
    self-disclosure and power, 241
Family origin issues, 229
Family systems therapy (FST), 80
Family therapy, 208, 211, 214, 217–220
  APA, 7
  charismatic proponents, 6
  history, 4

mental health treatment, 6
negative consequences, 4
networker, 249, 259
origin, 4
research, 4–5
theories and models, 5–6
Female sexuality, 106–107
Feminist literature, 274, 282–283
Feminist therapy
  connection as focus and process
    couple therapy, 277–278s
    redefining sex, 277–278
    same-sex couples, 279
    sex therapy, 278
  cultural diversity, racism and couples
    community support, 276
    heritage, feminist goals, 274–275
    pressures of racism, 275–276
    therapist self assessment, 273–274
    uniqueness, transitions, and innovations, 275
  deconstruction gender
    deconstruction to reconstruction, 272
    roles, 272–273
  pervasiveness of power
    couple violence, 281–283
    deconstruction to reconstruction, 279–280
    negotiating family and work, 280–281
    power and gender communication, 281
Franklin, Benjamin, 323
Functional family therapy (FFT), 149

G

Gamblers anonymous (GA), 83
Gambling, 83
Gay and lesbian violence, 281–283
Gay couples, 272, 276
Gender power, 279–280
Gender role bias, 228–229, 272

H

Heterogamy, 262
Heterosexism, 272–273, 275–276, 279–280, 282
Heterosexual relationship, 215, 218–219
History of Sexuality (Foucault), 105

350 • Index

Hormones, 31
Human diversity, 271–272, 274
Human Sexual Inadequacy (Masters and Johnson), 100–101
Humor, 36–37

I

IBCT, *see* Integrative behavioral couples therapy
Impact of culture, awareness
  context, 211
  cultural differences, 210
  culture and making meaning, 220–221
  definition, 209
  gender, 215–217
  majority culture, 210
  minority culture, 210
  overlap of cultural variables, 220
  race and ethnicity
    Asian American couples, 212–213
    assessment, 214
    couple and therapist role, 213
    homeplace, 212
    religious diversity, 213–214
  sexual orientation, 218–220
  socioeconomic class, 217–218
  values and beliefs, 209–210
Impact of divorce
  children
    affection and welfare, 175
    depression and emotional problems, 176
    positive and negative effects, 175–177
  partners
    benefits from divorce, 173
    divorcees, 173
    divorce process, 173
    economic impact, 174–175
    fewer benefits, 174
    negative effects, 171
    positive effects, 172
    re-marriage, 172
Implicit memory, 29–30
Infidelity
  Bowen family systems theory, 149
  couple characteristics, 148
  definition, 146–147

  development, within relationship, 147
  functional family therapy, 149
  individual characteristics, 147–148
  Internet
    research, 156
    treatment, 156–157
  postmodern movement, 149
  research, 151–152
  systemic/multigenerational characteristics, 148–149
  techniques and frameworks
    deficit model, 156
    eight-step model, 152–153
    extramarital relationship, 152
    integrative behavioral couple therapy, 156
    intersystem approach, 154
    post-traumatic stress disorder, 154
    Spring's model, 153
    three-stage integrative model, 155
  treatment
    forgiveness, 150–151
    multiple dimensions, 150
    society, 150
    therapists, values and beliefs, 151
  typologies, 147
Integrative behavioral couples therapy (IBCT), 13–15, 64–65
Interactional therapy (IT), 78
International Association of Marriage and Family Counselors, 255
Internet infidelity
  research, 156
  treatment, 156–157
Interracial same-sex couples, 234
Intimate partner violence (IPV)
  battering intervention programs, 116–117
  conjoint couples treatment
    Ackerman Institute program, 122
    assessment and contingency plans, 125
    behavioral couples therapy, substance abuse, 119–120
    clinical specialty, 123
    coordinated community response, 123–124
    Domestic Conflict Containment Program, 120

domestic violence-focused
couples treatment, 121
intimate terrorism, 117–118
navy couples, experimental
study, 122
physical aggression couples
treatment, 120
screening, 124
situational violence, 118
treatment structure modification,
124–125
intimate terrorism, 117–118
male-only treatment, 116
situational violence, 118
Intimate terrorism, 117–118
IPV, *see* Intimate partner violence
IT, *see* Interactional therapy

J

Journal of Family Psychotherapy, 259
Journal of Marital and Family Therapy,
250, 257, 259
Journal of Systemic Therapies, 251

L

Lesbian couples, 218–219, 272, 275–276,
278–279, 282
Lesbian, gay, bisexual, transgender
(LGBT), 219–220
Limbic brain system, 24–25

M

Marital Adjustment Test (MAT), 8–9
Marital therapy, 165
Marriage and family therapists, 248,
250, 260–261
Marriage and family therapy
education, 255, 260–261, 265
mental disorders, 42
Marriage counseling
AAMC, 2–3
AAMFC, 3–4
AAMFT, 4
COAMFTE, 3
training standards, 3–4
Marriage counseling movement,
247–248
Marriage education, 296
Marriage expectations, 294–295, 298

MAT, *see* Marital Adjustment Test
Maudsley model, 84
Medical family therapy
biopsychosocial model, 57
breast cancer
body image and sexuality, 65–66
emotional distress, depression,
and anxiety, 66–67
life cycle transitions, 67–68
long-term adjustment, 67
sexual dysfunction, 66
couples therapy, 68–69
illness, psychosocial demands
caregiving, 63–64
partner to patient, 61–63
integrative behavioral couples
therapy, 64–65
mental disorders, 44–45
research, couples and health
endocrine system, 60
gender difference, 60–61
health habits, 60
marital conflict, 58–59
survival/recovery rates, 59
Mental disorders
anxiety disorders
agoraphobia, 50
couple intervention, 49–50
posttraumatic stress disorder,
50–51
relationship satisfaction, 49
bipolar disorders, 47–49
comorbid, 41
couple therapists
diagnosis, 44
medical family therapy, 44–45
stress-diathesis model, 45
symptoms, 43–44
depressive disorders
marital discord and
depression, 46
systemic approach, 47
treatment, 46–47
emotion-focused therapy, 45–46
marriage and family therapy training
programs, 42
Minimal spouse involvement (MSI),
78–79
Multicultural counseling models, 219
Multiculturalism and cross-cultural
issues, 222

352 • Index

N

Negative communication, 299
Neocortex, 25–26
The New Sex Therapy (Kaplan), 101

O

Oriented therapists, 329

P

Paleolimbic brain system, 25
Panic disorder, 50
Partner abuse, 283
Pathological gambling, 83
Patriarchal terrorism, 117–118
Physical Aggression Couples Treatment
    (PACT), 120
Post-traumatic stress disorder (PTSD)
    infidelity, 154
    mental disorders, 50–51
Practical Application of Intimate
    Relationship Skills (PAIRS),
    299, 314
Pragmatic/experiential therapy for
    couples (PET-C), 33
Premarital counseling
    challenges, 321–322
    church setting
      cleagy, 315–316
      daylong workshops, 316
      engaged encounter, 316
      mentor couples, 316
    couple care, 317
    divorce rate, 311, 322
    effectiveness of, 318–319
    empirical support for programs,
      319–320
    Family and Couples Education,
      2007, 318
    first dance, 318
    inventory, 314–315
    premarital counselor, 316
    research on designing premarital
      programs, 320–321
    skills-based programs
      couple communication, 312–313
      PAIRS, 314
      PREP, 313
      relationship enhancement (RE), 312

solution-focused approach, 317
    SYMBIS, 317
    videotape, 317
Pressure to change (PTC), 77
Prevention and Relationship
    Enhancement Program
    (PREP), 313
Procedural unconscious, 29
Professional competence in supervision
    ambiguity, unpredictability and
      patience, 337
    co-therapists explore, 340–341
    prevent hope, 338–339
    sensitive areas, 339
    supervisory response, 339–340
    work with emotion, 336
Psychoeducation, 137–138

R

R-complex, 25
Recommendations for clinicians
    assessment of family system,
      196–197
    education, 197–198
    new family identity, 200–201
    strengthen and develop parents,
      197–200
RELATE-couple CARE program,
    302–306
Religious beliefs, 249–250, 255
Remarital issues, couple therapy
    clinical findings, 190–191
    cohabitating couples, 189
    legal marriages, 189
    recommendations for clinicians
      assessment of family system,
        196–197
      education, 197–198
      new family identity, 200–201
      strengthen and develop parents,
        197–200
    remarriage and stepfamily
      ethnic minority stepfamilies,
        195–196
      family boundary issues, 194–195
      family relationships, 193–194
      multiple losses, 191
      relationship of couple, 192–193
      unrealistic expectations, 191–192
    roles of first marriage, 190

Index • **353**

second marriages, 189
stepfamilies, 190
Remarriage and stepfamily
ethnic minority stepfamilies,
195–196
family boundary issues, 194–195
family relationships, 193–194
multiple losses, 191
relationship of couple, 192–193
unrealistic expectations, 191–192

S

Same-sex couples
family formation and membership
children, 235–236
diversity, 230–233
marriage/civil unions, 233–234
origin of, 234
relationship satisfaction, 229
U.S. census, 229
family function
applications, 227–228
potential bias, 228–229
family strength and resiliency, 226
family structure, 225
nurturance, education and
socialization
family support, 240
gender roles, 236–238
sexual fulfillment, 239–240
spirituality and religiosity,
238–239
vulnerable members protection
legal protection, 241–242
self-disclosure and power, 241
Same *vs.* opposite-sex couples, 229
SCT, *see* Systemic couple therapy
Sex addict, 263
Sexology, 97
Sex therapy, 260
Sexual abuse, 282
Sexual arousal, 279
Sexual Behavior in the Human Female
(Kinsey), 99
Sexual Behavior in the Human Male
(Kinsey), 99
Sexual behaviors, 278
Sexual compulsivity/addictions, 82–83
Sexual Conduct (Gagnon and
Simon), 104

Sexual disorders, 134–135
Sexual fulfillment, 239–240
Sexual issues, 278, 282
Sexuality theory and therapy
biphasic model, 102
female sexuality, 106–107
by Foucault, M., 105–106
Freudian psychology, 97–98
Gagnon and Simon, 104–105
Judeo-Christian religion, 96
medical professions, 96–97
normal sexual behavior
by Johnson, V.E., 100
by Kaplan, H.S., 101–102
by Kinsey, A., 99–100
by Masters, W.H., 100
systems theory, 102–104
postmodern approaches, 107–109
social constructionism, 104–105
SIT, *see* Systemic individual therapy
Situational violence, 118
Social construction sex therapy,
104–105, 108
Social identities, 330
Spiritual belief system, 253
Spirituality and religion, couple therapy
definition of, 248–249
first wave 1990–1994
research, 257–258
therapy and training, 253–256
marriage counseling movement,
247–248
recommendations
couple therapy model, 264
expanding research, 264–265
religious groups, 264
research utilization, 265
training and supervision,
265–266
second wave 1995–1999
research, 248–258
therapy and training, 253–256
surveys of MFT, 248
third wave 2000-present
research, 261–263
spirituality into therapy, 259–260
spirituality into training,
260–261
Stress-diathesis model, 45
Substance abuse, 81–82
Systemic couple therapy (SCT), 85–88

354 • Index

Systemic individual therapy (SIT), 87–88
Systems theory, 102–104

T

Therapeutic alliance, 333–334
Traditional inpatient program (TIP), 79
Trailer-parkism, *see* White trashism
Transgenerational theory, 157
Transsexual, 230
Trauma and recovery
acute stress disorder, 131
avoidance and emotional numbing, 131
care and understanding, 138
childhood maltreatment
anger, 136
anxiety, 136
boundary issues, 134
cognitive distortions, 135
communication difficulties, 134
depression and suicide, 135
grief sharing, 133
hypervigilance, 135
increased relational conflict, 133
reduced relational intimacy, 132–133
sexual disorders, 134–135
spirituality, 136
tension reducing activities, 136
couples, 131–132
emotional responses, 131
eye movement desensitization and reprocessing, 140–141
interpersonal traumas, 132
posttraumatic stress disorder, 131
primary emotions, 140
psychoeducation, 137–138
reexperiencing traumatic event, 131
stressors, 130
touch techniques, 141

U

Unilateral family therapy (UFT), 77

W

White-collar professions, 217
White feminist, 274
White trashism, 217